D0904872

No Ordinary Women

Women played a major role in the fight for Ireland's freedom, risking loss of life and family for a cause to which they were totally committed. They came from every class in society and all walks of life: titled ladies and shop assistants, doctors, housewives, laundry workers, artists and teachers. Some were married with children, others widowed and some mere schoolchildren. But while the names of their male counterparts are writ large in the history of those years, the women have never received the same recognition.

This is their story.

Above: Margaret Pearse's spectacles and locket with pictures of her husband James and sons Patrick and Willie.
Following page: Maud Gonne in her presentation dress.

NO ORDINARY WOMEN

IRISH FEMALE ACTIVISTS in the Revolutionary Years 1900–1923

Sinéad McCoole

The University of
Wisconsin Press

The University of Wisconsin Press
1930 Monroe Street
Madison, Wisconsin 53711

www.wisc.edu/wisconsinpress/

A Cataloging-in-Publication record for this book
is available from the Library of Congress

ISBN 0-299-19500-7 (cloth)

First published by The O'Brien Press, Ltd., Dublin, Ireland

Editing, typesetting, layout and design: The O'Brien Press Ltd
Printing: Eurolitho, Milan (Italy)

Cover Illustrations
Front cover, clockwise from top left: Hanna Sheehy Skeffington, courtesy of the Sheehy Skeffington family; Bridie Halpin, courtesy of Chris Halpin/KGC; Cumann na mBan brooch from the Kilmainham Gaol Collection; Countess Markievicz with her daughter and stepson, MacMahon family/KGC. Back cover: (top) Nora Connolly O'Brien, courtesy of Seamus Connolly/KGC; Harriete Lavery, courtesy of Dr Mary Heffernan; (background): Nora Connolly O'Brien's Webley from the Kilmainham Gaol Collection. Spine: Maggie Craven's Cumann na mBan brooch, Joe Craven/KGC.

This publication would have not have been possible without the financial assistance and encouragement of the Department of the Environment, Heritage and Local Government.

Left: Cumann na mBan membership card.
Opposite page: Margaret Pearse's hair accessories.

Acknowledgements

The research on this book began before the birth of my children, Eve (b.1998) and Edward (b.2001), and as the mother of small children, the task of writing this book at times has been overwhelming. To the women in my life who made it possible, my mother Barbara, my sister Fiona, my mother-in-law Ann, Dorothy and Valerie, I would like to express my deep gratitude; to Gráinne Blair and Carla Briggs who worked for long hours at the computer when I was despairing; to Niamh O'Sullivan, who played a major part in the creation of this story in her capacity as archivist in Kilmainham Gaol, but whose assistance to me went above and beyond the remit of simply doing her job; to Paul Turnell who undertook research on my behalf in London. Thank you to Margaret O'Sullivan and Dr Margaret Ward for reading the manuscript. I am grateful to Loretta and Gerald Murray and Francis McKay for allowing access to their important collections. To Sheila Pratschke, Director of the Tyrone Guthrie Centre at Annaghmakerrig, for giving me a place of solitude to complete the manuscript. And thank you to Dr Margaret MacCurtain for inspiring me to study women's history and to Diane Lyden Murphy who suggested that I write this book. Thank you also to Dr Robert Mandel, Sandy Sternlicht and Amy Farranto.

To those individuals who assisted with information, in locating pictures and documents, I extend my thanks. I wish to thank in particular those who shared their own research, some of it unpublished: Jill Andrews, Eileen Bostle, Eamonn Browne of Tralee Library, Peter Beresford Ellis, Ann Clare, David Chapman, Dolores Doyle, Anne Fagan, Margaret Franklin of Limerick County Library, John (Buddy) FitzGerald, Alan Hayes, William Henry, DJ Hickey, Cormac Lowth, Donal Lynch, Aoife MacEoin, Aoife MacMahon, Ann Matthews, Mike McCormack of Limerick City Library, Helen Meehan, Catherine Morris, Fr Brian Murphy OSB, Geoffrey O'Connor, Tom O'Donovan, Proinnsíos Ó Duigneáin, Tove O'Flanagan, Louise O'Hanrahan, the Ó Loingsigh Family, Marie O'Neill, Sr Martha Magdalan Power, Colin Sagar, Patricia Sharkey of Searc's Web Guide, Dr Geraldine Stout, Betty Sheehy, Imogen Stuart, Ruth Taillon, Mary Talbot, Isabel Treacy and Dr Anne-Maree Whitaker.

Many of those who willingly gave of their time and provided material for this publication were descendants of the women featured in the book. I wish to thank Con Brady, Oliver and Cheryl Brosnan, Bernard Browne, the Burke family, Ann Clarke, Dr Emmet Clarke, Joe Comerford, Seamus Connolly, Joe Craven, Margaret Cullinane, Melissa Llewelyn Davies, Nora and Mairead de hÓir, Celine Doyle, Rhoda Draper, Úna Dunne, Sheila Fortune, Sally Feore, Buddy FitzGerald, Frances Fleming, Mary Grant, Noel Guilfoyle, Dr Phyllis Gaffney, Ann Gallagher, Chris Halpin, Dr Mary Heffernan, Eleanor Hunt, Deirdre Jordan, JJ Kelly, Eibhlin Kenny, Laurie Lawless, Helen Litton, Kate Lowe, Manchán Magan, Ann MacDonagh, Christopher McCann, Mike McCormack, Domhnall McCullough, Delia McDevitt, Bill McDonald, Myra McGowan, Iseult McGuinness, Eamon McHale, Ann, Aoife, Laura and Bairbre MacMahon, Laura McGuirk, Eitne McKeown, Deirdre McKervey, Seamus Murphy, Brother Fintan Norris,

Michael Norris, Honor O'Brolchain for allowing me access to material from the Geraldine Plunkett Dillon Collection, Máirín O'Connor, Patrick Pearse O'Daly, Rita O'Daly, Teresa O'Dwyer, Kathleen O'Farrell, Marie O'Kelly, Esther O'Moore, Conor O'Neill, Eoin P O' Neill, Blon Uí Rathaille, Rita O'Toole, Moira Phillips, Robert Prole, Michael Purcell, John Power, Anthony J Roche, Kevin Rooney, Odran Seeley, Sally Smyth, Micheline and the Sheehy Skeffington family, Joe Tierney and Anna MacBride White.

A number of people who assisted me are now deceased. I would like their contribution noted: the late Nora Brosnan, Maureen Cashman, Maeve Donnelly, Ita O'Gorman Draper, Sheila Fortune, Peggy Jordan, Aodogán O'Rahilly, Tiernan MacBride, Louie O'Brien, Teresa O'Connell, Pádraig Ó Loingsigh, Andrée Sheehy Skeffington, Cissie and Lily Thewliss.

I am grateful for the assistance of the staff of the National Library of Ireland, in particular Joanna Finegan, Tom Desmond and James Harte; Commandant Victor Lang and Commandant Pat Brennan of the Military Archives; the Irish Labour History Society, in particular Theresa Moriarty; Ian Lee of the RTÉ Sound Library & Archives, the National Museum of Ireland, Sandra McElroy and Michael Kenny; Noelle Dowling of the Allen Library, Jean Hazlett and Derek G McCleane of Alexandra College; University College Dublin Archives Department, in particular Orna Somerville and Seamus Helferty; Mary Doherty of the Royal College of Surgeons of Ireland; Carol Murphy of SIPTU; Robert Mills of the Royal College of Physicians of Ireland; Cara Rowan and the staff of Kilmainham Gaol.

For granting me copyright permission, I wish to thank Bernard Browne for allowing me to quote the unpublished letters of Kathleen Browne; Terry O'Flaherty for permission to quote his aunt, Hanna O'Connor; Dr Simon Keane for allowing me to quote from his mother Hannah Moynihan Keane's unpublished diary; Anthony J Roche for permission to quote his grandmother Nora Gillies O'Daly; Cróine Magan for allowing me to quote her mother Sighle Humphreys O'Donoghue, her grandmother Nell Humphreys and her grandaunt Áine O'Rahilly; Eitne McKeown for permission to quote her mother Anne Cooney and for giving me access to the diary of Rose McNamara; Sean Finlay and Tom Connelly for permission to use material from the *Irish Echo*, Declan Malone for use of material from the *Kerryman*.; RTÉ for use of recordings from the Sound Library & Archives, The Board of Trinity College for allowing me to quote from the diary of Cecilia Gallagher, The Mercier Press for permission to quote from Kenneth Griffith and Timothy O'Grady, *Curious Journey*; The O'Brien Press for permission to quote from Brian Feeney, *Sinn Féin, A Hundred Turbulent Years*; Cormac O'Malley for allowing me quote from Ernie O'Malley, *The Singing Flame*, Dublin, 1978; Uinseann MacEoin and Argenta Press for permission to reproduce excerpts from *Survivors;* permission to quote extracts from *Inside Ireland* is courtesy of the Estate of Eilís Dillon, www.eilisdillon.com, thank you to Cormac O'Cuilleanáin for his assistance; the material from the National Archives, Kew, is reproduced with thanks to the Keeper of Public Records. I would also like to thank the Old Dublin Society for permission to reproduce a picture of Madeleine ffrench-Mullen and Dr Kathleen Lynn from the *Dublin Historical Record*. Every effort has been made to contact the copyright holders of original material in this book, but in some cases it has proved unsuccessful.

My thanks to Pat Cooke, Manager of Kilmainham Gaol, who facilitated the start of this research in 1994; Jim Larner, Head of Publications at Dúchas The Heritage Service, who has assisted me on numerous occasions; also to Dermot Burke, Gerry Bourke and Sheila Clifford for their assistance. Thank you also to the photographic department of Dúchas, Con Brogan, Tony Roche and John Scarry. In particular I wish to thank Síle de Valera, TD, who during her term as Minister for Arts, Heritage, Gaeltacht and the Islands provided funding for this book.

Finally I wish to thank Michael O'Brien and all the staff at the O'Brien Press: Íde ní Laoghaire, Mairéad Ashe FitzGerald, Caitríona Magner; Emma Byrne, David Houlden and Ivan O'Brien who expertly designed this book and Mary Webb, my editor, for her skilful guidance throughout this complex project.

Left: An autograph from Cumann na mBan member Nellie Merrigan.
Opposite page: Margaret Pearse's drawer.

Dedication

For my family, Eamon, Eve and Edward Howlin.
Thank you for living with me and 'my ladies'.

Annie Derham *née* Hampton in her Cumann na mBan uniform *c.* 1916.

Contents

Maud Gonne's belt; tortoishell purse belonging to Mrs Margaret Pearse.

Cumann na mBan hat and gloves
belonging to Sighle Humphreys.

Introduction

Ireland in the late nineteenth century was a conservative and male-dominated country – in politics as well as in religion. Irish nationalist organisations, both those that favoured physical force as a method of achieving their aims and those that favoured the constitutional path of change through the Westminster parliament, were almost entirely male in composition. Ireland was ruled by Britain and women in Britain and Ireland were denied the vote and ignored by parliamentarians. There had been many outspoken women writers in the ranks of the nationalist United Irelanders in the 1840s, but in the 1860s the new generation of revolutionary nationalists (known as Fenians after the Fianna, warriors of ancient Ireland) formed themselves into the Irish Republican Brotherhood, a conspiratorial organisation with membership confined to men. Women were not eligible to take the oath of membership but some, mostly female relatives, formed a Ladies' Committee which devoted its time to supporting imprisoned Fenians.

The one exception and, indeed, challenge to the politically marginalised position of women during the nineteenth century occurred during the Land War, at a time when the dangers of famine, which had so devastated the country in 1845-49, once again threatened the Irish countryside. In 1879 the small farmers and peasantry mobilised against the high rents charged by Irish landlords, through the formation of the Land League – a political alliance of Fenians and the Irish Parliamentary Party. While largely male, the few women who controlled their own farms (mainly widows of farmers) were allowed to join. However, when the British government, in an attempt to quell the agitation, declared the Land League an illegal organisation and began to arrest its membership, the male leadership, most reluctantly, agreed to the formation of a new organisation that would be outside the terms of the British proscription. The Ladies' Land League was headed by Anna Parnell, the sister of Charles Stewart Parnell, leader of the Irish Party. For a period of eighteen months the women's organisation took over the leadership of the Land War and proved to be effective and determined opponents of landlordism and of British control over Ireland. It was this militancy that led to their demise. Under the 'Kilmainham Treaty' the British government released the men, one of the conditions of release being that the women's organisation would be disbanded. For their part, many of the women decided that they had no wish to serve in a subordinate role under a male organisation with whose policies they disagreed. Those political differences had serious consequences. An

Irish National League was formed to replace the Land League. It was closely linked to the parliamentary party and voteless women were irrelevant. It was 'an open organisation in which the ladies will not take part.' The next generation of women found themselves barred from membership of all Irish political and cultural organisations.

When the young English heiress, Maud Gonne, attempted to gain membership of the National League she was told by Tim Harrington, its head, that the Ladies' Land League had done 'too good work and some of us found they could not be controlled.' Instead, Gonne found herself working, as she put it, as 'a freelance', campaigning for evicted tenants in Donegal and publicising the plight of the 'treason felony' prisoners, imprisoned after an unsuccessful dynamiting campaign in England in the 1880s. Significantly, Annie Egan, wife of James, one of the men released from Portland Jail, was to become one of the first women to join Inghinidhe na hÉireann, the group formed by women who 'resented their exclusion' from all other groups.

Before the emergence of Inghinidhe, one other organisation to admit women to its membership had been formed. The Gaelic League came into existence in 1893 with the intention of reviving Irish culture and language. While its acceptance of women helped to challenge some of the prejudice that existed regarding women's right to take part in public life, its remit did not extend beyond the cultural. Women were still impatient to be given an opportunity to take part in a political movement. They were ignored by the Irish Party and its offshoots and the physical force tradition within nationalism had not yet regrouped following the failure of its bombing campaign. Discussion groups like the Celtic Literary Society were male-only affairs, leaving the sisters and girlfriends of the members impatient to have an outlet of their own. However, Irish society was gradually changing. In the 1880s and 1890s, convent schools providing education to large numbers of Catholic girls spread throughout Ireland, in the wake of Protestant secondary schools. The Intermediate Education Ireland Act of 1878 and the Royal University of Ireland Act 1880 recognised for the first time that girls and women had the right to sit for public competitive exams and to take university degrees. As employment opportunities became available in shops offices and schools, the world of work was opened up to women of the middle class. A few women were obtaining degrees and some who qualified as teachers were able to put their experience to use in the Gaelic League.

The spark that was, at long last, to lead to the formation of a woman's organisation came in 1900, in nationalist reaction to the visit to Ireland of Queen Victoria, whom Maud Gonne had dubbed, memorably, as 'the Famine Queen'. It was the time of the Boer War and opposition to the threat of conscription to the British army was having an impact in reviving public enthusiasm for the Irish cause. A children's picnic had been organised to persuade the Irish populace to come out and cheer the aging monarch. In response, a small group of women came together to consider the possibility of a 'Patriotic Children's Treat', to reward those children who had not cheered for Victoria. Over a period of three months, a 'Ladies' Committee' organised a mammoth event that captured the imagination of nationalist Ireland. Amongst the donations of food were forty thousand buns, given by a variety of bakers, including the Fenian, John Daly of Limerick, whose niece Kathleen was soon to marry Tom Clarke, the man with whom he had been imprisoned. Arthur Griffith estimated that 30,000 children paraded the streets of Dublin, many of whom were later to become involved in resistance to British rule over Ireland.

It was evident, when the Ladies' Committee met to settle their accounts, that these new activists in Irish political life would not be content with merely a single event. They decided to form a permanent organisation. Inghinidhe na hÉireann was the outcome. Fourteen years later, in very different circumstances, Cumann na mBan would be formed, as nationalist Ireland prepared for war against British rule.

The role of women in revolutionary Irish nationalist movements is still under-researched and underestimated. In 1983, when I published *Unmanageable Revolutionaries*, I anticipated (wrongly) that it would be soon followed by other studies into the role played by women in the long struggle to achieve national self-determination. I was conscious, in developing the broad parameters of women's activities, that the rank and file women who provided the backbone of resistance, often at some considerable personal cost to themselves, remained 'hidden from history'. The work of recovery requires painstaking detective work, perseverance and considerable powers of persuasion, particularly in convincing many veterans (or their families) that their story is worthy of being told. Sinéad McCoole has uncovered the hidden stories of so many women, from all over Ireland, and from an incredible variety of backgrounds. We can see not only the actions they performed and the resistance to oppression they engaged in, but also glimpses of the 'Free State' in which they lived out their lives after the excitement of war. For those who had rejected the Treaty and found themselves on the losing side in the ensuing civil war, it was not a welcoming state. In the atmosphere of bitterness following the republican defeat, women were condemned by the victorious Free State as 'furies' and blamed for having set brother against brother. It is hardly surprising that too few felt their lives would be of interest to future generations. Most seem to have kept silent about their past life. It is remarkable how many lived companionably with the friends with whom they had fought alongside, maintaining woman-centred lives amidst a harshly masculine public sphere. Even those who had children were unlikely to have had their papers kept by family members, who seem not to have grasped the importance of their mother's contribution. Sinéad McCoole has succeeded in bringing to life many of these women. Here at least, their existence is recorded and their memory assured.

Margaret Ward
Belfast 2003

Foreword

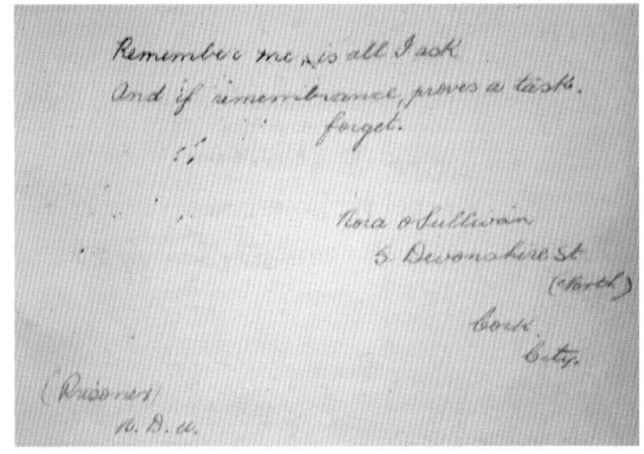
Remember me is all I ask
And if remembrance proves a task.
forget.
Nora O'Sullivan
5. Devonshire St
(North)
Cork
City.
(Prisoner)
N.D.U.

Remember me is all I ask
And if remembrance proves a task, forget.
Nora O'Sullivan
Prisoner, North Dublin Union and Cork City
(An entry in the autograph book of Kitty Coyle)

Finding women

Fifteen days before Christmas, Aunt Bridie died. She was 85 years old and had lived a good life, but the holiday was a sad one for the Halpin family because Aunt Bridie was the loved and respected matriarch of the clan in America. A strong and independent woman, she was the first to 'come over'. In 1937 she had emigrated to Canada to work in the De Havilland aircraft factory, and in 1946 came to New York ... There were no memories of Bridie as a young woman; no one knew her dreams and wishes ... Aunt Bridie was the typical spinster aunt of many an Irish family in America ... After the funeral came the sorrowful task of clearing out the little apartment in upper Manhattan that Aunt Bridie called home. That job was left to Christy. With fond recollections, he examined each item and trinket that she had kept over the years. Then he saw the suitcase under the bed. He lifted it onto the table, opened it, and began to go through photos, newspaper clippings, and papers brown with age. As each document unfolded, a totally different picture of Aunt Bridie emerged. Now why, he wondered, would Aunt Bridie have a copy of the Constitution of Cumann na mBan ... Then he found the newspaper clippings of the troubled 1920s in Ireland of Black and Tan raids, of Civil War strife ... The next item stunned Christy – it was a detention order dated 8 August 1923, declaring Bridie Halpin a dangerous person and ordering her imprisonment ... Each piece of paper was a personal memoir; a vignette weaving a biographical portrait of a time and person that – until now – he thought he knew well ... Then he came across a frail collection of papers, hand-sewn together ... to form a ...

> makeshift booklet... It was Aunt Bridie's jail journal – Christy couldn't believe what he was reading ... 'Far better the grave of a rebel without cross, without stone, without name than a treaty with treacherous England that can only bring sorrow and shame. Bridie Halpin, Kilmainham Jail.' This was not the Aunt Bridie he had known ... Christy left the apartment with an entirely new impression of the loving old woman he knew as Aunt Bridie.

This account of how Christy Halpin stumbled upon his aunt's secret past was written by Mike McCormack in the *Irish Echo* in New York on 2 April, 1988, in a piece entitled 'Aunt Bridie – A Woman of Ireland'.

When I began research into women prisoners in Kilmainham Gaol, such stories became familiar tales to me. Many of the women who had participated in Ireland's fight for freedom never spoke about this period of their lives. This was particularly true of those imprisoned for their part in the Civil War. The bitterness of those years and their experiences at the hands of fellow countrymen meant that it was an episode best concealed. Also, it had been a source of extreme embarrassment to some families that their womenfolk had been in prison. In many households the Civil War was never discussed.

The subject was taboo in many social circles. Fintan Norris, son of Éilis Robinson Norris, told me that his mother never mentioned the troubled times to him, either during his childhood or later. Her story came to him in snatches, secondhand.

Even as late as the 1950s, the history of the Civil War was considered too controversial and emotive a subject to be taught in schools in Ireland. When I spoke to Anna MacBride White, daughter of Seán MacBride and Catalina Bulfin, and granddaughter of Maud Gonne MacBride, she told me that, although the past was discussed in the house, she had to resort to textbooks to disentangle the complex story of the War of Independence and the Civil War in Ireland.

This book tells the story of the Irish revolutionary period 1900–1923, from the perspective of female activists. It is not meant to be a definitive account of the history of the period, but focuses on a time when vast numbers of Irish women were politicised and sent to jail for their beliefs, with a special emphasis on their imprisonment in the aftermath of the 1916 Rising, and during the War of Independence and the Civil War.

Kilmainham Gaol, Inchicore, Dublin, which was one of the main places of detention, is now a museum run by the state heritage service. Built between 1787 and 1796, it was in use until the end of the Civil War in 1924. By the 1960s it lay in ruins and over the next decade was restored by the Kilmainham Gaol Restoration Society, a group of voluntary workers, many of whom had fought for Irish freedom. It has become a national monument, having housed hundreds of Irish men and women freedom fighters during the 114 years that it was Dublin's county prison.

In 1994 I set out, on behalf of the heritage service, to gather material on women who had participated in the struggle for Irish independence, to be included in a permanent exhibition on the history of Kilmainham Gaol. The award-winning exhibition opened in 1996. By then enough material had been sourced to hold an additional temporary exhibition, *Guns & Chiffon,* devoted to the role of women in the revolutionary period. Mary Robinson, Ireland's first woman president, launched this exhibition and an accompanying catalogue entitled *Guns & Chiffon: Women Revolutionaries and Kilmainham Gaol 1916–1923.*

My research on the women of this period, originally expected to be of six months' duration, became the occupation of almost a decade. While I was collecting objects and mementoes of these women, I gathered stories. This book is based on this oral history, which includes interviews with surviving activists, their children, grandchildren, nephews and nieces, grandnieces and grandnephews. The information thus gathered would otherwise have been lost to the historical record, as many of the people mentioned in this narrative were not recorded in any other source. While the names of the high-profile women, such as Countess Markievicz and Maud Gonne MacBride, are well known, the rank and file had not warranted any mention in mainstream history textbooks. This book seeks to redress this omission, and in order to provide the reader with more than just names of the scores of women who took part, biographies of seventy-four have been included.

These short biographies provide information on some of the women mentioned in the main text, and what their lives were like before and after they took part in the pivotal historical events that helped shaped the Ireland of today. A number of the stories are compiled from information contained in scattered published accounts, others are based on information given to me by family members and published here for the first time. Some of the women, such as Maud Gonne and Markievicz, already have books devoted to them, so I have tried to weigh the biographies in favour of those women about whom less is known. Many of the women in this book have lived lives which merit full books, but in a number of cases, such as Dorothy Macardle, Margaret Buckley, Margaret Skinnider, Kathleen Browne and Moya Llewelyn Davies, this task is hampered by a lack of personal papers.

What emerged from researching the women who were politically active in this period was that they were not confined to a particular social grouping, but represented a cross-section of Irish life. They were shop assistants, doctors, housewives, laundry workers, artists, teachers and even mere schoolchildren. There were married women, mothers, single and widowed women. They came from the gentry and professional classes as well as from the poorest sections of Irish society. A number were titled women. Some had not even been born in Ireland, and not all were Catholic; there were Protestants, Quakers, Jews and atheists.

The vast majority of the rank and file who are mentioned in this account became involved because of familial links to the nationalist movement, but their commitment to the cause and the sacrifices they made were in no way inferior to those of the male members of their households. They were willing to give their lives for their ideals, and, while imprisoned, endured the full rigours of hunger strike and separation from family and friends for their beliefs. However, history has not remembered them in the same way as their patriotic brothers.

In 1994 I had been working as a guide in Kilmainham Gaol for over three years. On my tour of the prison the only women I mentioned were Countess Markievicz, Second-in-Command at the Royal College of Surgeons/St Stephen's Green garrison during the 1916 Rising, and Ann Devlin, the confidante of Robert Emmet, who had been imprisoned in Kilmainham Gaol following the ill-fated Rebellion of 1803. Telling the story of other female activists who had been political prisoners, and their involvement in the shaping of modern Irish history, simply did not occur to me. However, there had always been reminders of the women's imprisonment – paintings and inscriptions in cells and the recollections of visitors who came to the prison. These hinted that there was a story waiting to be told.

My research began as a discovery of women; their names and stories emerged slowly. Trying to tell their story was a little like trying to walk into the mists of time. The material relating to women in the archives of Kilmainham Gaol was, by and large, a collection of photographs of unidentified women and objects relating to individuals whose participation in the fight for freedom was unknown. One of these items was a group photograph of women, some of whom were wearing military uniforms. It later transpired that these were women who had participated in the 1916 Rising and had been photographed in the summer of that year. This information came from a caption in a newspaper clipping from the *Irish Press* of 9 April 1966, which featured the picture. For the first time I saw the faces of these women, I could put names on them, and to me they became real people.

Lists of the women arrested in 1916 were available from contemporary newspapers, but no such record was available for women arrested during the Civil War. To construct the list of those women I consulted autograph books in the Kilmainham Gaol collection and also ones in private collections. This information was later correlated with lists of prisoners contained in the Military Archives and is included here as an appendix. It is not a definitive list as it was limited to those who had signed the autograph books surveyed, and to the incomplete records compiled by the military – such as lists of some released prisoners and those who had received parcels and telegrams.

In order to find out more about the items in the Kilmainham Gaol Collection and the women who had been imprisoned, I made appeals on national radio and wrote letters to national and regional newspapers, as well as to Irish newspapers in Britain.

I requested any information on women who had been imprisoned in Kilmainham Gaol during the 1916 Rising and the Civil War. In July 1994 Teresa O'Connell answered my letter to *The Irish Times*. She wrote:

'I was interested to see your letter in the *Irish Times* ... about an exhibition you were planning on political prisoners. As an ex-prisoner of Kilmainham Gaol I am afraid I have no records left as things were confiscated ... As far as I know many of my friends there are now happy with God ... I have often wondered in these later years what happened to all the ex-prisoners ... It is good to see that the women will be remembered too ... Thank you very much for remembering Ireland's dead.'

Over the next five years I met with Teresa often. As she recounted her memories of those times, she was transformed from an old lady in her nineties to a young girl once again. She recited poetry, sang songs and told me about the conditions and lives of her fellow inmates with a vividness that can never quite be conveyed in the written word. When she attended the launch of the *Guns and Chiffon* exhibition in 1997 I saw her glancing around the main compound of the gaol with a look of nostalgia as if she could see the laughing and smiling faces of her comrades who were imprisoned there with her almost seventy-five years before.

I spoke to Nora Brosnan on a cold winter evening in 1994. I was sitting in my office, a cell on the second floor of the East Wing of Kilmainham Gaol, while thousands of miles away in the United States she told me that she could picture exactly where I was in the prison. She told me how the prisoners cooked in their cells, and laughed at the memory of events that had happened in prison in her youth.

Lily Thewliss was living in the same house in Chapelizod in Dublin that she had left on the day of her arrest. Although a local historian introduced me to her, I was nevertheless viewed with suspicion. Far from being the one with the questions, I found myself being interviewed, but I understood that she was speaking of times and events when everyone was a potential enemy. Political affiliations had been a secret subject for much of her youth, when to talk to strangers would have put people in danger. She did not invite me to have tea; the understanding was that I was being vetted, next time we would be friends and she would tell me more. These women entrusted me with their stories and I saw events with an immediacy that would have been lacking from this narrative if I had not heard their firsthand accounts.

Only a few women out of the hundreds of prisoners had survived into their nineties, but relatives of other women came to the Kilmainham exhibition. Men and women visited from all over Ireland as well as from England, Australia and America. With tears in their eyes, they told me stories of their mothers and aunts. They delighted in the remembrance of these women, and of their importance to the story of Irish freedom. They presented flags, embroidery, handwritten journals, diaries, drawings, memorial cards, tattered newspaper clippings and photographs. Through these objects, a picture emerged of the lives, personalities and activities of these women during the time of their imprisonment.

Much of the material from this period has been lost, mostly destroyed by the participants through fear of reprisal or imprisonment. Some had been captured during raids or, more recently, discarded due to lack of interest. The son of one of the women of the rank and file was asked if he had a picture of his mother in her Cumann na mBan uniform. He told me that there had been a large framed picture of her in the uniform, which had hung in the hall of his childhood home. When I asked eagerly if he had any idea of where it was now, he replied that it was on the dump. When they had cleared out his mother's house in the 1970s, nobody had any interest in keeping it.

By the mid 1990s the political climate had changed, with the first IRA ceasefire taking place in the North of Ireland. It had become easier to discuss the story of Irish Republicanism. As the events passed into the realm of history, the time had come to write it down. I was fortunate enough to have been given the job of collecting the mementoes of this period, and through them to encounter the brave women who had played such a crucial role in their country's fight for freedom.

This is their story.

Sinéad McCoole
Ballybrack
County Dublin.
June 2003

CHAPTER 1

Women Activists (1900–1916)

'Unladylike and Desreputable'

In 1900 nationalist women found an unlikely champion in a British soldier's daughter, Maud Gonne, who established Inghinidhe na hÉireann (Daughters of Erin). The aims of the organisation were the complete independence of Ireland, the popularisation of goods of Irish manufacture, the revival of the Irish language and the restoration of Irish customs, games, music and dancing. Twenty-nine women attended the first meeting. They elected five vice-presidents: Jennie Wyse Power, a former member of the Ladies' Land League during the Land War of the 1880s; Anna Johnston, better known by her pen name, Ethna Carbery, who in the 1890s had produced the nationalist newspaper, the *Shan Van Vocht* (Poor Old Woman); Annie Egan, wife of the Fenian James Egan who had been imprisoned in England as a 'Treasonable Felon'; and Alice Furlong, who had been a key member of the Patriotic Children's Treat Committee, a nationalist riposte to the visit of Queen Victoria in 1900.

Above:
Masthead of the *Shan Van Bhocht*, March 1896.

Members of Inghinidhe were asked to 'combat in every way English influence' which was 'doing so much injury to the artistic taste and refinement of the Irish people'.[1] One of the decisions taken at the first meeting was that members would stop wearing their hair puffed over their ears as this was deemed an English fashion.[2] A programme was drawn up to provide free classes for children over nine years old. That winter, Inghinidhe members commenced classes for children on Irish history and the Irish language. These subjects were not part of the curriculum in government schools of the time. The objective of the classes was to educate children – in particular boys – from the poorer regions of Dublin city, which traditionally had provided recruits for the British army. Ella Young told ancient Irish sagas to a roomful of eighty young boys and girls, whom she described as 'untamed Dublin', who could 'scarcely write their own names' but who, as a result of these classes, began 'to adventure with ancient Irish heroes'.[3] Indeed, many of those who attended the classes took part in the fight for Irish freedom in the decades that followed.

Presentation case for brooch commemorating visit of Queen Victoria, 1900.

One of the other activities undertaken by members of Inghinidhe na hÉireann was the distribution of leaflets to young women who were seen in the company of soldiers. One of the leaflets advised: 'Irish girls who walk with English soldiers, remember you are walking with your country's enemies, and with men who are unfit to be companions of any girl'.[4] Others highlighted the dangers of venereal diseases and having illegitimate babies. The leafleting activity frequently resulted in fights,

Left:
Inghinidhe na hÉireann members 1905-1906. Maud Gonne is centre, holding banner.

Maud Gonne MacBride, with son Seán and daughter Iseult.

as Maud Gonne recounted in her memoirs, and it was often necessary for the Inghinidhe women to have male protection. Despite this, they managed to distribute thousands of flyers.[5]

A small drama company was formed by members of the organisation. The group began with the staging of *tableaux vivants* (living pictures), which recreated an event in Irish history, Irish song, or an Irish legend. Works by the nineteenth-century composer Thomas Moore were among those staged. The actress Máire Nic Shiúbhlaigh recalled how Moore's poem '*Rich and Rare were the Gems she Wore*' was adapted into a tableau in which 'would appear a lady, richly bejewelled and garbed in silks, wooed by a glittering Sir Knight to the accompaniment of appropriate choral music.'[6] Alice Milligan, writer and poet, became a director of these tableaux. William Fay was appointed producer and stage manager with the Inghinidhe players. His brother Frank taught the players stagecraft and elocution. Occasionally the company produced full-length plays. Their efforts were 'received with interest in Nationalist circles' but they 'did not have much of a following amongst regular theatre goers' who enjoyed an ample choice of productions by professional companies in the bigger and better equipped theatres in the city.[7]

When William Butler Yeats saw the Inghinidhe players' performance of Alice Milligan's *The Deliverance of Red Hugh* he decided that he wanted to hear the words of his own plays spoken with an Irish accent. The first efforts of the Irish Literary Theatre had failed in 1901, as the plays written by Yeats and Edward Martyn had not been successfully produced by English players. In 1902, Inghinidhe na hÉireann subsidised the production of two plays: George Russell (Æ)'s *Deirdre* and WB Yeats's *Cathleen Ní Houlihan*, at St Teresa's Hall in Clarendon Street, Dublin.[8] Maud Gonne had convinced Yeats to give the rights of the production to her group under the direction of the Fays. For a short run of three nights Maud Gonne performed the leading role of the Old Woman. Although she was considered a great success, she believed that her future was not in the theatre.[9] The result of these performances was the formation of the Irish National Theatre Society, which evolved as the Abbey Theatre. The participation of Inghinidhe na hÉireann members in the fledgling stages of the creation of a national theatre meant that a number of these women, including

Below:
Alice Milligan (left) and Anna Johnston (Ethna Carbery).

Sara Allgood and Máire O'Neill, were to become the first actresses in the Abbey Theatre.

Membership of Inghinidhe na hÉireann was open to those of Irish birth or descent. Numbers soon increased, and women who later contributed much to the political life of Ireland became members: Marcella Cosgrave (a member of the Ladies' Land League who would fight in the Marrowbone Lane garrison in 1916); Marie Walker – better known by her stage name of Máire Nic Shiúbhlaigh (Jacob's Factory garrison 1916); Mollie Gill (imprisoned during the Civil War) and Jennie O'Flanagan, who became well known under the Gaelic version of her name, Sinéad, and would later be First Lady as wife of President Eamon de Valera. Branches were formed in Limerick, Cork, Belfast and in Ballina, County Mayo. The Cork branch was highly successful under the guidance of Margaret Goulding. As Margaret Buckley, she was to become president of Sinn Féin, 1937–1950. In 1903 the Cork branch reported that they had 100 children in their Irish language and history classes.

Many who joined Inghinidhe were young working women who discovered unprecedented freedom as they attended lectures, céilís and monthly debates. By taking part in the organisation these women were stepping outside the norms of a time when such political activity was seen as irreconcilable with the feminine aspects of their personalities and with their role as mothers, wives and sweethearts. According to one contemporary, Inghinidhe na hÉireann accomplished much in a period 'when to hold an Irish outlook or to profess Nationalism was not only "unladylike" but "disreputable".'[10] Ella Young recalled in her memoirs that Inghinidhe na hÉireann was 'composed of girls who work hard all day in shops and offices owned for the most part by pro-British masters who may at any moment discharge them for "treasonable activities".' These girls dared to do it, she concluded, despite the fact that being dismissed for having a nationalistic outlook could result in 'semi-starvation or long continued unemployment'.[11]

Eamon de Valera and his wife, Sinéad (née O'Flanagan).

There was no uniform for Inghinidhe members, but they had a badge, which was a replica of the penannular (gapped-ring) brooches worn in ancient Ireland. They also wore a blue sash embroidered with an emblem of a golden sunburst. The absence of a uniform had a very practical explanation: a uniform would have identified the women as members of a nationalist organisation, and for those who worked in unionist firms it might have invited their dismissal. To further ensure anonymity, the members adopted ancient Gaelic names: Maud Gonne was 'Maeve' and Constance Markievicz, who joined in 1907, became known as 'Macha'.[12]

Countess Markievicz, like Maud Gonne, was a highly unconventional figure. Born into the Anglo-Irish Gore-Booth family of County Sligo, she was an artist, an actress

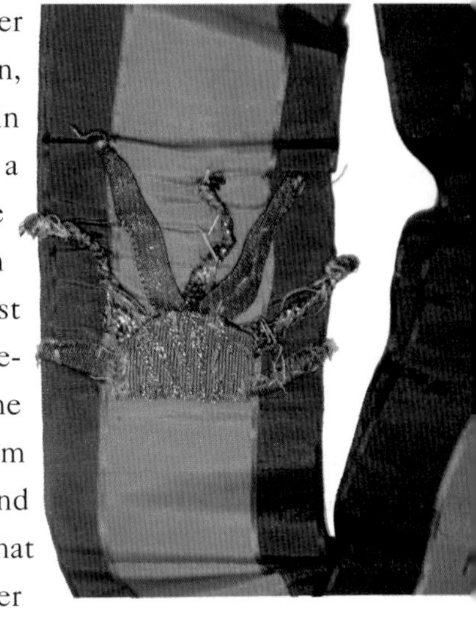

Inghinidhe na hÉireann sash belonging to Maud Gonne.

and the wife of a Polish count. She arrived at her first Inghinidhe meeting in an evening gown, having come straight from a function in Dublin Castle. During the meeting she offered to sell a diamond brooch to raise funds. Many of those present thought that she was an English spy. In time she was to become one of the group's most committed members and an activist for Irish independence, with the result that she shunned the world of her childhood, became estranged from her husband, gave up the care of her daughter, and died in reduced circumstances. When she left that meeting she made the prophetic statement to her companion that she would not have much time in the future for wearing fashionable clothes.[13] By 1915 she was encouraging women to 'dress suitably in short skirts and strong boots, leave your jewels and gold wands in the bank, and buy a revolver.'[14]

Countess Markievicz designed the masthead for the first issue of the Inghinidhe na hÉireann newspaper, *Bean na hÉireann* (Woman of Ireland) which appeared in November 1908. The newspaper sellers joked that it was 'the women's paper that men buy'.[15] Along with articles on politics, there were regular features such as 'Hints on Home Furnishing', 'Cookery Notes' and gardening advice with a nationalist flavour. Readers were advised: 'It is a very unpleasant work killing slugs and snails but let us not be daunted. A good Nationalist should look upon slugs in the garden in much the same way as she looks on the English in Ireland …'[16] Fashion and dress were frequent topics. According to its editor, Helena Molony, the paper 'was a mixture of guns and chiffon'.[17] The commitment to the use of Irish goods and dress expressed at the first Inghinidhe na hÉireann meeting continued to be promoted. The style of 'Irish' dress favoured by many of the women was Irish fabric adorned with Celtic designs. The January 1909 issue of *Bean na hÉireann* contained an article entitled 'How Irishwomen should Dress', which advised that 'the average Irishwoman, in common with the women of every European country likes to follow the fashions set by Paris; but if she adapted them to Irish materials, she would evolve a style that would be at once modern and original.'

Inghinidhe na hÉireann brooch.

Although Helena Molony's position was secretary of Inghinidhe na hÉireann, by 1902 she was effectively running the organisation as Maud Gonne spent much of her time in Paris, where she had a home. (It was in Paris, a year later, that she married Irishman Major John MacBride, who had led the Irish Brigade against the British in the Boer War.)

Helena Molony was one of the women whose participation in politics was not confined to the pursuit of nationalist aspirations. The labour movement was attracting a large following of women, particularly in Dublin, and Helena was among those who became involved. As the new century opened, young working women joined the trade union movement. Dublin's workforce was made up primarily of unskilled labourers – dockworkers, carters and railway workers. This workforce united with a common voice on the formation of the Irish Transport and General Workers' Union (ITGWU) in 1909 by James Larkin and James Connolly. By 1913 it had a membership of 10,000 and a headquarters at Liberty Hall on the Dublin quays. In 1911, the Irish Women Workers' Union was established. In a bid to get better working conditions, a number of strikes were organised by the ITGWU. Thirty different strikes took place in Dublin in 1913. One of the main employers in the city was William Martin Murphy, chairman of the Dublin United Transport Company, whose business interests included proprietorship of a large department store and ownership of *The Freeman's Journal* newspaper. Murphy got together with other employers and refused to employ any worker who was a member of the ITGWU. A showdown was inevitable. At the end of August 1913 there was a general strike, to which the employers responded by closing their businesses and locking out workers. Over 20,000 workers were involved in what became known as the 1913 Lockout, which lasted until the early months of 1914, when starvation forced the workers to return to their jobs.

Countess Markievicz in her Irish Citizen Army uniform.

Women who were out of work at this time became politicised. And others such as Madeleine ffrench-Mullen and Fiona Plunkett joined the labour movement to give assistance, working in soup kitchens and distributing food in Connolly's Free Food Organisation set up for unemployed workers and their families.[18] Many women also

Vol. I, No. 4. Feabra — FEBRUARY, 1909. Price—One Penny.

MADE IN IRELAND.

THE KILKENNY WOODWORKERS

Manufacturers of

Bedroom Suites.

Editorial Notes.

Alas, our statements on Women's Suffrage have got us into serious trouble. We carelessly stated in our December issue that there was nothing illegal in electing a woman to the Civic Chair of Dublin. This, it seems, is not so. Mrs. Sheehy-Skeffing-

they are not agitating for the Parliamentary vote because it is a desirable thing to have, but simply because men have it. We respectfully submit to the Irish Women's Franchise League that this is an unworthy and humiliating position for them to take up. If the English Parliamentary vote is not, in itself, a source of power, then we

Masthead of *Bean na h Éireann*.

joined the Irish Citizen Army (ICA), which had been formed in November 1913 for the protection of workers, following incidents of brutality suffered by workers at the hands of the police force. James Connolly, one of the founders of the ICA, saw to it that women were treated equally in the movement, and women's equality was an integral part of its philosophy. It was James Connolly's daughters, Nora and Ina, who founded the first and only girls' branch of Fianna Éireann, which they named Betsy Gray, after a heroine of the 1798 Rebellion. In 1909, Countess Markievicz, along with Bulmer Hobson, had founded Fianna Éireann, a 'boy scout' movement. Girls were admitted to the Belfast branch, but only after 'endless opposition', according to the Countess.[19]

By this stage other organisations were attracting female members. Arthur Griffith's *Sinn Féin* (Ourselves Alone) was a broadly based, non-extreme organisation committed to a policy of economic nationalism to be achieved by 'passive resistance, boycotting and non-violent agitation'.[20] Women were voted on to its executive, truly a novel idea for any organisation in 1907. Jennie Wyse Power, a founding member and vice-president of Inghinidhe na hÉireann, was one of those elected to the executive of Sinn Féin. However, Hanna Sheehy Skeffington, a founding member of the Irish Women's Franchise League, was sceptical of Sinn Féin's promotion of women, believing it to be no more than a movement in its infancy looking for all the support it could get.[21]

Nora Connolly O'Brien c.1916.

Hanna Sheehy Skeffington felt that until they were allowed to vote, women would remain on the fringes of political life.[22] Interestingly, the suffrage movement was not supported by Inghinidhe na hÉireann, who objected to the vote being granted by 'a hostile parliament'.[23] Countess Markievicz asked women to pause before they joined a franchise movement that did not include in its programme the freedom of the nation.[24] Unionists too, had put their cause before the 'Votes for Women' campaign.[25] Sinn Féin initially offered its support to the franchise movement, provided women did not undermine nationalist objectives, but withdrew its support later when the suffragettes did begin to do this. Individuals from the different nationalist organisations supported the franchise cause, but many felt that the issue should not be addressed until Ireland had her own government.

Nationalist politics were radically changed by the response to the third Home Rule Bill of 1912. Under Home Rule, Ireland would have remained part of the United Kingdom, but would have a separate parliament based in Dublin, with jurisdiction over all thirty-two counties. Ulster was vehemently opposed to any suggestion of

Home Rule from Dublin. On 28 September, designated Covenant Day, 218,206 unionist men expressed their opposition to Home Rule by signing a Solemn League and Covenant, many in their own blood, and 234,046 unionist women signed a women's declaration. Signatories of the covenant pledged to 'defend their cherished position of equal citizenship in the United Kingdom' and to use all means necessary to defeat the 'present conspiracy to set up a Home Rule Parliament in Ireland'. The covenant ended with the words 'God Save the King'. In January 1913 the Ulster Volunteer Force (UVF) was formed to oppose Home Rule. Among those who enlisted were 3,000 women, taking up duty as dispatch carriers, intelligence gatherers, fundraisers and medical workers in areas such as first aid and home nursing. Nationalist men reacted to the formation of the UVF by setting up the Irish National Volunteers in November 1913 with the aim of furthering the Home Rule cause.[26]

Countess Markievicz, second row centre, with a group of Fianna Éireann.

In his presidential speech at the first meeting of the Volunteers, Eoin MacNeill had told the gathering, (including a large number of women, who occupied a space specially reserved for them[27]): 'There would be work to do for large numbers who could not be in the marching line. There would be work for the women.'[28] The women decided to form a separate organisation, and, a few months later, a new women's nationalist organisation called Cumann na mBan (The Irishwomen's Council) came into being.

According to Barry O'Delany, secretary to Maud Gonne's French newspaper, *L'Irlande Libre* (Free Ireland) the idea for such an organisation had been floated in

Maud Gonne's drawing-room some time earlier.[29] A preliminary meeting was held in Harcourt Street, attended by Maud Gonne, Countess Markievicz, Mary Colum, Louise Gavan Duffy, Agnes (Una) O'Farrelly and Marcella Cosgrave. On 13 December 1913 there is a reference in *The Irish Citizen* to women who were refusing to work in a subsidiary capacity and had decided to form a Volunteer corps of their own with their own aims. Maud Gonne believed that the new organisation should be run along the lines of the French Red Cross, which taught first aid and nursing. So one of the earliest acts of the group was to write to the Red Cross in Geneva. The reply from Geneva said that the Red Cross could not accept a country which did not have a standing army of its own and suggested that Cumann na mBan apply for affiliation to the English Red Cross.[30]

Cumann na mBan ribbon belonging to Kathleen Clarke.

Jennie Wyse Power recorded in *Leabhar na mBan* in 1919 that a number of informal meetings had been held to discuss the formation of a woman's society. Those who attended had been women of 'all shades of nationalist thought', but they finally joined together for a meeting in April 1914.

The inaugural meeting of Cumann na mBan was held on 5 April 1914 at Wynne's Hotel in Dublin. Although held in the afternoon, it attracted an attendance of 100 women. Agnes O'Farrelly MA, later a professor in the National University, presided over the meeting. She ruled out the possibility of women taking part in the defence of Ireland, saying that the women's role was to help arm the men. The aims of Cumann na mBan outlined in their constitution were to advance the cause of Irish liberty and to assist in the arming and equipping of a body of Irishmen.[31] The first provisional committee consisted of Agnes O'Farrelly; Agnes MacNeill (wife of Eoin MacNeill, the leader of the Volunteers); Nancy (Nannie) O'Rahilly, (the American wife of Michael O'Rahilly who had instigated the foundation of the Volunteers); Mary Colum, (whose poet husband Padraic Colum was also in the Volunteers); Jennie Wyse Power; Louise Gavan Duffy, whose father had been a nationalist and member of the Young Irelanders; a Mrs Tuohy and a Mrs MacDonagh O'Mahony. Louise Gavan Duffy and Mary Colum were made Honorary Secretaries. As Maud Gonne was then living in France, the position of President of Cumann na mBan was given to Countess Markievicz.

Cumann na mBan raised money by organising céilís, concerts and other social events for the purchase of arms and ammunition. This collection was known as the 'Defence of Ireland' fund. The organisation adopted a green uniform with a slouch hat. Members were honour-bound to use material of Irish manufacture. In the early years many members made their own uniforms in 'Volunteer' tweed. When Cumann na mBan first paraded in uniform they were pelted with mud and stones by wives of British soldiers and called by 'the undignified name of grasshoppers.'[32] Despite the fact that they were not viewed as freedom fighters, their militarism was evident in their symbolism. Their banner and badge carried the motif of a rifle with the initials of the organisation intertwined. Patrick Pearse, who was now rising to prominence in the Irish Volunteers, is said to have commented: 'I would not like to think of women drilling and marching in the ordinary way, but there is no reason that they should not learn to shoot.'[33]

By October 1914 Cumann na mBan had sixty branches and a headquarters had been established in Dublin. Mary Colum spoke for many women in the organisation when she stated in *Irish Freedom* that Cumann na mBan members were not 'the auxiliaries or the handmaidens or the camp followers of the Volunteers – we are their allies'.[34]

When the Ulster Volunteer Force imported guns and became an armed force in April 1914, southern nationalists also sought to be armed. A plan to smuggle arms from Germany was masterminded by a group of Anglo-Irish nationalists. The idea came from the Honourable Mary Spring Rice, daughter of Lord Monteagle, a County Limerick landlord. In April 1914 she wrote to Michael O'Rahilly, Director of Arms of the Volunteers (who had adopted the style of The O'Rahilly), and this letter was the start of preparations. She considered one thing essential to making her plan a success: that Erskine Childers would be in charge of the project.[35] Childers, a British civil servant and former member of the British Army, was the son of an Irishwoman and was sympathetic to Home Rule for Ireland. He was a keen yachtsman; his famous book, *The Riddle of the Sands*, published in 1903, told the story of a yachtsman who discovers German preparations for an invasion of Britain. Although a work of fiction, it was credited with causing the British to increase the size of their fleet. Mary Spring Rice suggested that a fishing boat, the *Santa Cruz*, should be used, but when Childers inspected the boat at Foynes harbour, County Limerick, he decided that a yacht would be better, as it would attract less attention if the smuggling took place during the yachting season. The vessels chosen were the

Molly Childers and Mary Spring Rice on board the *Asgard*.

Kelpie (owned by Conor O'Brien, a cousin of Mary Spring Rice who had been organising the Volunteers in Limerick) and the *Asgard*, the Childers's own gaff-rigged ketch, a wedding gift to the couple from Molly Childers's father, Dr Osgood. In July 1914, the *Asgard* set sail on a nineteen-day voyage. Mary Spring Rice and Molly Childers were on board. Molly Childers, who had been crippled after a skating accident when she was three years old, was seated at the helm, wearing a flamboyant red skirt.[36] The mission was completed successfully; on 26 July 1914 the *Asgard* landed a cargo of 900 rifles and 29,000 rounds of ammunition at Howth, County Dublin. Meanwhile, the *Kelpie* had acquired a consignment of 600 rifles, which it offloaded onto another boat to be brought ashore in Kilcoole, County Wicklow.

When the ratification of the Home Rule Bill was postponed until the end of the Great War that had begun in August 1914, John Redmond, leader of the Irish Home Rule Party, called on the Irish Volunteers to join the war effort in support of small nations. This caused the Irish Volunteers to split. The vast majority – Redmond's Nationalist Volunteers – went to assist the war effort, while Eoin MacNeill's Irish Volunteers remained opposed to Ireland's involvement in the war.

The Cumann na mBan convention of November 1914 voted to support the minority Irish Volunteer force headed by Eoin MacNeill. Mary MacSwiney from Cork and Madge Daly from Limerick 'led the Convention by their strong denunciation of using the organisation to help the side that had gone over to recruiting for England.'[37] Cumann na mBan issued a statement in the *Irish Volunteer* in October 1914:

> **We came into being to advance the cause of Irish liberty ... We feel bound to make the pronouncement that to urge or encourage Irish Volunteers to enlist in the British Army cannot, under any circumstances, be regarded as consistent with the work we have set ourselves to do.**[38]

No branch of Cumann na mBan became associated with Redmond's Nationalist Volunteers.[39]

While the aim of MacNeill's Irish Volunteers was that there would be a Home Rule parliament in Dublin, militant nationalists, led by the Irish Republican Brotherhood (IRB), championed the cause of an Irish republic, to be achieved by armed rebellion. The IRB was a secret, oath-bound revolutionary organisation, founded in 1858. It viewed England's war with Germany as a situation that Ireland could take advantage of – 'England's difficulty as Ireland's opportunity'. Members of the IRB infiltrated a number of societies, including the Irish Volunteers, planning to use them as a platform from which to stage a rebellion. Among the IRB leaders in MacNeill's Volunteers were Patrick Pearse, Joseph Mary Plunkett, Eamonn Ceannt and Seán MacDiarmada.

Opposite page: (top) Inghinidhe na hÉireann sash; gold Cumann na mBan brooch. Anne Cooney's 1916 uniform, which she made herself.

At the beginning of 1915, the executive of Cumann na mBan appointed Florence McCarthy as organiser with responsibility for establishing a better system of communication between the branches and the executive. She undertook a lecture tour around the country, encouraging women to set up branches in towns and villages.[40] By the end of 1915 branches of Cumann na mBan were again increasing in number; members were divided into sections, and military titles such as 'squad commander' and 'section leaders' began to be used. Members were trained in first aid, signalling and drilling. The Limerick Branch availed of monies available from the Department of Education for each woman who was trained in first aid. As Madge Daly later recalled, the British Government thus unwittingly contributed to the arms fund of the Volunteers.[41] At Cumann na mBan's second convention, held in 1915, attendance was up by fifty percent on the previous year.[42] In May, 1915 Inghinidhe na hÉireann became a branch of Cumann na mBan.

An old Fenian leader named Jeremiah O'Donovan Rossa died in New York in 1915, and his body was brought back to Dublin for burial. The funeral was used as a propaganda exercise by the IRB. This was a seminal moment for many nationalists, in particular because of the stirring speech made by Patrick Pearse at the graveside, in which he proclaimed that 'Ireland unfree shall never be at peace'. The nationalist movement enlarged further. By 1916 there were four branches of Cumann na mBan in Dublin working with the four battalions of Irish Volunteers, and forty-three branches throughout Ireland.

Meanwhile, James Connolly was also making militant speeches and calling for an uprising to take place. His Irish Citizen Army was active in the early months of 1916. Although women were treated equally with the men in the Irish Citizen Army, some of the men ad complained that the women's section would be an encumbrance in the event of an uprising. To this, James Connolly responded that if none of the men turned out, the fight would go on with the women.[43]

The basement of Liberty Hall was turned into a munitions works, where scores of enthusiastic women and girls prepared bombs, cartridges and bullets.[44] Brighid Lyons Thornton remembered: 'We were all

CONSTITUTION, CORUGHADH.

Cumann na mBan is an independent body of Irishwomen pledged to maintain the Irish Republic established on January 21st, 1919, and to organise and train the women of Ireland to work unceasingly for its international recognition. All women of Irish birth or descent are eligible for membership, except that no woman who is a member of the enemy organisation or who does not recognise the Government of the Republic as the lawfully constituted Government of the people can become a member.

OBJECTS: **(Cuspora)**

1. (*a*) The complete separation of Ireland from all foreign powers.
   (*b*) The Unity of Ireland.
   (*c*) The Gaelicisation of Ireland.

II. **MEANS**: **(Slighthe).**

1. To maintain the Republic by every means in our power against all enemies, foreign and domestic.

2. To assist Oglaigh na h-Eireann, the Irish Volunteers, in its fight to maintain the Republic.

3. That at elections, Cumann na mBan, as such, give no assistance to any Organisation which does not give allegiance to the Government of the Republic.

4. To become perfect citizens of a perfect Irish Nation by :—
   (*a*) Taking Honour, Truth, Courage and Temperance as the watchwords of Cumann na mBan ; (*b*) by fostering an Irish atmosphere, politically, economically and socially ; (*c*) discouraging Emigration by brightening the social life of the district ; (*d*) supporting Irish industries.

5. At all times and in all places to uphold the spirit and the letter of the Cumann na mBan Constitution.

6. The Constitution of Cumann na mBan may not be altered except by a two-third majority vote of a Convention.

Cumann na mBan Constitution.

geared up and training and preparing for a rebellion. I didn't know what a rebellion would mean, but it would mean a change. After that we might have our freedom and the world would be a different place.'[45] Meanwhile, the Military Council of the IRB co-opted Connolly and told him of their plans to stage a rebellion, and asked him to join them.

The absence of female members in the IRB[46] meant that few women knew about the actual plans for the Rising. In this ignorance they were no different from most ordinary members of the Irish Volunteers or from their leader, Eoin MacNeill. But among those privy to the plans was Kathleen Clarke, wife of Tom Clarke, a member of the Military Council. Kathleen (née Daly) was in her native Limerick in the days before Easter 1916, which had been the date set for the Rising. She later recalled that she was with the members of Limerick Cumann na mBan on Good Friday 'Though none of them except my sisters knew that the manoeuvres which were to take place on Easter Sunday were really a rising, they seemed to sense a crisis, which made them very anxious and troubled.'[47]

New Ross, Co Wexford Cumann na mBan flag.

CHAPTER 2

The Women of the Rising

'Of all ranks from titled ladies to shop assistants'

Nell Humphreys stated that the Rising of 1916 had had the potential to be 'the best organised universal Rising that was ever in Ireland',[1] but in fact, the rebellion of Easter week, 1916 was attended by so much confusion and misadventure that it is astonishing it actually went ahead at all.

Above:
Marcella Cosgrave's armband, with image of women who participated in the 1916 Rising in background.

The Military Council of the IRB had sought the assistance of the German High Command in staging the planned rebellion. They requested that 12,000 German troops land at Limerick in the southwest of the country, bringing with them 40,000 rifles to arm Volunteers in the provinces of Connaught and Munster.[2] It was proposed that this force, led by the Germans, would then travel east to Dublin and would support an insurrection in the capital during Easter week, 1916.

Julia Grenan's 1916 brooch.

While no troops were sent, 20,000 rifles and one million rounds of ammunition were provided by the Germans and brought by submarine to the Kerry coast.[3] Sir Roger Casement, who was retired from the British colonial service and had been knighted in 1911 for exposing abuses of native workers in the Belgian Congo and in Peru, accompanied the shipment to Ireland.

But when the shipment arrived, on Holy Thursday, 20 April it was intercepted by British naval services and Casement was captured. He was later charged with treason and hanged. The loss of the arms was a severe blow, which changed the course and ultimately the outcome of the Rising.

Another plan of the IRB-led Military Council also failed. Eoin MacNeill, Chief of Staff of the Irish Volunteers, would support military action only if there was sufficient provocation, such as the British attempting to disarm the Volunteers. Hoping to dupe MacNeill into thinking that the time was right for an uprising, IRB leaders produced the so-called 'Castle Document', which indicated that the authorities in Dublin Castle were about to clamp down on the Volunteers. However, on Saturday, 22 April, just one day before the date chosen by the Military Council for the Rising, MacNeill discovered that the document was a forgery. He sent messages to battalions throughout the country and had a notice printed in the *Irish Independent* rescinding all orders, and stating that no parades, marches, or other movements should take place on Easter Sunday.

Determined not to abandon the insurrection, the Military Council immediately sent dispatch carriers around the country informing Volunteer units that the Rising would now take place on Easter Monday instead, under the guise of routine manoeuvres. The couriers were mainly women, as they could travel more freely than men, although the danger of arrest was still high. Teenager Eily O'Hanrahan, sister of Michael (later executed for his part in the Rising), dressed in furs and posed as an adult to deliver a dispatch to Enniscorthy, County Wexford. Julia Grenan was sent to Dundalk, County Louth, and Mary Perolz to Cork, while others went to County Kerry, County Waterford and County Carlow.

The garrison at Ashbourne, County Meath received confirmation of the Rising from a Miss Adrian who cycled from Dublin with a message from Patrick Pearse. Miss Adrian, a middle-aged woman, made this long and arduous journey several times during the week of the Rising but still managed to evade arrest.[4] James Connolly's daughter, Nora, was in charge of bringing the message to the Northern divisions of the Volunteers. She described the women as: 'a band of couriers sent to all parts of Ireland, trying to avert disaster, to countermand the countermand.'[5] In fact, the women's efforts did little to override the confusion caused by Eoin MacNeill's order. The result was that the Rising was confined to Dublin city and some areas in the counties of Wexford, Cork, Meath and Galway.

At 11am on Easter Monday, 24 April 1916, a large number of Volunteers and members of the Irish Citizen Army, male and female, met at the Liberty Hall headquarters of the ITGWU and marched from there to posts at various key buildings in the centre of Dublin city. The headquarters selected for the Rising was the General Post Office (GPO) located on Dublin's main street, Sackville Street (now O'Connell Street). Members of the Military Council, James Connolly, Patrick Pearse, Tom Clarke, Joseph Mary Plunkett and Seán MacDiarmada – calling themselves the Provisional Government of the Irish Republic – were stationed at the GPO. A group of Volunteers rushed the doors and occupied the building. Shortly afterwards, a Proclamation of Independence was read out outside the GPO. Links to militant nationalists in America and support from Germany were mentioned in this document, addressed to Irishmen and Irishwomen:

> **... Having organised and trained her manhood through her secret revolutionary organisation, the Irish Republican Brotherhood, and through her open military organisations, the Irish Volunteers and the Irish Citizen Army, having patiently perfected her discipline, having resolutely waited for the right moment to reveal itself, she now seizes that moment, and, supported by her exiled children in America and by gallant allies in Europe, but relying in the first on her own strength, she strikes in full confidence of victory.**

At 12.10pm on Easter Monday a group of ten men and nine women of the Irish Citizen Army, led by Sean Connolly, marched on Dublin Castle, the centre of British administration in the country. The guard at the gate was shot and Connolly ordered the remainder of the guards in, but the members of his garrison hesitated and 'in that moment a soldier clanged the gate.'[6] When they failed to take the Castle, they took other buildings in the area in addition to the building beside the Castle entrance, City Hall. The City Hall garrison was soon supplemented by a group of women who had gathered at Christ Church Place awaiting instruction. When they were told of the outpost at City Hall they entered the building by climbing the railings and iron gates.

Dr Kathleen Lynn, a captain in the Irish Citizen Army, joined the City Hall garrison instead of her initial posting at the Royal College of Surgeons, as she was required to attend to the first casualty, Sean Connolly, who had been shot by a sniper. Connolly died at 2pm, within hours of the Rising commencing. The women used a room on the top floor of City Hall as a cooking and first aid station. Helena Molony found some oatmeal and made porridge. Later, Helena Molony and Molly O'Reilly went to the GPO looking for reinforcements, but the garrison was unable to spare anyone.[7] City Hall was in a vulnerable position, and the rear of the building was shelled by troops from the Castle during the first night of occupation. Some of the defenders were on the roof and some inside, but no real defence was possible, recalled Helena Molony. She thought every moment would see the end.[8] City Hall was recaptured early in the morning of Tuesday, 25 April.

Dr Kathleen Lynn's medical box, used in 1916.

Michael Mallin departed Liberty Hall for St Stephen's Green with a detachment of Citizen Army members and began occupation at noon. Countess Markievicz arrived shortly afterwards and took up her post as Second-in-Command. Many of the women who were unable to locate their own scattered battalions found their way to St Stephen's Green, among them Nora O'Daly, Bridget Murtagh and May Moore of the Fairview Branch of Cumann na mBan. Nora O'Daly, who had left her three small children in the care of her sister[9] to take part in the fight, was understandably apprehensive about their location:

> **The Green, even to a mind untrained in military matters, looked a regular death-trap, and although I was quite willing to die to help to free Ireland I saw no reason for doing so if I could help it before I had accomplished the purpose which had brought me hither, namely, to render all the assistance possible to the wounded and to save life wherever possible.**[10]

Fifteen women, under the command of Madeleine ffrench-Mullen (who was later promoted to sergeant), commandeered vehicles, removed civilians from the Green, guarded the gates and tended the wounded. The first-aid post was located in the bandstand with the Red Cross flag flying for protection. The women involved on the Irish side in 1916 were not official members of the Red Cross. To British soldiers these women were, therefore, legitimate targets. Their white dresses with red crosses provided an easy target for the army marksmen. Amazingly, none of them were injured, although a bullet passed through one woman's skirt and another had the heel of her shoe shot off. By Tuesday, the British military had occupied the Shelbourne Hotel and other buildings around the Green, forcing the insurgents to relocate to the Royal College of Surgeons on the west side of St Stephen's Green.

The First Battalion under Commandant Edward Daly established its headquarters at Church Street on the north side of the river Liffey. A short time later the garrison seized the Four Courts on the quays in the northwest section of the city. Small outposts were held nearby at North Brunswick Street, the North Dublin Union, North King Street and at Father Mathew Hall in Church Street where some of the women activists had established a first-aid station.

The Second Battalion under the command of Thomas MacDonagh assembled at St Stephen's Green before taking over Jacob's factory in Bishop Street. When the women arrived they were told that no provision had been made for them. But Máire Nic Shiúbhlaigh persuaded MacDonagh to let herself and five others: Sara Kealy, Kathleen Lane, the two Pollard sisters, and Annie McQuade, cook and take care of casualties.[11] The Clann na nGaedheal girl scouts attached themselves to this Battalion. Clann na nGaedheal had been founded in 1910 by May Kelly. The scouts, like their comrades in the Irish Citizen Army and Cumann na mBan, were trained in first aid and signalling.[12]

The only food that could be located in Jacobs, a biscuit factory, was the confectionery it produced and the women made use of whatever was available: cream crackers, fruitcake, shortbread. Máire Nic Shiúbhlaigh recalled in her memoir, *The Splendid Years* that they were quartered downstairs during the period of occupation. Unaware of what was going on, they listened to 'the constant crack of rifles overhead.' News of the progress of the fight was brought to them by means of rumours but 'wild stories sped through the rooms each day.' Among the false rumours that circulated was that German troops had landed in County Wexford and that Dublin Castle was on fire.

Eamon de Valera commanded the Third Battalion, which seized Boland's Mill on the southeast side of Dublin in addition to locations situated along one of the main routes into the city from Kingstown (now Dun Laoghaire), the main port for passenger embarkation. De Valera refused to have women participate at his outpost. He did not want women who were untrained for soldiering. Afterwards he admitted that he was sorry that he had not used their help, as some of his best men were engaged in cooking rather than fighting. However, years later he still maintained that women were 'at once the boldest and most unmanageable revolutionaries'.[13]

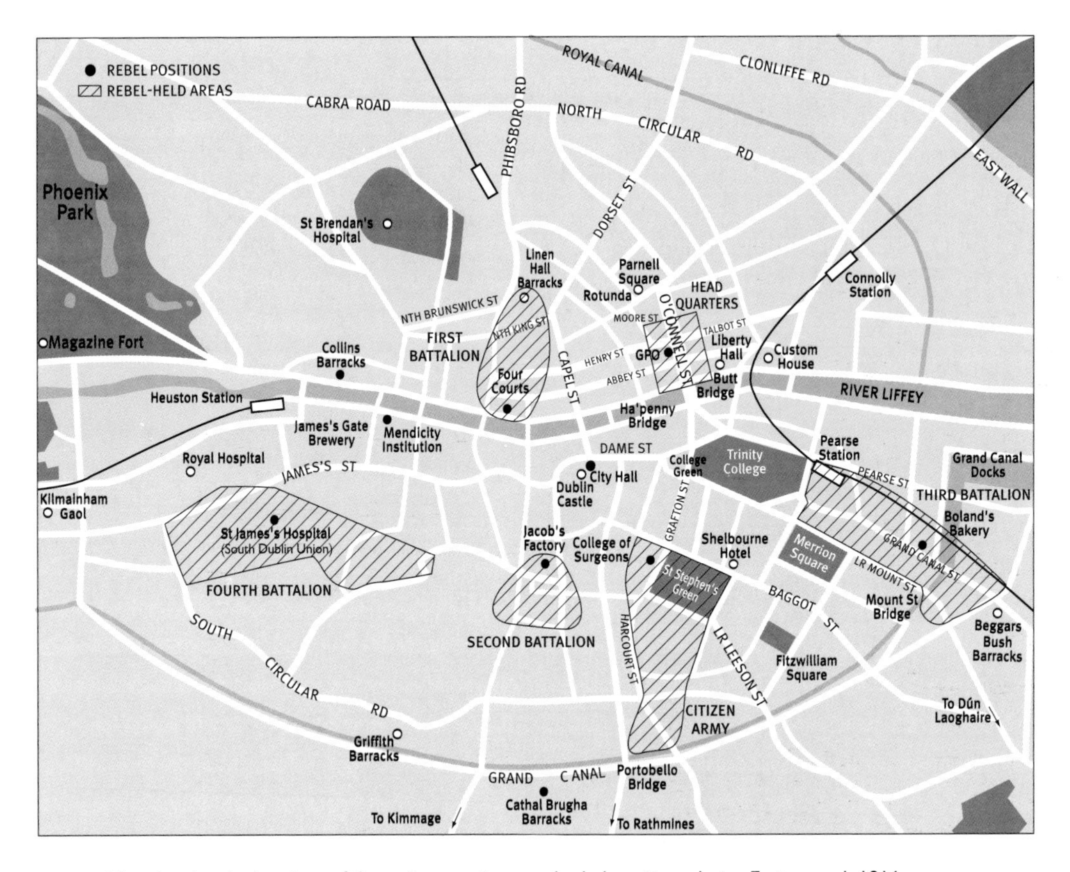

Map showing the locations of the various garrisons and rebel positions during Easter week 1916.

Eamonn Ceannt was in charge of the Fourth Battalion with headquarters at the South Dublin Union, a workhouse located in the south west of the city (now St James's Hospital). The women's headquarters was at the distillery at Marrowbone Lane, where they guarded the rear of the South Dublin Union. Captain Murphy, who was in charge of the Volunteers, had arrived there at 12pm on Easter Monday, 24 April and demanded that the gate be opened in the name of the Irish Republic. Twenty-two women followed the Volunteers into the garrison. Rose McNamara was in command, with Marcella Cosgrave as Quartermaster. Lily O'Brennan, a sister-in-law of Eamonn Ceannt, was part of the garrison. She had no Cumann na mBan uniform so dressed instead in a coat and skirt that she used for mountain walks. She had secured her nephew's schoolbag in which she placed rations, a water bottle and first aid equipment.[14] There were a number of siblings in the garrison at Marrowbone Lane: sisters Anne, Lily and Eileen Cooney; the Quigleys – Cilla and Maria; May and Winnie Byrne; Emily and Josie O'Keeffe; the O'Flaherty sisters, Cissie and Margaret.[15]

Anne Cooney (foreground) with sisters Lily and Eileen, c.1916.

Small groups of men took over the Mendicity Institution on the quays and commandeered buildings and houses in prime positions on approach roads into the city. The intention was to encircle the city, but plans had to be modified when the numbers who took part were reduced to about 1,600[16] owing to the confusion over MacNeill's countermand, and the loss of the German arms.

While the garrison in Jacob's factory survived mainly on cakes and biscuits, and the City Hall garrison were eating porridge, the Marrowbone Lane defenders fared considerably better. On Wednesday the garrison captured nineteen chickens from a messenger boy. Rose McNamara recalled that they did not have any utensils so the chickens were taken from the pots with bayonets.[17] On Thursday the women appropriated a cow and two calves and made butter with the milk.[18] A Volunteer who was a butcher killed one of the calves, and the following day there were veal cutlets for breakfast.[19] The garrison was also doing well in the fighting. On Thursday they resisted an attack by British troops. Fighting lasted into the afternoon, when the South Staffordshire regiment was forced to withdraw. The women announced their intention of holding a victory céilí on the following Sunday.[20]

At first, members of Cumann na mBan were turned away from many posts, including the GPO.[21] When this news filtered back to the leaders a directive was sent to accept any of the women who wished to take part. For a time Winnie Carney was the only woman in the headquarters at the GPO, but throughout the next two days women continued to arrive. Julia Grenan and Elizabeth O'Farrell, members of Inghinidhe branch of Cumann na mBan, became attached to the Irish Citizen Army. 'We saw no objection to this,' Julia Grenan related, 'because the

Winnie Carney.

Volunteers weren't taking any notice of us, didn't care whether we were there or not.'[22] They then made their way to the GPO. By the end of the week the number of women in HQ had risen to about forty. May Gibney was among them:

On Easter Monday 1916 I volunteered for service at the GPO. I was not a member of the Republican organisation at the time but as a reference I mentioned the name of a Volunteer officer whom I knew would be on duty at one of the points ... I asked to be allowed remain at (the) GPO and was lucky enough to be accepted as a member of the garrison.[23]

Edward Daly was another who only accepted women into his garrison upon receipt of the directive from the GPO. One of those women was a young medical student from Longford, Brighid Lyons, a member of Cumann na mBan in Galway where she was at university. She had come to Dublin on Easter Tuesday with her uncle, Frank MacGuinness, and they joined another uncle, Joe, who was in the Four Courts.[24] Fierce fighting with heavy casualties raged in the vicinity of the Four Courts but the women nevertheless carried dispatches between the various outposts in this area. Years later Brighid Lyons Thornton recalled how she and another Cumann na mBan member were selected to go to provide first aid in a house in Church Street:

Elizabeth O'Farrell, *c.*1916.

... someone said, 'Let that fat girl from the country go, she's not tired like the rest of us.' ... So of course I was up like a shot and the two of us went out ... we had a very hazardous trip ... we went along cops and robbers, stopping and going along the side, with the sniping going on around us.[25]

Fifteen tenement dwellers were killed in the fighting in North King Street, but none of the dispatch carriers sustained injury.

The involvement of women in combat bemused observers, and they were at a loss to explain their presence. In the *Weekly Irish Times*, a newspaper with a loyalist perspective, a colourful description was given of the activities of the women in the GPO:

> **The girls serving in the dining room at the Post Office were dressed in the finest clothes, and wore knives and pistols in their belts. They also wore white, green and orange sashes.[26]**

In reality the women's role was, as ever, practical. Some staffed a field hospital established at the rear of the building. The kitchen of the GPO was placed under the control of Desmond FitzGerald and Louise Gavan Duffy. Louise, a founder member of Cumann na mBan, had abandoned writing her MA thesis to go to the GPO. She had not approved of the Rising going ahead, but after voicing her opinions to Patrick Pearse, she joined the garrison.[27] Catherine Byrne entered the GPO through a window on Prince's Street. She was immediately called upon to tend to Liam Clarke who had been injured when a homemade bomb accidentally exploded near him. There were no bandages to hand, so Catherine tore her petticoat and used it to dress his wound.[28]

During the Rising many women acted as dispatch carriers and also as 'basket girls', walking or cycling to bring food to the garrisons. They made their way through broken walls, burning houses and barricades, at all times targets for snipers and arrest. One observer recorded that 'Cumann na mBan girls did practically all the despatch carrying ... none of them returned unsuccessful. That was a point of honour with them – to succeed or be killed.'[29] Chris Caffrey was one of the women arrested by the military. She was stripped and searched by British soldiers, but by that time she had already eaten the dispatch![30] When Catherine Byrne was being sent by Patrick Pearse from the GPO to the Four Courts, he commented on her ingenuity when she rolled the note into her hair bun.[31] An eyewitness account described the female activists as 'of all ranks, from titled ladies to shop assistants' who 'worked on terms of easy equality, caring nothing apparently but for the success of the movement'.[32]

Julia Grenan.

Heedless of the dangers, the women left their garrisons 'under the deadliest fire to bring in wounded Volunteers'.[33] A Red Cross nurse attached to the British Army complimented their bravery in a letter to her friend in England: 'These Irish women, who did their work with a cool and reckless courage, unsurpassed by any man, were in the firing line from the first to the last day of the rebellion ... I never imagined that such an organisation of determined fighting women could exist in the British Isles.'[34]

And there were, of course, women who carried weapons and fought alongside the men; women who were trained snipers. In Cumann na mBan there had been classes in the use of weapons, but training in setting up a field hospital had proved more popular in some branches, so members were more or less proficient in arms depending on the branch to which they belonged. Accounts of the period describe Winnie Carney, who acted as secretary in the GPO during the Rising, as being armed with a Webley and a typewriter. In her Cumann in Belfast she had achieved outstanding results in rifle practice.[35] There were others in the GPO willing to use weapons. An observer later wrote, 'Many of the women were snipers, both in the Post Office and in the Imperial Hotel'. They were on guard with rifles, relieving worn-out Volunteers.[36]

Helena Molony, stationed at City Hall during Easter Week, was equipped with her own revolver and ammunition. She had been taught to shoot by Countess Markievicz. During the Rising she was dressed in an Irish tweed costume with a Sam Browne belt.[37] There is no question that she wished to be active in the firing line; as she later recounted, 'part of our military duty was to knit and darn, march and shoot, to obey orders in common with our brothers in arms'.[38]

Margaret Skinnider, a twenty-three-year-old schoolteacher from Glasgow, and a private in the Irish Citizen Army, had joined the snipers on the roof of the College of Surgeons. In her memoir she wrote: 'It was dark there, full of smoke and the din of firing, but it was good to be in action ... More than once I saw the man I aimed at fall'.[39] Not content with this activity, on Wednesday, 26 April she insisted on being allowed go to bomb a house near St Stephen's Green. She was wounded, shot in three places, but her only regret was to be disabled so early in the fight.[40]

As a result of the confusion over MacNeill's countermanding order, few of the battalions outside Dublin were active during Easter Week. On Thursday, 27 April, members of Cumann na mBan were involved in the seizure of the Athenaeum and the skating rink in the centre of Enniscorthy, County Wexford. They were commanded by Mary White and included Úna Brennan, Eileen O'Hegarty, Marion Stokes and Gretta Comerford.[41]

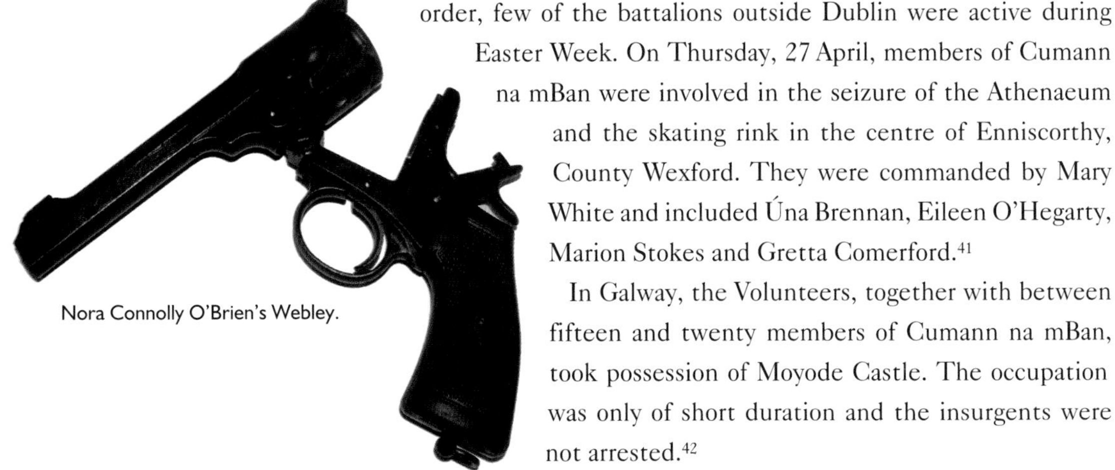

Nora Connolly O'Brien's Webley.

In Galway, the Volunteers, together with between fifteen and twenty members of Cumann na mBan, took possession of Moyode Castle. The occupation was only of short duration and the insurgents were not arrested.[42]

Observers' accounts show that when the Rising actually began, Dubliners were taken by surprise. They were used to seeing the Volunteers and the Irish Citizen Army marching in uniform through the streets, so on Easter Monday there did not appear to be anything unusual happening. It was a public holiday and many people who would normally have been in the city were off work. Lilly Stokes wrote in her diary that the first indication that something was amiss was when there was no public transport. The initial reaction of people was that the fighting was related to the war in Europe. On her way through the city, Lilly encountered 'a very befuddled recruiting Sergeant' who told her that the Germans had taken over St Stephen's Green. In her diary account she recorded how the Volunteers came into town unobtrusively, as Bank Holiday visitors, attracting no attention. 'What they hope to accomplish, one has no idea', she commented.[43]

And the Rising also came as a surprise to many of the Volunteers. This is illustrated in a letter written by a Volunteer named Joe in the days following the Rising, which was intercepted and found its way into the papers of British Prime Minister H H Asquith:

> We were no doubt deceived and taken by surprise by our leaders. I have not yet met one member of the rank and file who was aware that the Republic was to be proclaimed. Of course we expected trouble from the military if there was an attempt to disarm the country, that was the policy of McNeill [sic] ... and everyone was with him ... It can be plainly seen that Connolly and Clarke and the extreme men of our [IRB] Supreme Council got control of the movement and rushed matters ... The yarn about 20,000 Germans landing put great spirit into our lads. They feared nothing but God and really thought that Ireland's hour had come ...[44]

Even at the highest levels of command the plans had not been fully communicated. During his court martial, Ned Daly, commander of the battalion at the Four Courts, stated in his defence that he had no knowledge of the insurrection until Monday morning, 24 April:

> The officers including myself when we heard the news held a meeting and decided that the whole thing was foolish but that being under orders we had no option but to obey.[45]

The sense of disbelief that a Rising would take place when the eagerly awaited promises of the Home Rule Bill seemed imminent was expressed by people at all levels of Irish society. This view was shared by the Chief Secretary, Augustine Birrell, and his Under Secretary, Sir Matthew Nathan, and may explain why they failed to act despite being surrounded by a climate of rumours and counter rumours.

Marcella Cosgrave's 1916 medal.

Nathan is aid to have had a growing feeling that 'everything is not quite right' but nonetheless, on Saturday, 22 April he wrote reassuringly to his superior: 'I see no indications of a rising.'[46] Although communications between the Irish and the Germans had been intercepted, this information had not been forwarded to either Birrell or Nathan. Reports from the Inspector General of the Royal Irish Constabulary warning Dublin Castle that there was evidence that a Rising was being planned were ignored.

By Thursday, 27 April it was clear that the GPO could not be held for much longer. Patrick Pearse gathered the women together and told them that 'without the inspiration of their courage the Volunteers could not have made their stand. They deserved, he said, a foremost place in the history of the nation.[47] He then asked them to leave. At first they all refused, but finally a number of them were persuaded to go. Even then many of them were reluctant to go home and reported to the Four Courts garrison. They were present for the final stages of the fight, and were arrested and brought to Kilmainham Gaol.[48] Others, including Gertie Colley, made their way home but were held up by the military and detained for a short time at Broadstone Railway Station.[49]

When fire broke out in the GPO on Friday, 28 April it was decided that the remaining women should leave under the protection of the Red Cross flag. A small group, led by Louise Gavan Duffy, took the wounded to Jervis Street Hospital via passages broken through buildings in Henry Street.[50] They sheltered in the hospital for the night.

Three women remained in the GPO: Winnie Carney, Julia Grenan and Elizabeth O'Farrell. They stayed to nurse the wounded, including James Connolly, who had been shot while inspecting barricades. He later remarked to Julia Grenan and Elizabeth O'Farrell, who had delivered several dispatches from the GPO, 'When I was lying there in the lane I thought of how often you two went up and down there and nothing ever happened yez!'[51]

By Saturday morning, it was clear that the plan for the GPO garrison to join with that of the Four Courts would be impossible. The entire city was surrounded by troops. Aware of the loss of life among the civilian population, the decision was taken to surrender. While Elizabeth O'Farrell was chosen to deliver the surrender documents, Julia Grenan and Winnie Carney were arrested and taken with the men to the Rotunda Gardens where they spent the night.

At 12.45pm on Saturday, 29 April Elizabeth O'Farrell left Moore Street and approached the British Army post, carrying the surrender documents. An observer recalled, 'Inside, her two companions watched her breathlessly, with lumps in their throats, afraid that every minute they would see the gallant little figure totter and fall. But as she advanced, the fire slackened and finally stopped'. [52]At first she was thought to be a spy and the red cross was cut off her apron and sleeve. O'Farrell was held prisoner until 2.25 pm when it was decided that she would be sent back to Pearse, who would be asked to tender his unconditional surrender. She returned with Pearse at 3.30 pm.

While her comrades from the GPO were surrendering, O'Farrell set out for the various outposts with the surrender documents from Pearse and Connolly. There were so many snipers in the area around Boland's Mill that she was accompanied by a British Officer, Captain Wheeler for only part of the journey.

> **So I started through the firing line from Butt Bridge to Boland's ... This was a very difficult job and I had to take my life in my hands several times. When I came into Westland Row the military were lined across the top, and they were screaming at me to go back, but I kept on waving my white flag and the paper ... crossing Grand Canal Street Bridge the firing was terrific. At this point a man crossing the bridge about half a yard behind me was shot.**[53]

By dusk that evening Elizabeth O'Farrell had completed her task without injury. After a short period of imprisonment she was released.

The following day, when Louise Gavan Duffy and the other members of the GPO garrison who had sheltered at Jervis Street Hospital were making their way home, they passed their surrendering comrades. They evaded capture by saying that they were Red Cross nurses. The military were suspicious and took their names and addresses. Some were later questioned, but were released without charge.[54]

Dr Kathleen Lynn and the women of the City Hall garrison had been imprisoned in Dublin Castle since the early hours of the previous Tuesday morning. Dr Lynn, the highest-ranking officer following Connolly's death, offered the surrender. When asked if she was engaged in Red Cross work, she replied that she was 'a Red Cross doctor and a belligerent'.[55] At first the British did not know if they could accept capitulation from a woman, but in due course the insurgents were arrested. When the doctor was searched she was found to have an automatic revolver and fifty rounds of ammunition.[56] The prisoners were removed to Ship Street Barracks behind the Castle and held there until 1 May. Kathleen Lynn noted in her diary 'All women taken to Ship St. about 8.30 [pm] ... We were locked up in a filthy store, given blankets thick with lice and fleas ...' [57]

War of Independence medal belonging to Marcella Cosgrave.

When the time for surrender came at the Jacobs Factory garrison, Thomas MacDonagh called all the Volunteers together and told those who were not in uniform that they could leave. He wanted all the girls out of the building before he surrendered, as he was particularly concerned that the women not be arrested. Máire Nic Shiúbhlaigh later recalled that when she gave MacDonagh's order to the girls they did not want to obey it.

> If this had been the only consideration, I would have ignored his plea, and stayed; but he thought that the sight of the girls being arrested might upset the men — he wanted everything to go as quietly as possible.[58]

Kathleen Lynn (left) and Madeleine ffrench-Mullen, *c.*1916

At the College of Surgeons the women were arrested when Michael Mallin and Countess Markievicz surrendered to Major Wheeler at 2pm on Sunday, 30 April. Nora O'Daly recalled:

> On Sunday to us came news of the surrender which had already taken place the previous days at some other posts ... We were marched ... men first, women following. I carried the Red Cross flag, as some extraordinary stories were afloat to account for the presence of women amongst the garrison ... On the way soldiers going the opposite direction frequently shouted, 'Wot you goin' to do with this lot?' and the rejoinder was invariably 'Ow, goin' to biyenet 'em like the rest'.[59]

A number of women who had taken part in the fight in both Dublin and in Enniscorthy, County Wexford managed to evade arrest, but those in the Four Courts were taken under guard to Keogh Square, Inchicore and from there to Kilmainham Gaol.[60]

Meanwhile, at Marrowbone Lane, and unaware of the surrender, Anne Cooney recorded on Sunday, 30 April that 'things seem to have quietened down and the shooting had diminished. It was so quiet in comparison to the rest of the week that we decided to relax ...'[61] At four o' clock Thomas MacDonagh came to let the garrison know that they had to surrender. During the week the men of the garrison had constructed a tunnel so that the women could escape if necessary. The Cumann na mBan members were not pleased and would not make use of it. The women did not try to avoid arrest; Rose McNamara went to a British Officer and informed him that the women were part of the garrison.[62] As she recorded in her diary: 'we were all marched under military escort to Richmond Barracks, the girls were singing all the time in amidst the insults of the soldiers and the people along the route.'[63] As they came close to Kilmainham Gaol they met Major John MacBride, who was also being marched to the prison. He had been second in command at Jacob's Factory; he was not a member of the Volunteers but had been in Dublin when fighting began and volunteered. Major MacBride told the girls to keep on singing. Then he turned to Rose McNamara and said 'You'll be alright, you'll be out tomorrow'. When she asked 'what about you?' he said sadly: 'Ah no, we won't be out, we'll be shot.'[64] Although Ceannt's Volunteers had met with 'marked enthusiasm' when they surrendered from their post at the South Dublin Union,[65] in the main there was hostility from Dubliners as the garrisons surrendered. Immense damage had been done to the city and its everyday functions were brought almost to a complete halt. Lilly Stokes recorded in her diary on 2 May: 'One has some idea now how the Belgians and French feel, seeing their towns laid in ruins. Over 180 buildings have been burnt.'[66] The cost in damage to property in Sackville Street (O'Connell Street) alone was estimated at £1 million and £750,000 in lost stock.[67]

Looting had taken place on a major scale during the week of the fighting. On Wednesday, 26 April, Robert Livingston Chapman, an observer of the Rising, recorded in his journal: 'Noblett's looted and small boys smashing up everything breakable.'[68] Noblett's confectioners, located on the corner of Sackville Street and North Earl Street had its plate-glass frontage broken, and once one shop was looted, there was no halting the destruction.

The Government figures for casualties among civilians and insurgents came to 318 killed and 2,217 wounded. Civilian casualties were high, owing to the high concentration of dwellings in the vicinity of the fighting as well as the 'insatiable curiosity of the citizens of Dublin and their apparently fatalistic acceptance of the dangers involved in watching the spectacle.'[69]

The anger of people towards those who had taken part in the rebellion was heightened by the fact that the Rising had taken place while there was a war on — a war in which many Irishmen, in particular Dubliners, were involved. By the end of 1915 there were at least 85,000 Irishmen enlisted in the British Army, and over 16,300 of these men were from Dublin.[70] Anne Cooney's memory of the journey to Kilmainham Gaol was of being taunted by the 'separation women',[71] who, through the disruption caused by the Rising, were deprived of the allowance paid to them by the British Army as wives of men fighting in the Great War. They and their families faced hunger and hardship until the city began to function normally again. May Gahan was pelted by bottles and horse dung as she walked to Kilmainham Gaol.[72]

Maggie Craven's 1916 Cumann na mBan commemorative badge; Winnie Carney's pendant made from a Volunteer button.

On Friday, 28 April, General Sir John Maxwell had arrived from England to take up command of the British Army in Ireland. He oversaw a wide-scale round up of all those who were involved, or suspected of involvement, in the insurrection. Leaders of the Rising were court-martialled and sentenced to death by firing squad: Patrick Pearse, Thomas Clarke, Joseph Plunkett, James Connolly, Thomas MacDonagh, Seán MacDiarmada and Eamonn Ceannt were members of the Provisional Government of the Irish Republic. Others who received the death penalty included Willie Pearse (brother of

Patrick Pearse), Michael Mallin, Cornelius Colbert, Ned Daly, John MacBride, Michael O'Hanrahan, Seán Heuston and Thomas Kent. The first to be executed were Patrick Pearse, MacDonagh and Clarke, who were shot in the stonebreaker's yard in Kilmainham Gaol at dawn on 3 May 1916. The remainder of the executions took place between 3 and 12 May. James Connolly, who had been wounded in the GPO, was too ill to stand and was shot while strapped to a chair. Although seventy-five more revolutionaries had been sentenced to death, there was such an outcry after the first executions that their sentences were subsequently commuted to penal servitude for life.

The exact number of women who participated in the 1916 Rising remains unclear. If one uses the official figure for those imprisoned in Kilmainham Gaol following the

1917 propaganda postcard, depicting General Maxwell being haunted by the widows of the executed 1916 leaders.

Rising, the figure is seventy-seven [see listing Appendix 1], but because the vast majority of the women were not arrested, this is not a true reflection. Surviving documentation and oral accounts seem to suggest that out of an estimated total of 1,600 people involved in the Rising, as many as 200 were women.[73]

Kilmainham Gaol had ceased to function as a convict prison in 1910 and was taken over as an army detention barracks at the outbreak of the First World War. It presented a grim and forbidding picture to the arriving 1916 prisoners, made worse by the fact that there was no lighting or heating because the gas supply had been cut off during the fighting. Nora O'Daly remembered 'arriving after dusk and being received by the light of candles, which only served to intensify the gloom.'[74] Many of the women were housed in the older west wing, built in the 1790s, which was in a state of disrepair, with poor sanitary facilities. Anne Cooney remembered seeing an inscription that read 'Sin no more lest worse shall come to thee.'[75]

Upon her arrival, Elizabeth O'Farrell recorded that she was stripped and searched, but it does not seem as if other women were given the same treatment. Rose McNamara noted that those who came from the Marrowbone Lane garrison were lined up, searched and had their names taken. The women gave their names in Irish and the soldiers could not understand them.[76] Nora O'Daly recalled that during her questioning she was asked to make a statement about her involvement with these 'frightful rebels'. The soldiers were mainly curious about the Rising, asked what the women were 'in' for, and gave them gratuitous information about their own sentences and their sergeant's character.[77] Brighid Lyons Thornton recalled:

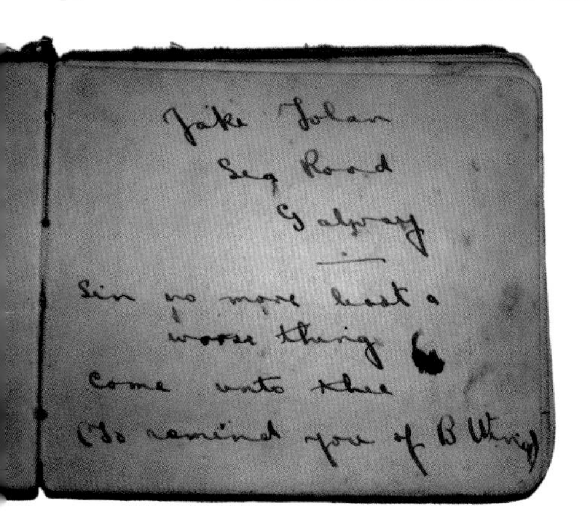
Jake Folan
Sea Road
Galway

Sin no more lest a
worse thing
come unto thee
(To remind you of B Wing)

Left: Katherine (Jake) Folan recorded the Kilmainham Gaol inscription in an autograph book.

> Kilmainham ... was a dismal, dreary, frightening place to be on a lovely summer evening. We went in and there were officers inside ... they tried to get more details out of us and then somebody said, 'Take them up and throw them into the cells, we can't get anything.' ... then we were marched upstairs and thrown three or four into a cell. We didn't care where we got so long as we got lying down. We were very exhausted and very tired.[78]

The daily routine of the prisoners began at 7am, although breakfast was not until 9.30am.[79] Elizabeth O'Farrell described the dinner as 'awful stuff, neither soup nor

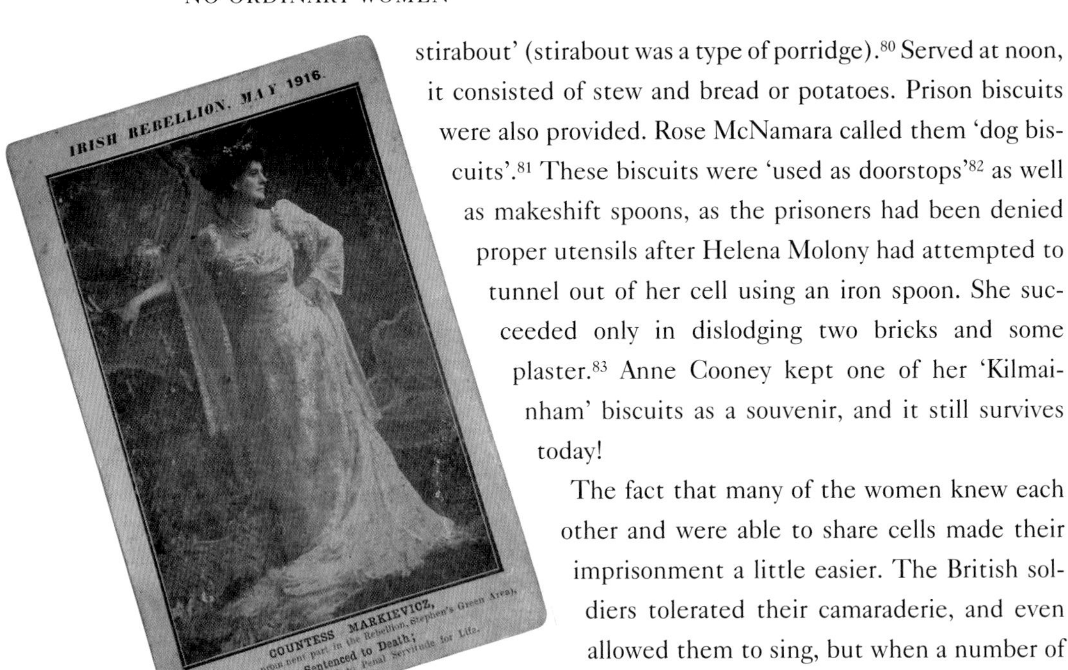

Countess Markievicz portrayed on one of a series of commemorative postcards of 1916 leaders.

stirabout' (stirabout was a type of porridge).[80] Served at noon, it consisted of stew and bread or potatoes. Prison biscuits were also provided. Rose McNamara called them 'dog biscuits'.[81] These biscuits were 'used as doorstops'[82] as well as makeshift spoons, as the prisoners had been denied proper utensils after Helena Molony had attempted to tunnel out of her cell using an iron spoon. She succeeded only in dislodging two bricks and some plaster.[83] Anne Cooney kept one of her 'Kilmainham' biscuits as a souvenir, and it still survives today!

The fact that many of the women knew each other and were able to share cells made their imprisonment a little easier. The British soldiers tolerated their camaraderie, and even allowed them to sing, but when a number of the women did the Sixteen Hand Reel in the exercise yard,[84] that was a little too much for the authorities, who then forbade Irish dancing at exercise hour on penalty of being kept in their cells.[85]

Countess Markievicz was held in solitary confinement, and not allowed to exercise with the other women.[86] As one of the leaders of the Rising she had been sentenced to death, but the charge was commuted to penal servitude for life because she was a woman. The verdict of Markievicz's court martial was unique; having been found guilty and sentenced to be shot, the court recommended mercy for the prisoner 'solely and only on account of her sex'.[87] In October 1915 the Germans had executed Edith Cavell, a nurse who had harboured British soldiers in occupied Belgium, and the British had protested against her execution.[88] It may, therefore, have been politic to commute the Countess's sentence.

Some of the women were unaware that the Volunteer leaders were also in Kilmainham Gaol. But when they heard gunshots at dawn on 3 May they suspected the worst. 'At first the wardress said it was distant fighting. But we knew the truth', recalled Julia Grenan.[89] Nora O'Daly was not aware of what had happened until the prisoners were told by the military on Monday, 8 May:

> **...we learned for the first time, with heavy heart, of the executions which had taken place, and this news sent my mind back to an occurrence during our detention and which had remained unexplained up to now. One morning we were awakened at the first grey dawn by a shot, which appeared to be within the building.**[90]

General Maxwell ordered an examination of intelligence reports to ascertain what information was available on the women arrested.[91] From the intelligence reports it was concluded that the majority of the women belonged to the Sinn Féin ambulance society, and that this organisation did not entirely confine itself to Red Cross work, but was in fact the women's branch of the Irish Volunteers and was highly seditious in its activities.[92]

The British were already facing a logistical nightmare in dealing with the vast numbers arrested after the Rising. One estimate is that 134 were condemned to penal servitude, and 2,650 were deported without trial.[93]

Late on the evening of 8 May, when the women were preparing to go to bed, the cell doors were opened and they were ordered into the central hall. Downstairs there were a number of British officers, the Governor of the gaol and Father Eugene McCarthy from the nearby St James's Street parish.[94] Those whose names were called out had to cross to one side of the room. Rumour spread among the women that they were going to be deported and shipped to Jamaica to pick oranges.[95] However, after being cautioned as to 'their future behaviour',[96] the women were informed that they were being released.

General Maxwell clearly saw their gender as the decisive factor in letting them go free. Writing to the Secretary of the War he stated: 'In view of their sex ... I consider that it would be desirable that they should be granted their liberty.'[97] He had sent William Wylie, a prosecution counsel, to interview the women being held in Kilmainham Gaol and Wylie was given the power to conduct a selection process. With a few exceptions, he decided to release them. Maxwell agreed with his decisions and told Wylie that he did not know what to do with 'all these silly little girls'. He was sure that 'the right thing to do was to send them home.'[98]

Nevertheless, a number of women were detained, among them Helena Molony, Brigid Foley, Nellie Gifford, Madeleine ffrench-Mullen and Dr Kathleen Lynn. Mary Mac Swiney was arrested in Cork. These were women who were known to the British authorities in Ireland, and the reports that they were 'merely Red Cross workers could not be sustained'.[99] General Maxwell was adamant that 'had they been male prisoners, I would at least have recommended for internment.' He believed that it would be unwise to have them 'at large' in Ireland while such an 'unsettled state of affairs' continued.[100]

Helena Molony, Madeleine ffrench-Mullen and Dr Kathleen Lynn had all been prominent in the Irish Citizen Army during Easter week. Helena already had a police record, having been arrested during a protest against the state visit of King George and Queen Mary to Ireland in 1911. She had been caught throwing a stone at a picture of the King that was displayed in a shop window in Grafton Street.[101] Her association with the Labour movement, her position as editor of *Bean na hÉireann*, and her career as an actress made her a well-known figure.

Brigid Foley was a member of Inghinidhe na hÉireann. Before the Rising she brought dispatches to Cork. She also belonged to the Irish Citizen Army and had reported to the GPO on Easter Monday.[102] During the fighting she was stationed at St Stephen's Green.

Nellie Gifford was with the Irish Citizen Army in St Stephen's Green. She had been a founder member of the Irish Citizen Army and her family were well known to the authorities. Her sister Muriel was married to Thomas MacDonagh, and a second sister, Grace, had married the poet Joseph Mary Plunkett, another of the leaders, on the night before he was executed. Winnie Carney, from Cumann na mBan's Belfast branch, had been stationed in the GPO during the Rising.

Some of the prisoners held in Kilmainham had been dispatch carriers but had not taken part in the actual fighting, and there were a number who had not taken part at all. One of these was Nell Humphreys, sister of Michael O'Rahilly, and mother of nineteen-year-old Dick Humphreys of the GPO garrison. Although she had visited the GPO several times during the week of the Rising, her capture came about when there was fierce fighting in the vicinity of her house at 54 Northumberland Road. Number 25 had been occupied by rebels and there were a number of engagements with the military on Wednesday, 26 April. The Humphreys house was pointed out to the troops as the home of sympathisers to the rebels, but the military mistakenly riddled a neighbour's house instead, where the occupants were actually pro-British. After the fighting on their street, Nell Humphreys was arrested and taken to the nearby Royal Dublin Society grounds. There she was held in a horsebox during the day and at night she was taken home and a soldier slept outside her bedroom door.[103] After a few days she was brought to Kilmainham Gaol and from there transferred to Mountjoy Jail. Later, Timothy Healy, the Cork-born Home Rule MP, asked the Under Secretary for War why she was arrested, stating that there was no evidence that she had participated in the Rebellion. She was released on 16 May.[104]

Helena Molony with Maud Gonne MacBride (seated).

Annie Higgins, a music teacher at a school in Carrickmacross, County Monaghan, had been on holiday in her native Dublin when the Rising occurred. She had spent Tuesday and Wednesday of Easter week cooking for the Volunteers at the Hibernian Bank until they evacuated to the GPO. She was then sent on a courier mission to Monaghan. Although there was a cordon around the city, she managed to get past the military by showing her return train ticket to Carrickmacross. However, her activities were noticed and she was arrested in Monaghan and brought to Armagh Jail.[105]

Count and Countess Plunkett, with daughter Mimi (left), dressed for a function at Dublin Castle.

Mary Perolz had not taken part in the fighting. She had been a dispatch carrier to Cork before the Rising but was unable to return to Dublin and went instead to Tralee, County Kerry where she was arrested on 1 May. She was brought to Dublin Castle and later to Mountjoy. Mary Perolz was a member of a number of organisations including Inghinidhe na hÉireann and the Irish Citizen Army. It was entered into the evidence of the Rebellion Commission that she was the registered owner of the 'seditious weekly paper', *The Spark*, with a circulation of 2,382.[106]

Countess Plunkett, mother of Joseph Mary Plunkett, was arrested on 7 May and brought to Kilmainham Gaol where her son had been shot a few days previously.[107] She had played no part in the Rising. In the aftermath of the Rising she had gone from official to official, desperately looking for information on the whereabouts of her husband, Count Plunkett, and her three sons, George, John and Joseph who had all taken part in the Rising. It was at this time that she was herself taken prisoner.[108]

Kathleen Browne and Ellen (Nell) Ryan, from County Wexford, both from nationalist families, were making their way to Dublin after the Rising when they

were arrested near Bray.[109] Kathleen Browne had made no secret of her sympathies during Easter Week when she flew the tricolour from the roof of her ancestral home, Rathronan Castle, Wexford.[110]

Nell Ryan was one of a family of twelve children from Tomcoole, County Wexford. A number of the Ryans were involved in nationalist politics. The report submitted by the County District Inspector at Gorey, County Wexford, to the Chief Secretary's office at the time of her arrest gives a picture of how the Ryans were viewed by the authorities: The 'O'Ryans are industrious people and quiet. They are interested in Irish politics and are inclined to extreme views.'[111] He recommended Nell's continued internment as he felt that in her position as a clerk with the County Wexford National Insurance Committee she was' in a position to spread the extreme views she holds.'[112]

That the intelligence on which some of the arrests were made was very arbitrary is evidenced by the treatment received by the Ryan sisters. Nell had not even been in Dublin during the Rising, but was arrested because she was found to be in possession of correspondence with 'extreme Sinn Féiners' such as Seán MacDiarmada. Yet her sister, Mary Josephine (known as Min) was MacDiarmada's girlfriend, mentioned in his final letter to his sisters as: 'Miss Ryan, she who in all probability, had I lived, would have been my wife.'[113] Min and another sister, Phyllis, had been messengers during Easter week and had visited the GPO daily up to and including Thursday when the GPO was evacuated.[114] They also visited MacDiarmada in Kilmainham Gaol just before he was executed[115] but still they evaded arrest. Min, who was a founder member of Cumann na mBan, even managed to get out of Ireland. On the instructions of the executive of Cumann na mBan she travelled to America in the weeks following the Rising; she was the first to bring news of the Rising to Irish supporters in America.[116] However, another of the Ryan sisters, Mary Kate (known as Kit) was arrested following the Rising. There is no record of her participation in the Rising but like many of the others arrested she must have been named in the intelligence reports received by Maxwell.

The Ryan family of Tomcoole, Wexford, c.1910.
Standing (left to right): Jim, Chris, Jack, Kate, Mick, Nell, Min.
Seated: Liz, Father Martin, Elizabeth Ryan, John Ryan, Joanna (Mother Stanislaus), Aunt Jane.
Front: Agnes and Phyllis.

Certainly, neither Kit nor Nell knew why they had been arrested, as attested to by their sister, Phyllis, who wrote on 19 May 1916 'Kate and Nell are both in Mountjoy ... They have no idea of what they are being kept for, or for how long.'[117] It could be argued that Kit was arrested instead of Min as they both had the same Christian name of Mary. Kit was at the time acting Professor of French at University College Dublin[118], and the house that she shared with her siblings, 19 Ranelagh Road, was frequented by many activists. Two years later she married Seán T O'Kelly, who had served in the GPO during the Rising, and was later to become President of Ireland.

The remaining prisoners were kept at Kilmainham Gaol for about ten days and then moved to Mountjoy Jail. Conditions for the women in Mountjoy were not too harsh. They were allowed to exercise together twice a day,[119] to have visitors and accept clothes and food parcels. They were given the concession of a room in common so they could spend the evenings together. At the end of May the authorities gave the women a choice of internment or exile to England to serve out the remainder of their sentence. On 23 May Kathleen Browne wrote to her mother:

> **... we have not been asked yet for our decision as to whether we shall take up our residence in holy England or go into internment — which of course is quite a different thing from imprisonment. Five or six of us have decided to take the latter ...**[120]

Opposite: Central staircase, East Wing of Kilmainham Gaol.

However, the internment did not happen and, on 4 June, Kathleen Browne was released along with Kit Ryan, Madeleine ffrench-Mullen, Annie Higgins and Nellie

Gifford. Nell Ryan wrote to a friend that the remaining prisoners were hoping for their 'liberty every day since', but that 'each day's sun sets on disappointed hopes.'[121] She wrote that she was pleased that her sister had been released: 'I was very happy once Katie (Kit) was set free for she looked so badly. I was afraid she would not be able to stand it much longer.' Nell described herself as in the 'best of spirits' and said that she and the other prisoners had 'no complaints to make of their treatment', but concluded that 'of course one must remember prison at any time is not home.'[123]

At the direction of Prime Minister Asquith and under the provisions of Regulation 14 of the Defence of the Realm Act, General Maxwell sent Countess Plunkett to live in Oxford with her husband. Count Plunkett, a learned man, was the former Director of the Arts and Science Museum in Dublin and had chosen to go to Oxford because he wanted the chance to read at the Bodleian library. However, when he arrived in Oxford, he was denied this opportunity when the librarian — an Irishman who did not approve of his politics — refused him a reader's ticket.[124]

Dr Kathleen Lynn was deported to Abingdon, near Bath. Her father used his connections as a rector in Cong, County Mayo which was under the patronage of Lord and Lady Ardilaun of the nearby Ashford estate, to spare her incarceration in an English prison. The Lynn family's solution, she later described, was to have someone take her in, on the basis that she was some kind of 'lunatic'.[125] As doctors were in short supply due to the ongoing war, it was arranged by a friend that she would be given a position with a Doctor Cusack, originally from Galway, who had a medical practice at Abingdon.[126]

Nell Ryan, Helena Molony, Winnie Carney, Mary Perolz and Brigid Foley were deported to England on 20 June to serve sentences in Lewes Prison in Sussex.[127] Following their arrival in England, the prisoners were given seven days in which to appeal their sentences.[128] The appeal was referred to an Advisory Committee presided over by a Judge of the High Court. After questions in Parliament and a short court appearance, Brigid Foley and Mary Perolz were released.[129] They were issued with travel warrants and told to return to Ireland via Kingstown (Dun Laoghaire).[130] The case of the continued imprisonment of Nell Ryan was discussed in the House of Commons in August 1916 and it emerged that the evidence against her consisted of two documents that had been sent to her — a letter referring to a resolution that was to be passed by the Wexford Board of Guardians and another which was an invitation to a picnic. In reply to the question: was Miss Ryan to be held responsible for other people's words? Mr Samuel, the Secretary of State for the Home Department, replied that 'after personally hearing Ellen Ryan and carefully considering the evidence against her' he had recommended that her internment be maintained.[131]

In July, Kathleen Lynn was allowed back to Ireland to nurse her sister who had taken ill. Questions continued to be raised in Parliament as to why these 'Irish lady prisoners' were detained without trial for 4 months.[132] As a result of the growing dissatisfaction that the women were held without trial, Kathleen Lynn received word in early August that she did not have to return to Abingdon. Maxwell gave his authorisation, stating in a memo that there was 'no great objection to this lady remaining in Ireland.'[133]

Nell Ryan, Winnie Carney and Helena Molony were sent to Aylesbury Jail in Buckinghamshire at the end of July 1916, where Countess Markievicz was already interned.[134] In Aylesbury, Countess Markievicz was held in a wing with thieves, prostitutes and murderers. While male prisoners arrested for their part in the Rising had won the right of association, the Countess was not allowed to converse with fellow inmates as a rule of silence was imposed.

When the Irish women arrived in Aylesbury they were put in a different wing from the Countess as they were untried prisoners. They petitioned the Secretary of State for the Home Department to allow them to join the Countess, in accordance with the rights granted to the male prisoners. They offered to forego their privileges and accept the same treatment as Countess Markievicz, but were refused permission to do so.[135] Nell Ryan was finally released on 13 October.[136] That same month Countess Plunkett was also permitted to return home.

In early November, Helena Molony and Winnie Carney were told that if they wished to be released they should sign an undertaking 'not to engage in any act of a seditious character'.[137] Both women refused to sign. Helena Molony told her Military Tribunal that the Irish Citizen Army had organised the Rising and would do so again.[138] On 21 December, 1916 the British Government decided to release 600 untried male prisoners from Frongoch Detention Camp in Wales, and on 23 December others were released from Reading Jail, Berkshire.

During the general amnesty on Christmas Eve 1916, Helena Molony and Winnie Carney were finally released. Helena Molony's letter to Nell Ryan describes their departure from Aylesbury.

Spiral staircase, East Wing of Kilmainham Gaol.

You can't imagine anything so sad as the morning we left. They were all so helpless, and hopeless. Paula in hysterics and floods of tears, Mrs Herbert at the piano, playing and singing hymns and patriotic songs ... If I had my choice I think I would rather have stayed over Christmas. They were all so overwrought that we both hated leaving them. Mrs Herbert played from 11 o'clock, and it was like a county pub to see them singing and shaking hands with us and their eyes flooded

> **with tears the whole time, you'd think we were their nearest relations. Miss Carney collapsed on the table sobbing, and even I felt a bit damp.**[139]

Countess Markievicz was still held in the prison. The treatment was telling on her health. According to Helena Molony, the company was awful.[140] According to a biographer, Diana Norman, her title and reputation marked her for grimmer treatment than other inmates.[141] Her sister Eva campaigned for her, and after a couple of months in prison, she was allowed a notebook in which to sketch and write — this was to occupy the long hours after 5.30pm when she was locked in her cell. Among her prison duties was sewing work, and later she worked in the kitchen. In August 1916 she wrote to her sister from Aylesbury: 'Don't worry about me. I am quite cheerful and content, and I would have felt very small and useless if I had been ignored. I am quite patient and I believe that everything will happen for the best.'[142] It would be a year before the Countess, convict G-12, was released. When she emerged from prison Ireland was a very different place.

Women who took part in the Easter Rising, photographed in the garden of Ely O'Carroll's house in Peter's Place, Dublin, during the summer of 1916.

Standing (left): A. Tobin, Aoife Taaffe, Marcella Cosgrave, Kathleen Murphy, Bridget Foley.

Standing (right): M. Kelly, Máire Nic Shiúbhlaigh, Lily O'Brennan, Elizabeth O'Farrell, Nora O'Daly, Mary Murray.

Back row: M. Kelly, Brigid Brady, Jeannie Shanahan, Kathleen Barrett, Rosie Hackett, Margaret Ryan, Brigid Davis, Chris Caffrey, Patricia Hoey.

Fifth row: Lucy Smith, Nora Foley, Pauline Morecombe, D. Sullivan, M. Elliott, Mary Sullivan, Tilley Simpson, Catherine Treston.

Fourth row: Nora Thornton, Rose Mulally, Sheila O'Hanlon, Maria Quigley, Margaret O'Flaherty, Josie McGowan, Eileen Cooney, Josie O'Keefe.

Third row: M. Moore, K. Lane, Sarah Kealy, Gertie Colley, Mary O'Hanrahan, Amee Wisley, Bridget Murtagh, Cilla Quigley, Julia Grenan, Statia Twoomey, B. Walsh.

Second row: Rose McNamara, Kathleen Kenny, M.J. Walsh, Mrs Lawless, Jenny Milner, Eileen Walsh, K. Kennedy, May Byrne, Eileen Cooney, Annie Cooney.

Front row: Madeleine ffrench-Mullen, Miss Foley, Dr Kathleen Lynn.

ST COLMCILLE'S STATUE,
LONG TOWER CHURCH, DERRY.

Lá na mBan
A Solemn Pledge for
The Women of Ireland.
Inaugurated on St. Colmcille's Day.

"Because the enforcement of conscription on

CHAPTER 3

Women and the Road to Independence (1917–1921)

'Let us show our enemy what we women can do.'

In the months following the 1916 Rising, women provided a communications system that brought together disparate elements gathering under the umbrella of Sinn Féin. Although Sinn Féin had not been behind the Rising – which was planned and carried out by the Irish Republican Brotherhood – it was called the Sinn Féin Rebellion by the authorities and the press.

> **Sinn Féin, with its dozen or so councillors and its newspaper, would have been the only separatist organisation known to the civilian administration in Dublin Castle that had any political presence in Dublin.[1]**

The work of Cumann na mBan in the aftermath of the Rising had a major effect in shaping the revolutionary spirit of the years 1917–1921. While the internment

Above:
Pledge signed by the women of Ireland, Lá na mBan, 1918.

camps have been termed the 'universities of revolutionists', producing men who returned to Ireland as 'a core of dedicated politicised soldiers and idealists',[2] it was the women who spread the doctrine of Republicanism throughout the country during the period when the men were interned.

Immediately after Easter week, women activists set about the destruction of any papers of an incriminating nature[3] and they delivered messages to the families of men who had been interned. Others searched for the dead and the injured in the hospitals[4] – work that was vital in compiling a register of those who had been widowed and orphaned or were otherwise in need of support. Many of those in prison had made no provision for their families and, as there was no welfare system in place, these families were now destitute. On the instructions of the Irish Republican Brotherhood, Kathleen Clarke, widow of Tom Clarke, had not joined in the Rising. An official confidante of the Supreme Council of the IRB, she had been given 'detailed information of all their decisions and plans and the names of people with whom she should communicate in the event of the members of the Military Council all being arrested or killed. They were determined that the work would go on even if they were all dead.'[5]

Kathleen Clarke.

Kathleen Clarke had been left £3,000 by the Military Council for relief aid.[6] Despite her double bereavement (both her husband and her brother, Ned Daly, had been executed) and the fact that she suffered a miscarriage in the weeks following the Rising, she took a leading role in coordinating the relief operation. In this she was joined by Sorcha MacMahon, who resigned her job and postponed her marriage in order to concentrate on setting up a system for the distribution of funds.[7] Within a fortnight, two organisations had been established: the Irish National Aid Association and the Irish Volunteers' Dependants' Fund. Cumann na mBan encouraged and facilitated their amalgamation into the one organisation, The National Aid and Volunteers' Dependants' Fund (NAVDF). The huge task of administrating the collection and distribution of the money was undertaken mainly by Cumann na mBan members. The women formed Distribution Committees, appointing to each district a secretary and a staff of five or six visitors. The coordination of the distribution 'rounds' was highly organised. Visits took place once or twice a week, often after the working day was over.[8] Apart from the distribution of funds on a weekly basis to those on the register, women were involved in committee meetings, the distribution of handbills promoting their work, and fundraising through

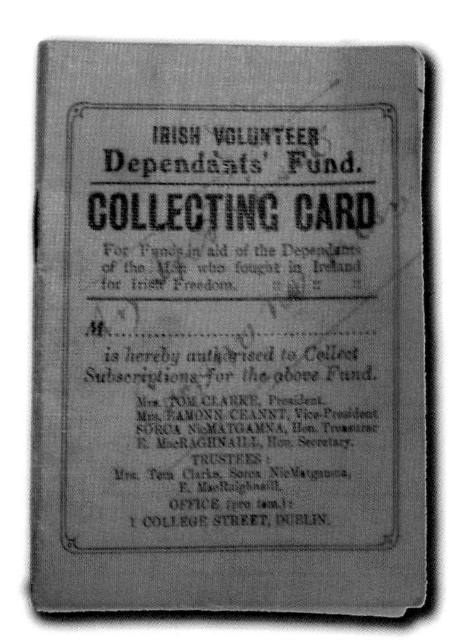

Irish Volunteer Dependants' Fund Collecting Card.

concerts, collections and the selling of commemorative material.

Seventy-eight Volunteers had lost their lives during the Rising and the number of those interned reached 2,300 at its height 'affecting the means of some 10,000 persons'.[9] The National Aid and Volunteers Dependants' Fund aimed to provide money for the welfare and education of the families of all those killed and interned, as well as creating employment for those victimised as a result of their involvement in the Rising.

Many of the women who had been involved in nationalist organisations lost their jobs. Eileen Dempsey (GPO garrison), managed to avoid arrest but lost her job at McCrad Collar Manufacturers as a result of her membership of the Citizen Army.[10] Éilís Ní Chorra, a member of Cumann na mBan in Belfast, never got the opportunity to join in the fight, but her sympathies were nevertheless known to her employers and they dismissed her for being absent without leave.[11]

An Employment Registry Office was established. The register at one point contained almost 500 names of those unemployed as a result of their participation in the Rising. The committee approached employers on an individual basis and managed to get many reinstated in their jobs. For those unable to regain their positions, grants were given to start businesses that included boot repairing, tailoring and wheel and wagon works. However, applications for fares to the United States of America were turned down.[12]

Eamonn and Áine Ceannt c.1908. (Áine is on the right.)

The position of secretary to the National Aid and Volunteers' Dependants' Fund became vacant shortly after Michael Collins was released from Frongoch Internment Camp in Wales. Collins had emerged as a leader among the internees, who had become a united force and were committed to fighting for Irish freedom with 'a sense of belonging and a sense of purpose'.[13] He went to Kathleen Clarke and sought her support in reorganising the Irish Republican Brotherhood and the Volunteers.[14] Kathleen assisted by giving him her husband's Irish Republican Brotherhood contacts. She believed that Collins was the man who could strike another blow for Ireland.[15] Thus, from February 1917, Collins's work as Secretary of the NAVDF helped in his dual roles as Director of Organisation for the Irish Volunteers and Chairman of the Supreme Council of the IRB. Having access to the records of all the activists and their families who were obtaining funds, he was able to establish a network of supporters throughout the country. Collins went on to become the key figure in what became known as the Irish War of Independence.

The first meeting of the Central Branch of Cumann na mBan after the Rising was a very stormy one. Kathleen Clarke chaired the gathering and later recalled a motion being proposed to the effect that those who had not fought in the Rising should be expelled. She called on the women present to forget about the failures and get to work, urging them: 'let us show our enemy what we women can do.'[16]

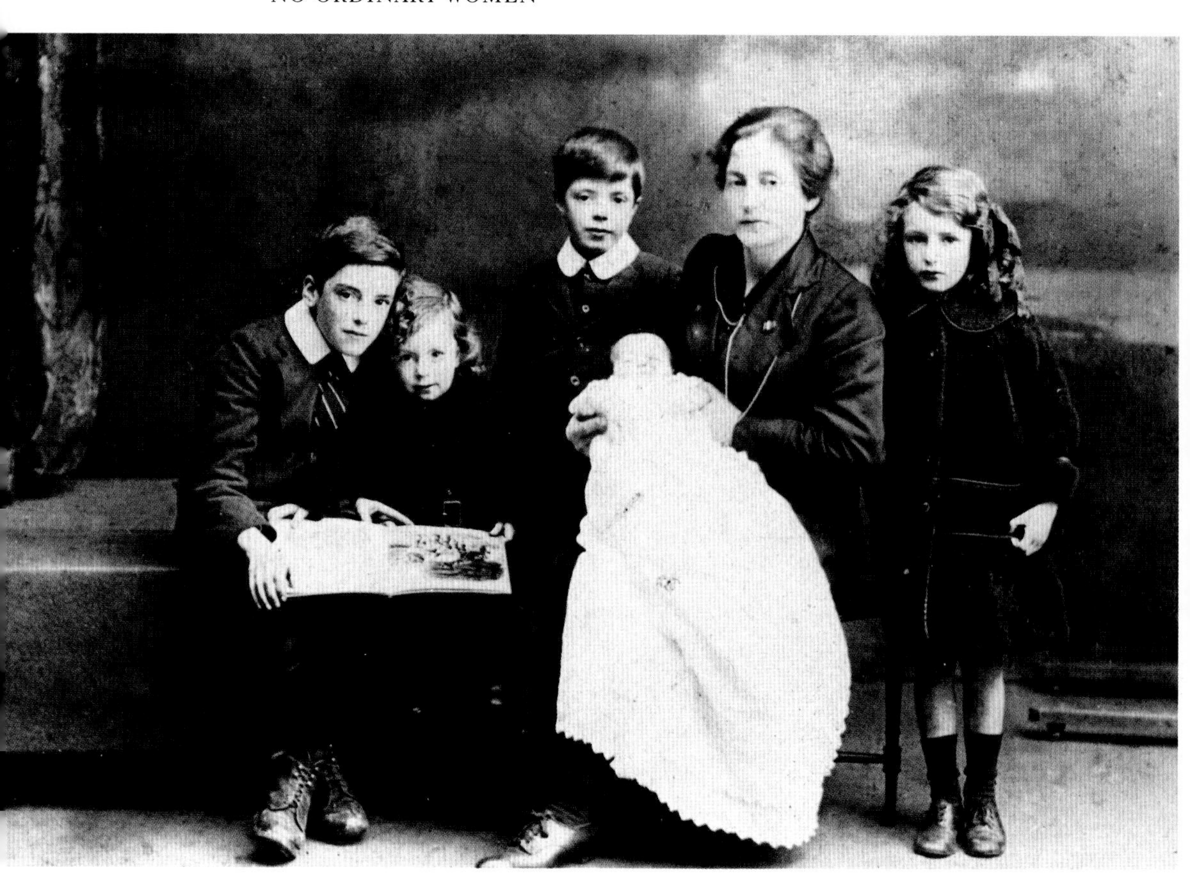

The Mallin family, 1916. Seamus, Joe, Sean, Agnes holding baby Moira, and Úna.

In the autumn of 1917, Countess Markievicz was re-elected President of Cumann na mBan. Relatives of men executed or killed in the Rising were elected as vice-presidents, including Nancy (Nannie) O'Rahilly (widow of The O'Rahilly who had been killed during the fighting of Easter Week), Margaret Pearse (mother of the executed Patrick and Willie Pearse), Áine Ceannt (widow of Eamonn Ceannt) and Kathleen Clarke.

The widows became a tangible symbol of the 1916 leaders' sacrifice. They were public figures and gave a powerful focus to the highly emotive commemorative Masses that marked the first and subsequent anniversaries of the executions. The Christmas 1916 issue of *The Catholic Bulletin* contained photographs of the widows and their children. Agnes Mallin is pictured holding her four-month-old baby Moira (born in August 1916) and surrounded by her other children, Seamus (12), Seán (10), Úna (7) and two-year-old Joe. Nannie O'Rahilly's baby son, Rory (born July, 1916) is pictured with his four older brothers – the eldest just thirteen years of age. Other families included those of Kathleen Clarke (three children), Mrs Philip Clarke (eight children) and Mrs Richard O'Carroll (seven children). These images brought a human face to the tragedy of Easter week and highlighted the sacrifices that had been made in the struggle, particularly by the families who were left behind.

Opposite (below): The altar of the chapel in Kilmainham Gaol where Joseph and Grace were married hours before his execution.

Another event that changed public opinion in favour of the leaders and their families was the marriage of Joseph Plunkett and Grace Gifford in Kilmainham Gaol just hours before Joseph was executed. The couple had arranged to marry on Easter Sunday, 23 April 1916 but their plans were thwarted by the upheaval of the Rising. When Joseph was sentenced to death, they asked for permission to marry in Kilmainham. Grace entered Kilmainham Gaol on 3 May at 6pm and was kept waiting there till about 11.30 pm. She did not see her fiancé until she entered the prison chapel, which was lighted only by a candle carried by a soldier.[17] There were no friends in attendance, although Grace's sister Nellie was a prisoner in the gaol. The witnesses to the wedding were two soldiers, John Smith and John Carberry of the Third Battalion of the Royal Irish Regiment.[18] During the marriage ceremony the couple were not allowed to speak except to recite the words of the ceremony. Immediately afterwards Joseph was taken back to his cell and Grace left the prison. At 2am Grace received a letter granting her permission to visit her husband before his execution. Later she recalled their last meeting: 'I saw my husband in his cell for ten minutes. During the interview the cell was packed with officers and a sergeant, who kept a watch in his hand and closed the interview by saying "Your ten

Commemorative poster featuring Joseph Mary Plunkett and Grace Gifford Plunkett, c.1916.

Letter of Freedom issued to Joseph Plunkett and Grace Gifford by the parish church in Rathmines, Dublin.

Bmæ et Imm.

Virginis Mariæ, Peccatorum Refugii,

APUD RATHMINES.

Testimonium Status Liberi Ad Matrimonium Proxime Contrahendum.

Præmissis opportunis diligentiis, nulla tamen, ob rite obtentam dispensationem, facta bannorum proclamatione, testatur infrascriptus Ecclesiæ B.V.M. Vicarius *nullum fuisse detectum impedimentum Canonicum quod obstat quominus, servatis ceteris de jure servandis, tuto possit ad Matrimonii celebrationem procedi inter*

Joseph Plunkett.

de ______ *filium* ______

de ______ *Orthodoxæ fidei ac hujus, Parochiæ sub titulo B.V.M. Pec. Ref. a*pud Rathmines.

incolam et Grace Gifford.

e Parochia, ut exponitur Rathmines.

filiam ______ *de* ______

modo ipsa sit ab omni impedimento Canonico similiter soluta.

In fidem, etc. [illegible]

Dat. Ap. Eccl. B.V.M., Rathmines,

die 3 Maii *19*16.

Rdo. Dno.

minutes is now up".'[19] It was a story of such romance and heartbreak that even today the tragic marriage is remembered in a popular song.

The first anniversary of Easter week 1916 was marked by the holding of commemorative Masses. Limerick Cumann na mBan arranged that a Mass would be held at dawn on 4 May 1917 at Saint John's Cathedral in the city, marking the first anniversary of the executions following the Rising. Madge Daly recalled, 'Hours before daylight Saint John's Square was packed by a dense crowd of people … from streets and lanes and the suburbs they came to honour the memory of our latest martyrs.'[20] In Dublin, women were instrumental in the re-flagging of the 1916 outposts. Helena Molony got a steeplejack to climb up on the roof of the GPO and hoist the tricolour. It was placed in such an awkward location that it took until six o'clock that evening to remove it.[21] Against the wishes of the Irish Transport and General Workers Union, Helena accompanied Rosie Hackett and hung a banner from Liberty Hall, with the inscription 'James Connolly – Murdered 12 May.'[22] The Proclamation was reprinted (copies of this reprint are now as rare as the original 1916 Proclamations themselves) and posted up around Dublin city.

In April 1917 meetings were convened to discuss how nationalist groups would come together to form a united force. Negotiations were conducted by the Council of Nine, which involved only one woman, Countess Plunkett; her husband, Count Plunkett, was one of the main negotiators. She was selected rather than elected, and action was required to make sure that women were not marginalised.[23] A number of politicised women from groups such as the Inghinidhe branch and the executive of Cumann na mBan, members of the Irish Women Workers' Union and women from the Irish Citizen Army came together to form the League of Women Delegates (the name was later changed to Cumann na dTeachtaire). They were determined that the promise of equal opportunity and equal citizenship contained in the Proclamation would be adhered to by those fighting for independence. The aim of this organisation was to 'secure women's role in the national movement and to promote their claims for equality, including suffrage.'[24] Lobbying by Cumann na dTeachtaire resulted in four women (not six, as they had requested) being co-opted onto the executive of Sinn Féin.[25]

The activists who had supported the Easter Rising now became Sinn Féin candidates in by-elections for vacant seats to the British Parliament. The candidates agreed to abide by the Sinn Féin policy of abstentionism; if they were elected, they would not take their seats. Count Plunkett, father of the executed Joseph Mary Plunkett, successfully contested the Roscommon by-election. In June 1917 Eamon de Valera, who had been a garrison leader in the 1916 Rising but had escaped execution, was elected for Sinn Féin in County Clare.

In July of 1917, following years of parliamentary agitation, the British government set up an Irish Convention to implement some form of home government, but Sinn Féin boycotted it. In the same month, Sinn Féin held their first Ard Fheis [Convention]. Arthur Griffith, the founder of Sinn Féin, stepped aside to allow Eamon de Valera to become its President. The organisation was restructured and Sinn Féin clubs were now coordinated from a central body and given clear aims. Women were vocal and visible at the Sinn Féin Convention, but there were only twelve female delegates among the thousand male delegates. Countess Markievicz, together with Kathleen Clarke, Kathleen Lynn and Grace Plunkett, were voted on to the executive.[26] Later, Áine Ceannt became Director of Communications and Hanna Sheehy Skeffington became Director of Organisation.

The Irish Volunteers reformed to become the military wing to Sinn Féin's political wing; they were now becoming known as the Irish Republican Army (IRA). The recruiting drive begun after the Rising by Cumann na mBan was so successful that by 1917 one hundred branches of the organisation had been set up. The following year it had grown to 600 branches. Min Ryan, Jennie Wyse Power, Lily O'Brennan, Louise Gavan Duffy and Áine Ceannt were among those sent to recruit in different parts of the country.[27]

Pledge signed by the women of Ireland, Lá na mBan, 1918.

St Colmcille's Statue, Long Tower Church, Derry.

Lá na mBan

A Solemn Pledge for The Women of Ireland.

Inaugurated on St. Colmcille's Day.

"Because the enforcement of conscription on any people without their consent is tyranny, we are resolved to resist the conscription of Irishmen.

"We will not fill the places of men deprived of their work through refusing enforced military service.

"We will do all in our power to help the families of men who suffer through refusing enforced military service."

The above was signed by me

at ....

on ..... day of .... 1918.

Name ....

Address ....

St Colmcilles Cross Durrow King's Co.

St Colmcilles Tower Swords Co Dublin.

The City Hall, Dublin. Where the women's Pledge was signed on St. Colmcille's Day.

Up and down the country they travelled, helping with affiliation forms containing inventories of the arms and equipment, which were scant and obtained mainly by raids on barracks or police personnel. The forms included details of stretchers, bandages, and signalling equipment, even pikes.[28]

When the government attempted to introduce conscription to Ireland in 1918, following the huge losses in the Great War, now in its fourth year, women were prominent in the anti-conscription movement; such an emotive issue attracted many who otherwise would not have been politicised. In Cork, members of Cumann na mBan sought to do their part by agreeing not to assist in filling the jobs of men who had joined the war effort, and pledged not to do work, or 'even to learn to do, work that was being done by the men of Ireland.[29] On 9 June 1918 Cumann na mBan organised 'An Ireland Women's Day' (Lá na mBan) as part of the campaign. The following day, the *Freeman's Journal* reported that more than 40,000 signed the anti-conscription pledge at City Hall, Dublin, as well as at other locations around Ireland. Several thousand women paraded in the towns of Waterford and Tipperary.[30] In Dublin, the first to sign at City Hall were 700 members of Cumann na mBan. Other women's groups who supported anti-conscription included the Irish Women Workers' Union, the Irish Drapers' Assistants' Association and the women of the Irish Citizen Army.[31]

The issue of conscription united Sinn Féin and the Irish Parliamentary Party, which had withdrawn from Westminster in April 1918 when conscription was extended to Ireland. In the face of such opposition the British Government dropped its plans. The result was that Sinn Féin gained more supporters, and members of the Irish Parliamentary Party were no longer present at Westminster.

On 11 May 1918, Lord French was appointed Viceroy. Lord French had a military background, held the rank of Field-Marshal, and had been commander-in-chief of the British Expeditionary Force in France in 1914. His appointment signalled a change in policy towards Ireland. His objective was to re-establish law and order. During September and October 1918 there were continual arrests: 973 men, women and children were sentenced to various prison terms during that year.[32] Their crimes were varied; one boy was given a month's sentence for carrying a Sinn Féin flag, another was given two years for singing 'The Felons of our Land', a rebel song written fifty years previously.[33] It became illegal to collect on the streets without a permit, and as a result a number of women were arrested and fined. There were jail sentences for those who refused to give their names in English or for those resisting arrest. Maisie O'Loughlin of Milltown in Dublin was held for a week after kicking an officer who was arresting her for selling flags without a permit.[34]

In what became known as 'The German Plot', the British authorities alleged in 1918 that Sinn Féin was engaged in a new conspiracy with Germany. This accusation of treason was used to justify the mass arrest of key activists. They recommended that the Sinn Féin leadership be deported and interned. Among the seventy-three people who were deported were Countess Markievicz, Kathleen Clarke and Maud Gonne MacBride, who had just returned to live in Ireland after many years residing in France. Activists knew of the round-up in advance and it was decided that prison terms would serve their cause. Kathleen Clarke was urged to 'go on the run' but this was impractical for a mother with three young sons. She believed she was 'neither temperamentally nor physically fit' for life on the run.[35] Her children's lives were nevertheless disrupted when she was imprisoned for nine months.

Hanna Sheehy Skeffington, a widow with a nine-year-old son, later joined the women in prison. Sheehy Skeffington had been widowed during the 1916 Rising, when her husband, Francis, a well-known pacifist, was shot by a deranged military officer. He had been on the streets trying to get recruits for his citizen militia to prevent looting, when he was arrested, 'unarmed and unresisting'.[36] Hanna was arrested under the terms of the Defence of the Realm Act in 1918 and deported. Immediately after her imprisonment she went on hunger strike, thus gaining her freedom in a few days. The newspapers stated that the British Government would not have wanted another Sheehy Skeffington tragedy.[37] Other women were suffering from ill health and could not resort to hunger strike. Maud Gonne MacBride was released in December 1918, Kathleen Clarke in February 1919, and Countess Markievicz in March 1919. While she was still in prison, the Countess had been elected to Westminster, thus becoming the first female to be elected as a Member of the British Parliament. She never took up her seat.

In the General Election of November 1918, when women over thirty were granted the vote, Sinn Féin fielded candidates who advocated an abstentionist policy. With so many of Sinn Féin's key activists in prison, the women organised a cohesive strategy for the election. Their tasks may have been mundane but they were practical and ultimately effective. Apart from canvassing and distributing propaganda, members of Cumann na mBan looked after children so other women could record their vote, and escorted the elderly and invalids to the polling booths. They provided food for agents at polling booths and others working for Sinn Féin candidates.[38] The result of this election was a gain of seventy-three seats for Sinn Féin, with Unionists winning twenty-six seats. The Irish Parliamentary Party, who a few short years before had seemed as if they would bring Home Rule to Ireland, were reduced to a party of the past, attaining only six seats.

Countess Markievicz and Winnie Carney were Sinn Féin's female candidates. Cumann na mBan had issued a pamphlet, *The present duty of Irishwomen*, which claimed that failing to cast a vote for Sinn Féin was nothing short of treason.[39] The fact that women were now entitled to the vote must have had an effect on the successful outcome for Sinn Féin candidates, even though Winnie Carney failed to get elected. She was not as well known as the Countess, and with her trade unionist background was advocating a 'workers' republic', which gained her little support in the Victoria division of the Central/East Belfast constituency where she stood for election. [40] This was a predominantly Unionist area. She felt her defeat was due to the fact that she had not sufficient support from the Sinn Féin party. She wrote:

> **I had neither personation agents, committee rooms, canvassers or vehicles, and as these are the chief agents in an election, it was amazing to me to find that 395 people went to the ballot box of their own initiative ....** [41]

Having received a mandate from the people, (over sixty percent of the electorate voted for Sinn Féin candidates) Sinn Féin established a parliament in Dublin called Dáil Éireann. It was not a parliament that unified the entire country. The division that would colour Irish politics for the century to follow was already in evidence. In Ulster, Sinn Féin had been victorious in three of the nine Northern counties. The Unionists held the majority in the remaining six counties. During the 1918 election Sinn Féin fought its case even in hard-line Unionist constituencies. The Sinn Féin leaders

> **... did not seem to realize that they were ignoring unionist sensitivities by their emphasis on the Irish language and their virulent anti-British and anti-war propaganda, especially when thousands of unionist men were fighting at the front and Sinn Fé in was seen as a supporter of the Germans.**[42]

At the first session of Dáil Éireann, held on 21 January 1919, only twenty-six of Sinn Féin's elected ministers were present. The others were in prison, and members of the Unionist Party and the Irish Parliamentary Party refused to attend. The Unionists had been invited to take part in Dáil Éireann through invitations written in Irish – the sort of occurrence that confirmed them in the belief that 'there was no place for them in Sinn Féin's Ireland.'[43] Eamon de Valera was elected President. In his cabinet were Arthur Griffith (Secretary for Home Affairs), Cathal Brúgha (Defence), Count Plunkett (Foreign Affairs), Eoin MacNeill (Industry), Michael Collins (Finance), and WT Cosgrave (Local Government). Countess Markievicz became Secretary for Labour. In holding this post she became the first female cabinet minister in Western Europe.

Propaganda cartoon by Grace Gifford Plunkett for North Roscommon by-election, 1917.

As well as establishing the Dáil, Sinn Féin obtained control in a number of county councils and rural district councils. With the exception of Belfast and Derry, all the mayors in the country were Sinn Féin members.

There were a growing number of women in public life. In the January 1920 local government elections, forty-three women were elected to borough and urban

Councils. As Máire Comerford stated: 'the job fell to them mainly because it was difficult at the time for any courageous or public-spirited man to perform the duties of office.'[44] Women worked for the Dáil departments and County Councils that were set up by the provisional government.

Eamon de Valera was absent from Ireland for much of this period. He was imprisoned in Lincoln Jail in England from May 1918 until February 1919, when he escaped from prison by a plan credited to Michael Collins. After his election as President of Sinn Féin and the Dáil he travelled to the United States of America. One of the aims of Dáil Éireann was to 'seek international recognition for the Irish Republic'. To this end de Valera stayed in America from June 1919 until December 1920. Although he raised millions of dollars for the Irish National Loan and addressed meetings all over the country, he failed to meet President Wilson and secure recognition for the Irish Republic. However, Cumann na mBan had succeeded in presenting President Wilson with a petition putting forward Ireland's claim to self-determination. Hanna Sheehy Skeffington, although not a member of the organisation, had secured a meeting with the President while on a lecture tour in America in 1918. Hanna took on the task of delivering the document to him. She was, as she described herself: 'the first Irish exile and the first Sinn Féiner to enter the White House'. She proudly wore the badge of the Irish Republic pinned on her coat.[45]

On 21 January 1919, the day Dáil Éireann first met in Dublin, two members of the Royal Irish Constabulary (RIC) were shot by Irish Volunteers in an ambush in Soloheadbeg, County Tipperary. This was the first of a number of incidents where the Volunteers, who began to call themselves the Irish Republican Army (IRA) acted without any reference to the Sinn Féin leadership and the newly-created Dáil Éireann. This episode is now taken as the beginning of the War of Independence, a guerrilla war between the Volunteers (IRA) and British defence forces, which lasted until a Truce was called in 1921.

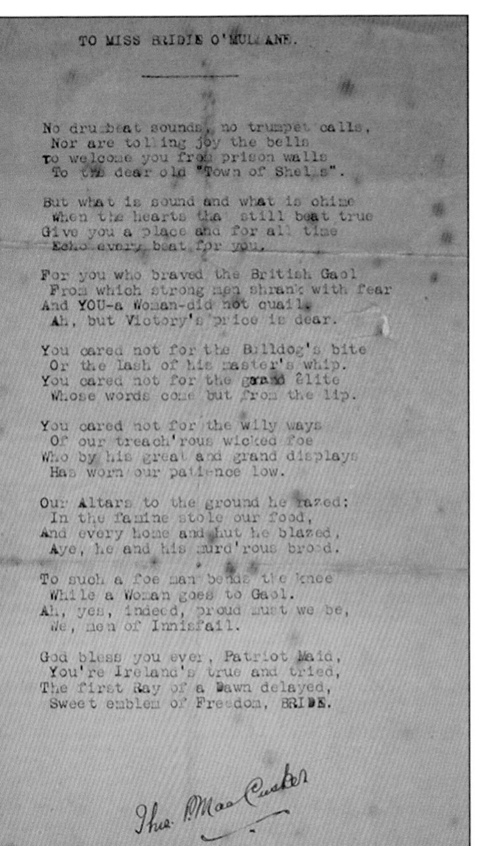
TO MISS BRIDIE O'MULLANE.

No drumbeat sounds, no trumpet calls,
Nor are tolling joy the bells
To welcome you from prison walls
To the dear old "Town of Shells".

But what is sound and what is chime
When the hearts that still beat true
Give you a place and for all time
Echo every beat for you.

For you who braved the British Gaol
From which strong men shrank with fear
And YOU-a Woman-did not quail.
Ah, but Victory's price is dear.

You cared not for the Bulldog's bite
Or the lash of his master's whip.
You cared not for the grand élite
Whose words come but from the lip.

You cared not for the wily ways
Of our treach'rous wicked foe
Who by his great and grand displays
Has worn our patience low.

Our Altars to the ground he razed:
In the famine stole our food,
And every home and hut he blazed,
Aye, he and his murd'rous brood.

To such a foe man bends the knee
While a Woman goes to Gaol.
Ah, yes, indeed, proud must we be,
We, men of Innisfail.

God bless you ever, Patriot Maid,
You're Ireland's true and tried,
The first Ray of a Dawn delayed,
Sweet emblem of Freedom, BRIDE.

Thos. P. MacCusker

Poem written in tribute to Bridie O'Mullane by Thomas MacCusker.

It was considered essential to break down the system of British authority in Ireland. By April 1919, Sinn Féin had advocated the ostracisation of the Royal Irish Constabulary (RIC). A document was issued by Cumann na mBan that month stating that President de Valera had asked for a boycott of the police. Members were told not to speak to the police unless absolutely necessary. If they should have occasion to converse with them the conversation had to be reported to the Captain of their Cumann na mBan branch. Members were to avoid entertainments where police might be in attendance. They were not to share a bench with a policeman at Mass and if a policeman entered a social event they were to leave it. The directive concluded: 'The responsibility for carrying out this order ... rests more on the women than on the men of Ireland. Let us prove that we can render this order effective and do so alone if necessary.'[46] Brighid (known as Bridie) O'Mullane recalls how she got Cumann na mBan members to refuse to dance with police, or to greet them on the street; she also encouraged shopkeepers not to do business with them and advised mothers to pull their children in from the street if the police were passing.[47]

By March 1920, the British had begun drafting in reinforcements to bolster the regular police force. The first batch were ex-British Army men who were so hastily assembled that they wore a mix of uniforms: khaki army trousers and black RIC jackets. As a result they became known as the 'Black and Tans'. They were an undisciplined force that quickly acquired a notorious reputation for brutality. In August 1920 a smaller force of 1,500 men, recruited from ex British Army officers, arrived to back up the RIC. Called the Auxiliary Constabulary, they were known as the Auxiliaries.

In March 1921, the Lord Mayor of Limerick, George Clancy and former mayor Michael O'Callaghan were gunned down in front of their wives by masked men, believed to be Black and Tans. Kate O'Callaghan recalled: 'I flew at him. I had the strength of a maniac ... I tore at their faces and heads ...we fell against the umbrella stand and at last, with an effort they threw me off. I crawled back to my husband and fell across his body ...' Mrs Clancy was wounded in the attack.[48] Although no woman in public office was shot, they were subjected to continual harassment. Maria Curran, who chaired Arklow's Urban District Council from the parlour behind her shop, was raided on a weekly basis.[49]

Local units of the Volunteers, now known as the IRA, operated as 'flying columns' and initiated attacks in their own areas. A key centre of activity was the province of Munster. The success of this type of warfare depended on widespread popular support. In this context the role of women was crucial in providing a network of support in the community. The task of finding 'reliable girls' to be recruited to the fight fell mainly to the Cumann na mBan organisation, although there were those who took part and never joined the organisation. Bridie O'Mullane from Sligo became an organiser for Cumann na mBan at the end of 1918. From then until 1921 she travelled the country, mainly on a pushbike, recruiting members in counties Sligo, Fermanagh, Down, Armagh, south Derry, Westmeath, Cavan, Kildare, Louth and Wexford. Some women had difficulties in convincing their parents that they should join Cumann na mBan and take part in the fight. Women being involved in an army was a new idea and Bridie O'Mullane encountered parents who 'did not mind their boys taking part in a military movement, but who had never heard of, and were reluctant to accept, the idea of a body of gun-women.'[50]

In July 1919 Lord French declared Sinn Féin clubs and organisations, the Irish Volunteers, Cumann na mBan and the Gaelic League illegal in the Munster county of Tipperary, where action in the War of Independence had begun. Later in the year this ban was extended to the entire country. Cumann na mBan's main office was closed. Despite the difficulties of communication, the organisation still maintained control over the activities of its branches. This was due in the main to the calibre of its members. As Bridie O'Mullane said, 'I was determined to carry on the work of forming and reorganising branches, which was my main objective, although I would have had an easier time in jail if I had allowed myself to be arrested.' [51]

All over the country branches were established. They maintained a separate identity, but worked with the local IRA units. Women and girls provided safe houses and sheltered wanted men. In doing so they risked their lives and the welfare of their families, homes and businesses. Women provided food and clothing to men who were often hiding in isolated places in the countryside. The women brought them much needed sustenance as well as cigarettes and tobacco.[52] They also provided much of the medical attention to the wounded and tended the sick. They acted as lookouts and scouts, hid weapons and documentation and, when the need arose, they formed guards of honour at funeral processions.[53]

In the cities the women did similar tasks. The anonymity of the city meant that the police did not know nationalist sympathisers like they did in the country. Also, females were rarely stopped and searched. In the Liberties area of Dublin they were called 'the handbag ladies'. When there was an ambush the women would wait up the road with their handbags open, the men would come running, drop the guns in the handbags and escape. The women would then go up to the soldiers and say 'Bloody bowsies, shooting at the poor soldiers.' And the soldiers would reply: 'Mind your own business girls, go on home.'[54] The fashion of the day facilitated the women's role as couriers; their long clothes enabled them to carry weapons.[55] Anne, Lily and Eileen Cooney were often called upon to carry guns. On one occasion they were approached by a member of the Fourth Battalion and told to be 'ready at University Church' as 'there was a big job on.' Having heard shooting in the area, they knew that 'operations were in progress.' Anne Cooney later recounted 'after waiting during what seemed to be an eternity, the three fellows came along walking pretty smartly and handed over their guns to us, one each, in a laneway between the church and Harcourt Street corner.' The men then walked behind them, until they reached a point a safe distance from the 'scene of operations.'[56]

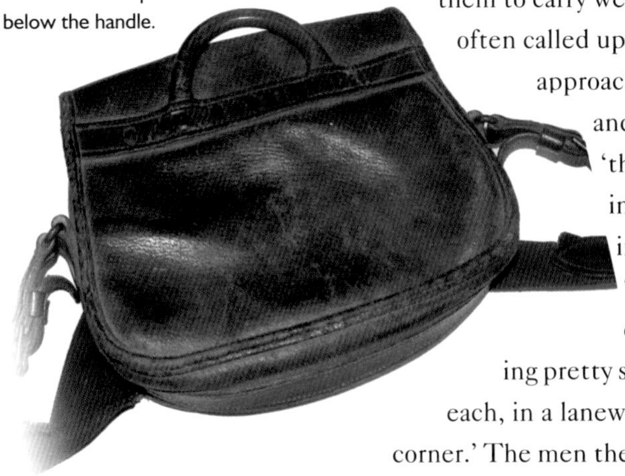

Countess Markievicz's dispatch bag. Her name is inscribed in the panel below the handle.

Members from branches in Scotland and England smuggled in arms at huge personal risk. Couriers included Pidge Duggan, Lizzie Marrin, Mollie Duffy, Mary Nelson and Julia Foy.[57] The Commander of the First Western Division of IRA later wrote:

> In my area there was no question of the girls only helping. In dispatch carrying, scouting and intelligence work, all of which are highly dangerous, they did far more than the soldiers ... were it not for the assistance of the women, organised and unorganised ... at the height of the terror we found that the more dangerous the work the more willing they were to do it.[58]

Bag made for Máire Comerford by a prisoner in the Curragh.

Drill training took place in most branches and instruction was given in the care of arms, map reading, signalling, first aid and home nursing. In some branches discipline was rigid; one Cumann na mBan member attending a first-aid demonstration remained at 'her post of instruction' after hearing news of her brother's death in action until she received official permission to leave.[59]

The difficulty of sustaining these activities was intensified when curfews and other restrictions were imposed. The situation became more dangerous for Cumann na mBan members after the arrival of the Black and Tans. They patrolled the country in their Lancia cars, raiding, shooting and looting. For the women organisers, who were solitary cyclists and whose work entailed being out late at night, there was continuous danger.[60] Although Cumann na mBan meetings were forbidden, they continued to be held, under the guise of a 'Baby Club'.[61]As many members were young mothers, this was an ideal way to explain a gathering of women.[62] Unlike the men on the run, during this entire period women continued with their daily home routine. 'The boundaries of private home and political battlefield became blurred.'[63] Throughout the war, Cumann na mBan and other nationalist organisations were the public face of opposition to the ruling administration. They distributed propaganda and engaged in bill posting, selling Dáil Bonds door-to-door and continuing to collect and distribute money for the dependants of Republican prisoners.

One of the reasons that women were not arrested more frequently was that many of them collected and distributed material from their babies' prams. They showed no compunction in using their children to allay suspicion; on one occasion, Catherine Wisely O'Daly, a member of Inghinidhe na hÉireann and later Cumann na mBan, carried twenty rounds of ammunition hidden in her baby son's clothes.[64] Áine Heron's house was under constant surveillance, as many known activists frequented it. However, the authorities did not suspect the mother of six young children, and instead

Unidentified Auxiliary befriended by Ita O'Gorman for intelligence purposes.

arrested her apolitical husband George who ended up serving a prison sentence. One of the warders, aware that Mr Heron was not 'one of the boys', took pity on him and would unlock his cell door so they could share a cigarette together.[65]

During the War of Independence the tasks undertaken by female activists were those which left them vulnerable to raids, to arrest, attack, and as time went on, to reprisals. Yet for those women who had young families, it was essential that their political activities were incorporated into their daily lives. When Áine Heron was appointed as a District Justice in the Republican Courts she liked the work because she could do it while her children were at school.[66]

These Republican Courts were set up in 1919 to provide a legal system for Ireland that would replace the existing system operated by the British administration. They came into effect in all areas with the exception of the North-Eastern region. The courts were organised at a local level through Sinn Féin Clubs. The court decrees were executed by police provided by the Dáil on the basis of one officer for each brigade area. There were a number of courts in operation: Parish Courts, District Courts, and Circuit Courts, which were held three times a year and were presided over by a Circuit Judge. Áine Ceannt and Kathleen Clarke were among the District Justices hearing petty cases, while other women, including Madge Clifford, Catalina Bulfin and Nora Brick filled secretarial roles.[67]

As the war continued, violent punishment was used for young women who were socialising with 'the enemy'. In March 1920, a 'young girl who was keeping company with a local policeman was seized by a number of men, who forcibly cut off her hair.'[68] Any young women consorting with 'the enemy' were inviting isolation for themselves and their families. Therefore Cumann na mBan members who befriended British personnel as a means of gathering intelligence were engaging in a precarious activity. When Ita O'Gorman, a woman in her early twenties from the Dublin suburb of Ranelagh, encouraged the attentions of a British Auxiliary she was taking a great risk. While she was working as a secretary in an office in Dublin city centre during the War of Independence, an Auxiliary became a regular customer. She recalled that he became 'very fond of her'. From the information he shared with her about his job she obtained valuable knowledge of military manoeuvres. On one occasion, Ita persuaded him to take her to witness an arrest. She accompanied him to Greystones, County Wicklow where he was arresting a father of five children. The reason Ita was anxious to accompany him was because she had already foiled the raid by contacting her 'real' boyfriend, a member of the Irish Republican Army.[69]

The IRA also used haircutting as a punishment for informers, but on two occasions they resorted to the ultimate punishment, death. The two women executed by the IRA as spies were Mrs Noble and Mrs Lindsay.[70] Mrs Lindsay was identified as a spy and shot for conveying information to the British authorities. The IRA gave the British authorities the opportunity to save her life in exchange for the lives of IRA prisoners, but when they refused she was killed. [71] In the main, suspected women were ordered to leave the country. Bridie O'Mullane was almost shot by the IRA as a spy in County Kildare. There was a spy operating in the area and suspicion fell on Bridie. Fortunately, a Volunteer came and told her of the plan to shoot her without giving her a court martial, and she was able to make her escape.[72]

As hostilities continued, raids became a regular occurrence, especially for those whose political affiliation was known to the authorities. By February 1920 there had been five thousand raids. The frequency with which these raids took place meant that much damage was done to property and many people lived in terror. When Min Ryan and Richard Mulcahy (Chief of Staff of the Volunteers from 1918, later Assistant Minister for Defence in the Dáil) were first married, they lived in a flat in Oakley House (now Cullenswood), Ranelagh, owned by Patrick Pearse's mother, which had been the site of his first school. After yet another raid on the flat, Min was asked by Mrs Pearse to leave the premises because of the damage that was being caused to the property. Min pleaded with her, saying 'who would take in a man like that, if you didn't?'[73] In fact, Richard Mulcahy would spend much of the period from 1919 to 1921 on the run, making infrequent visits to his wife and the two children who were born during this time. Min was not intimidated by the raiders – she was known to have used her 'sharp tongue', telling them 'they were pursuing poets and educated men who were perfectly in the right to seek the freedom of their country.'[74]

Hiding weapons and documentation and providing safe houses were all essential activities in the continuation of the war. Providing accommodation where men could hide out was vital as returning to their own homes would mean certain arrest. In certain houses some windows were kept open for men to come in at any time of the day or night.[75] Those women who kept safe houses for the most wanted men had to be of a certain disposition. It was essential that they did not gossip and that they kept their nerve in difficult situations.[76] Female ingenuity was called into play when raids occurred unexpectedly, as papers had to be hidden and uniforms concealed at a moment's notice. When four IRA activists were taking shelter in an upstairs bedroom of the Punch family home in County Clare and the house was raided, the young women of the house immediately invited the soldiers to join them for tea and began an impromptu singsong. The result was that the house was never searched and the men evaded arrest.[77]

Ita O'Gorman in Cumann na mBan uniform.

When Michael Collins was looking for a trustworthy woman to pose as his aunt, Máire Comerford suggested her mother. But the arrangement only lasted a couple of weeks when it became apparent that Mrs Comerford, as former Ladies Captain of the Greystones Golf Club and the winner of numerous tennis championships, 'was not the best person as she was really quite well known.'[78]

Homes of known nationalists were constantly raided, so it was often the houses of people assumed to be pro-British that were favoured by the wanted men. The safe house occupied by Austin Stack, Deputy Chief of Staff of the IRA during the War of Independence, was that of the respectable Winifred (also known as Úna) Gordon, widow of a District Inspector in the police force. In her house, Batt O'Connor had constructed a recess that was accessed by a trap door over the bathroom. On one occasion when it was raided, Austin dislodged some plaster but the members of the raiding party were not observant enough to notice.[79] On another occasion he escaped arrest by climbing over the rooftops. Austin Stack married his 'Winnie dearest' in 1925 but their marriage was short-lived, as he died prematurely four years later.

Una Gordon, later Mrs Austin Stack.

Many women, unable to go on the run, had to come face-to-face with their attackers. Hundreds of women were living this existence all over the country, with no male member in the household to protect them, as they were imprisoned, on the run or deceased. Lil Conlon from Cork Cumann na mBan recalled: 'To intensify the reign of terror, swoops were made at night, entries forced ... and women's hair cut off in a brutal fashion as well as suffering other indignities and insults.'[80]

The fact that they were mothers with young children was not enough to prevent some women from being arrested. When Geraldine Dillon, daughter of Count and Countess Plunkett, was arrested following a raid during which literature on the White Cross was discovered, she was separated from three small children.[81] The baby, who became the well-known writer, Eilís Dillon, later recalled the events of that period:

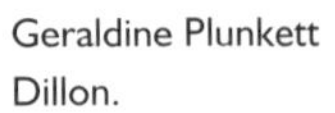

Geraldine Plunkett Dillon.

> ... my earliest memory dates from about my first birthday, March 1921, when a party of soldiers broke into the house, upset the furniture, threw the books down from the shelves, lifted the floorboards in their search for hidden guns, and finished by taking my mother away with them on their lorry, surrounded by fixed bayonets ... My older sister, then four, knew just what was afoot because on another occasion, not long before, she had been compelled by a party of Black and Tans to lead them out into the garden where my mother was, so that they could kill her. My mother argued them out of their intention then, saying that it would be objected to in England if they were to shoot down a young woman in the

> **presence of her child. But now they had gone off with our mother, and my sister understood that we would never see her again.**[82]

The children were left in the care of a young maidservant, Peggy, as their father was already on the run. Eilís's father was Thomas Dillon, a Professor of Chemistry in Galway University, and a political activist who spent much of this period in jail or in hiding. As Eilís Dillon recalled 'My father was on the run, a familiar expression to me as a child, meaning that he had left home and gone into hiding in fear of being murdered.'[83] Geraldine Dillon remained imprisoned for three months in Galway Gaol 'loudly demanding' that she should have her child with her in prison 'as the tinkers were allowed to do.' When a question about the case was raised in the House of Commons, she was released. Eilís Dillon remarked: 'I lost my only chance of being able to boast that I had been imprisoned for my country.'[84]

Some of the Daly family, Limerick, after the Easter Rising. Left to right: (back) Madge, Mrs Catherine Daly, Agnes; (front): Laura, Nora, Carrie.

The British forces in Limerick frequently targeted the Daly family. Madge Daly was president of the local branch of Cumann na mBan, her brother Edward (Ned) had been executed in 1916 and her sister was Kathleen Clarke, so the family's politics were well known. The Daly sisters were targets of official and unofficial raids day and night from 1916 onwards, which culminated in a vicious attack on Agnes (Úna) and Carrie Daly when they were alone in the house in October 1920. Madge Daly later recounted:

> **Masked and armed men came to our house at 12 pm, attacked both my sisters, putting revolvers to their faces. My sister Úna was knocked, and dragged out by the hair out of the house and down the garden path ... her assailants cut off her hair and slashed her hand with a razor from the back to the palm, severing an artery. Fortunately my sister Carrie's knowledge of first aid enabled her to stop the bleeding, thereby saving Úna's life.**[85]

The newspapers of the period, in particular the newspaper of Dáil Éireann, the *Irish Bulletin*, reported these raids in their propaganda war which documented the brutality of the British military's treatment of the civilian population. In August 1920 an American Commission on Conditions in Ireland was set up in Odd Fellows Hall, in Washington DC. This commission, which operated until January 1921, recorded the atrocities taking place in Ireland. They recorded many accounts, including those of Americans who visited Ireland.[86] Among those who gave testimony in Washington in December 1920 was Muriel MacSwiney.[87] The Commission's interim report, released early in 1921, brought pressure to bear on the British government to ceases hostilities.

In 1920, an American committee also began fund-raising for the estimated 100,000 people who had been left destitute as a result of the war situation in Ireland.[88] In January 1921, the White Cross was established in Ireland to distribute these funds. The committee was comprised of well-known women, including Molly Childers, Mary Spring Rice, Hanna Sheehy Skeffington, Kathleen Clarke, Áine Ceannt and Maud Gonne MacBride. Cumann na mBan administrated the fund. Their members carried out mundane but essential tasks, which included locating those eligible and assisting in filling out forms to obtain the allowance.[89] The task of visiting and assessing cases fell to the women. In her history of the organisation, Áine Ceannt recounted the heart-rending stories of some of those helped by the White Cross: husbands shot at their own front doors; family members driven to insanity by the terrorism of the Black and Tans. Many of the victims were not members of the IRA, but were targeted because they were known to be sympathetic to the nationalist movement.[90]

Muriel MacSwiney, widow of Terence MacSwiney, with her daughter, Máire Óg, early 1920s.

As the war progressed, more attention gradually focused on the women. The intelligence division discovered from information contained in captured documents that women were playing a major part in the campaign. As Lil Conlon recorded, General Macready (Commander-in-Chief of the British forces in Ireland) knew that women 'co-operated in no small degree with the Volunteers, even though his tributes were not too complimentary.'[91]

Michael Collins, whose roles in 1920 included Adjutant General of the Volunteers, Director of Organisation, Director of Intelligence and Minister of Finance, had developed a spy network, and had many uses for the women's talents. Eileen McGrane, Kathleen McKenna, Patricia Hoey and Sinéad Mason worked for him as administrators and secretaries. Máire Comerford, Sighle Humphreys and Leslie Price acted as couriers, and other women assisted him in the gathering of intelligence. Among these key figures were Jennie Wyse Power, Márie Comerford, Brigid Lyons Thornton and Moya Llewelyn Davies. Moya, the wife of the Solicitor General of the British Post Office, was an unlikely spy, but she was also the daughter of James O'Connor, a former Fenian and nationalist MP. Her family background made her a nationalist, but her husband's connections meant that she moved in the highest levels of British society.

Collins was also fortunate to have the support of women who worked with the British administration in Dublin Castle and were willing to take part in espionage. When Nancy O'Brien (Michael Collins's cousin) was given the job of decoding secret messages, Collins could not believe his luck.[92] Another of these spies was Lily Mernin, a typist. She compiled a list for Collins of intelligence officers who dressed as civilians and lived outside the barracks. Despite her activities she was not suspected until after the Truce of July 1921, when she was dismissed from her post.[93]

May Gibney in her Cumann na mBan uniform.

Information such as that provided by Lily Mernin made possible the elimination of eleven members of British Intelligence. On Sunday morning, 21 November 1920, Collins's Squad (an elite group he had specially trained for this type of operation) assassinated the intelligence officers. The immediate aftermath of the events of that day, dubbed 'Bloody Sunday', was the entrance of a group of Auxiliaries into Croke Park Stadium, Dublin, where a Gaelic Athletic Association (GAA) match between Dublin and Tipperary was taking place. The Auxiliaries killed twelve spectators and injured sixty others in what is believed to be a search operation that went wrong. In the eyes of the Irish people it was a reprisal.

Also in November, May Gibney's fiancé, Dick McKee, Commandant of the Dublin Brigade, was shot in Dublin Castle. The circumstances of the death of McKee were particularly tragic for his fiancée. When his body was laid out in the Pro-Cathedral it was mutilated and his face had the expression of one who had been tortured.[94]

Young women found independence and adventure in their work, and the sense of freedom in an era when women's social life was highly restricted. Many of the women were to marry men that they met at this time through their work for the 'movement' although some of their romances were doomed as so many men were killed in the fighting. Leslie Price had been engaged to Charlie Hurley of the West Cork Brigade, who was killed in the Crossbarry ambush. He had foretold his own death, telling Tom Barry that he would die fighting, and asking Tom to look after his fiancée. When Charlie was buried, Tom stood beside Leslie at the Clogagh graveside and, in a gesture that touched her deeply, gave her a piece of the tricolour that had draped the coffin.[95] After a whirlwind romance, Leslie and Tom were married on 22 August 1921.

Early in the new year of 1921, martial law, already in force in the counties of Cork, Limerick, Kerry and Tipperary, was extended to Clare, Waterford, Wexford and Kilkenny. Attacks on the military resulted in counter-attacks on individuals. Mrs Kelleher's home in Kilmichael, County Cork was burnt in reprisal for an attack

Charlotte Despard outside Mountjoy Jail.

on Auxiliaries at Macroom, County Cork on 29 April 1921.[96] Whole communities were affected by other incidents, such as the sacking of the village of Balbriggan in County Dublin on 20 September 1921 by the Black and Tans.

One opponent of the British administration's policy, who came to Ireland to see the atrocities herself, was Charlotte Despard, sister of the Viceroy, Lord French. Mrs Despard, a widow in her seventies, was a suffragette who had undertaken philanthropic activities among the poor in Battersea in London. In addition to her charity work, she was a member of the Indian Independence Movement, and involved in a host of other global causes. She also became a member of Sinn Féin and the Irish Self-Determination League, which was formed in London in March 1919. Her family, in particular her brother, Lord French, considered that she 'had always mingled with subversives, but now she was emphatically one of them.'[97] When she came to visit Ireland in 1920 she joined Maud Gonne MacBride on a fact-finding mission in County Cork. Her status as the Viceroy's sister gave them access to places that, according to Maud Gonne MacBride: 'I should never have been able to get to alone in the martial areas.'[98] After her visit to Ireland she decided to move to Dublin. By the time she took up residence in Ireland, during the summer of 1921, her brother no longer held the position of Viceroy.

Despite the scope and nature of their activities, very few women were arrested at the beginning of the War of Independence, but arrests increased as the war continued and by 1921 an estimated fifty women were imprisoned.[99] Many of these women were untried prisoners. Amongst this group were Eily McAdam, who was held in Armagh,[100] Miss Burke and Miss Fenton in Limerick and Miss Byron in Tipperary.[101] Others had fines imposed for collecting money without a permit, and, on refusing to pay the fines, were imprisoned. In Galway, Dr Ada English, Medical Superintendent at Ballinasloe Asylum, was arrested when a printed document with 'Cumann na mBan' on it was found in her sittingroom.[102] The women's sentences ranged from three days to life imprisonment. In Edinburgh, twenty-year-old Jean Quinn was found in possession of ammunition and Sinn Féin literature. She was sentenced to twelve months' imprisonment.[103]

The majority of the women arrested for political crimes were held in Mountjoy Jail, Dublin. Anne Cooney, aged twenty-five, was picked up in February 1921. She had previously been a political prisoner, having spent time in Kilmainham Gaol in the aftermath of the 1916 Rising. Arrested after a raid on the family home at Upper

Basin Street, Dublin, she was first brought to the Bridewell and then on to Mountjoy. She later wrote:

> **I was surprised at the cleanliness of Mountjoy after my experience in Kilmainham ... We were let out for exercise for two hours at a time ... we were allowed to associate with the other political prisoners.**[104]

One of her fellow inmates in Mountjoy was Eileen McGrane, serving a sentence of four years. Eileen had served part of her sentence in Mountjoy before being transferred to Walton Prison in Liverpool, only to be returned to Mountjoy to complete her sentence. When arrested, she was found to be in possession of six revolvers and a quantity of ammunition. Her rooms at 21 Dawson Street were described as 'a complete temporary office full of papers belonging to Michael Collins.' Among documents found were plans for 'introducing typhoid bacillus into the troops' milk'.[105] Other political prisoners were Lily Dunne and Kathleen Brady, who were serving a two-year sentence. During Anne's imprisonment the number of female political prisoners increased with the arrival of 'the two Sharkey girls from Strokestown, County Roscommon and Peg McGuinness from Roscommon who was a courier for Seán McKeon's column.'[106] Aileen Keogh from Wexford, housekeeper to the nationalist Fr Sweetman in Gorey,[107] was sentenced to two years. Some time after that, Frances Brady from Belfast arrived to serve her two-year sentence.[108] Molly Hyland joined them later.[109]

Anne Cooney was brought to trial in April 1921. She had been coached in her responses by the Officer in Charge in the prison, Eileen McGrane, who told her to say 'that she did not recognise the court to try her, and that the only authority to do so was a court of the Irish Republic.'[110] Her sentence of six months' imprisonment was reduced to four months, to date from her arrest in February. She was transferred to the Tried Wing, which held Countess Markievicz and a Dublin woman named Máire Rigney – known to fellow inmates as 'the gunwoman'.[111] Eithne Coyle (later President of Cumann na mBan) was also tried and transferred to that wing. She had received a one-year sentence for activities prejudicial to the defence of the realm and was accused of having in her possession a plan of a military barracks, in addition to other seditious material.[112] The prisoners in that section of the jail were not allowed to mix with other women prisoners and were not allowed any parcels.

Another prisoner held in Mountjoy Jail at the time was Moya Llewelyn Davies, described by Anne Cooney as 'a mysterious character':

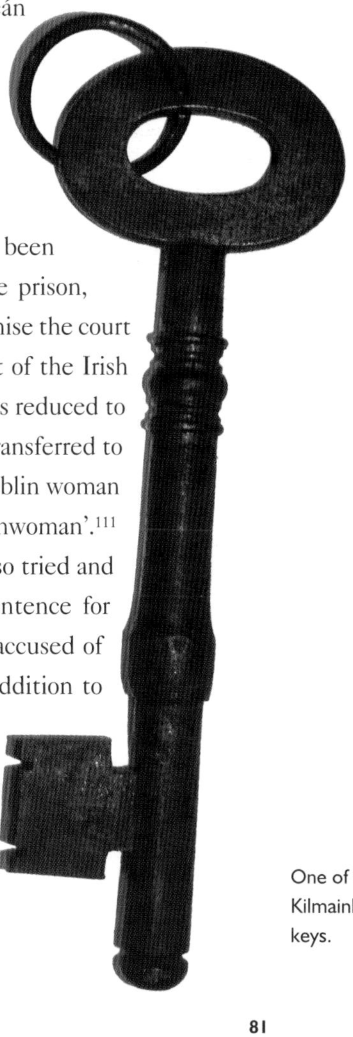

One of the Kilmainham Gaol keys.

> **I never could quite place her. Very often she mixed with us young girls and asked us quite a lot of questions. She seemed so curious that I got on my guard. Her questions were too pointed to my mind. She wanted to know all we knew about the leaders. She questioned me closely about Bloody Sunday ... I gave her no information and said I knew nothing about it.**[113]

In March 1921, through what Michael Collins described as 'a frightful example of carelessness and thoughtlessness', premises used for propaganda purposes had been hired under Moya Llewelyn Davies's name. It brought her to the attention of the authorities and led to her arrest. Her husband, Crompton Llewelyn Davies, was promptly dismissed from his job, with the loss of an annual income of £2,500. Crompton's position as solicitor to Lloyd George made this situation highly embarrassing for the British Government, and so the matter received very little publicity.[114] While she was in prison, Moya told her fellow inmates the story:

> **She spoke of ... her husband, told me what his position was and that he was very well in with some members of the British cabinet – I think she mentioned Lloyd George. She said he used to write some of the speeches for them. I don't know whether she was boasting. But I don't think that she was that type of woman.**[115]

Michael Collins took 'the arrest and dismissal to heart'.[116] He made repeated efforts to get Crompton Llewelyn Davies employed by the Dáil, and used his network of warders to make prison life easier for Moya, Patricia Hoey and Eileen McGrane. ' Mick saw to it that little comforts such as woollen rugs, good books, food, China tea, which she preferred, sweetmeats were smuggled in to her and her companions.' [117] Anne Cooney noted this and wrote: 'She was able to get letters in and we were always wondering how she managed that. Also she had other little facilities that were denied to us.'[118] Moya was released in June and deported to England.

Moya Llewelyn Davies.

Other Mountjoy inmates were two elderly sisters, aged seventy and eighty respectively, from Ballinalee, County Longford, but after a few days, when the authorities could get no information from them, they were released.[119] There were also three teenagers from Cork: Lily (17) and Madge Cotter (19) and their cousin Kate Crowley (19), serving sentences of penal servitude for life (they were released during the Truce). They had been weeding turnips in a field when a lorry full of Black and Tans had been blown up nearby. The survivors identified the young girls as being involved.[120] However, their fellow prisoners knew that they were not members of Cumann na mBan and believed them to be innocent.[121]

On 13 September 1921 Linda Kearns arrived in Mountjoy Jail to serve the remainder of a ten-year sentence. On the night of 20 November 1920 Linda had been driving to Sligo in a car full of arms, and with three IRA men as passengers. About a mile from the town they encountered a military roadblock. When the car was searched and ten rifles, four revolvers, and 500 rounds of ammunition were discovered, Linda and her companions were arrested.

> **... our treatment was pretty rough. I've often heard of the bad treatment of prisoners but that half-hour – that half-hour I want to forget.**[122]

Linda Kearns Mac Whinney, with daughter Ann.

Linda was sentenced to ten years' penal servitude. She was imprisoned first in Sligo Barracks, then transferred to Sligo Jail, where she wrote that she feared for her life as another victim of the British authorities 'shot while trying to escape.'[123] After this she was brought by gunboat to Buncrana in County Donegal and from there by lorry to Derry Jail. She was admitted to this jail with some reluctance, as it was for men only. Later she was taken to Armagh Jail and held there on remand until her trial in March 1921. Her sentence was supposed to be served in Walton Prison in Liverpool, but she went on hunger strike to get transferred to a prison in Ireland, and after ten days, when she had become extremely weak, it was decided to grant her request. It was felt that had she died, a female martyr would have had a huge impact on the Irish cause.[124]

After two and a half years of war, a Truce was declared on 11 July 1921. By this time Cumann na mBan was affiliated to IRA battalions around the country and had more than 1,000 branches. Forty women remained in detention.[125] Because of her position as a TD (Dáil Deputy), Countess Markievicz was released, along with 'important people' like Arthur Griffith and Robert Barton who might take part in talks.[126]

The Truce brought concessions for the prisoners. They were allowed to see visitors in the comfort of the solicitor's room and even the watch had become somewhat relaxed. Eithne Coyle later recalled: 'Although the Truce was now on for four months we had not been released. ... We were fed up anyway, and although I had only a few months to go, I never ceased looking for a means to escape.'[127]

Political prisoners were allowed to associate in the yard and conversations often turned to the topic of escape. Eileen McGrane and Kay Brady refused to get involved, and they decided the three Cork prisoners were too young to take part. However, Eithne Coyle, Aileen Keogh, Linda Kearns and May Burke from Limerick decided to attempt it.[128] Eithne Coyle made contact with a friend who brought in a flask and a

(Left to right):May Burke, Eithne Coyle and Linda Kearns at Duckett's Grove, Carlow, 1921.

piece of dental wax. The wax was kept in the flask so that it could be used when required to make an impression of a key. When everything was ready, the escape date was set for Halloween, 31 October.[129] That evening, a football match was arranged, Cork against 'the Rest of Ireland'. The Rest of Ireland beat the Corkonians and in the midst of the cheers and shouting the key was fitted and it turned. The four women ran until they reached an agreed spot. Linda Kearns, Eithne Coyle, May Burke and Aileen Keogh were to escape by climbing a rope ladder that had been thrown over the wall.[130] Linda was allowed to go first as she was serving the longest sentence. A man was waiting on the other side to take her by motorbike to a house where the well-known surgeon and writer, Oliver St John Gogarty, was waiting. Gogarty brought Linda and May Burke, who was the second to escape, to a safe house.[131] They were followed by Aileen Keogh and finally Eithne Coyle. Eithne later recalled:

> **We only had minutes before the military would appear. To save time each of them dropped from the twenty-two foot wall, hanging on their fingers as far down as they could go. When my turn came to climb up – having no one to hold the ladder back – my knuckles took a rasping against the rough wall, but I persevered, and dropped down upon the soil of somebody's garden.'[132]**

After a couple of days in safe houses in Dublin, it was discovered that a reward had been posted for their recapture, so it was felt that they should leave the city. Aileen Keogh decided to return to her job as housekeeper in Father Sweetman's school in County Wexford. Eithne Coyle, Linda Kearns and May Burke were first brought to the convent of the Cross and Passion in Kilcullen, County Kildare, but the British authorities were informed of their whereabouts and they were brought to a hideout at Duckett's Grove, Carlow which was an IRA training camp. Linda remained in hiding until the signing of the Treaty in December 1921.[133]

De Valera had travelled to London during July of 1921 as head of a delegation that met with Lloyd George on four separate occasions to discuss terms to determine 'how the association of Ireland with the Community of Nations known as the British Empire may best be reconciled with Irish national aspirations.' [134] The proposals put forward in these meetings, which advocated dominion status for Ireland and a swearing of allegiance to the crown, were officially rejected on 10 August. A second delegation was sent to London to negotiate in early October. Arthur Griffith headed the delegation, which included a reluctant Michael Collins, Robert Barton, Eamon Duggan, George Gavan Duffy and Erskine Childers as secretary of the delegation. No women were among the delegates, although there were a number of female secretaries, including Lily O'Brennan. Mary MacSwiney had asked de Valera to appoint her as a plenipotentiary but he would not agree, telling her that she was 'too extreme'.[135] De Valera did not travel with the second delegation. He opted to stay in Ireland as 'a symbol of the Republic'. Austin Stack and Cathal Brugha also refused to join the delegation.[136]

The Irish delegation was pitted against experienced negotiators: the Prime Minister, David Lloyd George (who had been the principal delegate at the Paris Peace Conference of 1919), Austen Chamberlain, Lord Birkenhead, Winston Churchill, Sir Lamer Worthington Evans, Sir Gordon Hewart and Sir Hamar Greenwood.

The Treaty resulting from these negotiations with the British Government, which lasted from October to December 1921, did not grant Ireland a Republic. It required members of the Dáil to take an Oath of Allegiance to the British monarchy. The Government of Ireland Act 1920, adapted from the pre-war Home Rule Bill, which provided for a parliament in the North – to govern counties Down, Antrim, Derry, Tyrone, Fermanagh and Armagh – and a parliament in Dublin to govern the twenty-six other counties, remained in place. Eithne Coyle was at home in Donegal when the proposals were outlined in the newspaper. Her

Members of the Treaty Delegation and staff, 1921. Lily O'Brennan is seated on left.

mother, 'a great old Republican'[137] reacted immediately, saying 'throw your hat at that, it is no settlement.'[138]

Opposition to the Treaty was intense. Unable to accept the compromise of the Treaty, Cumann na mBan voted 419 to 63 against its ratification. It was the first organisation to declare against the Treaty. All women deputies in the Dáil also opposed its acceptance: Countess Markievicz, Margaret Pearse, Kathleen Clarke, Mary MacSwiney, Kate O'Callaghan, and Dr Ada English who, unlike the others, was neither a widow nor a relative of any person killed in the fighting of the previous five years. As she stated in Dáil debates, she was not a relative of any dead men, and could not be accused of being embittered by personal loss, therefore she asserted her right to speak on behalf of other women.[139]

'The women of An Dáil are women of character, and they will vote for principle, not for expediency'[140] declared Kate O'Callaghan, widow of the former Mayor of Limerick, Michael O'Callaghan. Mary MacSwiney, sister of Terence, who had died on hunger-strike in Brixton Prison during the War of Independence, stated that if the Treaty was accepted she would be the Free State's 'first rebel' and that they would have 'the pleasure or the pain' of imprisoning her as 'one of their first and most deliberate and irreconcilable rebels.'[141] Countess Markievicz echoed her: 'I am pledged as a rebel, an unconvertible rebel, because I am pledged to the one thing – a free and independent Republic.'[142]

However, these formidable women were no longer representative of the opinions of the majority of Irishwomen, who wanted peace and supported the Provisional Government's stance, believing that the Treaty would be a stepping-stone to gaining more freedom and eventually an Irish Republic. The wives of men taking a pro-Treaty stance generally followed their husband's views; a notable exception was Mabel FitzGerald. Mabel, despite her Northern unionist background had become an ardent Republican and maintained her allegiance despite her husband Desmond's support for the Treaty.[143] Among the prominent members to leave Cumann na mBan were Louise Gavan Duffy and three members of the Executive. Min Ryan, a founder member and long-time member of the executive, joined her husband, Richard Mulcahy, who became Minister of Defence in the Provisional Government, in supporting the Treaty. The other executive members to leave were Jennie Wyse Power and her daughter, Nancy.[144]

Jennie Wyse Power was at first unable to decide which side to take, writing in December 1921: 'It is the first time in my life that I hesitated to take sides and until I know all I cannot have my mind easy on the subject.'[145] Later she argued for the Treaty, saying that it seemed to her easier to get the Republic from a Government worked in Ireland by Irishmen than from an Ireland under British rule.[146] She had grave misgivings about the stance taken by Cumann na mBan. Some years later she reflected:

It is to be regretted that this splendid force of women should have been the first body to repudiate the National Parliament, and thus initiate a policy, which has had such disastrous results. The decision had the further effect of limiting Cumann na mBan to purely military work.[147]

These pro-Treaty women formed a new organisation called Cumann na Saoirse [Freedom Group].[148] The rejection of the Treaty saw the departure of moderates from Cumann na mBan. It had become a more hard-line Republican organisation as the Civil War loomed.

Cumann na mBan Convention, 5 February 1922. Countess Markievicz is seated, front row, centre.

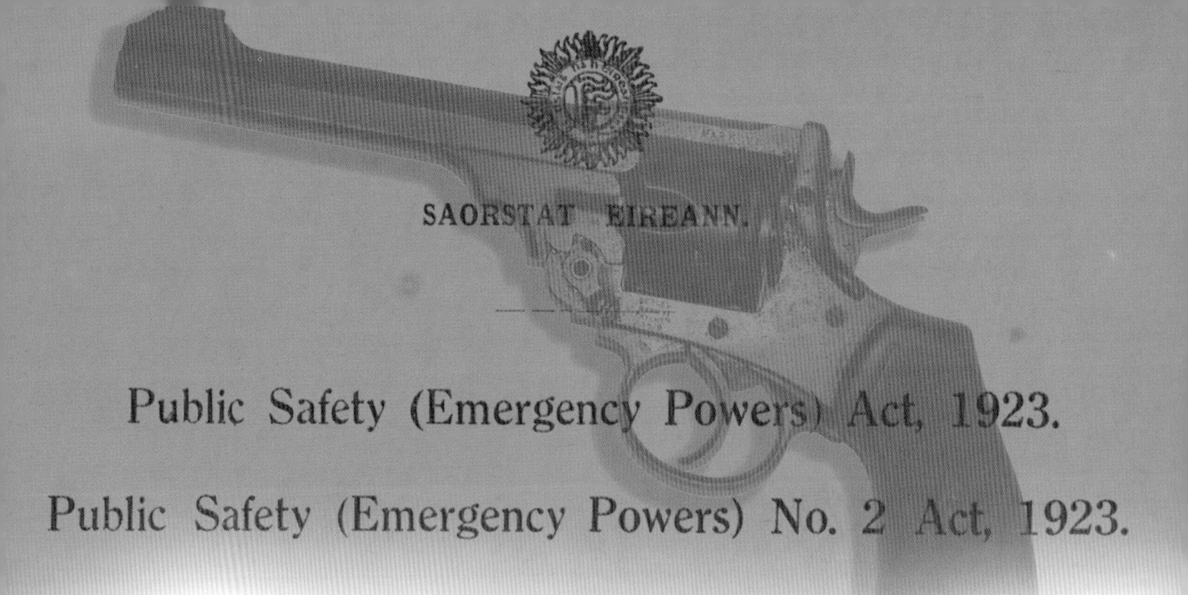

CHAPTER 4

The Civil War (1922–1923)

'Far better the grave of a rebel, without cross, without stone, without name than a treaty with treacherous England that can only bring sorrow and shame.'

Bridie Halpin,
Kilmainham Jail.

The new year of 1922 brought with it an acceptance of the Treaty by the majority of Dáil Deputies. Eamon de Valera resigned his presidency of the Dáil, and after he failed to get re-elected on 10 January he and his followers who opposed the Treaty left the Dáil. The Provisional Government of the Irish Free State was established in January 1922, with Michael Collins as Chairman and W T Cosgrave, Kevin O'Higgins, Eamon Duggan, Joe McGrath, Patrick Hogan, Eoin MacNeill and Fionán Lynch as Ministers without portfolio. These set about the transfer of power from the British authorities.

Cumann na mBan held a convention in early February 1922. Members of the organisation reaffirmed their allegiance to the Irish Republic and passed a resolution that they could not support the Articles of Agreement signed in London on 6 December 1921. The convention decided 'that the acceptance by the Irish people of any measure of Dominion Home Rule' was 'a denial of the Republic' and 'hence treason to it.'[1]

From the outset, a formidable number of IRA and Cumann na mBan members opposed the workings of the Provisional Government. Those who opposed the Treaty had to be referred to in the newspapers as the Irregulars, to differentiate them from the regulars of the Irish Free State Army. An Army Council of the Irregulars was formed and on 14 April 1922 a number of them, including some women, seized the Four Courts, the centre of the Irish judiciary, as well as buildings on the east side of O'Connell Street, the Kildare Street Club and the Ballast Office. They issued a declaration

Anti-Treaty deputies, including Countess Markievicz, leaving the Dáil.

refusing to recognise the Provisional Government. Tensions escalated as 1922 progressed and more Irregulars joined the garrisons. There were several skirmishes and anti-Treaty forces succeeded in capturing arms.

Some republicans still continued to attend Dáil meetings. A dual administration existed: the Dáil, now headed by Arthur Griffith, and the Provisional Government with Collins as Chairman. A Dáil Committee chaired by Kathleen Clarke tried to work out a diplomatic resolution. Michael Collins and Eamon de Valera worked on a pact, which, following the election in June 1922, would have created a coalition government, but at the last moment it was abandoned. The election was a victory for the government and confirmed that the majority of the country was anxious to return to peace. Anti-Treaty women members of the Dáil, Countess Markievicz, Kathleen Clarke, Dr Ada English and Margaret Pearse, lost their seats.

In this period of transition the Provisional Government was aware that the peace brokered with the British could fail and war with Britain could resume. Protests from Westminster regarding the republicans' stance became more intense when General Sir Henry Wilson (security advisor to Northern Ireland) was assassinated in London, and two IRA members were arrested for the crime. The Provisional Government still had not decided to move against the Irregulars in the Four Courts, but when General J J O' Connell of the Free State Army was kidnapped, confrontation became inevitable.

Ina Connolly and Archie Herron, who she later married.

The Civil War began with the shelling of Republican headquarters in the Four Courts on 28 June 1922. The bombardment continued for two days. Two hundred men were arrested but some managed to make their way to O'Connell Street where several buildings were occupied by fellow republicans. There were a number of women among the garrison, including Madge Clifford, Máire Comerford and Bridie Clyne. Bridie later recorded that on the morning of the attack of the Four Courts 'I rushed the Free State barricade and got into the garrison.' During her time in the Four Courts her tasks including carrying guns, medical supplies and clothing to the various garrisons. 'In the closing scenes I was asked by Rory O'Connor and Liam Mellowes if I thought I could break through to get news back as to the outside situation – things were then desperate.' Bridie made several attempts, and finally she made it through by driving an ambulance. She assessed the situation in the other garrisons and reported back. She was arrested at the surrender but released after a couple of hours.[2]

As had happened during the 1916 Rising, Cumann na mBan members provided nursing care. Ita O'Gorman administered first aid[3], as did Nora and Ina Connolly, the daughters of James Connolly, executed in 1916. The Connollys set up a first aid centre in Tara Hall, Talbot Street. The sisters raided a chemist shop for supplies;

Ina had trained as a midwife, so she was able to identify what was needed.[4] Other women took over the large kitchen in Moran's Hotel and some of the small rooms in the basement were used to treat the wounded. Ernie O'Malley recalled how some of the women had trained to be couriers:

> **Cumann na mBan girls had learned to drive motor-cars under fire; they practised gear changes up and down streets and back lanes until they felt themselves sufficiently skilled to act as despatch carriers.[5]**

Women were also involved in the fighting. Countess Markievicz reported for duty at Moran's Hotel, which was under the command of Oscar Traynor.[6] She took up position as one of the snipers. One of the members of the garrison later described how, when he was due to be relieved, he was surprised to find that his replacement was none other than Countess Markievicz:

Countess Markievicz with her daughter, Maeve c.1904.

> **Played-out as I was after two or three hours up there under continuous fire, I didn't like the idea of a woman taking over that position. But Madame just waved me to one side ...[7]**

Maud Gonne MacBride headed up a delegation of women, The Women's Peace Committee. Charlotte Despard, Hanna Sheehy Skeffington and a number of pro-Treaty women such as Agnes O'Farrelly and Rosamund Jacob tried to broker a peace. They sent a proposal to both sides – a cessation of hostilities to be settled by a meeting of the Dáil – but Collins, Cosgrave and Griffith rejected their proposal. Maud Gonne MacBride insisted on seeing her old friend Arthur Griffith, but he refused to help, saying that he was now part of the government and that they had to keep law and order.[8]

Cartoon of the period, entitled 'The Voice of the People'. Text underneath read: *'She must have a job in the Free State'*

The fighting continued in Dublin, and as the days passed, those who had been in Moran's Hotel moved to the Gresham Hotel but soon that was also evacuated. Groups of Republicans still occupied Whelan's Hotel, the Hammam Hotel and other buildings in the area. C S Andrews later recalled: 'Thanks mainly to the presence of the girls, I suspect, we were not at all down hearted although recognising quite well that militarily we were in a hopeless position.'[9]

The forces held out until 5 July when the government troops pumped petrol into the O'Connell Street positions from armoured cars and the buildings were set on fire. A white flag was raised over the Hammam Hotel. Once again the women were asked to leave prior to the surrender. Ernie O'Malley wrote:

> The girls had refused to leave. They recited the proclamation of Easter Week: 'The Irish Republic is entitled to, and hereby claims, the allegiance of every Irishman and Irishwoman. The Republic guarantees religious and civil liberty, equal rights and equal opportunities to all its citizens'. Why, if men remained, should women leave? The question was debated with heat in rooms of burning buildings, under the noise of shells and the spatter of machine-guns. Cathal Brugha had to exert his personal influence to make them go.[10]

Cartoon by Countess Markievicz of the attack on a meeting in O'Connell Street, November, 1922. Charlotte Despard, shawled, is shown addressing the meeting, with Maud Gonne MacBride standing beside her.

Máire Comerford left on the day before the surrender. She believed 'there was no point in remaining just to make a bigger bag of prisoners for the Free Staters.'[11] Three women remained: Linda Kearns and two of those who had suffered the loss of relatives in the War of Independence – Cathleen Barry, whose brother Kevin, an eighteen-year-old medical student had been hanged, and Muriel MacSwiney, the widow of Terence, who had died on hunger strike in Brixton Prison in 1920. Most of the buildings in that part of O'Connell Street were destroyed. Sixty-four people were killed, including Cathal Brugha (Minister of Defence in the first Dáil), and over a hundred wounded. Many key people within the Republican camp were imprisoned following the fighting, including Rory O'Connor, Liam Mellowes, and Tom Barry.

Having been lost in Dublin, the remainder of the conflict was played out in the countryside. Republicans returned to the fighting they knew best and a guerrilla war commenced. Fighting concentrated in the so-called 'Munster Republic' – an area stretching from County Limerick in the southwest to County Waterford in the southeast. With the capture of many of the Irregulars, Liam Lynch became Chief of Staff. Although the cities of Limerick and Waterford were soon under the control of the Free State troops, the Irregulars held the 'Munster Republic' for almost ten months.

As time passed, the Free State grew in strength, and following a recruitment drive, 500,000 men swelled the ranks of the National Army. The troops were supplied with weaponry by the British, which included 240 machine guns and 10,000 rifles. The republican side had to rely on bank robberies for money, and raids for weapons.

During the War of Independence, women had shown how vital their role could be to the success of a guerrilla campaign. But the republican women were now well known to their former comrades on the pro-Treaty side, who were quick to appreciate the threat they represented. The mass arrest of women supporters of the IRA from the outset of the Civil War must be seen as a major factor contributing to the eventual defeat of the Republicans.

Bridie Clyne, who had been in the Four Courts, joined the fight in the Dublin Hills, going firstly to Blessington in County Wicklow and then down to the south of the country and finally back to Dublin city. For the next number of months she 'worked underground living in "dumps", typing, cooking, nursing for the Chief of Staff and the Director of intelligence.' She was arrested in 1923 in a raid on a house on Strand Road, Sandymount and held for a number of months in Kilmainham Gaol. However, she had given a false name, Annie Hardwicke, so she managed to conceal her identity and when she got out of prison she continued her work for the IRA.[12]

Booklet written by Countess Markievicz.

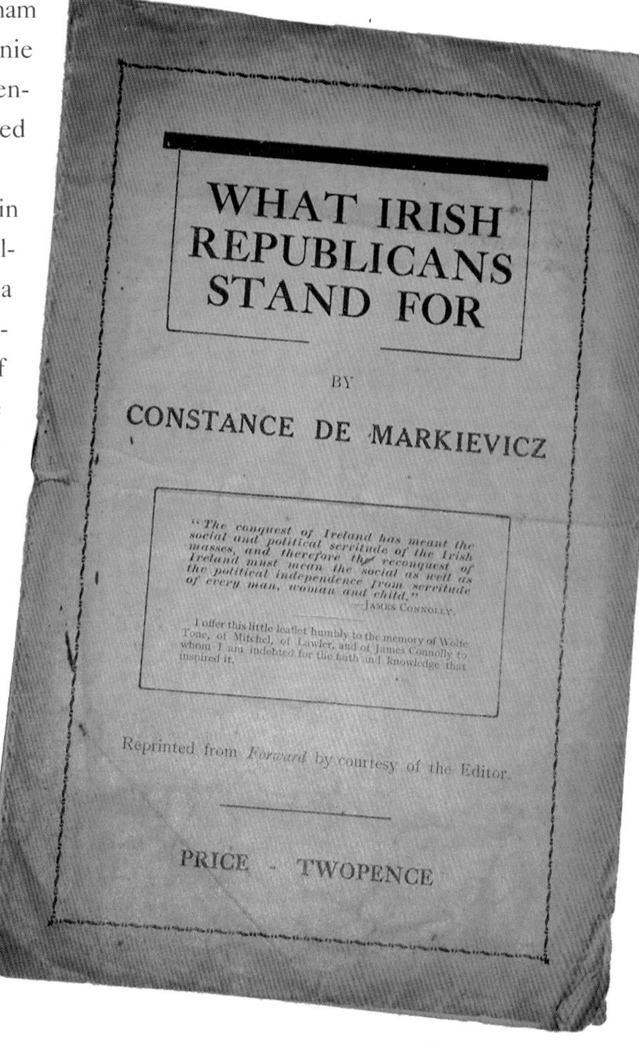
WHAT IRISH REPUBLICANS STAND FOR

BY

CONSTANCE DE MARKIEVICZ

"The conquest of Ireland has meant the social and political servitude of the Irish masses, and therefore the reconquest of Ireland must mean the social as well as the political independence from servitude of every man, woman and child."

—JAMES CONNOLLY.

I offer this little leaflet humbly to the memory of Wolfe Tone, of Mitchel, of Lawler, and of James Connolly to whom I am indebted for the faith and knowledge that inspired it.

Reprinted from *Forward* by courtesy of the Editor.

PRICE - TWOPENCE

Arthur Griffith died on 12 August 1922 of a brain haemorrhage. When, ten days later, Michael Collins was shot dead in an ambush at Béal na mBlath, County Cork, events took a more draconian turn. W T Cosgrave became President of the Executive Council of the Irish Free State and, following an intensive campaign, all major towns in Munster were brought under government control by the end of August.

Public support for the Republicans had almost gone, and the destruction of roads and railway lines; robbing banks, blowing up bridges and unofficial billeting that were all tolerated during the War of Independence now seemed pointless.[13] The actions of the Irregulars caused annoyance to the general public, who would have considered the departure of British troops from the country as a successful outcome and wanted to work with the government of the Irish Free State. Brighid Lyons Thornton, who had been an activist in the 1916 Rising and the War of Independence supported the Treaty.

> **I didn't think we should have to pay any tribute to the King of England ... I thought that this wasn't the Republic we'd fought so hard for. But then I began to think, what is the alternative ... All through the previous years we'd had the support of the people, both young and old. It was the support that kept us going, not the guns or the grenades. The people really had to bear the brunt of the suffering ... If there was any hope of peace you couldn't blame them for taking it.**[14]

Support for those who opposed the Treaty was dwindling daily. In October the Catholic clergy came out against the Irregulars with a pastoral letter condemning them for waging 'a war of wanton destruction, of murder and assassination against the people and the people's government.' It went on to say that those who took part in these crimes were deemed to be guilty of the 'gravest sins and may not be absolved in Confession, nor admitted to Holy Communion.'[15] In Ireland of the 1920s, when Roman Catholicism was the majority religion and the Hierarchy was revered and all-powerful, this excommunication had a profound effect. In this climate the position of the Irregulars seemed hopeless, as Máire Comerford recorded:

> **I felt discouraged at times during that long autumn of 1922, as the Republican Army broke up everywhere into smaller and less effective units. There was no part of Ireland now in which a column of twenty or thirty men might shelter safely ... Of the half dozen houses in any one neighbourhood which might have sheltered them before, only one was open to them now and it was well watched and spied upon. A column now was four men, short of ammunition, hiding in a dripping dug-out ... I was a courier now, trying to maintain links between these disintegrating groups. Sometimes I would return to a place to find that the unit was no longer there.**[16]

Richard Mulcahy was appointed General Commander in Chief of the Free State Army. In October an amnesty was declared for those who would lay down their arms, while those who continued to oppose the working of the Government were dealt with severely. The Army Council was given special powers to deal with those whose offences were deemed to be 'aiding and abetting any attacks on the National forces' [17]and imposed a number of sanctions, including the death penalty, for the possession of a weapon without proper authority.

There were few places left where men on the run could hide out. Ernie O'Malley, the Assistant Chief of Staff of the IRA, took refuge in Ballsbridge, Dublin at the home of the widowed Mrs Humphreys and her family. Nell Humphreys lived there with her three children, Sighle, Dick and Emmet, and her sister, Áine (Anna) O'Rahilly. Ernie O'Malley stayed there because he believed that the household was too frankly Republican to be considered a likely safe house. He wrote: 'Surely the Staters would never think that we would have the hardihood to use such a well-known house again.'[18] O'Malley lived in a hidden room in the house for a number of weeks.

Sighle Humphreys was one of the most active of the Cumann na mBan in Dublin. Her jobs included looking after the wounded and finding safe houses for the men on the run as well as carrying dispatches and painting slogans. When on slogan duty she would set off at 6am and have her messages finished before people were up and about. She was arrested one morning while daubing on a favourite location – the boundary wall of Trinity College in the centre of Dublin. Somehow she and her companions managed to conceal their paints and brushes. When they arrived at Portobello Barracks and were locked in a room they quickly got to work. Soon the walls were covered in green-painted slogans such as 'Call off the Murder Gangs' and 'The Irish Republic Lives'. Some time later an officer came into the room. He asked them why they had been brought to the barracks and they told him to look at the walls and he would find out.[19] He mustn't have understood what they meant, as he released them and let them go home.

Nell Humphreys with her children, Dick (standing), Sighle and Emmet.

On 4 November 1922, the Humphreys home was raided. Ernie O'Malley decided that he wanted to go down fighting, so he came out of the secret room shooting. He accidentally shot Áine O'Rahilly through the chin. Nell and Sighle Humphreys were arrested and spent the next year being moved from prison to prison. Áine was brought to hospital for treatment and in the following April she joined her sister and niece in prison. Writing from her cell, Nell described her situation: 'Don't imagine that I am to be pitied in here. I have been here before … I would be almost enjoying myself, everything is so much easier than at home … I am sure I will get fat, everybody does in prison, now my anxiety about Anna (Áine) is over.'[20]

Another house targeted on 4 November 1922 was 40 Herbert Park, Ballsbridge, the home of Nell and Áine's sister-in-law, Nannie O'Rahilly, and her young family. Mary MacSwiney was arrested there. Immediately after her imprisonment in Mountjoy Jail she began a hunger strike. Her fellow inmates made a report on her condition:

> **For the first fourteen or fifteen days her vitality seemed remarkable. She conversed, read, and wrote letters at intervals and, though each**

day her voice and movements grew fainter, and the periods for which she could exert herself shorter, and the exhaustion which followed more distressing, her mind was alert, cheerful and at peace.[21]

It was at that point that the prison doctor, Dr O'Connor ordered a waterbed for her. Sighle Humphreys felt that this 'of course was a great boon to Mary MacSwiney but put the heart across me as I took it to be a sign that she wouldn't be released.'[22]

Michael O'Rahilly (The O'Rahilly) and his sister, Anna.

Cumann na mBan organised meetings outside the prison and marched on government offices. A nightly vigil of the rosary was held at the prison gates. Free State troops fired shots over the heads of the protesters, and hosed and harassed them, which served only to enhance the publicity surrounding their protest.[23] At one of the meetings in O'Connell Street, fourteen people were seriously wounded and hundreds hurt in a stampede that occurred when Free State soldiers opened fire on the crowd. The gathering had been organised by Maud Gonne MacBride and Charlotte Despard under the auspices of a new organisation, the Women's Prisoners' Defence League, formed by them in August 1922 to protect the prisoners' rights. 'Outside the jail gate there were crowds of women endeavouring to obtain news of their missing sons, husbands and daughters ... no visits were allowed, no information supplied.'[24] The League, affectionately known as 'the Mothers', charged a halfpenny a week and organised vigils, traced missing Republicans, located information on prisoners, and publicised the plight of prisoners. They spoke from moving lorries, outside courtrooms, prisons, the Dáil and street corners. They worked tirelessly for prisoners' rights.[25]

Maud Gonne MacBride and Charlotte Despard became the public voices of opposition to government policy. Dubliners christened them Maud Gonne Mad and Madame Desperate.[26]

On 21 November 1922, when Annie MacSwiney, the youngest of the family, was refused permission to see her sister, she encamped at the prison gates and went on hunger strike also. In protest at the exclusion of her sister, Mary MacSwiney refused to have nurses or doctors attend her. She was then cared for by her fellow prisoners. On 22 November they reported that on her eighteenth day of hunger strike her agitation about her sister had produced 'a marked and rapid change.'[27]

She had clearly resigned herself to death. 'A Message from Mountjoy', signed by all the female prisoners in Mountjoy Jail, stated:

> **Whichever way the struggle ends, victory will be with her who can endure so much and with the cause for which she is going to her agony, joyous if her death will bring back her fellow-countrymen to their ideals and make them brothers-in-arms again.**[28]

On the twentieth day of her hunger strike Mary MacSwiney's condition became critical. She was given the Last Rites. People from both Ireland and abroad lobbied the government for her release, and four days later she was set free. 'Another death of a well known Republican leader, this time a woman, may have proved too harsh an obstacle to overcome for maintaining governmental credibility.'[29] Henceforth, going on hunger strike was seen as an effective weapon against the Free State Government.

On 17 November 1922, the first executions under the new sanctions for illegal possession of a weapon were carried out. Four young men – Peter Cassidy, James Fisher, Richard Twohig and John Gaffney – all under the age of twenty-five, were shot in Kilmainham Gaol. Erskine Childers, Chief of Propaganda for the Irregulars, was shot on 24 November 1922 for being in possession of a revolver. The pearl-handled revolver had been a present from Michael Collins. In early December, the Irregulars assassinated Sean Hales, a member of the Dáil. The Government's reaction was to select four republican prisoners: Rory O'Connor, Liam Mellowes, Joseph McKelvey and Dick Barrett – each from a different province of Ireland – and execute them.

Although the death penalty for carrying a gun had not so far been enforced on women, it was always a possibility that a woman might be the next to be executed. This did not deter the more committed from carrying weapons, one of those being Máire Comerford. Máire was involved in a plot to kidnap W T Cosgrave. On 8 January 1923, she and her accomplice, Paddy McGrath, were en route to Dublin to carry out the kidnapping when their car, nicknamed 'Cupid', broke down in Loughlinstown, on the road from County Wicklow to Dublin. They were forced to hail a taxi already carrying passengers. Her old comrade, Min Ryan, now Mrs Richard Mulcahy, was in the taxi. When they saw her, Paddy and Máire quickly went in different directions and Min Mulcahy, suspecting they were up to something, informed on them at the first police checkpoint.[30] Máire and Paddy were arrested and Máire was found to have a revolver in her possession.[31] She was taken to Mountjoy Jail.

Annie MacSwiney (with blanket) on hunger strike outside Mountjoy Jail, 1922. Charlotte Despard is seated, right.

Suspected anti-Treatyites could be arrested and detained without charge under the terms of the Emergency Powers Act, and women were more vulnerable to arrest than men on the run. The government was well aware of the importance of the women to the IRA's communications network. W T Cosgrave commented that 'the mainstay of the trouble we have had was the activity of the women'.[32] When there were complaints in the press of 'a war on women' Cosgrave countered that it was 'not possible to consider these women as ordinary females'.[33] Women were now legitimate targets for some members of the Free State Army. Mrs Hartney, a Cumann na mBan member from Limerick was shot dead while she was assisting the IRA in Adare, County Limerick. The mother of two small children, she had been an active member of Cumann na mBan for many years. Both she and her husband had taken the Republican side and she paid for this with her life.[34]

The Government had increased the powers of the military courts and issued a statement that any person found in the possession of a 'plan, document or note, for a purpose prejudicial to the safety of the State or of the National forces' would be executed.[35] The arrests began at the end of 1922. Eithne Coyle had been arrested and released so many times in 1922 that 'she began to think the Free State authorities did not intend to imprison Republican women.'[36] Now, however, Republican women were arrested and incarcerated in prisons all over the country, usually in the county prison or police barracks. As Eithne Coyle recalled, when the Volunteers 'were being rounded up wholescale' she had been working with the Third Western Division of the IRA in Sligo. She decided to return home to Donegal, and attempted to enter the county by boat at a quiet spot outside Donegal town, but the Free State soldiers were waiting for her; they had in fact lain in wait for her for all night. They were hoping to find arms and documents in her possession but as she had 'dumped her war luggage on the Sligo side'[37] she was caught empty-handed. In Rock Barracks, Ballyshannon she was detained in a room next to the guardroom for six weeks. With her past history of escaping from jail they were not taking any chances. Her cell was 'invaded at all hours of the night by members of a drunken guard, an undisciplined mob.'[38] She went on hunger strike in a bid to be transferred to Mountjoy Jail where other members of Cumann na mBan were being held. She was brought instead to Drumboe Castle but, still refusing to eat, she was brought to Buncrana Barracks and from there to Dublin. When she arrived in Mountjoy Jail, Deputy Governor Paudeen O'Keefe greeted her with 'By cripes, here is Eithne Coyle from Donegal!' His familiarity was checked by a dark look from Eithne and henceforth he referred to her as 'Miss Coyle'.[39]

Raids on the homes of well-known republicans became a common occurrence. The Intelligence Department was run from Oriel House, Westland Row, Dublin and a special force known as the Criminal Investigation Division (CID) took charge of dealing with the policing of the anti-Treatyites. Women searchers started a

Áine Ceannt and her son, Ronan, after the Rising.

particular type of raid known as a 'sit-down raid'. They entered the house, locked the family in the back, and spent a day or two enjoying the freedom of the house, eating, drinking and taking souvenirs.[40]

During one month in 1923, the home of Áine Ceannt, widow of Eamonn Ceannt, was raided on three separate occasions. The house in Ranelagh that she shared with her seventy-two-year-old mother and teenage son was ransacked and most of their possessions were destroyed. After one raid Áine wrote to her sister Lily in prison:

> We have now fixed up the kitchen but the house is not habitable. Eamonn's photo is disfigured beyond recognition ... when the Black and Tans raided they did not destroy it. You cannot imagine the house or the minuteness of the destruction ... the marble wash stand, chest of drawers, wardrobe ... in your room are in splinters, and the dining room beggars description.[41]

Just over a month later, the house was raided again. Áine described the event to Lily: 'I believe that they dressed up in your clothes and then jazzed in my bedroom; I thought that the dining room ceiling would come down ... when ten people take possession of your house and eat everything in it – by order as they said, it does not encourage one to spend money. '[42]

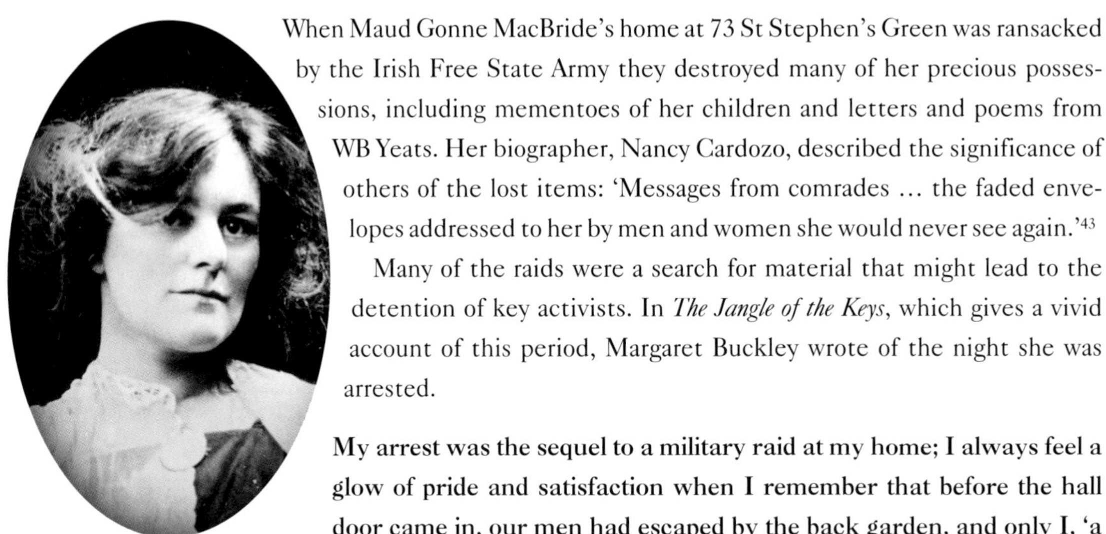

Maud Gonne.

When Maud Gonne MacBride's home at 73 St Stephen's Green was ransacked by the Irish Free State Army they destroyed many of her precious possessions, including mementoes of her children and letters and poems from WB Yeats. Her biographer, Nancy Cardozo, described the significance of others of the lost items: 'Messages from comrades ... the faded envelopes addressed to her by men and women she would never see again.'[43]

Many of the raids were a search for material that might lead to the detention of key activists. In *The Jangle of the Keys*, which gives a vivid account of this period, Margaret Buckley wrote of the night she was arrested.

My arrest was the sequel to a military raid at my home; I always feel a glow of pride and satisfaction when I remember that before the hall door came in, our men had escaped by the back garden, and only I, 'a woman of no importance', was there to greet the raiders when they trooped in ... Having failed to make the capture they expected, they spent nearly four hours going through papers ... and finally took me away ...[44]

When Margaret Buckley arrived in Mountjoy Jail there were eighteen women there. The number had increased suddenly with the arrest of the staff of the Sinn Féin office in Suffolk Street on 9 November. [45] They named the big cell in which they were held 'Suffolk Street'[46] The 'Suffolk Street' women included Lily O'Brennan, Dorothy Macardle, Teresa O'Connell, Rita Bermingham, and Kathleen Devaney, and they stayed together as a group for their period of imprisonment. On the day of the Sinn Féin office arrests, Rita O'Farrelly and Kathleen O'Carroll had met on Grafton Street and, hearing that Suffolk Street was being raided, had gone down to have a look, where they were promptly arrested. Their curiosity earned them eleven months and nine months respectively.[47]

The Governor of Mountjoy Jail was Phil Cosgrave, but it was Deputy Governor Paudeen O'Keefe who was in charge of the women. He was well known to many of them, as he had been an activist during the War of Independence and had worked with Margaret Buckley as Secretary for Sinn Féin. Although some of the inmates thought that he had 'no love' for his former comrade,[48] Margaret Buckley felt that she could get around him, and at her request he gave the women many concessions. On one occasion he got them the ingredients for pancakes and at another stage he agreed to their request for a gas stove. But Margaret Buckley went too far when she asked for a typewriter; he replied: 'Lord God, the next thing you'll want is a machine gun'.[49]

Other members of the group had a different approach as to how they would conduct themselves in prison. They advocated a 'perpetual row' and favoured a 'state of war' being maintained.[50] Objecting to overcrowding, Nell Humphreys,

Sighle Humphreys, Rita O'Farrelly and Bridie O'Mullane, who were all sharing a cell, decided to barricade themselves in when they heard the governor and soldiers bringing in yet another prisoner. When it was discovered that the door could not be forced open, Paudeen O'Keefe broke the gas globe and mantle, leaving the inmates in darkness. Still they refused to admit the new prisoner. Suddenly the prisoner outside – Máire Comerford – shouted for them to take cover. They had barely dropped to the floor when a shot came through the keyhole. After firing, Paudeen O'Keefe said, 'I hope that there will be three dead bodies in there in the morning.' The women remained barricaded inside for several days. There were no more prisoners placed in their cells.[51] Sighle Humphreys and Máire Comerford were held in solitary confinement for three months because of their defiant attitude. They saw the other women only on Sunday mornings.[52] Despite not taking part in these obstructionist tactics, the other prisoners refused to disassociate themselves from them and, as a result, all the female prisoners were subjected to random searches and had shots fired at them. These were blank shots, but Máire Comerford was shot in the leg by a real bullet when she was seen waving to other prisoners.[53]

On one occasion the women had all the furniture taken from their cells. They went on hunger strike to have the furniture returned. According to Margaret Buckley: 'The hunger strike was the only weapon we could wield, and we felt justified in using it. … We were being deprived of common necessities, which are accorded to the most depraved criminal prisoners. '[54] They succeeded in getting the return of the furniture as well as a supply of newspapers, food parcels and letters. Throughout 1923, in all the detention camps, both male and female prisoners would use hunger strikes to obtain concessions.

Depiction of women prisoners playing rounders in the Invincibles yard, Kilmainham Gaol.

As the months passed, the numbers of prisoners increased; the CID were arresting as many members of 'the movement' as possible. The extent to which whole families were involved in anti-government activities is illustrated by the familial links among those imprisoned throughout 1923. There were the Gifford sisters from Dublin, Kitty and Josie Falkner, Jenny and Kitty Coyle, also from Dublin; the McGee sisters from Donegal and the Power sisters from Tralee, as well as fellow Kerrywomen Julia and Pauline Hassett. Tessie and Angela Doyle from Dublin were cousins; Harriette and Maynie Lavery were mother and daughter. For the most part, the offences were comparatively minor: being found in the possession of republican literature, attending Cumann na mBan meetings, collecting for the prisoners' dependants. The women were held without trial under the terms of the

Jo Power (Siobhán de Paor).

Emergency Powers Act. They were told that they could obtain their freedom by signing a document in which they gave an undertaking that they would not oppose the working of the Free State. This was known to the prisoners as 'the form' and over the months many women did sign it. However, as some of them found out, it was not always a guarantee of freedom.

Many of those arrested were the mothers, sisters, daughters or girlfriends of republican men who were imprisoned or on the run. One such prisoner was teenager Annie Moore of Kildare. Her brother Brian, a labourer, and her fiancé Patrick Nolan were executed at the Curragh Camp on 19 December 1922 for possession of arms and ammunition.[55] When Margaret Buckley met her in Mountjoy Jail later that month she described her as 'an inconsolable looking girl'.[56] Sighle Humphreys wrote: 'Her story was the saddest of all ... if anyone ever got our sympathy she certainly got ours but I wonder did it give her any comfort.'[57] Annie was transferred to Kilmainham Gaol in February 1923 and to the NDU in April.

Cecilia Gallagher was arrested despite the fact that she was apolitical; her crime was to be married to Frank Gallagher, a well-known republican who at that time was assistant editor of the newspaper *Poblacht na hÉireann* (The Republic of Ireland). A family story tells of how, shortly after Cecilia was arrested, her mother was stopped on the street in Cork by a woman who asked after Cecilia, saying: 'I hear that Cecilia is in prison for Ireland'; to which Mrs Saunders replied, 'She is not – she is in prison for Frank Gallagher.'[58] Cecilia was arrested on 9 November 1922[59] along with her landlady, May Langan, who had no political associations except for having the Gallaghers in her house.[60] They were brought to Mountjoy Jail, where Frank was already a prisoner; each morning Cecilia would wake her fellow prisoners as she climbed the bedsteads to shout 'good morning' to Frank when he emerged to do his orderly duties. The couple spent their first Christmas as a married couple in different wings of Mountjoy Jail.[61] As the year passed and many of the prominent members of the movement were executed, Cecilia's constant fear was that Frank would be next to be killed. In June 1923, by which time he had been moved to Gormanstown Camp, she wrote of him: 'I am so grateful that he is still alive that I am content to abide indurance (sic) vile till it pleaseth the Lord to deliver us and give us once more to each other.'[62] They were reunited the following year and lived on into old age together.

Cis Power (Mairéad de Paor).

In the early months of 1923 over 13,000 male and female republican prisoners were being detained by the Free State. The prisoners came from every part of Ireland as well as from abroad. Among the inmates in Mountjoy Jail were ten women from London, five from Liverpool[63] and four from Glasgow. Members of the Scottish and English branches of Cumann na mBan and the Irish Self-Determination League had been deported to

Ireland on His Majesty's Battle Cruisers 'Castor' [64] and 'Wolfhound', under clause 14b of the Restoration of Order in Ireland Act.[65] The English political prisoners were all 'old campaigners for the fight for freedom': Mrs Eileen Barrett (sister to Seán Connolly, killed in 1916), Aggie Sheehan (known as Big Aggy) and Sorcha MacDermott. Margaret Buckley described them as 'well known to the junta that now jailed them.'[66]

Cecilia Gallagher.

Paudeen O'Keefe hated the deportees as some of them had pronounced English accents and that got on his nerves. And the deportees did little to ingratiate themselves with him when they presented a list of demands on their first morning in Mountjoy Jail. One of them had even asked for a corset. He cursed when he read it and Margaret Buckley chastised him, reminding him that ladies were about. He retorted: 'Ladies be damned, would you believe that one of those English so and so's has asked to bring her in a stays?' He left, banging the door, and snarling 'Ladies how are ye!'[67] It is not recorded what his reaction was when the 'Scotch' girls taught their fellow prisoners to whistle 'Rule Britannia'. The Scottish prisoners were members of the Anne Devlin Branch of Cumann na mBan in Glasgow. Hannah Duggan (known as Pidge), Lizzie Marrin, Mollie Duffy and Mary Nelson had been deported from Glasgow on the destroyer 'Wolfhound' and brought to Mountjoy Jail to serve their sentences. An action was later taken against the illegal deportations of these women, and the British government had to compensate them.[68]

The Glasgow women had been active couriers during the War of Independence and the Civil War, supplying much-needed ammunition during the fighting in O'Connell Street in July 1922.[69] On one occasion, when Pidge Duggan and Lizzie Marrin arrived from Glasgow to a safe house in Dublin, they were detained by Free State soldiers. The military were looking for Joe Robinson, the head of the IRA in Glasgow, and they knew that he was Pidge's fiancé. They tried all kinds of tactics to find out information on Joe's movements, including bringing the girls up to the Dublin mountains and threatening to shoot them. Three times they stopped the lorry, got out their guns, made the girls kneel, and avised them to say their prayers, telling them they would shoot them on the count of ten. Eventually they dragged Pidge and Lizzie to their feet and threw them up on the lorry. The women were imprisoned for a couple of hours and then brought to a boat that was sailing for Glasgow that night. They were warned not to return to Ireland, under pain of death. The

Hannah (Pidge) Duggan, left.

two ladies arrived home, slept for a few hours, got up, packed their waistcoats with guns and were back again in Dublin the following evening.[70]

The huge numbers being arrested created immense pressure on the prison accommodation. By March 1923, Mountjoy Jail was not accepting any more female political prisoners. In early February, Kilmainham Gaol (which had been used since 1916 as a place of detention for army deserters and male political prisoners during the War of Independence) was made ready for female prisoners. Inmates from Mountjoy Jail and from prisons in other parts of the country were moved to Kilmainham. Between February and September 1923, over 500 women and girls[71] aged between twelve and seventy were incarcerated in Kilmainham Gaol.[72]

Lily O'Brennan, who had been in the Marrowbone Lane Garrison in 1916 and a secretary on the Treaty Delegation, was among the first group of women to arrive in Kilmainham on 6 February, 1923. As she and forty-two others were transported from Mountjoy Jail at one o'clock in the morning in an open lorry they shouted 'Up Dev', 'Long Live the Republic' and other slogans.[73]

Lily was already familiar with Kilmainham Gaol, having been imprisoned there in 1916, but for others, like Cis and Jo Power from Tralee, who saw it for the first time in March 1923, it was a formidable place:

> When we got inside, the interior looked grim and forbidding and our spirits by now were sinking to zero to be somewhat revived again by the strains of the hymn 'Hail Glorious St Patrick' sung with great volume and devotion. We were marshalled along a stone passage and came to a big iron gate when the singing ceased and the prisoners came to the gates to discover who the latest arrivals were.[74]

Suddenly they heard a shrill voice, asking, 'Are ye prisoners?' When they replied that they were, the voice said: 'Up the Republic', 'No surrender'.[75] Then they saw two wild eyes glaring through the grating of a door by the entrance to the main jail.

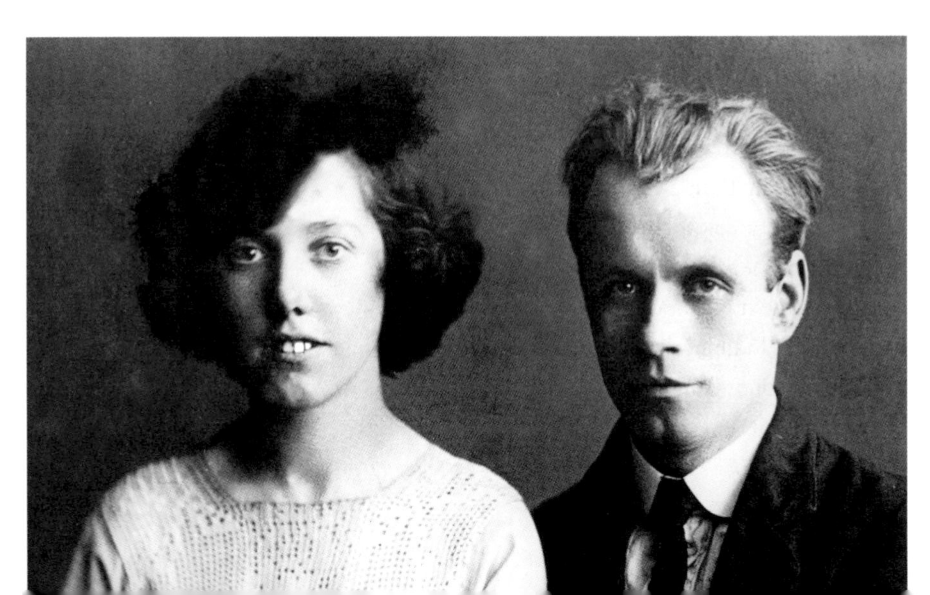

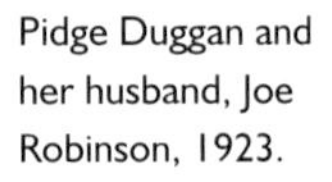

Pidge Duggan and her husband, Joe Robinson, 1923.

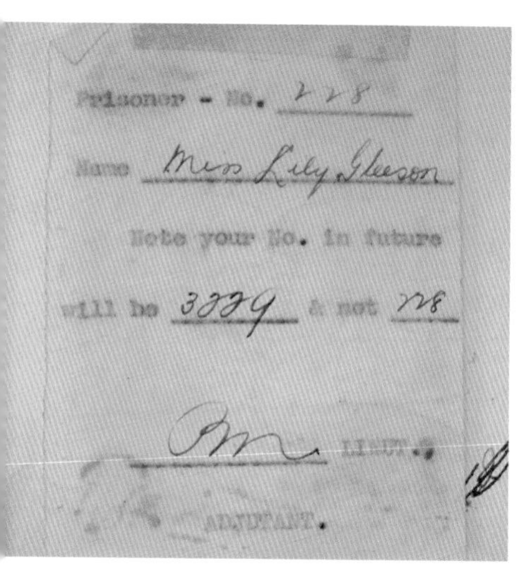
Prisoner - No. 228

Name Miss Lily Gleeson

Note your No. in future

will be 3339 & not 228

LIEUT.

ADJUTANT.

Lily Gleeson stuck the notification of her new prisoner number into her autograph book.

'God' said Cis 'Are we to join that hysterical woman?' One of their escorts, Deputy Ryan overheard and hastened to reassure them. 'No', he said 'You won't join her until morning, but don't let the thought disturb you, you'll all be hysterical by then.'[76] The sisters later discovered that the 'hysterical' woman was Nora Rogers from Tipperary. 'No Surrender' was the watchword that she used at every opportunity. As she told her fellow inmates, the explanation for her behaviour lay with her mother. When her mother was dying she had said to her daughter: 'Nora Rogers, as long as John Bull has the tip of his big toe on the shores of Ireland let there be for you No Surrender.'[77]

The Powers had been involved in producing a propaganda paper called *The Invincible*. Working only with a typewriter, they could make just four or five legible copies at a time, so were anxious to acquire a duplicator. They wrote a letter requesting one, and asked a Mrs Eileen O'Connor to carry the message with her to Dublin. However, she was arrested at Tralee Station and the letter was found in the lining of her hat. She was taken to Tralee Jail. Later that same day the Power sisters were also arrested and brought to the jail.

Having Mrs O'Connor in their company had a sobering effect on the girls, who had thought of the whole experience as a 'great adventure'.[78] Mrs O'Connor was the widow of Sean O'Connor, a victim of the infamous Ballyseedy Cross massacre on 7 March 1923, when nine Irregulars were tied together by Free State troops and a mine was detonated. One of the men, Stephen Fuller, was miraculously thrown clear by the force of the blast and lived to tell the story. Dorothy Macardle gave a graphic account of the event in her book *The Tragedies of Kerry*, when she wrote: 'for days afterwards the birds were eating the flesh off the trees at Ballyseedy Cross.'[79]

Mrs O'Connor had come to Ireland from Liverpool to claim her husband's body. While in Tralee she had met the Power sisters, and in the course of conversation told them how her husband had promised their little daughter that he would bring her back a doll from Ireland. Somehow, they managed to procure a doll and have it clothed by a dressmaker in the town. Mrs O'Connor had the doll with her in Tralee jail and on the journey to Kilmainham, a fact that intrigued another prisoner from Kilkenny who saw them at Kingsbridge (Heuston) Station. She thought it 'most unlikely that prisoners would be travelling flaunting a doll in their possessions.'[80]

Mrs O'Connor was finally released from prison in Dublin on 22 March after she became ill. As Hannah Moynihan recorded: 'Had she been detained any longer, she would have lost her job in Liverpool – her only means of support, now that her husband was dead.'[81]

There were other Civil War prisoners who, like Mrs O'Connor, had little interest in the fight for a Republic, but had simply been caught up in the struggle. Hannah O'Neill, a widow from the Liberties area of Dublin, was arrested on 6 February 1923 when detectives came looking for her son. When they could not find him they arrested her.[82] The three youngest of her children were put into the care of her married daughter. In the week of her arrest Mrs O'Neill was due to have an operation on an ulcerated stomach. During her incarceration in Kilmainham and the North Dublin Union (NDU) she continued to suffer from her stomach complaint, as well as arthritis and other ailments. Her period of imprisonment did nothing to convert her to the Republican cause.[83]

There were especially large numbers of women prisoners from the Republican strongholds of Kerry and Cork. As well as the Power sisters, there was Hanna O'Connor, a twenty-two-year-old from Ballymullen, County Kerry, who had been transported from Fenit in County Kerry with a number of other prisoners, including Hanna Mullins, Julia Hassett, Maimie McSweeney and Bunty Barrett. Their very undignified mode of transport was 'The Slievegalleon' cattle boat. Its cargo was described as livestock and women! Hanna had been held in Mountjoy Jail until Kilmainham Gaol opened its doors to women prisoners. Her impression of Kilmainham was of an 'edifice of gloom and misery,' the 'huge iron gates, the clang of the keys in the rusty locks, the dim gaslight.'[84] She wrote in her memoir that she was struck by the size of the building in contrast to the comparative smallness of Tralee and Mountjoy jails. Here she was allocated her own cell, whereas in Tralee and Mountjoy all the 'Kerrys' were housed together in one room. The regional divisions were still maintained in the grouping of the women's cells in Kilmainham. Though the new cells seemed bigger than their old ones, the windows left something to be desired. 'We missed the big windows of Mountjoy,' wrote Hanna O'Connor, 'instead we had a small window high up, which left in very little light and which could not be opened.'[85]

Hanna O'Connor's autograph also gives details of her various imprisonments.

N.D.U. 5th May 1923.

Now Jennie, my dear, always be of good cheer,
And don't let the "Union" oppress you,
There are great times ahead when the Slave State is dead,
And an Irish Republic will bless you."

Hanna Connor,
"Kerry No I."

Tralee Jail 24th Oct. 1922.
Mountjoy " 23rd Nov. 1922
Kilmainham 5th Feb. 1923.
N.D.U. 1st May 1923.

The cells in Kilmainham Gaol were small and basically furnished with a table, a stool and a mattress on the floor. Those without gas in the cells got a large candle, which had to last for two nights.[86] Many of the women decorated their cells. Hannah

Moynihan and Cis Power busied themselves 'making their "house" beautiful, putting down floor mats made of prison blankets'. They spent all day on 17 April decorating their cell, 'covering it with pictures – mostly magazine cuttings and some pictures of food – mouth watering dishes'. Hannah noted in her diary: 'All combined to produce a very pleasing effect.'[87] The women gave their cells different names: 'Barry's Own', 'The Flying Squad', 'The Snipers', 'The Republican Sisterhood' and 'The Barbarians'.[88] Jo Power and Hannah Moynihan christened their cell 'The Invincibles' after the newspaper that they had been producing in Tralee. Norah Hurley, who had been arrested with the Powers and Hannah Moynihan in Tralee, called her cell 'Mistaken Identity'. When her friends were being escorted to Tralee Jail, Norah had crossed the street to speak to them, not realising their situation, and was promptly arrested by the escorting officer. She always maintained that it had been a case of mistaken identity.[89]

A cell window in the West Wing, Kilmainham Gaol, today.

Kilmainham Gaol was run by Governor Corri and staffed by Free State soldiers and female warders, all of whom, according to Hanna O'Connor, were 'well seasoned warriors'. She described the warder, Miss Dill, who to her dismay was said to be a fellow-Kerrywoman, as being 'as stiff as she could be, never smiled and never budged an inch to be helpful to us.' Loath to see her as one of her fellow countrywomen, she called her 'another specimen of the British type.'[90] The staff was not all so unpleasant. Margaret Buckley described one of the warders, Miss Wilson, as kind and considerate. She was slow to ask the wardresses to take out messages as she felt it was not fair to jeopardise their jobs, especially as it was only 'the decent ones who would agree to chance it.' She broke her resolve only once while she was imprisoned in Mountjoy Jail, when all parcels were stopped and the women were starving. When one of the warders told her that she was buying a coat in Arnotts department store, Margaret asked her to bring a message with her, knowing that many of the shop assistants were supporters of the prisoners. Her SOS was rewarded when the wardress brought back a selection of food in her Arnotts' parcel.[91]

Seventeen-year-old Sheila Hartnett, one of the younger inmates, also attested to the compassion of one of the warders. Sheila had been forced to move to Dublin when the family home and chemist shop, 'The Medical Hall' in Kenmare, County Kerry, was burned down by Free State troops on suspicion of being a bomb factory.[92] A red-haired wardress gave her homemade sandwiches and Sheila always remembered her acts of kindness.[93]

One of the medical officers who attended the women was Brighid Lyons Thornton, who as a young medical student had fought in the Four Courts garrison in 1916. Now a qualified doctor, she was the only female recruited as a First Lieutenant in

Newspaper cutting kept by Brighid Brophy, indicating the location of her cell in the East Wing, Kilmainham Gaol.

the Free State Army. She had been a prisoner in Kilmainham Gaol in 1916[94] but, having become a supporter of the Free State, she was now on the opposite side politically to her former comrades.

The women won their status as political prisoners by a constant fight against the rules and regulations. When Bridie O'Mullane arrived in Kilmainham she was appointed Officer Commanding in A Wing. She decided that she would protest against the women being locked up in their cells at night. She organised that locks would be removed from the cell doors on an agreed date. She showed her fellow inmates how to loosen the screws and take off the padlocks. They then put the locks in the ventilators. On the arranged date, eighty locks were removed and a search made by the prison staff failed to find them. When Bridie was called into the Governor's office, an agreement was reached that if she returned the prison property the women would not be locked in the cells again. The locks were handed over and the women gained their concession.[95] They were able to leave their cells during the day and the only check was a daily roll call.

Female convicts were brought from Mountjoy Jail to Kilmainham to do the cooking and general cleaning. This concession had been won in Mountjoy Jail when the inmates refused to be 'charwomen'.[96] The convicts also worked the furnace, so the women were able to take a bath each morning with warm water. The convicted prisoners from Mountjoy Jail 'were glad to be there, as they had a much better time: tea, instead of cocoa, less work and altogether freer conditions.'[97]

One of the convicts engaged Hannah Moynihan in conversation. She enquired from Hannah where she was from, and when she discovered it was Tralee, she asked Hannah if knew her uncle, Billy Flynn. It transpired that Hannah did know him – as

'Fling-a-ling' the tinker. Having discovered a mutual acquaintance and enjoyed their conversation, the convict's parting remark was 'Ah, Miss it's the cream of the country that's in jail now'.[98]

The convicts brought up the meals. Breakfast came at 8.30am, dinner at 1pm, tea at 5pm, and there was always something for supper.[99] For the Power sisters, the most memorable thing was the soup. It had to be fished out of a large container with tin mugs. It was served in a very unhygienic fashion, which they ignored when they were hungry.[100] Fanny Kelly added Bovril to hers and she thought that it improved the flavour.[101] Some prisoners refused to eat prison food and survived on the food parcels sent into them. Food parcels were accepted by a sentry at the prison gates, but could be withheld subject to the prisoners' behaviour, and these rules were constantly changing.[102] Those who could afford it could have a standing order at the local shop for 'essentials' such as cigarettes.[103] The women devised an ingenious way of cooking in their cells. There was a gas jet in an aperture behind the cell door that could be reached by placing a stool on top of the small table. A can of water held over the flame gave boiling water for tea, while food was cooked on a large enamel plate set over the flame. Nora Brosnan, a prisoner from Castlegregory in County Kerry, thought it was a wonder they were not all burnt to death.[104]

It was the job of Peadar Kearney (composer of *The Soldier's Song*, now Ireland's national anthem) to censor all the post that came into Kilmainham. The state of parcels depended upon the temper of the censor; if news from prison was published outside, a close search of the contents was carried out for a week or so.[105] Parcels and letters could be halted without explanation. At one stage they were stopped for a three-week period. And the parcels that did arrive were not always complete. One inmate was deprived of her birthday cake, although the letter describing how it had been iced and decorated got through.[106]

Prisoners were normally allowed to write a specified number of letters per week, but had to use special notepaper. Each letter was limited to one page, to be written on one side of the paper only.[107] They could, however, receive any number of letters; this was considered an essential concession of their political status. Dorothy Macardle received supplies of books and writing materials from her former pupil in Alexandra College, Lillian Dalton Soiron. Lillian told of having received a letter from Dorothy requesting a copy of Plato's *Republic*; the censor had crossed out the word 'Republic'.[108] Hanna O'Connor recalled receiving a letter from a friend in which everything was cut out except 'Cheer Up Hanna, it's all for Ireland – Mollie.'[109]

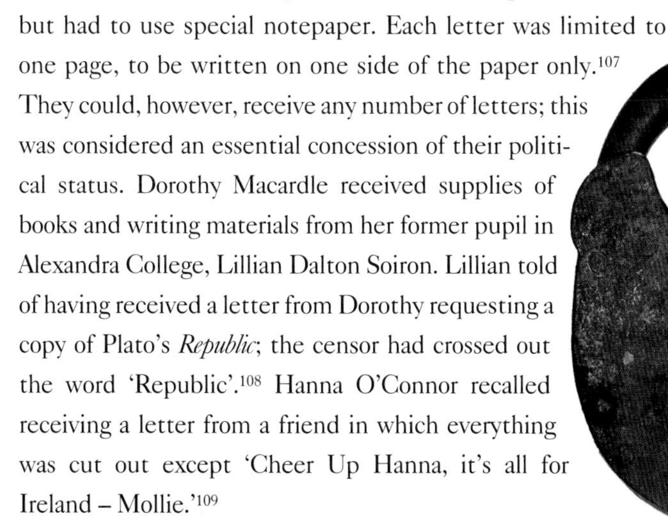

Old lock from Kilmainham Gaol.

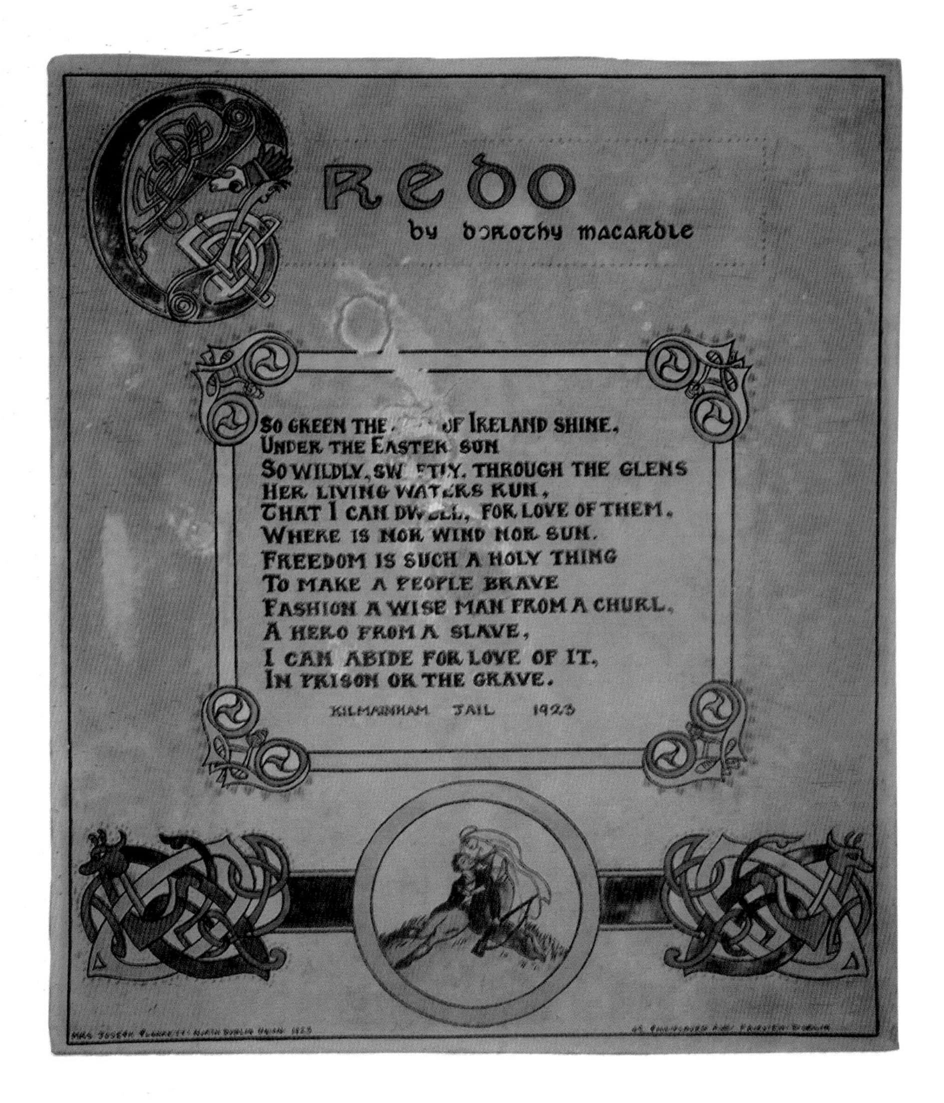

Poem by Dorothy Macardle, illustrated by Grace Plunkett.

Throughout the Civil War no prison visits were allowed. From November 1922 executions of men were frequent, and families feared for the lives of the women prisoners. The considerable strain this imposed on relatives is reflected in the stream of telegrams sent to the authorities begging for news of the prisoners.[110] The execution of a woman was a real possibility. According to Eithne Coyle, Paudeen O'Keefe 'always carried two revolvers, one at his belt and another at his thigh', and was constantly warning the women that they would be shot.[111] Rumours constantly circulated that a woman would be executed 'just for an example.'[112] The Kilmainham prisoners were fortunate, as friends could gather outside the gaol. Inmates were able to converse with those outside by shouting down from the third floor windows of the East Wing. It was difficult for those outside to recognise people at a distance, but when the name of a prisoner was shouted, a message was relayed and she would be brought to the window. There was quite an amount of competition to get the prime vantage points at the windows. This pastime was the subject of a painting by Jack B Yeats entitled 'Communicating with Prisoners', now in the Model Arts and Niland Gallery in Sligo. A group of seven women are depicted standing beside an advertising billboard looking up at the East Wing of the Gaol, where figures are visible in the windows.

The inmates could spend hours chatting to friends and watching the world go by. Lily O'Brennan wrote in her diary for Tuesday, 13 February that she and another prisoner called Betty passed the time by reading advertisements on hoardings nearby. [113] However, when on one occasion an over-zealous sentry strafed the walls with rifle fire, 'it curbed the flow of information for a time'.[114] Eileen Tucker was shot in the hand at the base of the thumb. Years later her daughters remembered her having bits of the bullet extracted when they came to the surface of her skin.[115]

Although the regime for these prisoners was more relaxed than for ordinary convicts, the members of Cumann na mBan imposed their own rules in Mountjoy, Kilmainham and the North Dublin Union, where women were also held. The highest-ranking Cumann na mBan officers drew up a set of rules and these were read to the prisoners. A Prisoners' Council was formed. Commanding Officers and Quartermasters and Adjutants were appointed. These were usually the older women such as Nell Humphreys, Margaret Buckley and Katherine Wilson. Tasks of the Quartermaster included the distribution of food, candles, soap and notepaper.[116] An Adjutant was in charge of the collection and distribution of post. The highest-ranking officers made representations to the Governor.[117]

When Hannah Moynihan attended her first meeting with the Prisoners' Council, she was most impressed by Bridie O'Mullane, and wrote in her diary that she 'spoke vehemently, fired by a righteous indignation and a determination to improve conditions or die in the attempt. She fired my blood too, as I listened, not so much with what she said as the way she said it. Oh! to be like her, a leader of women.'[118]

The Prisoner's Council kept in touch by letter with their comrades in Cumann na mBan outside the jail. Messages were smuggled in, along with daily bulletins that gave them information on the political situation from the Republican standpoint. Secret dispatches were sent out looking for information on certain inmates and asking for suggestions on how the Council in the jail should deal with troublesome prisoners.

If prisoners were unknown to the senior members of Cumann na mBan they fell under suspicion. When Sadie Dowling and Esther Davis were arrested for hitting a policeman and brought to Mountjoy Jail, Sighle Humphreys recorded: '... they were unknown to us, it used to be wondered if they were Republicans at all, but the fact that they never signed the form may be proof enough.'[119]

One of the secret dispatches sent from Kilmainham Gaol refers to a certain prisoner 'continually trying to stir up a mutiny against the Council, and encouraging irresponsible girls to escape by means which the Council knew to be unsafe.' 'Very often we have to keep watch all night to prevent some of the youngsters from being led into a trap.'[120] The Council also requested that Cumann na mBan members outside the prison make enquiries about certain inmates to ascertain information about them. They wished to find out the truth about a woman who was accused by a fellow inmate of having informed on the six railway workers (including Annie Moore's fiancée and brother) who were subsequently executed.[121]

The Councils in Mountjoy and Kilmainham organised classes according to the educational standards of the prisoners. The highest-ranking Cumann na mBan members came from educated middle and upper class backgrounds. In a period when university education was open only to the privileged few, such women were well represented among the Civil War prisoners and included Katherine Wilson, the Power sisters and Dorothy Macardle.

Lessons ranged from the 'Three R's' – Reading, Writing and Arithmetic – to subjects of university matriculation standard.[122] Intermediate French was taught. There was also a dancing class for those less interested in study.[123] In keeping with the educational objectives of women's groups since the turn of the century, Irish language and culture was keenly promoted. Three nights a week, Dorothy Macardle gave Irish history lessons,[124] under the title 'Revolutionist History Class'.[125] All the prisoners were encouraged to speak and read Irish. Many of the women converted to the Gaelic versions of their names. Lily O'Brennan was proud of her progress and wrote to her nephew Rónán: 'I am reading Irish well now – almost without a dictionary.'[126]

Above: Autograph book cover. Opposite: autographs from Nora Spillane, Nellie Lambert and Neans Ní Fhlannachadha. Nora Spillane has written over a British stamp bearing the words Saorstát Éireann (Irish Free State).

The women prisoners spent a period of time out of doors each day. In Kilmainham the time allowed in the yards was 11am to 1pm and 4pm to 6pm.[127] Outside, the women played rounders and handball. The sentry in the crow's nest was in a good position to catch high handers. Games of rounders had begun as a pastime in Mountjoy Jail and became very popular. Inter-county matches were held, advertised in advance with posters announcing the day, time and members of the teams. All the teams wore the colours of their respective counties. Hanna O'Connor described how the Kerry team 'wore blue and gold ribbons in our hair'. She also recalled in her memoir that 'it's not a boast to say Kerry invariably emerged victorious.'[128] Other prisoners devised their own entertainments; fifteen-year-old Jake Folan's favourite pastime was to go into the padded cell in B Wing and bounce around.[129]

Indoors, the prisoners passed the time visiting – invitations to tea in each other's cells were a way of sharing the goodies sent in from relatives and friends. Other women read fortunes in teacups or using cards. One of these was Lucy Bermingham, of whom Hanna O'Connor wrote: 'How we listened to her "prophecies".'[130] Card games such as whist helped to while away the long hours.[131] Ghost stories were also very popular. Dorothy Macardle wrote down some of her best stories and had them published in America in 1924 in a book entitled *Earthbound.* Each of the stories was dedicated to one of her fellow inmates.

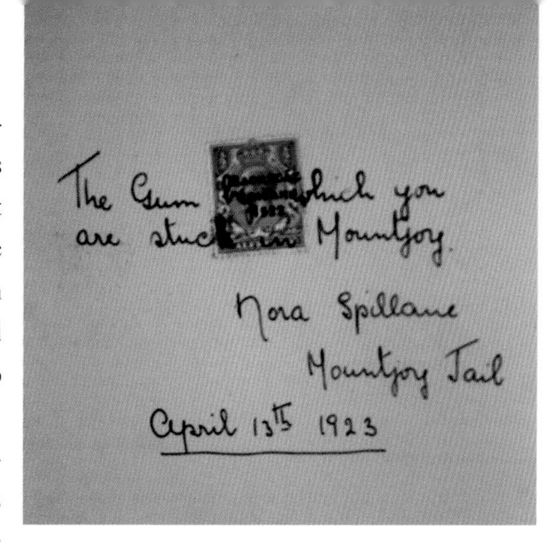

The Gum which you are stuck in Mountjoy.
Nora Spillane
Mountjoy Jail
April 13th 1923

Most Irish women of the time would have possessed autograph books. These were not used as they are today, to collect the signatures of the famous, but rather as keepsakes that held verse, humorous rhymes and greetings contributed by friends, especially friends who had departed for America and other foreign shores. Many of the women prisoners had autograph books sent into them. These became filled with patriotic verses, Republican slogans, comments on prison life, and sometimes the details of the sentences being served by various prisoners. The entry from Maggie Timmins of Irishtown, Dublin, dated 2 June 1923 reads: 'May the rivers of England cease to flow, May the shamrocks of Ireland cease to grow, May the coal fields of Scotland cease to give fuel, Until Ireland is under Republican Rule.'[132] Often, standard autograph-book doggerel was customised to suit the circumstances. On 30 September 1923, Nora Brosnan from Castlegregory in Kerry wrote in Fanny O'Connor's autograph book: 'Think of me now, Think of me ever, Think of the days we spent in NDU together.'[133]

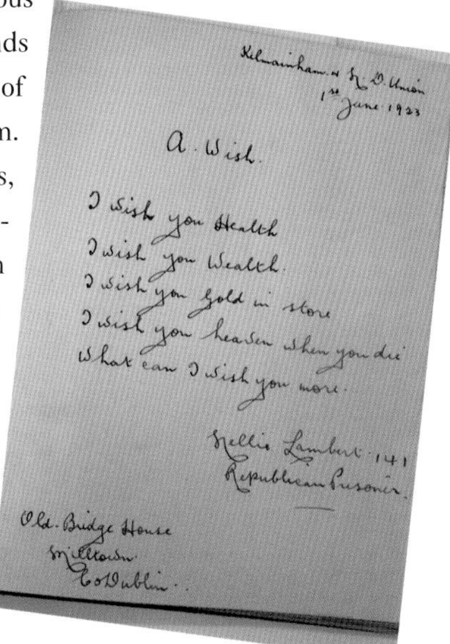

Kilmainham & N.D. Union
1st June 1923

A Wish.

I wish you Health
I wish you Wealth
I wish you gold in store
I wish you heaven when you die
What can I wish you more.

Nellie Lambert 141
Republican Prisoner.

Old Bridge House
Milltown
Co Dublin.

Knitting and needlework were common occupations; the prisoners were allowed to have wool, materials and sewing kits sent in to them. Sixteen-year-old Essie Snoddy from Carlow was very productive; she brought home souvenirs such as tea cosies, golliwogs and dolls, as well as a crocheted top.[134] Many prison blankets were also sacrificed to make keepsakes of imprisonment. These were mostly slippers and small items, but the more enterprising ones tried larger garments.[135] Such misuse of prison property was frowned upon and, when discovered, there was a penalty to pay. When one of the wardresses – a Miss Higgins – found a dress made by Mrs Rogers and a

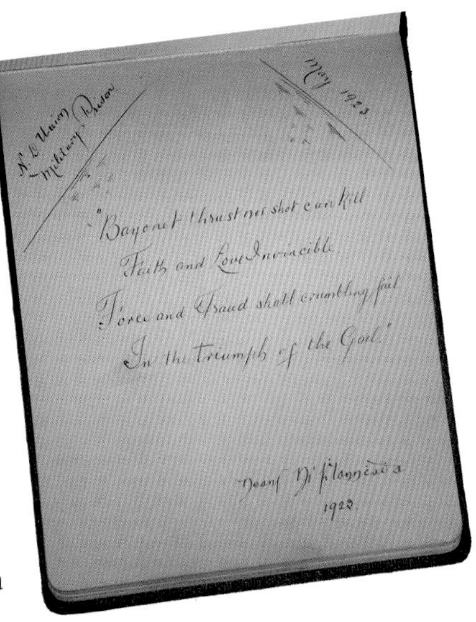

N.D. Union Military Prison
May 1923

"Bayonet thrust nor shot can kill
Faith and Love Invincible.
Force and Fraud shall crumbling fail
In the triumph of the Gael."

1923.

dressing gown made by Monica Doyle, letters and parcels were stopped for a week.[136]

Together with Brid Brophy, another member of Carlow Cumann na mBan, Essie Snoddy became involved in an ambitious project – the making of a tri-colour with the Cumann na mBan initials embroidered in the centre. This flag was used to drape over the coffins of Carlow activists killed in combat.[137] Subsequently, Eamon de Valera came to occupy Essie's cell in Kilmainham Gaol and found a thimble bearing the inscription E Snoddy. After his release he made a point of finding out who she was. He returned the thimble and they became lifelong friends.[138]

Art materials were also among the items sent in to the prisoners. Grace Gifford, widow of Joseph Mary Plunkett, was an artist who had made her living outside of prison as a cartoonist and caricaturist. She made good use of her talents, drawing and painting on walls in many of the areas of the gaol as well as decorating the inside and outside of her cell. Among her creations were a portrait of her cellmate Sheila Bowen, whom she depicted as a dancer, and an image of the Madonna and Child. She also painted the fourteen Stations of the Cross as devotional aids for her fellow-prisoners[139] and decorated the altar erected to Our Lady of Perpetual Succour on the second landing of the main compound (A wing).[140] A vigil was held at this altar day and night. However, some inmates were not so pious. One night, when it was the turn of Cis Power and Hannah Moynihan to do the vigil, Mrs Humphreys allocated them a two-hour shift, from 3am to 5am. The girls decided to split the vigil; Hannah did the first hour while Cis did 4am to 5am.[141]

Laundry bag embroidered by Sighle Humphreys with the words 'Cill Mainginn' (Kilmainham), 1923.

Crochet top made by Essie Snoddy in Kilmainham Gaol.

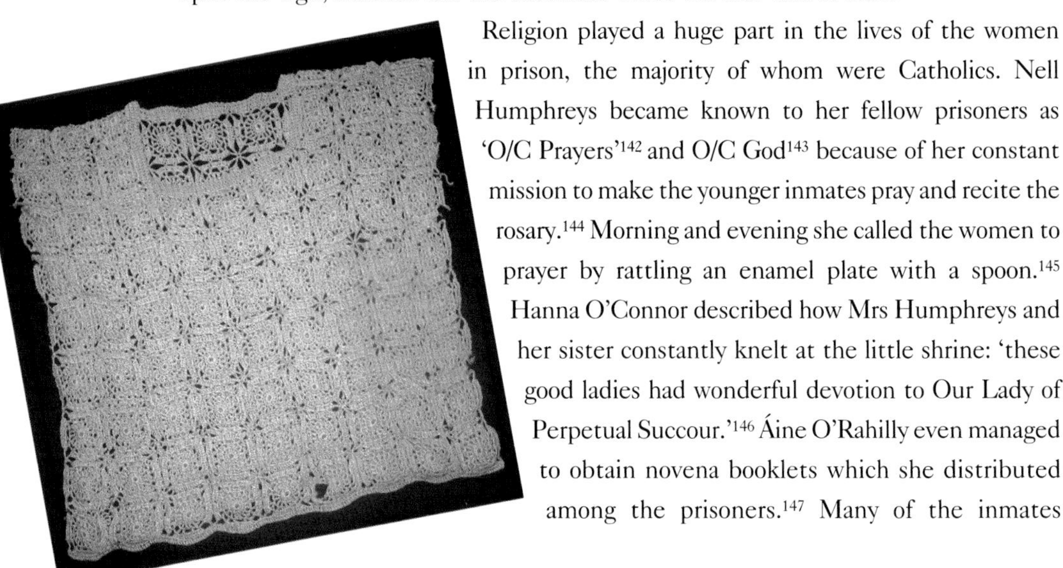

Religion played a huge part in the lives of the women in prison, the majority of whom were Catholics. Nell Humphreys became known to her fellow prisoners as 'O/C Prayers'[142] and O/C God[143] because of her constant mission to make the younger inmates pray and recite the rosary.[144] Morning and evening she called the women to prayer by rattling an enamel plate with a spoon.[145] Hanna O'Connor described how Mrs Humphreys and her sister constantly knelt at the little shrine: 'these good ladies had wonderful devotion to Our Lady of Perpetual Succour.'[146] Áine O'Rahilly even managed to obtain novena booklets which she distributed among the prisoners.[147] Many of the inmates found that prayer was a comfort; Fanny Kelly wrote to a friend, 'the Rosary ... is really the only consolation we have here ...'[148]

Many women were deeply affected by the bishops' excommunication pronouncement and its description of republicans as carrying on 'a system of murder.' Dorothy Macardle, who had recently converted to Catholicism, was later to renounce her new faith in protest.[149] When the female political prisoners attended Mass in Mountjoy Jail they were refused Holy Communion.[150] A priest came to Kilmainham Gaol each Saturday but the women's confessions were not heard. There was no absolution given to the hunger strikers.[151] It was common that a priest would not give absolution if one refused to sign the form undertaking not to oppose the workings of the Free State, presumably on the basis that this meant one had not repented of one's actions.[152] The strict enforcement of the excommunication of republicans was later relaxed, and Ellen Masterson attended Mass and received Holy Communion after ten months of being denied the sacrament.[153] Despite their exclusion from the church, their religion was the women's mainstay during their imprisonment. Margaret Buckley later wrote of this time '... our religion was our bulwark, our food and our stay. We never confused the Creator with His creatures. Though denied the holy Sacraments by human agency we were in close communion with God; nobody could deny us access to Him ...'[154]

Kilmainham Madonna painted on her cell wall by Grace Plunkett.

Conditions in the almost derelict Kilmainham Gaol caused much hardship for the women. By March 1923 the area known as A Wing was filled to capacity, and B Wing (the older, westerly section of the prison) was brought into use. As the Power sisters described:

> **This was really a condemned part of the jail ... We learned afterwards that some of these cells had housed patriots down the ages and that the 1916 men occupied them for some days before their execution. However having no knowledge of this time at the time, there was no sense of atmosphere to make us feel that we were following, even at a far off distance, in the footsteps of the great patriots. It is more likely that we were thinking of the rats and mice that might be running over us and our mattresses during the night but even these visitors did not trouble us and we never saw one of their kind during our time in Kilmainham.**[155]

Sanitary conditions here were poor and it was described as smelling horribly. 'The cells were placed along narrow corridors, and all the passages were stone.[156]...The

Patrick Pearse quote: 'Beware Of the Risen People', in Kilmainham Gaol today.

lavatory was on the corridor, quite close to the cells, and as the weather became warmer, the air became foetid.' The prisoners were supplied with disinfectant, but when this had little effect they removed the glass from some of the windows. This made some improvement at the time, but later when the weather got colder the prisoners regretted that they had taken out the glass, as they had no protection from the wind. The Governor was asked to replace the glass, but he refused, remarking that as it was they who took it out, it was they who could put it back.[157]

As a result of the poor sanitary conditions in Kilmainham, many of the previously healthy women became ill, and the condition of those who were already in ill health worsened. Although none of the female prisoners died while they were in jail, one of B Wing's inmates, Angela Doyle, was in bed for much of her time in Kilmainham. She was just sixteen when she was arrested with her cousin Tessie in St Stephen's Green on 21 February 1923.[158] When a new doctor arrived to examine her, he made a complaint to his superiors about the sanitation problems. The Medical Officer came to inspect the conditions in which the prisoners were held, but nothing happened as a result of his inspection.[159] Angela was subsequently transferred from Kilmainham to the North Dublin Union.[160] Angela Doyle's stay in B Wing did not lengthen her life; she died in September 1925, just two years after her release, eighteen years old, and her family always believed that her imprisonment brought about her premature death.[161]

The prison doctor and Governor also recommended the release of Chrissie Stafford, who was suffering from acute sciatica. A fellow prisoner massaged her but this gave her no relief. A nurse was brought from St Bricin's military hospital and the doctor prescribed morphia for the pain.[162] Finally, when a letter about her condition was smuggled out of the prison and was published in *Éire* she was let go free.[163] Cecilia Gallagher referred in her diary to the sad condition of a girl called Rosaline Kinsella, who suffered from epilepsy: 'One of the girls from A Wing had been very bad with epileptic fits ... [she] can be heard moaning and choking ... It is dreadful to listen to her and how shockingly inhuman to keep her at all when she is like that.'[164]

Visits from outside doctors were not allowed in Kilmainham Gaol. When Margaret Burke's family asked for a specialist to be allowed to examine her, the request was denied.[165] There were two doctors among the prisoners: Dr Elenora Fleury, who had been Medical Superintendent in Grangegorman Mental Hospital before her arrest for treating a number of wounded Republicans,[166] and Dr Elsie Murphy, a sister of Kate O'Callaghan[167] They administered what relief they could to their fellow inmates, but, lacking medicines, it was difficult for them to provide adequate assistance. There were hospital sections in all of the jails, but there were insufficient beds to cope with demand, in particular during the frequent hunger strikes.

The action of hunger strike was never adopted as a formal policy by the Republican leadership, but it came to be used frequently by prisoners during the Civil War to ensure that they were awarded political status and to hasten their release. The hunger strike was, of course, voluntary, but as the Power sisters recalled:

> **It was amazing how quickly many of the prisoners suggested this deadly weapon as a means to redress grievances, and these were generally the ones who were on hunger strike before, and knew its full rigours.**[168]

Only a few days after Kilmainham admitted female prisoners, on 24 February 1923, a hunger strike was begun by Annie MacSwiney, sister of Mary, and now a prisoner herself. She was released after fifteen days.[169] Ninety-seven women went on hunger strike for a week in March 1923 after all their privileges had been denied without explanation on St Patrick's Day.[170] Hannah Moynihan was of the belief that withholding letters and parcels was not a good enough reason to go on hunger strike. She described it as 'such drastic action' and mused: 'We must consider the moral aspect – is one justified in dying for letters and parcels?[171]

Sighle Bowen on a Harley Davidson, *c.*1923.

That hunger strike ended with the restoration of privileges on 22 March, but already Nell Ryan had started another strike. Her plan was to continue it until she was given her release.[172] Nell was the sister of Min Ryan, now married to Defence Minister Richard Mulcahy, and this gave her strike great publicity value. Min received many appeals from her family to persuade Richard to have Nell released. However, he refused to be influenced.[173] Another Ryan sister, Kit, spent her days meeting anyone whom she felt might help, including priests, the Assistant Medical Officer of the Free State and the Deputy Governor, in the hope of gaining her sister's release. She met the Deputy Governor of Kilmainham when Nell had endured thirteen days of hunger strike, and described the outcome to another sister, Liz:

> **He was full of her praises – she was such a soldier, not grumbling or tormenting other people, but determined not to give up the strike ... She is too well of course – too strong to show the required signs of weakness so far for release. She is most cheerful.[174]**

Two other prisoners, Kitty Costello and Annie O'Neill, soon joined Nell Ryan in her hunger strike. Kitty Costello was 'a bad subject' for hunger strike and was suffering a great deal from the ninth day.[175] Father Costello, Kitty's brother, wrote to President W T Cosgrave and appealed to him to have his sister released, reminding Cosgrave that during the War of Independence the Costello family had sheltered him and he had used Father Costello's clothes as a disguise.[176] But the Civil War had already led to bitter strains and divisions in friendships and families, and Cosgrave refused.

Mary MacSwiney and Kate O'Callaghan arrived in Kilmainham Gaol on 10 April having been arrested en route to Liam Lynch's funeral[177] and immediately joined the protest. The redoubtable Mary MacSwiney was not daunted by the prospect of another hunger strike. She later wrote that the only kind of strike which would succeed was when the striker started out 'realising fully the probability of death and [was] ready for it.'[178] The same day Maud Gonne MacBride was arrested for engaging 'in painting banners for seditious demonstrations and preparing anti-governing literature'[179] Hannah Moynihan recorded in her diary:

Door and interior of a cell in the East Wing, Kilmainham, today.

> **Last night at 11pm, we heard the commotion which usually accompanies the arrival of new prisoners ... we pestered the wardress and she told us there were four – Maud Gonne MacBride, her daughter Mrs Iseult Stuart and two lesser lights ... Early this morning ... we could**

> **see Maud walking majestically past our cell door leading on a leash a funny little lap dog which answered to the name that sounded like 'Wuzzo – Wuzzo'.[180]**

Maud Gonne also joined the hunger strike. As these women were well known, their protest had widespread propaganda value. Kate O'Callaghan was a Dáil deputy and the widow of a former Mayor of Limerick. Maud Gonne MacBride was one of the best-known women in Irish society. Yeats had immortalised her in his poetry, and he now urged the President to consider that, at fifty-seven, she could 'not be expected to stand the same strain as the younger women.'[181]

Illustrated page from autograph book.

Kate O'Callaghan and Mary MacSwiney were being held without charge, while the others on hunger strike had been arrested for the distribution of anti-Government propaganda, considered by many to be trivial crimes.[182] However, there was not the same public outcry that there had been for Mary MacSwiney's first hunger strike in 1922. Support for Cumann na mBan had dwindled as the Civil War dragged on and as the more active of the members were arrested.

The continued fighting often brought tragic news to those inside prison. On 4 April 1923 Mary Fleming got word that her brother Jackie had been shot by the Free State. Hannah Moynihan wrote in her diary: 'he had previously handed in his gun so there was no excuse.'[183] Sheila Nagle found out that her brother had been killed in fighting in Kerry[184] from a report in the *Sunday Independent* that had been smuggled into the jail.[185]

On the evening of 8 April a Cumann na mBan member was killed at Adrigole in County Cork. Free State troops from Glengarriff had had an encounter with two Irregulars, in the course of which one of the Free State soldiers was wounded. The Irregulars escaped. About ten minutes later, Margaret Duggan, a member of Cumann na mBan from Berehaven, County Cork was seen conversing with another Irregular and, without warning, Captain Hassett of the Free State Army shot her and she was fatally wounded.[186]

In April 1923, on the seventh anniversary of the Easter Rising, there were among the prisoners in Kilmainham Gaol a number of women who were related to the men executed in the stone-breakers yard after the Rising: Nora Connolly O'Brien, daughter of James Connolly, and Joseph Plunkett's widow Grace.

It was Nora who asked the Governor to commemorate the anniversary. She wrote to her mother from the prison on Good Friday: 'It is depressing and a bit of a strain to spend Easter in the jail where Papa was executed. I cannot forget that fact for one minute.'[187]

Lily O'Brennan wrote to her sister who had also been widowed in 1916: 'it is like Easter week 1916 all over again here. The women I met for the first time then are in here now again.'[188] One of those was May Gahan, now Mrs O'Carroll and the mother of two children, Eileen, aged three and Robert Emmet, aged two. Nell Ryan was another of those arrested after the Rising who was now serving sentences for their opposition to the Treaty.

At 3pm on Tuesday, 24 April, the 270 prisoners marched into the yard where the 1916 leaders were executed. Hanna O'Connor described how 'a deep hush seemed to pervade the whole prison – gone was the buzz and the chatter.'[189] Grace Plunkett laid an olive wreath to their memory and Nell Humphreys led the rosary in Irish. As Hanna O'Connor recalled it, there was 'no fanfare of trumpets – no bugle – instead the voices of hundreds of women prisoners, piercing the sky in recitation of the rosary in our mother tongue.'[190] After marching back to A wing, where the tricolour was unfurled, 'Faith of our Fathers' was sung and the Republican oath was recited.[191] Speeches were given by Lily O'Brennan and Nora Connolly O'Brien. Nora's speech spoke of the honour and privilege of being in the place of execution:

We had hoped that visit might be made when the hopes of those men were realised. To our sorrow that has been denied us. The enemy has not left us, and we, today are prisoners in the same prison ... because we are true to their cause and have striven to bring about the realisation of their dream.[192]

The East Wing, Kilmainham Gaol, today.

The speech was described by fourteen-year-old May Coughlan as 'lovely but very sad.'[193] The speeches were recorded by a prisoner in shorthand and were smuggled out of the prison and published in *Éire*.

Later that night a concert was held in the main wing of the gaol. Its horseshoe shape made it an ideal venue. Aoife Taaffe produced Patrick Pearse's play 'The Singer'. The cast included Sighle Bowen, Hanna O'Connor, Lily O'Brennan, Nellie

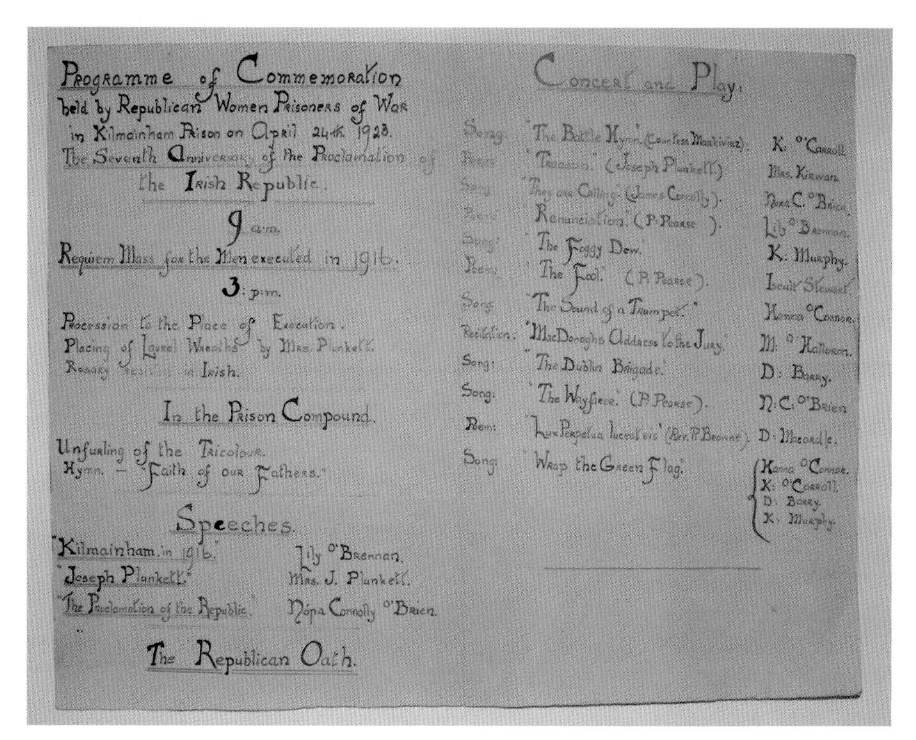
Programme of Commemoration
held by Republican Women Prisoners of War
in Kilmainham Prison on April 24th. 1923.
The Seventh Anniversary of the Proclamation of
the Irish Republic.

9 a.m.

Requiem Mass for the Men executed in 1916.

3: p.m.

Procession to the Place of Execution.
Placing of Laurel Wreaths by Mrs. Plunkett.
Rosary recited in Irish.

In the Prison Compound.

Unfurling of the Tricolour.
Hymn. – "Faith of our Fathers."

Speeches.

"Kilmainham in 1916."	Lily O'Brennan.
"Joseph Plunkett."	Mrs. J. Plunkett.
"The Proclamation of the Republic."	Nora Connolly O'Brien.

The Republican Oath.

Concert and Play.

Song:	"The Battle Hymn." (Countess Markievicz).	K. O'Carroll
Poem:	"Treason." (Joseph Plunkett.)	Mrs. Kirwan.
Song:	"They are Calling." (James Connolly).	Nora C. O'Brien.
Poem:	"Renunciation." (P. Pearse).	Lily O'Brennan.
Song:	"The Foggy Dew."	K. Murphy.
Poem:	"The Fool." (P. Pearse).	Iseult Stewart.
Song:	"The Sound of a Trumpet."	Hanna O'Connor.
Recitation:	"MacDonagh's Address to the Jury."	M. O'Halloran.
Song:	"The Dublin Brigade."	D. Barry.
Song:	"The Wayfarer." (P. Pearse).	N. C. O'Brien
Poem:	"Lux Perpetua luceat eis" (Rev. P. Browne).	D. Macardle.
Song:	"Wrap the Green Flag."	Hanna O'Connor. K. O'Carroll. D. Barry. K. Murphy.

Handwritten programme of commemorative events in Kilmainham Gaol, 24 April 1923.

Fennell, Maureen Power, Mary MacSwiney and Mrs Kirwan. It was followed by songs and poetry. Kathleen O'Carroll sang 'The Battle Hymn' by Countess Markievicz; Nora Connolly O'Brien sang her father's song, 'They are Calling'; 'Wrap the Green Flag round me' was the choice of Dotie Barry, Kathleen O'Carroll, Hanna O'Connor and Kathleen Murphy. Iseult Stuart recited 'The Fool' by Patrick Pearse; Kathleen Kirwan performed 'Treason' by Joseph Plunkett. 'Lux Perpetua Luceat eis' was Dorothy Macardle's contribution to the evening's entertainment.[194]

On the day following the concert, Nell Ryan was released from prison, having endured over thirty days on hunger strike. Another of the strikers, Kitty Costello, was released on 28 April. Maud Gonne MacBride was set free after twenty days in prison.[195]

Some months later, Maud Gonne spread a rumour that Nell had died as a result of the effects of her hunger strike. Cecilia Gallagher wrote in her diary: 'Very mean of Nell Ryan! She did not die after all! ... Very mean of Nell Ryan indeed to have taken such a great piece of propaganda from us.'[196]

The death of one hunger striker did occur in the weeks following her release from jail. Twenty-five- year-old Annie (Nan) Hogan, a native of Cratloe, County Clare, was arrested for trying to assist a group of Republicans escape from Limerick Jail. She was held in both Kilmainham Gaol and the North Dublin Union during 1923. She died four weeks after returning home, having been weakened by the hunger strike she had undertaken in jail.[197]

On Monday 30 April 1923 when Kate O'Callaghan and Mary MacSwiney were on their nineteenth day of hunger strike, the Governor told the prisoners that seventy of the 270 prisoners were being transferred to the North Dublin Union (NDU). Conditions were so bad in Kilmainham Gaol that the women would have ordinarily welcomed a transfer, but they were anxious for the two hunger strikers, fearing the consequences of leaving them without support and at the mercy of their gaolers in the empty prison.[198] At 4 pm, after a meeting held to discuss the situation, a message was sent to the Governor that no prisoner would consent to leave until the hunger strikers were released.

Just as a plan of resistance was formulated, Kate O'Callaghan was released, but Mary MacSwiney was still being held. It seemed to the prisoners that there was 'malice against Mary MacSwiney' by the authorities, who 'for all we knew, might intend her death' recalled Dorothy Macardle.[199] That evening, Governor replied to the prisoners' message, stating that eighty-one prisoners would be removed – by force if necessary. The women were locked in their cells for some time and then removed by the CID and women from Cumann na Saoirse, known by the inmates as 'Cumann na Searchers'. They gave the prisoners five minutes[200] to make up their minds whether they were going to co-operate or be forcibly removed. The Power sisters recalled how Mary Bourke Dowling, 'a deep-voiced ex-militant suffragette', advocated a technique that had been used by Irish suffragettes in resisting removal: grouping 'in mass formation, four deep with linked arms'.[201] The removal began at 11.30pm. The prisoners positioned themselves at the top floor of the main wing, and the fight began with their war cry 'No Surrender'. [202] The women had agreed to resist but not to attack; they were not to come to one another's rescue; no missiles were to be thrown, and for Mary MacSwiney's sake, whatever was done to them, they must not cry out.[203] One of the prison matrons came up the stairs to plead with the women not to go ahead with their plan of resistance, but to no avail.

The women were dragged down the metal staircase in Kilmainham and forcibly removed to the North Dublin Union.

Some of the CID men and military police had their faces blackened in order to avoid recognition. Hanna O'Connor recalled: 'like ravening wolves they rushed upstairs – guns in hand – ordering us all down'.[204] Some of them were drunk and cursing. Their attack was violent but disorganised. Bridie O'Mullane and Rita Farrelly, the first to be seized, were crushed and bruised 'between men dragging them down and men pressing up the stairs'.[205] Úna Gordon was next, and Dorothy Macardle recalled that it was hard not to go to her assistance. She clung to the iron bars of the stairs and the men beat her hands with their fists. When they were unable to make her loosen her grip she was hit twice in the chest.[206] As she was being dragged down the stairs by her hair, her head was beaten against the iron bars of the staircase.[207] Unconscious, she was hauled across the hall and out the gate. Some of the women went quietly but most were pushed and beaten.[208] May Zambra was struck on the head with an iron bar.[209] Jake Folan was badly hurt and she always believed that the injuries she suffered during this episode were responsible for her numerous miscarriages in later years.[210] A number of girls fainted and were carried away in a state of collapse.[211] A cheer was raised when Nora Brick used her suitcase to hit her attacker as she was pulled down the stairs. Dorothy Macardle recalled her own experience:

> **... after I had been dragged from the railings, a great hand closed on my face, blinding and stifling me, and thrust me back down to the ground, among trampling feet. I heard someone who saw it scream, and wondered how Miss MacSwiney would bear the noise. After that I remember being carried by two or three men and flung down in the surgery to be searched.**[212]

Bridie O'Mullane created such a racket that she was not searched. She had a poker and some other weapons concealed on her person and later recalled that she 'arrived safely at the North Dublin Union' with her weapons intact.[213]

Onlookers had various reactions. 'Some soldiers who were on guard there looked wretched; the wardresses were bringing us cups of water; they were crying; the prison doctor looked on smiling, smoking a cigarette, he seemed to have come for entertainment ...'[214] Despite the scenes she had witnessed, teenager Hannah Moynihan commented dryly in her diary: 'not sure which side had the toughest part!'[215] The women were removed one by one over a period of five hours. Finally, at 4.30am all sixty-five prisoners were on their way to the North Dublin Union.[216]

Mary MacSwiney was released from Kilmainham the following day.[217] The government resolved that the next prisoner on hunger strike would be allowed to die.[218]

On 1 May another fifty women were transferred from Kilmainham, but this was a peaceful departure.[219] By 3 May the number of women prisoners in Kilmainham Gaol was reduced to less than a hundred. It appeared that there were plans to close the gaol. The intention was to move all female prisoners from around the country to the one location – the North Dublin Union – described by Margaret Buckley as 'a sort of concentration camp for women.'[220]

At the same time, inmates from Mountjoy Jail were also being taken to the NDU. On 28 April prisoners in Mountjoy were told by the wardresses to get ready to be moved. A number of them gathered in the 'Suffolk Street' cell, and while they were waiting they began to dance 'The Walls of Limerick'.[221] The women were searched before removal. When Maura Deegan hit a number of the CID with the contents of a bucket of slops there was pandemonium. In the fight that followed, she got a black eye. From then on, each search was conducted with 'a row'. The women emerged with clothes torn, faces scratched. Judy Gaughran was flung down the stairs and only escaped injury by grabbing the banisters. Máire Comerford had to have three stitches in her head. Sighle Humphreys was taken out half conscious. Sorcha MacDermott from London was knocked to the floor by five female searchers. She was stripped of her shoes, stockings and her dress and held down by a prison adjutant while he beat her with one of her own shoes. Two other men then took her and twisted her wrists until she fainted. One wrist was badly sprained and in the end she was too weak to be transferred to the NDU.[222] When Margaret Buckley's turn came, she threatened the woman searcher: 'If you touch me, I'll choke the life out of you'. Meekly, the lady allowed her to pass on.[223]

The NDU had been used as a barracks for the Black and Tans during the War of Independence. The conditions were terrible and the new inmates thought the dirt of the place was beyond description.[224] The rooms were large and bare, and the floorboards were caked in mud. The women approached Governor O'Neill to have the place cleaned. He informed them that soldiers had been sent to clean it before the women's arrival. A number of women set about 'scraping pencilled obscenity off the walls, lest the younger prisoners should see it.'[225]

The women experienced 'every kind of discomfort, hunger, cold and dirt' in the months that they were incarcerated in the NDU.[226] There were no bathing facilities, so a basin of water would be placed in a corner of the room and two girls held up a blanket to make a curtain, which afforded some sort of privacy. For many this was too troublesome to undertake.[227] There was straw on the floor but this was dirty. Harriette Lavery, a widow in her fifties, contracted anthrax – a rare infection spread by spores – that her family always believed was the result of lying on contaminated straw. She died on 29 December 1923 shortly after her release from prison. Her daughter Maynie, who had also been in prison, was released only days before her mother died.[228]

Judy Gaughran.

The building was laid out in large dormitories, which housed twenty-five to thirty women in each unit. The dormitories acquired names, such as 'Barrie's Hotel', 'Devil May Cares', and 'Kilmainham Ward'.[229] There was no privacy. Nan Hogan wrote to her family: 'There are armed sentries on raised positions, several of who can ... see into the dormitories and even into the lavatories at night ...'[230] Every available spot was being utilised in the NDU to house prisoners. The new prisoners from Kilmainham Gaol brought the total to 321. The doctor at the NDU had already agreed that the dormitories were full, so when a lorry carrying a further sixty prisoners arrived from Kilmainham Gaol on 3 May, the existing prisoners protested. They threw out the additional beds and refused to allow the new prisoners to enter the building.[231] The doors of the Union building were barred and the would-be inmates forced to stay outside in the recreation ground. The prisoners inside called to them from the windows, saying that there was no accommodation. Hannah Moynihan was one of the new arrivals and she noted wryly in her diary: ‘A nice warm welcome. Well, principles are principles, so there was nothing in it but to walk around until morning.’[232]

Some of the women slept in the passages and on the landings, but the last lot of prisoners slept out in the open, on mattresses lined up against the wall. Cis and Jo Power recalled: ‘So we had only God’s sky and stars for a canopy … There was an outcry outside about the cruelty of making women and girls sleep out-of-doors. We were feeling very “heroic” …’[233] Kate Breen slept under a tree with an attaché case as a pillow.[234] During the nights that followed, the women slept on mattresses that were lined against the wall. The weather was very cold and although it was the month of May there were occasional showers of snow.[235] Indoors the women felt sorry to see their comrades getting wet and their beds drenched,[236] and some shared their blankets. The new prisoners were allowed in during the daytime to wash and change their clothes.[237] After a couple of weeks some prisoners were released and the women got beds inside.

The food was described as ‘unpalatable’, and, with the chronic overcrowding, there were not enough rations to feed all the prisoners. The prisoners themselves organised the distribution of food. The task of cutting the bread and buttering it for over 300 people was given to Margaret Buckley as Quartermaster, helped by nine orderlies. The women later won a significant victory when they were supplied with a cutting machine and a soldier to work it.[238] For a period of time food parcels were stopped, so many went hungry but generally they had the contents of food parcels to sustain them. One evening in late May, Jim Larkin, the trade union leader, led a crowd to demonstrate at the gates of the NDU. According to the inmates, ‘it seems he threatened to force an entrance to rescue the starving women.’ Hannah Moynihan remarked: ‘Thank heavens he failed. The moment would have been most inopportune as he would have been greeted by the whiff of rashers and eggs.’[239]

Memorial card for Harriette Lavery.

A number of prisoners had embarked on digging an escape tunnel shortly after they arrived in the NDU. The Power sisters recorded: 'Those who were in this enterprise were at it for some days, and it was very "hush hush", we only heard vague rumours about how it was progressing.'[240] The tunnellers were foiled in their plans when, having run into some problems in the construction of the tunnel, they smuggled out diagrams to an engineer for advice. When his office was raided, their plans were found. But Máire Comerford had seen a simple escape route from the NDU; she had noticed it immediately upon arrival but had waited a couple of days before trying it as she felt it was so easy that she suspected there might be a trap. The barbed-wire entanglements on the walls surrounding the compound had not been erected properly. At the top of the walls, rigid barbed wire had been stretched to meet the poles that had been placed in the ground a distance from the wall, therefore it was possible to climb over the entanglement to reach the top of the wall. The arrangement of poles and wires had unwittingly created a ladder for the women.[241] On Monday, 6 May Máire Comerford, Maura Deegan and AoifeTaaffe decided to make their escape.[242]

The breakout was successful. The women were not missed, and the following night, twenty-two prisoners took the same route out, planning to hide in Broadstone Railway Station, which was located alongside the NDU. Kathleen Coyle was the first over, as she knew the layout of the railway yard. However, in the darkness the women went in the direction of the platform rather than the workshops where they might have remained undetected. They hid in two empty railway carriages overnight, hoping to be able to mingle with the crowds in the station the following morning, but they were discovered and thirteen of them were recaptured.[243] The authorities assumed they had got all of the escapees as they had no idea how many had broken out. In fact, three got away – Kay Brady, Éilis Robinson and Maureen Power. Maureen Power hid beneath an empty carriage and remained undiscovered.[244] Éilis Robinson decided against staying in the station overnight, so she braved the curfew and set off for her house. Later she described her walk home as the longest and loneliest walk she ever made.[245]

Back in the NDU, the prisoners concealed the fact that three of their number were missing. 'We dodged count, and displayed quite wonderful agility in appearing in one part of the building, having just been counted in another. Except for this activity, we never, even to each other, made any reference to the fact that we were three less.'[246] Éilis Robinson's sister, Sinéad, concealed her sister's absence by answering for her at roll call.[247]

The result of the escape was a tougher regime for those who remained in the NDU. On Wednesday, 9 May Hannah Moynihan recorded in her diary: 'By way of reprisal for yesterday's happenings the soldiers blazed away all night long. It was raining too but through fear of being shot we didn't dare move from our mattresses to seek shelter.'[248] The women were informed by the governor that the camp would now be run along Internment Camp rules – one letter a week; inspections by the military. He insisted that the women be lined up and counted.[249]

One of the prisoners whose 'joy knew no bounds' to hear of the escapes was the Honourable Albinia Brodrick. Albinia (or Gobnait Ní Bhruadair as she preferred to be called) had arrived in the NDU on 2 May on a stretcher. She had been arrested in Cahirciveen in County Kerry having been 'fired at eight times by Free State troops, and wounded 3 times in the leg.'[250] Despite her injuries, she immediately went on hunger strike. According to Sighle Humphreys, her wounds were 'pretty bad as a bone had been shattered and going on hunger strike didn't help her recover. She was certainly no subject for a hunger strike as she had little spare flesh.'[251] The sixty-year-old vegetarian, who was known to eat raw vegetables from a sack, was a nurse who had set up a hospital for the poor in County Kerry.[252] Her accent, which was described as 'Oxford and Cambridge rolled into one'[253] and her title were the only things that gave any clue to her past. She was, in fact, the sister of the Earl of Midleton, leader of the Southern Unionists. When in later years politics estranged them, and people would ask if they were related, she would reply: 'he used to be my brother'.[254]

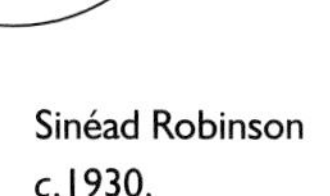

Sinéad Robinson c.1930.

Aware of the importance of keeping her fellow-prisoners women active and busy, Albinia initiated a prison newspaper, the *NDU Invincible*, as 'a chronicle of jail life.' Her strength of character and her dedication to the republican cause was evident in the piece she wrote for the *NDU Invincible*:

The Honourable Albinia Brodrick.

> **I want to express to you my sympathy with your long imprisonment, most of you have endured it for months and with it many difficulties and temptations ... belonging especially to prison life – the love of self, showing in petty disputes, petty jealousies, petty growls and grumbles, impatient of the faults of others ... above all want of discipline ... We are Republicans surrounded on every side by an enemy, keen to note any breach in the ranks, and even the least failure in our unity. To that enemy, we must present a united front.**[255]

On the thirteenth day of her hunger strike, as she grew increasingly weaker, Albinia told Margaret Buckley: 'An old woman is not much loss, but my death will be sure to make a noise, because of that wretched little prefix to my name, and in that way my death may do more good for Ireland than my life could do.'[256] She was released after fifteen days' hunger strike, on 11 May.[257] Despite her ordeal, she lived on to a ripe old age, surviving for another thirty-two years.

Outside of the prison the situation had steadily become worse for the republican side. They were chronically short of weapons and grossly outnumbered. The numbers of republicans in prison now far exceeded those in action. Meanwhile, the Free State Army grew in strength (the total number was estimated at sixty thousand). Support from the civilian population had dwindled; most people now wanted an end to the fighting. When Liam Lynch, the leader of the republican forces, was killed on 10 April 1923, republican morale was dealt a severe blow. Surrender was announced at the end of that month. On 24 May Frank Aiken, their new leader, ordered the IRA to dump arms. Eamon de Valera issued a message addressed to the 'Soldiers of the Republic, Legion of the Rearguard'. He told them 'further sacrifice would now be in vain' and suggested that 'other means must be sought to safeguard the nation's rights'. Although these declarations effectively ended the Civil War, there were still thousands of political prisoners in gaols around the country.

The death toll of those executed by the Free State Government continued to rise. According to official statistics, by the end of the Civil War seventy-seven men had been executed. There were many more unauthorised killings, which have been estimated to number as many as 153.[258]

Dorothy Macardle later wrote of this disillusioning period:

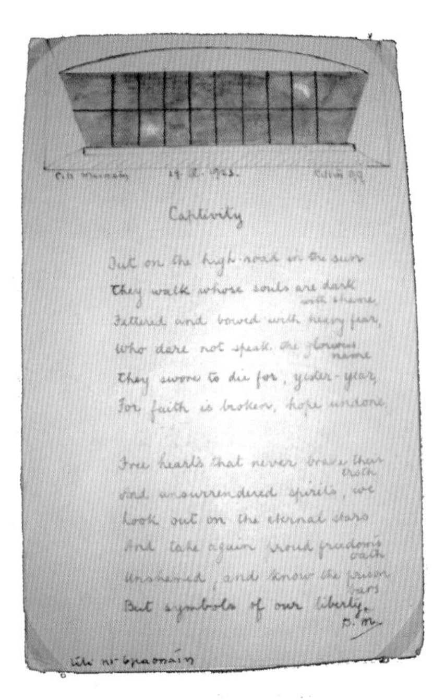
Captivity

Out on the high-road in the sun
They walk whose souls are dark with shame,
Fettered and bowed with heavy fear,
Who dare not speak the glorious name
They swore to die for, yester-year,
For faith is broken, hope undone.

Free hearts that never broke their troth
And unsurrendered spirits, we
Look out on the eternal stars
And take again proud freedom's oath
Unshamed, and know the prison bars
But symbols of our liberty.

D. M.

Dorothy Macardle's poem 'Captivity'.

For the defeat of the Republicans was a victory for England, not for Ireland; the leaders who had achieved it had defeated their own cherished ends. They, too, had desired the Republic; they had agreed to the Treaty only for fear that refusal would bring another war on Ireland, and, in consenting, had brought war on Ireland themselves. In this lay the tragic irony of their victory: they had accomplished for the English what the English might have failed to accomplish for themselves.[259]

There was a friendly rivalry between those who came from Kilmainham and Mountjoy Jails. One woman penned a verse:

Would you like to go back to Kilmainham jail,
Where you don't have to sweep the floors,
Stroll around the old compound
And take the hinges off the doors,
Where you get clean sheets every second week,
And letters each day without fail
When the tears come I know the heart aches to go
Back to Kilmainham jail.[260]

In the middle of June 1923 that is precisely what happened to Úna Gordon. She and Margaret Buckley left the NDU, having been told that they were being released. Their friends packed their bags and they departed, hearing the cheers and shouts of their companions. They were escorted in 'a beautiful big motor car'. Throughout the journey Úna Gordon was silent and Margaret realised that she was looking for an opportunity to escape. In order to assist her, Margaret Buckley suggested that they would be driven through the Phoenix Park. She recalled in her memoirs that 'the officer nearest to us replied politely that they would like very much to do so, but could not as they were acting under orders.' Their destination was not home. 'We dismounted at the jail gate and were delivered up to the charge of Commandant Corri, the Governor of Kilmainham. They were put in B Wing. Margaret Buckley was appalled and told her companion Úna Gordon that Kilmainham would be her grave: 'if we are to be here alone, just you and I, we will go mad.'[261]

There were some prisoners already in A Wing, and B Wing soon filled up as Margaret and Úna were joined by prominent Cumann na mBan members and members of the Prisoners' Council in the NDU: Judy Gaughran, Eileen McGrane, Mollie Hyland, Lily McClean and Bridie O'Mullane. The following day, Cecilia Gallagher, Nell and Sighle Humphreys, Miss Breen and Mrs Brown were also sent there.[262] The women were told that Kilmainham Gaol was now being used for prisoners on remand. Cecilia Gallagher's opinion was that there was an entirely different rationale for prisoners being returned to Kilmainham: 'It looks as if the "authorities" did this to lower the morale of the girls by breaking up Councils and removing Irish teachers and "dangerous" people (like myself!). To cloak their move they threw in a few children and harmless people.'[263] Hannah Moynihan noted her diary: 'Mrs Humphreys, Sheila (Sighle), Jenny Coyle, Kathleen, Bridie O'Mullane ... were moved this evening. Touching scene between Bridie O'Mullane and her satellites.'[264] There were a number of women who regretted Bridie's departure from the NDU. Mary Woods wrote to Bridie from the NDU, telling her that how lonely and sad it had become since she'd left, but 'please God I hope we will all meet again, not in jail I hope but in a grand and free Ireland.' [265]

Arrests continued, and on 1 June, escapee Máire Comerford had been picked up again. She had been staying in a flat in Nassau Street in Dublin and was caught one night when she went out for a walk. She felt that she was recognised because of her 'slouching country walk'.[266] She was brought to Kilmainham Gaol and immediately went on hunger strike. She was held for twenty-seven days before she was released.[267] The day before she was set free there had been a large protest at the gates of Kilmainham. Among the protestors were former prisoners Maud Gonne MacBride, Dorothy Macardle (who had been released from the NDU on 9 May),[268] and Iseult Stuart (released from the NDU 11 May).[269]

In late June 1923, a new Public Safety Bill had passed its first reading in the Dáil. It gave the government powers to continue the internment of republican prisoners for a further period of six months. The situation in the country was returning to normal and the unarmed police force, the Garda Síochána, was growing in number since its formation in the autumn of 1922. But there was always the fear that war would resume, as the Republicans had not surrendered their arms. Kevin O'Higgins wrote to his confidante, Lady Lavery:

> **... the twelve thousand prisoners – the vast majority of them harmless poor devils ... the victims of circumstance, but with a very nasty and dangerous sediment ... The National hysteria is almost gone – a few ladies drumming their heels on the ground but the acoustics for that kind of thing are not as good as they used to be.**[270]

On 28 June, the anniversary of the taking of the Four Courts, Cecilia Gallagher wrote in her diary from Kilmainham Gaol:

I fancy we might be out fairly soon after all, for there is a bit of agitation outside about us, and talk too in the Dáil. As Gavan Duffy said the other day, prison does not change one's convictions, it strengthens them. He is quite right. I have become far more a Republican since my arrest than I ever was before.[271]

A number of women had now 'signed the form' but despite this they were still held prisoner. In early July, four girls went on hunger strike for release; three of them had signed the form.[272] As Fanny Kelly wrote to her friend Crissie from the prison hospital in the NDU on 9 July: 'Miss Shortall wrote in several letters asking me to sign the form and come out. She seems to think that is all that is necessary but indeed she is greatly mistaken for unless you have Free State influence outside you may stay where you are no matter what signing you do.'[273]

As the months passed and releases and transfers took place, in the NDU the women were tireless in organising activities to keep up their spirits. Fancy dress parties, concerts and other entertainments were held regularly to try to cheer up the 'lonely' prisoners.[274] On another night prisoners were asked to come to a céilí in the 'Devil May Cares' wearing just red and black.[275] And not all the entertainments were conventional – beginning in June, there were regular wrestling matches. Margaret Skinnider was usually the one who took on opponents.[276] The prisoners celebrated American Independence Day on 4 July. Once again the blankets and sheets got cut up –making a naval uniform for one prisoner and a nun's habit for Connie Murphy.[277] But the women were not allowed to forget that they were still prisoners. On one occasion a sentry fired into one of the dormitories, laughing, and saying: 'It is the will of the people. It must be done.'[278]

The pressure on the government to release prisoners was mounting. There was a meeting in the Mansion House, Dublin in early July and talk of a labour strike if

SAORSTAT EIREANN.

Public Safety (Emergency Powers) Act, 1923.

Public Safety (Emergency Powers) No. 2 Act, 1923.

ORDER BY THE MINISTER FOR DEFENCE.

WHEREAS Teresa O'Connell 42 Oakley Rd Dublin (hereinafter referred to as the prisoner) was at the date of the passing of the PUBLIC SAFETY (EMERGENCY POWERS) ACT, 1923, detained in Military Custody.

AND WHEREAS the prisoner was not before the passing of the said Act sentenced to any term of imprisonment or penal servitude by any tribunal established by the Military Authorities.

AND WHEREAS I am of opinion that the public safety would be endangered by the prisoner being set at liberty.

NOW I RISTEARD UA MAOLCHATHA an Executive Minister within the meaning of the said Act do hereby order and direct that the prisoner be detained in custody under the said Act until further order but not after the expiration of the said Act.

Dated this 8th day of August 1923.

Signed Risteard Ua Maolcatha

Minister for Defence.

Member of the Executive Council of Saorstat Eireann.

Detention order for Teresa O'Connell.

untried prisoners were not released soon.[279] By the middle of the month, releases were happening on a daily basis. At 8.45pm on 18 July, the Governor came to tell Nell Humphreys that she was free to go. She was in the middle of making an omelette and just continued cooking as if he had not told her.[280] She left when she was ready.

Cecilia Gallagher was not so fortunate and the strain of long imprisonment was telling on her. She had been in prison since 9 November of the previous year, and wrote about her fits of depression and her longing to be reunited with her husband. On Sunday, 15 July, she had commemorated St Swithin's feast day by starting a calendar on the wall of her cell. According to the legend of St Swithin, if it rained on his feast day it would rain for forty days afterwards. And on St Swithin's day Cecilia duly recorded in her diary 'it has the temerity to rain!'[281] Over the following weeks, she meticulously recorded the weather, on her wall calendar. It was one of the few variables in a prisoner's daily routine.

The older women spent a lot of time keeping the teenagers and younger prisoners in check. A group of five young girls, May Jones, Angela Doyle, Mary Kenny, Tessie Doyle and Agnes Coyne, were called 'the Night Birds' because they stayed up late – laughing, talking and singing songs – long after the time they should have been asleep. The regime set by Mrs Buckley as their O.C. was that they were to be in their cells at 10pm and in bed by 11pm. She often had to bang on a plate with a spoon to remind them of their curfew. They would come down the corridors, singing 'Rolling Home'.[282] Hannah Moynihan and Margaret Skinnider were often in trouble for late night talking. After staying up until 3am one night, they were given a telling off and they promised to reform.[283] In the confined circumstances, 'clashes were bound to occur … even in a community of nuns' as Margaret Buckley commented in her memoir.[284]

In Kilmainham, days were spent once again playing rounders, handball and gymnastic lessons. The steadfast Sighle Humphreys started her Irish class again and even insisted that the women speak Irish during the excitement of playing rounders.[285] An escape plan was never far from the minds of the prisoners. The occupants of B wing hatched a plan to break out of Kilmainham. According to Margaret Buckley 'the time-honoured idea of digging a tunnel took root, and though outwardly, the usual routine of educational and physical culture went on, time was also found for deeper delving.'[286] The basement of the East Wing, also known as the 'dungeons', was accessible from the main exercise yard. One of the rooms, which had served as a laundry in the past, was the location chosen to begin digging. It was an optimistic plan, given that the foundations of Kilmainham's perimeter walls go several metres below ground level. Although there had been several escapes from Kilmainham Gaol during the 114 years that it was used as a prison, these escapes had always involved people getting out through doors and gates. A timetable was drawn up.

Senior officers were not involved, as their absence from exercises might have been noticed by the warders. The work was disguised by the din made by the handball and rounders players. Lookouts were posted; the song 'Kevin Barry' was the signal that warders were approaching, while another, older song, 'O'Donnell Abu' indicated that danger was averted.[287] The first task was to remove a large flagstone about five inches in thickness. As there were no tools available, the job had to be done with knives and spoons. The project added great excitement to the lives of the prisoners. By the time it was discovered by the matron, after a month's work, a long gaping hole, four feet deep, had been excavated. The Governor was not informed. The diggers took the discovery stoically. Judy Gaughran laughed and May Connolly simply said 'better luck next time'.[288] Sighle Humphreys wished to pass on the benefit of their efforts to future inmates, and wrote the location of the tunnel in pencil on her cell wall, an inscription that is still evident in the cell today.

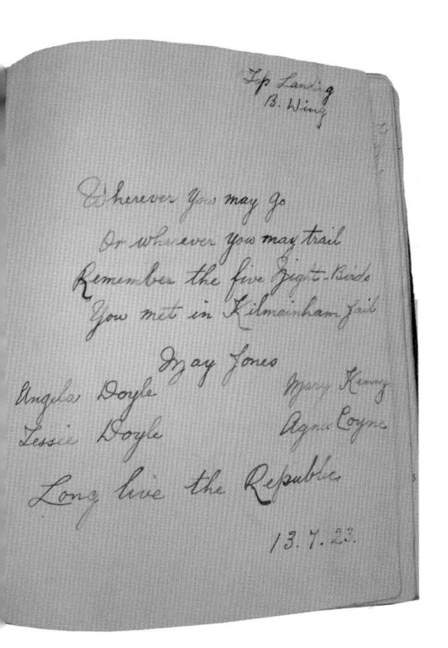
Top Landing
B. Wing

Wherever you may go
Or wherever you may trail
Remember the five Night-Birds
You met in Kilmainham Jail

May Jones
Angela Doyle
Mary Kenny
Tessie Doyle
Agnes Coyne

Long live the Republic

13.7.23.

The 'Night Birds' entry in Kilmainham autograph book.

De Valera urged republicans to contest the General Election of August 1923, although participation was contrary to the policy of non-recognition of the Irish Free State. Republicans polled well, despite having many of their supporters in prison. Cumann na nGaedheal, the government party, had sixty-three candidates elected, while Republicans had forty-four elected. However, the Republican deputies would not take their seats in the Dáil because of having to sign the oath of allegiance to the British monarch. The prisoners in Kilmainham held their own election meeting. Cecilia Gallagher was WT Cosgrave, Bridie O'Mullane represented Kevin O'Higgins, while other prisoners were the Civic Guard and the crowd.[289] In the NDU the election inspired inmates to hold mock election meetings, with women representing Kevin O'Higgins, Richard (Dick) Mulcahy, and President Willie Cosgrave. 'There were great cries of "Release the Prisoners".'[290]

One girl dressed up as one of the best known of the pro-Treaty women, Mrs Wyse Power, 'with a black eye after the elections!'[291] Maggie Timmins went as a gipsy, Maynie Lavery dressed as 'Winter covered in Snow', Sheila Hartnett was the Ace of Diamonds, Eileen Shelly represented Spring, Pollie McDonnell was costumed as a Dutch girl and Brighid Connolly as a cigarette.[292] Catalina (Kid) Bulfin went as a Black and Tan. [293] She reminisced years later: 'I remember Annie O'Farrelly as

Inscription in Sighle Humphreys's cell, giving location of escape route: 'Tunnel begun in basement laundry … may be of use to successors. Good Luck.'

Robert Emmet … the job she had to get the flour out of her hair – she had 'powdered' her hair in the style of his period and she looked splendid! '[294]

The biggest prison production was held in Kilmainham Gaol on Sunday, 19 August when three plays were staged. WB Yeats's *Cathleen Ní Houlihan* had a cast of Brigid Brophy, Bea Colfer, Claire Brady and Aoife Taaffe. A scene from *The Rising of the Moon* by Lady Gregory was also performed, with Eileen McGrane, Siobhan Clery and Josie McGrath taking part. The programme included more unusual accomplishments such as Maggie Fagan's rope dance.[295] The women attended in fancy dress. Many notable characters from Irish history were represented: Brian Boru, Saint Patrick, Sarah Curran, Queen Maeve, Lord Edward FitzGerald, Strongbow. Cecilia Gallagher dressed as Silken Thomas. She described it in her diary: 'I made quite a splash with my fairy pyjamas. I tied up the legs and made a frill with them below the knees; I wore a crêpe de chine blouse under the coat and had a gorgeous sash made out of chintz curtain.' A fellow prisoner's brightly coloured dressing gown was the cloak and she made a feather out of tissue paper. The women marched into A Wing in chronological order and Tessie Doyle acted as their herald.[296]

In August 1923, a barrister named Alex Lynn, originally from Belfast, brought a case of *Habeas Corpus* on behalf of Nora Connolly O'Brien and obtained her release. He proved that it was unconstitutional to have arrested her when the Act under which she was arrested had not been signed at the time.[297] Releases continued throughout September. The last of the female prisoners left Kilmainham Gaol on 28 September 1923. They were moved to the North Dublin Union to serve out the remainder of their sentences. They were replaced in Kilmainham Gaol by thirty male prisoners transferred from over-crowded camps and jails around the country.

By early October the atmosphere in the NDU had changed. At the time, a school friend of Jo Power's – Josephine Daly – was dying and kept asking to see her. Extreme pressure was put on the military authorities and she was given parole for a week. When she returned to prison her search was perfunctory, another indication that there was a change in attitude by the authorities. She had been asked to bring in a camera and managed to smuggle in a small Brownie. The photographs taken with this camera were featured in the *Kerryman* newspaper in December 1968 to illustrate the Powers' memoir of their imprisonment: *Blaze Away with your little Gun – A Story of Kerry's Patriot Girls*. These were unique images of this time. There had been an attempt once during the summer months to take photographs of the women in the NDU as they sat outside in their brightly coloured dresses. The prison authorities no doubt wanted to use these for propaganda purposes. But the prisoners were wise to the plan and kept moving whenever they thought the cameras were trained on them.[298]

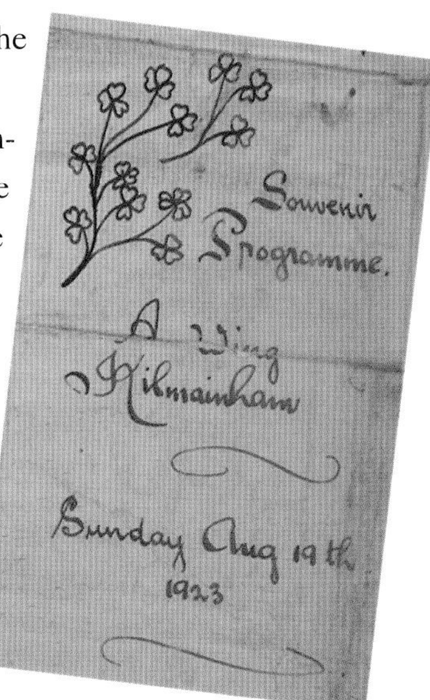

Cover of concert programme, 19 August 1923.

In October 1923, the government intimated that all prisoners would be released by Christmas; at that point there were still nine thousand prisoners in gaol. Releases began at the rate of 3,000 per month. Those who remained incarcerated grew daily more restless, as many of them had been in prison for almost a year. There were ongoing complaints about the quality of food, clothing, exercise rights, overcrowding and status as political prisoners. On 10 October, 300 male political prisoners in Mountjoy Jail went on hunger strike to 'protest at their continued detention'; by the end of the month 7033 prisoners, fifty of whom were women, were on a hunger strike in order to bring about a general release.[299]

Some of the female prisoners had been reluctant to join the hunger strike. A report from inside the North Dublin Union detailed the divided views. A small number of prisoners believed that this was a new phase of the war and that they would be shirking their duty to the Republic if they did not fall in with the men. Another group were opposed to sympathetic action, but were prepared to strike at any time for their own individual releases. There were also those who believed that as their conditions in the NDU were fairly decent, they had no logical reason for striking. A number who thought that it was a wrong move, but having no moral misgivings they were prepared

Programme, handwritten by May Gibney, for a staging of *Cathleen Ní Houlihan* and other entertainments, including a 'Rope Dance'.

to support the majority. The anonymous writer of the report was herself against the strike, believing that the remaining eighty-six women would be released in a matter of weeks. She wrote: '... very few of the girls here are fit subjects for a protracted hunger strike. If they were released after 30 or 40 days they would need a great deal of care and attention, which very few of them could afford. Most of them are in poor circumstances and practically all have to earn their own living.'[300]

However, when all the votes were added up, the majority of prisoners agreed to the strike. Some of the conscientious objectors then joined because they thought that they would be letting the others down by not doing so.[301] Áine O'Rahilly and her niece Sighle were among those on hunger strike. On 1 November, Áine wrote to her sister Nell: 'I was a bit seedy on the 6th day but am now quite well again. We had a lazy life, lie in bed most of the day and when up lounge on cushions before fine fires ... we don't even suffer. We talk about food and love to think of the things that we shall eat sometime ...'[302] But there was no public support for the hunger strikers and two weeks later the number on strike had dropped to 559.

On 20 November while the strike was still ongoing, Countess Markievicz, now nearing the age of sixty, was arrested while canvassing for the release of prisoners. She joined the prisoners on hunger strike in the NDU, but had endured only three days when the strike was called off. She wrote to her sister, Eva Gore Booth:

> **I did not suffer at all, but just stayed in bed and dozed and tried to prepare myself to leave the world. I was perfectly happy and had no regrets. I just seemed to be sliding along in a happy sort of dream. When Derrick (usually given as Derrig) came to me he woke me up with a jump and it was like coming to life again and I wanted to live and I wanted the others to live ...** [303]

Denis Barry, a hunger striker in Newbridge Camp, died on 20 November, and Andrew Sullivan died in Mountjoy Jail on 22 November. The deaths caused no major public outcry, so the remaining 167 prisoners were called off their fast.[304] On 23 November when Tom Derrig had come to the NDU with the announcement, he told the prisoners that 'it would not be worth sacrificing all our lives'.

A number of women prisoners, including Áine O'Rahilly, Maeve Phelan and Lily Dunne were in a very bad way.[305] Áine O'Rahilly wrote to her sister Nell, telling her that she and Sighle were fine: '... we are both climbing the hill again ... tho' we were both very near the bottom of the Valley ... I am glad not to be at home just yet as we are not fit to meet people'.[306]

The remaining women prisoners were finally released in December 1923. Sighle Humphreys, one of the last to leave, described how they felt: 'We were flattened. We felt the Irish public had forgotten us. The tinted trappings of our fight were hanging like rags about us.'[307]

For the rest of their lives the memory of their time in prison would stay fresh in the minds of those who had endured the rigours of Mountjoy, Kilmainham and the North Dublin Union. This was graphically expressed by Polly Cosgrave from Wexford in a letter written in July 1923 from the NDU to her former prison comrade, Bridie Halpin:

> **'my jail experience is written in letters of fire across my brain, never to be effaced.'**[308]

Illustrated autograph page by Eilís Dolan. Text reads: We will stand by 'Roisin Dhu' and the Irish Republic forever.

Biographies

Fairview Cumann na mBan *c.*1915.

BRODRICK, ALBINIA LUCY, THE HONOURABLE [GOBNAIT NÍ BHRUADAIR]

(1863–1955)

When the Honourable Albinia Lucy Brodrick died on 16 January 1955, aged ninety-three, she left her estate 'for the benefit of the republicans as they were in 1919–1921'. Albinia was born in London in 1863 into a wealthy Anglo-Irish family who claimed the town of Midleton, County Cork, among their possessions. She was the fifth daughter of the 8th Viscount of Midleton and his wife, Mary Freemantle. Her youth was spent in England on the family estate at Peper Harow. In 1897 Albinia accompanied her father on a visit to his estates in Ireland. But her first recorded interest in Ireland was in 1903, when she wrote an article on poverty in the west of Ireland. She returned to Ireland and trained as a nurse in the Rotunda, a maternity hospital in Dublin city. Interested in the Gaelic Revival, she joined the Gaelic League and succeeded in gaining an excellent command of the Irish language, albeit with an Oxford accent. Albinia then changed her name to the Irish, Gobnait Ní Bhruadair.

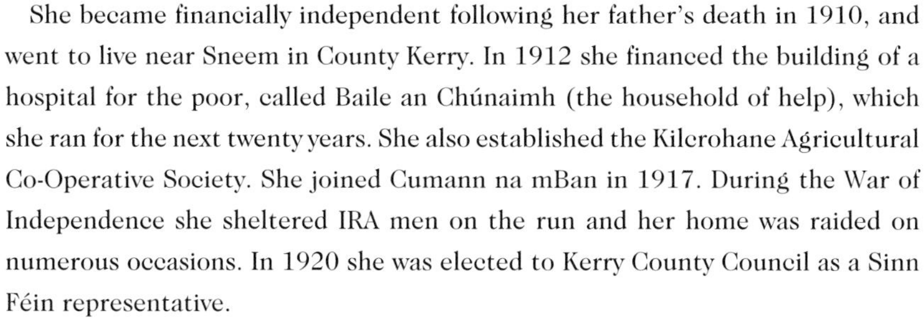

She became financially independent following her father's death in 1910, and went to live near Sneem in County Kerry. In 1912 she financed the building of a hospital for the poor, called Baile an Chúnaimh (the household of help), which she ran for the next twenty years. She also established the Kilcrohane Agricultural Co-Operative Society. She joined Cumann na mBan in 1917. During the War of Independence she sheltered IRA men on the run and her home was raided on numerous occasions. In 1920 she was elected to Kerry County Council as a Sinn Féin representative.

During the Civil War she was arrested by the Irish Free State Government and held in the North Dublin Union detention camp. In prison she organised the production of a jail journal called *The NDU Invincible* and took part in a hunger strike that lasted seventeen days. After the Civil War she continued to support Cumann na mBan and was subjected to raids and harassment by government troops, especially in the late 1920s when there was renewed republican activity. She resigned from Cumann na mBan in 1933 when the focus of the organisation moved towards social radicalism. The dissidents formed a group called Mná na Poblachta (Women of the Republic). From 1926 to 1937 she financed and ran a republican journal called *Saoirse* (Freedom). Gobnait died in 1955, and is buried in Sneem, County Kerry. Her papers disappeared after her death, but in 1958 a couple found her journal in the rubble of the ruined hospital, Baile an Chúnaimh. The journal is now in a private collection in England.

BROWNE, KATHLEEN

(1878–1943)

Born at Rathronan Castle, County Wexford, Kathleen Browne was descended from two of Wexford's oldest families. Her father was Michael Browne of Rathronan Castle and her mother was Mary Stafford from Baldwinstown Castle. Her father was involved in the early twentieth century cultural revival of the Irish language and customs and active in the local branch of the National Land League. His eldest daughter grew up to be a prominent member of the Gaelic League in Wexford and was its secretary. She was elected to the first Wexford County Council after the Local Governement Act 1898. She was a member of Sinn Féin prior to the 1916 Rising and was involved with the Irish Volunteers from 1914 to 1922. A concert that she staged in the hall at Common, County Wexford became one of the largest of the National Aid fundraisers, attended by an estimated 1,000 people. She was arrested after the Rising and held in Kilmainham and Mountjoy jails. After her release she returned to the family home of Rathronan Castle and managed the large mixed farm. She was prominent in the anti-conscription campaign.

Kathleen supported the Treaty and joined Cumann na nGaedhael. During the Civil War she assisted the National Army. She was a member of the Senate from 1929 to 1938. She was a regular contributor to senate debates on the issue of agriculture. She was a Peace Commissioner and a member of the management of the Loch Gorman Co-operative Society as well as belonging to the United Irishwomen (an agricultural association). Kathleen lectured in dairying at the Department of Agriculture in 1930 and went to London as an Irish delegate to the World Poultry Congress. She became one of the first beet growers in South Wexford.

Kathleen was passionate about history and in particular local history. In 1927 her book, *Wexford* was published and became a textbook for senior students in national schools. She was an expert in the ancient dialect of Yola from the baronies of Forth and Bargy in County Wexford. In the 1930s she recruited women to the Blueshirt movement and gained notoriety for wearing a blue blouse in the Senate chamber. In 1938 Kathleen was a key organiser of the 140th anniversary of the 1798 rebellion. She never married, but when her sister Margaret died at a young age she became involved in the upbringing of her five children. Kathleen died in 1943. She is buried in the family plot in Mayglass, County Wexford.

BUCKLEY, MARGARET NÉE GOULDING

(1879–1962)

Margaret Goulding was born in Mourne Abbey, a small community located on the railway line south of Mallow in County Cork. In her youth she became involved in amateur dramatics, music and choral work. She was a member of the Cork Celtic

Literary Society and a founder member of the Cork National Theatre Society. She joined Inghinidhe na hÉireann, and while she was still in her twenties she became president of the Cork branch. In 1905 she took part in the play *The Last Irish King* produced by Alice Milligan.

Margaret married Patrick Buckley in 1906 when she was twenty-six. He was described as 'a typical, rugby-playing British civil servant.' Little else is known of Patrick Buckley except that he died sometime before 1920. Margaret was left well off by her husband and moved to Marguerite Road, Glasnevin, Dublin. For a period during the War of Independence she returned to County Cork to nurse her father who was ill. At this time Margaret became active once again in nationalist circles and was closely associated with the MacSwineys and the MacCurtains. By 1920 Margaret had come back to Dublin and was a judge in the republican courts on the North City circuit. She was opposed to the Treaty and was imprisoned in Mountjoy Jail, Kilmainham Gaol and the North Dublin Union internment camp before being released in October 1923. In prison she held the posts of Officer Commanding and Quartermaster. She wrote an account of her prison experiences in *The Jangle of the Keys* published in 1938.

In 1925 Margaret took over the care of her ten-year-old nephew Seamus Goulding (better known by the Irish form of his name, Séamus Ó Goilidhe) whose mother had died of TB and whose father was working in Scotland. She was an active member of the Women Prisoners' Defence League, and an organiser of the Women's Workers' Union. She opposed Eamon de Valera when he entered Leinster House in 1926. In 1935 she became vice-president of Sinn Féin. Two years later she became president, a post that she held until 1950. During that time she lectured throughout Ireland and Scotland. When the Second War World commenced in 1939 she supported neutrality while remaining anti-British.

For five years of her tenure as president she was occupied with the Sinn Féin Funds' case, trying to secure monies belonging to the Sinn Féin organisation that had been vested in the High Court in February 1924. Ultimately, Sinn Féin lost the case, and not only did it not get the funds, but costs were awarded against it.

After 1950 she was again made vice-president, a position she retained for the rest of her life. When de Valera brought in internment, the first place to be raided was Sinn Féin's headquarters. In July 1957 the entire Ard Chomhairle of Sinn Féin was arrested, with the exception of Margaret Buckley, probably due to her advanced years, as she was then aged seventy-eight.

In her latter years she continued to write, using the pen name of Margaret Lee. In 1956 she published a short history of Sinn Féin 1905–1956. She died at her home in Glasnevin on 24 July 1962. She was buried in St Finbarr's cemetery in her native Cork.

BULFIN MACBRIDE, CATALINA

(1900–1976)

Catalina Bulfin was born on 19 December 1900 in Buenos Aires, Argentina, to William Bulfin and his wife Annie O'Rourke. Her parents had met in Argentina when they both worked on the Dowling Estate in the Pampas. Catalina, the youngest of their five children, was affectionately called Kid, a name that stayed with her for the rest of her life. Her father was a writer and journalist. He became editor of the *Southern Cross* newspaper in 1898, writing under the name of Che Buono. The family came back to Ireland in 1902 and lived in William Bulfin's childhood home in Derrinlough House, Birr, County Offaly. William divided his time between Argentina and Ireland until 1909 when he returned to live full-time in Ireland. He died the following year. Catalina's only brother, Eamonn, was sent to Patrick Pearse's school, St Enda's, in County Dublin. Catalina was kept closer to home and sent to boarding school in Bannaher, County Offaly.

In her twenties she moved to Dublin. Her contemporary, Tod Andrews, described her as sophisticated and well read. 'She was a typical woman of the Twenties, elegant, smoking cigarettes through a very long holder, short skirted and not sparing décolletage.' Catalina worked for Austin Stack while he was Minister of Home Affairs during the War of Independence and continued working for him when he opposed the Treaty during the Civil War. It was in his office that she was arrested on 6 April 1923. She was imprisoned in Kilmainham Gaol and later held in the North Dublin Union; she was released on 26 October 1923. The twenty-three-year-old was not a member of Cumann na mBan but she knew many of the activists. One of her fellow inmates and co-workers, Nora Brick, later married Catalina's brother.

On 26 January 1926 Catalina married another activist, Seán MacBride, the son of Maud Gonne and Major John MacBride. As a member of the anti-Treaty forces, Seán was on the run. The couple spent their honeymoon in France. Over the next year they divided their time between Paris and London. When Catalina became pregnant they returned to Ireland and went to live in Roebuck House, Clonskeagh with Seán's mother. On 24th November 1927 their daughter Anna was born. Catalina took over the running of the house and the jam making factory that had been set up by Mrs Despard as an industry for unemployed republicans. These were difficult years for Catalina; as a senior member of the Irish Republican Army (an outlawed organisation), her husband was on the run from the authorities and his visits home were sporadic. He was imprisoned in 1927 and again in 1929. Raids on Roebuck House were a feature of life through the late 1920s and 1930s. As Seán MacBride had no income during these years, it fell to his wife to provide. In 1932 she got the agency to run the Irish Hospital Sweepstakes, a fundraising lottery to raise money for hospitals. It gave employment to many of the women who had been imprisoned during the Civil War.

The couple's second child, Tiernan, was born on 19 March 1932. In 1937 Seán left the IRA and qualified as a barrister. Catalina and Sean continued to live in Roebuck House with Maud Gonne MacBride until she was in her late eighties. She died in 1956. Catalina suffered ill health in her later years and died in the winter of 1976, aged seventy-six.

CARNEY MCBRIDE, WINNIE

(1887–1943)

Maria Winifred Carney, always known as Winnie, was born on 4 December 1887 at Fisher's Hill, Bangor, County Down. She was the youngest of six children. Her mother, Sarah Cassidy, was a Catholic and her father, Alfred Carney, a Protestant. During her childhood her parents separated and her father went to live in London. Her mother maintained the family by running a sweet shop on the Falls Road in Belfast. Winnie trained as a secretary and shorthand typist. She joined the Gaelic League and began learning Irish. She was also involved in the suffrage and socialist movements. In 1912 she became secretary to the Irish Textile Workers' Union. She became a close friend and personal secretary of James Connolly, who was then living in Belfast. In 1913 she was actively involved in fundraising for the locked-out Dublin workers.

Winnie joined Cumann na mBan in April 1914. She was aware that the Rising was imminent. On 14 April she received a telegram from James Connolly asking her to come to Dublin immediately. When the fighting began she was stationed at the headquarters in the GPO and was the first women in the garrison. During Easter Week she was responsible for typing Connolly's dispatches. When Connolly was wounded she refused to leave. She was arrested and held in Kilmainham, Mountjoy and Aylesbury prisons until Christmas Eve 1916.

After her release her colleagues found her restless and uprooted. She took part in the Cumann na mBan convention in 1917, and became the Belfast delegate for the organisation, but her radical socialism alienated her from many of the members. Promoting a Workers' Republic, she stood unsuccessfully in the 1918 election as a Sinn Féin candidate in the Central/East Belfast Victoria Division. She was Belfast secretary of the Prisoners Dependants' Fund 1920–1922. Her energies were afterwards focused on labour and socialist activities, although she sheltered men on the run during the War of Independence and took the anti-Treaty side in the Civil War. During this time she was arrested and detained for eighteen days in Armagh Prison and fined for possession of 'seditious papers'. In the 1920s she was an active member of the Northern Ireland Labour Party. In 1928, at the age of forty-one, she married George McBride, a Protestant Unionist more than ten years her junior. McBride was a former member of the Ulster Volunteer Force who had fought in The Great War. The couple did not have children.

After years of ill health, possibly latent TB, she died in November 1943. She is buried in Milltown cemetery, Belfast. In 1985, the National Graves Association erected a headstone over her grave.

CEANNT, ÁINE (FRANCES) NÉE O'BRENNAN *(1880–1954)*

Frances (Fanny) O'Brennan is best known by her married name, Áine Ceannt, as the widow of Eamonn Ceannt, one of the leaders of the 1916 Rising.

Frances was born in Dublin on 23 September 1880, four months after the death of her father, Frank O'Brennan. Frank, an auctioneer by profession, was twenty years older than his wife, Elizabeth Butler. After her husband's death, Elizabeth got a job as a nurse in a workhouse.

At the turn of the century Fanny joined the Gaelic League and, like many of the other women who became interested in the Irish language, she adopted an Irish name, Áine. It was in the Gaelic League that she met Eamonn Ceannt. Their first encounter was on the annual excursion to Galway in 1901. Eamonn was said to have courted her by sending her romantic poetry. The couple married on 7 June 1905.

Their son Rónán was born on 18 June 1906. In the years following their son's birth Eamonn worked in Dublin Corporation. By 1916 he was assistant to the City Treasurer and commanded a substantial salary. He was a committed nationalist; in 1913 he joined the Irish Volunteers as a Private and rose to the rank of Captain. He was in charge of the South Dublin Union garrison in 1916.

Just before his execution on 8 May 1916, Eamonn Ceannt wrote a last letter to his wife: 'My dearest wife Áine, Not wife but widow before these lines reach you … Dearest 'silly little Fanny' My poor little sweetheart of – how many – years ago … Ever my comforter, God comfort you now. What can I say? I die a noble death, for Ireland's freedom … You will be – you are, the wife of one of the Leaders of the Revolution. Sweeter still you are my little child, my dearest pet, my sweetheart of the hawthorn hedges and Summer's eves … '

Like many of the other widows, Áine moved into a public role following the Rising. Although she had been a member of Cumann na mBan from its inception, she did not take part in the Rising. Her sister, Lily, was in the Marrowbone Lane garrison. Áine served as vice-president of Cumann na mBan from 1917 to 1925. Unlike other widows, she took an active part in the organisation. When Cumann na mBan organised key members to travel around the country recruiting members in 1918, Áine went to Tralee. She was a member of the standing committee of Sinn Féin from 1917 to 1925. In 1918 she contested the elections for the Urban District Council of Rathmines and was vice-chairman for a period. During the years 1920–1921 she acted as a District Justice in the republican courts in the Dublin suburbs of Rathmines and Rathgar. During the War of Independence she sheltered men on the run; one of the many who stayed with her was Robert Barton. She also acted as an arbitrator for the Labour Department of Dáil Éireann in wage disputes throughout the country.

In 1920 she became a founding member of the Irish White Cross and later was made administrator, with responsibility for the distribution of funds allocated for the benefit of orphans of wars in Ireland. She went on to become secretary of the organisation and later deputy vice-chairman. By 1941 the office had closed and all the papers were brought to her home. Áine wrote a history of the White Cross from 1920 to 1947. In its foreword Chairman James Webb wrote: 'One cannot imagine what the Children's Relief Association (a division of the White Cross) would have been without Mrs Ceannt. It would only be fair to say that SHE was the Association.'

In 1939 Áine was a founding member of the Red Cross. She acted as honorary treasurer of the society from its inception in 1939 until pressure of work compelled her to resign in 1947. In later years Áine and Lily talked about writing a biography of Eamonn Ceannt but never realised this ambition. Lily died in May 1948 and following her sister's death, Áine, now in her late sixties, suffered bouts of ill health. She died in February 1954. Her funeral took place in her local parish of Dundrum, County Dublin and she was buried in Deansgrange cemetery.

CHILDERS, MOLLY NÉE OSGOOD
(1877–1964)

Mary Alden Osgood (known as Molly) was born in Boston's Beacon Hill, one of twin daughters of Dr Hamilton Osgood and his wife Margaret Pearmain. The Osgood family traced their descent from passengers on *The Mayflower*. Her antecedents had been active in the American Revolution.

A skating accident at three years of age left Molly crippled. Both hips were damaged and developed tubercular abscesses. For a time she was only able to move her head and hands. She was what was then known as a 'basket case', as she had to be carried everywhere in a specially designed basket that also served as her bed. She had a number of operations. At thirteen she had an operation that enabled her to walk with crutches.

One of her favourite childhood occupations was to go to the library at Beacon Street. Even though she was young, she was entrusted with rare volumes. A very determined character, Molly managed to achieve many things despite her disability, including conducting a junior orchestra of thirty musicians. To give her greater mobility, she drove a horse and carriage. When she was a child, the Fenian John Boyle O'Reilly was a frequent visitor to her home. In 1867 Boyle O'Reilly had been sentenced to life imprisonment and transportation to Australia. He escaped and made his way to the United States.

Molly's meeting with Erskine Childers in 1903 was to change the course of her life. Robert Erskine Childers was visiting Boston in his capacity as a horse artilleryman with the Honourable Artillery Company of London. It seemed as though they were fated to meet; Molly's sister Margaret was invited to a dinner party to entertain the company, but when she became ill she asked her sister to take her place. Molly sat next to Erskine at dinner and there was a mutual attraction. Before returning to England he proposed to her. They were married in

Boston in January 1904.

The couple went to live in London, where Erskine worked as a committee clerk in the House of Commons. They had three sons, Erskine Hamilton (b.1905) (who later became President of Ireland) Henry (b.1908) who died after birth, and Robert Alden (b.1910).

Erskine Childers' mother was Irish and he had spent much of his childhood living with his cousins, the Bartons, in County Wicklow. In 1911 he published *The Framework of Home Rule,* showing his interest in Irish nationalism. In 1914 he was approached by Mary Spring Rice to undertake gun smuggling for the Irish Volunteers. An informal committee, composed of many anglo-Irish Protestant liberals, was set up, which raised funds for the purchase of the guns. Molly was secretary of the committee, with Alice Stopford Green as chairman. The Childers's yacht, the *Asgard,* was used to smuggle guns into Ireland and Molly took the helm on the voyage.

When Britain went to war, Erskine joined the British Naval Air Service. He served until March 1919, undertaking hazardous North Sea duty. He reached the rank of major in the Royal Air Force. During the war Molly was honorary secretary of a committee that looked after the welfare of Belgian refugees.

The Childers came to Ireland in 1919 when the War of Independence began and Erskine joined the IRA. At first Molly was opposed to the move to Ireland but then became as committed as her husband to the Irish fight for freedom. Childers worked as a propagandist, and his accounts were smuggled out to the press of a number of countries. Molly's activities during those years included running a clipping service from her home for the revolutionary papers of the period. On one occasion she published the *Irish Bulletin* single-handedly. She entertained foreign journalists and sheltered men on the run. She also worked with Michael Collins, sequestering and distributing vast sums raised by the Dáil Loan. From 1920 she was a Trustee of the White Cross.

In 1921 Erskine was a secretary on the Treaty delegation, although he opposed the Treaty. Molly was also against it, feeling that it had been signed under duress. Erskine spent months on the run during the Civil War. It is said that as republican fortunes declined his wife asked him to flee Ireland. He refused and was arrested at Glendalough House, Annamoe, County Wicklow in November 1922. He was one of the first men executed by the Irish Free State. Molly made a statement to the press following her husband's death: 'His sacrifice is as much a gift to me as it is to his comrades who serve Ireland's cause'. She maintained her commitment to the republican cause and continued to produce publicity material for Sinn Féin.

In 1921, Margaret Osgood, now a widow, came to live with her daughter in Bushy Park, Terenure, Dublin. She remained in Ireland until her death in 1934. For a while in the late 1920s Molly's eldest son, Erskine and his wife Ruth and children also lived in the house. In 1926 Molly was honorary treasurer of the Republican Daily Press Fund, which facilitated the founding of the *Irish Press* in 1931.

Her severe health problems often meant prolonged hospital care and Molly was a patient at Brookline Hospital in Massachusetts from 1947 until 1950. She returned to Ireland and survived to see eight grandchildren and twelve great grandchildren. Her final years were spent at Glendalough House, the home of her husband's cousin, Robert Barton. There she was confined to bed, surrounded by books and listening to the radio. She died on New Year's Day 1964 aged eighty-seven.

COGHLAN MACMAHON, MAY

(1907–1985)

May Coghlan, the eldest of nine children, was fifteen years old when she was imprisoned during the Civil War. Her family home, Frankfort House in Dartry, Dublin, was a boarding house for many activists. Countess Markievicz lived with the Coghlan family from the War of Independence onwards, her first permanent residence since the Rising. Years later, Dr Eleanora Fleury lodged with the Coghlans. The home was also used as a safe house and a meeting place for the Fianna.

After her fourteenth birthday May joined Cumann na mBan. She helped at the Department of Labour offices during the War of Independence. In January 1923 Countess Markievicz took May, then aged sixteen, with her on a ten-week propaganda tour of Scotland and England. Later that year, May was arrested while visiting the widow of the recently executed Erskine Childers, along with all the visitors to the house that day. Molly Childers was an invalid and May ran messages for her; many of which were of a political nature. She was known to have carried dispatches in her plaits. May spent almost a year in Kilmainham Gaol and the North Dublin Union.

In later years she worked with former activists who were given employment in the Irish Hospital Sweepstakes and in St Ultan's Hospital. She married Gerard MacMahon and had three sons. Throughout her life May remained active in the Fianna Fáil organisation in her local area of Dundrum in south County Dublin. In the early seventies she took care of her baby granddaughter, Aoife MacMahon. Aoife became a tour guide in Kilmainham Gaol seventy-five years after her grandmother had been a prisoner there.

COMERFORD, MÁIRE

(1893–1982)

Máire Comerford was born in Rathdrum, County Wicklow. Her father was James Comerford and her mother was an Esmonde from Wexford, the daughter of a District Inspector of the RIC (Royal Irish Constabulary), who had been awarded a Victoria Cross for his part in the Crimean War in 1854. James Comerford died when Máire was young. After a period living in London, Máire returned to Ireland in 1915 and lived in Courtown, County Wexford with her widowed mother, where it was their intention to open a private girls' school.

While training to be a secretary in London, Máire was given the task of taking down Sir Edward Carson's speeches in shorthand. Often gibed about her lack of knowledge of Irish history – she remarked that 'Home Rule, Sinn Féin, the Gaelic League had passed me by', she began reading on the subject. However, after witnessing the 1916 Rising, the course of Máire's life changed. She joined the local branch of Sinn Féin and Cumann na mBan in Courtown in 1918. During this time she was also an active member of the central branch of Cumann na mBan, and involved in collections for the prisoners' dependents. She also worked with the North Wexford branch of Cumann na mBan, organising branches in Brideswell, Craanford, Camolin, Castletown and Gorey. She was later made Officer Commanding for North Wexford. She carried dispatches and procured weapons.

Máire was living in Dublin during the War of Independence. In 1920 she became secretary to the historian Alice Stopford Green, and later worked for Áine Ceannt. She was appointed to the General Council of the White Cross in 1920 and became one of its main organisers, travelling all over the country and setting up committees to oversee the distribution of funds. This work facilitated her in her other role as courier for Michael Collins. At the weekends she continued her involvement with Cumann na mBan in North Wexford. In 1921 she was sent to organise Cumann na mBan in Leitrim. During this period she was appointed to the Dublin District Council of the organisation and later served on the executive. Máire was regularly entrusted with secret communications, which she delivered all over the country, gathering intelligence and assisting in key operations. On one occasion, when the Auxiliaries raided 90 St Stephen's Green, she was threatened and a revolver was shoved in her mouth.

At the outbreak of the Civil War, Máire attended the Treaty debates in her capacity as a member of the Cumann na mBan executive. She opposed the Treaty. She became director of propaganda and was active in obtaining arms in the early months of 1922. On 28 June she reported to the Four Courts garrison. From there she carried dispatches to other outposts. She was detained with other prisoners in Bachelor's Walk, but escaped under fire and joined the O'Connell Street garrison, where she took part in the fighting and rendered first aid to the casualties. She brought out Cathal Brugha's last dispatch.

As a courier in the winter of 1922 she was a critical part of the communication network between scattered and 'disintegrating groups of Republicans'. She took part in fighting in many areas, including Waterford, Wexford and Cork. She was one of a group who were ambushed by the Free State army in Camolin in County Wexford. In her account of her involvement she wrote: 'Shot through the hat, drove through and delivered the stuff.'

Following her arrest, Máire was held in Mountjoy Jail, Kilmainham Gaol and the North Dublin Union. She escaped from the North Dublin Union but was re-arrested. During her second period of imprisonment she went on hunger strike and was released after twenty-seven days.

In the election campaign of 1923, Máire was given a motorbike and was in charge of electioneering in County Cork. She was arrested and held in Cork Jail for a short time. In November 1923, posing as an artist, 'Edith Lewis', she was sent to the United States where she spent nine months fundraising. She was on the executive of Sinn Féin in 1926, and, like others who maintained their support for this organisation, she refused to sign an oath of allegiance to the British monarch. As a result, she was unable to obtain a job in the public service. While others emigrated, Máire returned to County Wexford where she ran a poultry farm, living in poverty.

She refused to join Fianna Fáil. She was arrested in 1926 for trying to influence a jury and was sent to Mountjoy Jail for several months. In the 1940s and 1950s she was one of the most prominent figures in the Anti-Partition League. She was women's editor of the *Irish Press* from 1935 and worked with the newspaper until her retirement in 1965. In the book *Curious Journey* she is described as having carried on 'a kind of cold war with all Irish governments since the establishment of the Free State.' As a committed and resolute republican she marched, wrote letters to the paper, spoke at public meetings and gave radio interviews expressing her opinions.

In 1969 her book *The First Dáil* was published. In 1974, at the age of eighty-one, she was arrested on a Sinn Féin platform in Dublin. Two years later she was convicted in a Dublin court for participation in a banned march to commemorate the Easter Rising. Although she refused to pay the fine imposed, the authorities did not sent the elderly woman to prison.

Máire never married. Uinseann MacEoin, who interviewed her for his book *Survivors*, wrote: 'She was interested in a number of men in the Movement but never allowed herself to fall in love until the struggle was over. And of course it was never over'. When she died in December 1982, a half-finished article supporting the H-Block hunger strikers was found in her typewriter.

CONNOLLY O'BRIEN, NORA
(1893–1981)

Nora was the second daughter of James Connolly (executed following the 1916 Rising) and his wife Lillie Reynolds. She was born in Edinburgh, but when she was three years old the family came to live in Dublin. Her father was an organiser for the Dublin Socialist Club. His trade union activities often brought him into conflict with his employers and he frequently lost his job or was unable to find work, so the family lived in poverty for much of her childhood. At one time the Connollys occupied a tenement room in one of the decaying Georgian houses in Queen Street, near Arran Quay, Dublin. Lillie Connolly taught her daughters at home before they went to school, and Nora could read at the age of three. Her English grammar was so advanced that her teacher called her 'Common Noun'

In 1902, when she was just eight years old, Nora's father brought her to Scotland where he was speaking at public meetings in Glasgow, Leith, Falkirk and Edinburgh. Henceforth Nora was a devotee of her father's politics. In 1904 the family moved to the United States. They settled in Troy and later moved to Newark in New Jersey. When Nora reached her teens she began accompanying her father to his meetings and was business manager of his publication, the *Harp*. At thirteen she left school and went to work in a millinery store and later worked as a dressmaker. The Connollys were better off than they had been in Ireland but it was in Ireland that James Connolly saw his future, advancing socialism.

In 1910 the family returned to Ireland and lived in Ringsend in Dublin. Nora could not obtain employment in Dublin so she went to Belfast and got a job in a factory, making blouses. By 1911 the family had moved to Belfast and made their home at Glenalina Terrace on the Falls Road. When her father was appointed organiser of the Transport and General Workers' Union in Dublin, Nora and the rest of the family remained in Belfast.

Nora was a founder member of the Young Republican Party, the girl's branch of the Fianna, and of Belfast Cumann na mBan. When guns were landed at Howth in 1914 Nora and her sister Ina couriered them to hiding places all over Dublin and were rewarded with two rifles, which they brought back to Belfast.

Before the Rising, Nora was sent to the United States with a secret message from her father; while there she met with Roger Casement. When she returned, she was brought directly to meet key members of the Military Council who were planning the Rising. When MacNeill nearly scuppered the Rising by issuing a countermanding order, Nora was sent to the North to try to persuade the leading activists there to join in the fight. Unsuccessful, she made her way back to Dublin by train, by car and on foot. By the time she reached Dublin with her sister the Rising was over and her wounded father was being held in Dublin Castle.

After James Connolly's execution Nora and the family wanted to return to America, but the authorities refused them permission to leave Ireland. The family was destitute and Nora was unable to find work, so she decided to travel alone to America under a false name. She was immediately in demand to speak about the Rising, and over the next year she lectured to thousands. She wrote an account of the Rising, published as *The Unbroken Tradition* in New York in 1918. While she was in America she met her future husband, Seumas O'Brien; he had been given the job of introducing her to people at a dance in Boston. Nora returned home in the summer of 1917, but being refused entry to Ireland, she went to Liverpool and made her way to Ireland as a stowaway, dressed as a boy. She had to go on the run when she got home and lived for a number of months in various safe houses in Dublin city. She was involved in electioneering for the 1918 election.

Nora opposed the Treaty. When the shelling of the Four Courts began on 28 June 1922, Nora and Seumas O' Brien, now married, immediately volunteered. Seumas was posted to the Gresham Hotel and Nora went to Tara Hall, which was a first aid post. When Margaret Skinnider was arrested in December 1922 Nora became paymaster general of the IRA. The O'Briens' flat was raided constantly and although the money was not located, Nora and her husband were arrested. As she later wrote 'they reckoned Seumas must have been working with me just because he was my husband.' Nora was held in the North Dublin Union and Kilmainham Gaol, from where she was released in August 1923. Seumas was imprisoned until November 1923. When he got out they took a flat in Lillie Connolly's house in Belgrave Square, Rathmines and Seumas found work as a commercial traveller with Cleeves, the toffee manufacturers.

The couple did not have children. In the 1930s they ran a newsagents in Rialto. Nora also operated a lending library from the shop. Difficulties in obtaining goods during World War II forced the closure of the shop. For the duration of the war Nora worked in the Post Office and later she was a secretary in Rathmines College.

Nora and Seumas devoted their energies to building up the Labour Party founded by James Connolly in 1912. This proved difficult. Nora also tried to reconstitute the Irish Citizen Army but this failed too. They moved to Drimnagh and ran a small branch of the Labour Party. In 1939, when the objective of a Worker's Republic was removed from the constitution of the party, she and her husband retired completely. Seumas died in June 1962. His wife of forty years, Nora, then aged sixty-nine, remarked that she had never argued with him except over politics.

Nora lived to see the fiftieth anniversary of the Rising in 1966 and in that year received an Honorary Doctorate of Law for her services to Ireland. In the 1960s she became a senator. She was also in receipt of a State pension for her participation in the fight for Irish freedom. During her nineteen years of widowhood she maintained a close friendship with Margaret Skinnider, spending weekends at Margaret's Sandycove home. In the 1960s and 1970s she was a member of the Kilmainham Gaol Restoration Society, which worked to renovate the gaol, which had been in a ruined state since it closed in 1924. In 1935 Nora had published *Portrait of a Rebel Father*, an account of her life with her father up until his execution in 1916. Another book, *James Connolly Wrote for Today – Socialism* was published in 1978 and *We Shall Rise Again* was published in 1981. She died in the Meath Hospital, Dublin on 15 June 1981.

COONEY MCKEOWN, ANNE
(1896–1959)

COONEY CURRAN, LILY
(1898–1980)

COONEY HARBOURNE, EILEEN
(1900–1982)

Twenty-year-old Anne Cooney and her younger sisters, Lily, aged eighteen, and Eileen, sixteen, were part of Marrowbone Lane garrison during Easter Week. Their father and brother were also active in the Rising. The family had a long tradition of nationalism; their grandfather took part in the Fenian rising in 1867.

Anne joined Cumann na mBan in the summer of 1915. Her first job was selling souvenir booklets at the funeral of O'Donovan Rossa. Through her work in Cumann na mBan she got to know Con Colbert from Limerick, a member of the Fianna who was later executed for his part in the Rising. Colbert was a frequent visitor to the Cooney home. Anne made her Cumann na mBan uniform (now in the Kilmainham Gaol Collection) the week before Easter, finishing it on Good Friday. Colbert and his men, including Denis O'Brien (whom Anne later married), joined the garrison at Marrowbone Lane. Anne, Lily and Eileen were among the twenty-one women arrested and brought to Kilmainham Gaol where they were held for the next ten days. Their father was also imprisoned in Kilmainham and was later transferred to Wakefield Prison in England. At Mass in the church in Kilmainham Gaol the Cooneys saw Con Colbert for the last time. Before he was executed (8 May 1916) he wrote to Anne and Lily and gave them his gloves and rosary beads as keepsakes.

Anne Cooney was one of the few women arrested during the War of Independence, serving a sentence in Mountjoy Jail. Eileen tended the wounded during the Civil War fighting in the centre of Dublin in July 1923. The Cooney sisters remained active in the Cumann na mBan movement in later years.

COSGRAVE, MARCELLA

(D.1938)

Marcella Cosgrave was born in Dublin in the late 1860s. Little is known of her early life, but she was active in all the women's political organisations that flourished during her lifetime. When she was in her twenties she became a member of the Ladies' Land League and was among those who joined the new organisation, Inghinidhe na hÉireann, founded by Maud Gonne in 1900. Marcella's Inghinidhe brooch is in the collection of the Allen Library, North Richmond Street, Dublin. As with so many of the activists, the existence of the brooch among their possessions is the only indication of their membership of the organisation.

Marcella was a founder member of Cumann na mBan, a fact attested to by her Cumann na mBan brooch, which is the original version. This early design was found to be impractical, as it caught on clothing, so later members wore a different version. The brooch is now in the collection of the National Museum of Ireland.

As a member of Cumann na mBan, Marcella took part in the 1916 Rising and was Second-in-Command at the Marrowbone Lane garrison. The garrison held out for the duration of the Rising. Marcella was arrested following the surrender of the garrison and imprisoned in Kilmainham Gaol for ten days. Her brother-in-law approached a British officer and succeeded in gaining permission to have her released, but Marcella refused to leave the prison. Her sister Ann was not surprised by her sibling's reaction, knowing her steadfast commitment to her political beliefs.

Marcella never married and lived for many years at 3 George's Quay, Dublin with Julia Maher, who ran a sweet and tobacco shop next door. Julia was also a member of Cumann na mBan. There are family stories that Julia Maher's shop in George's Quay had a trapdoor under the counter for hiding ammunition. The house and shop were frequently raided by the Black and Tans but Marcella somehow managed to conceal her uniform.

No surviving documentation gives an account of Marcella's participation in the War of Independence, but her medal acknowledging her role during that period is in the Kilmainham Gaol Collection. It is not known if she supported or opposed the Treaty of 1921.

Marcella maintained lifelong friendships with many of those who worked for Irish freedom, in particular Julia Grenan. When Marcella died, on 31 January 1938, her niece, Mary Agnes Fleming, declined a State funeral, stating that her Aunt Marcella was a quiet woman who 'did what she did for Ireland and would not have wished to have such an acknowledgement.' She is buried in Glasnevin cemetery, Dublin.

COYLE O'DONNELL, EITHNE [EITHNE NÍ CUMHAILL]

(1897–1985)

Eithne Coyle was born in Killult, near Falcarragh in County Donegal. She was the youngest of seven children of Charles Coyle and May McHugh. Her earliest memories were stories of the Land War, when the local landlord, Colonel Alphert, and the 'battering ram' had terrified the native population. Shortly after her birth, Eithne's father died, aged thirty-six. She later attributed his early death to 'hardship he suffered during the Land War.' Her mother managed the small farm and acquired more land during Eithne's childhood. Eithne wrote: 'My mother was a republican and nationalist and encouraged us in every way.' Eithne and her brother Domhnall became activists. Domhnall was a commandant of the First Northern Division and was imprisoned both in the War of Independence and the Civil War.

Eithne Coyle became a member of Cumann na mBan in 1918 and set up a branch in her local area. In 1920 she moved to Dublin to find work and became known to the key activists. She became a courier carrying arms and messages. She was one of the few women arrested by the British military during the War of Independence. She was at that time living in Ballagh, County Roscommon. Locally she was believed to be a Gaelic League organiser but this was merely a cover for her work with Cumann na mBan. She lived in Ballagh for six months but aroused suspicion and her cottage was raided. She was held in a barracks in Roscommon and later in Mountjoy Jail. She escaped from Mountjoy in October

1921 along with three other women and stayed in an IRA camp in Carlow until the Truce.

She was back in Donegal when news came of the shelling of the Four Courts. She immediately became active and was responsible for bringing messages from the First Northern and Third Western divisions of the IRA. Local newspapers referred to her as the 'Donegal Amazon' and 'the gunwoman'. She joined other members of Cumann na mBan and the IRA in occupying Glenveigh Castle in County Donegal, but with such a small force their resistance only lasted until the autumn. Eithne was arrested in November 1922 and was imprisoned in Ballyshannon Barracks, then in Drumboe Castle, then Mountjoy Jail and in January 1923 was sent to the North Dublin Union. She went on hunger strike in November 1923 and was released just in time to make her way home for Christmas. Early in 1924 she returned to Dublin, but, unable to find work, she lived with one of her sisters who kept a boarding house in Rathmines. She remained active in Cumann na mBan, becoming an executive member in 1924 and president of the organisation in 1926. From 1926 to1929 Cumann na mBan members wrote to jurors who were involved in political cases, seeking to influence them, an action which brought about the Juries Protection Bill in May 1929. She was imprisoned on three separate occasions in the late twenties and early thirties 'on various charges of not being a lady, although I never claimed to be one.'

In 1930, like so many other republicans, Eithne got her first steady job in the Irish Hospital Sweepstakes, run by Joe McGrath. In 1935, at the age of thirty-eight, she married Bernard O'Donnell from Moville in County Donegal. He too had been an activist and up until the mid thirties was attached to the Dublin Brigade of the IRA. In 1941 Eithne resigned as president of Cumann na mBan; she felt that 'the movement was fragmenting'.

She was now the mother of two children, a son, Christopher, and a daughter, Máire, both of whom entered the religious life. Her husband Bernard died in February 1968. In the 1970s she began to gather documentation for a history of the Cumann na mBan organisation, which can now be found in the Eithne Coyle O'Donnell Papers in the University College Dublin Archives. She died in January 1985.

DALY CLARKE, KATHLEEN

(1878–1972)

Kathleen Daly was born in Limerick into a nationalist family. She was the third of ten children of Catherine O'Mara and Edward Daly. Kathleen had eight sisters, Eileen, Madge, Agnes (known also as Úna), Caroline (Carrie), Laura, Nora, Eileen and Annie, and one brother, Edward (Ned), who was born after his father's death. Her father worked in Spaight's Timber Yard. Her mother had a successful dressmaking business until her brother-in-law, John Daly, was arrested and imprisoned in England for Fenian activities and she lost her clients. When Edward

Daly died in 1890 at the early age of forty-one, his daughter believed it was a result of his imprisonment for his Fenian activities. After his death, relations assisted his family financially. Kathleen was ambitious to pursue a career in music but her wealthy Uncle James would not finance it. By the time Kathleen was in her late teens the family was running a successful bakery under the proprietorship of her Uncle John. Kathleen wanted to be independent, and at the age of eighteen she set up a dressmaking business that she ran until she left her native city.

In 1901 she emigrated to the United States and married Tom Clarke who had been in prison with her uncle, John Daly. Tom Clarke had been released from prison three years previously at the age of forty, having served fifteen years. The couple's first son, John Daly Clarke, was born in Brooklyn in 1902. Throughout their period living in the United States Tom was an active member of Clan na nGael and worked as general manager of the organisation's newspaper, the *Gaelic American*. Following a period of ill health for Kathleen and her son, the Clarkes purchased a farm in Manorville, Long Island. Kathleen later wrote that she would have been content to stay there forever but Tom was anxious to go to Ireland. Their second son, Tom Junior, was born in March 1908 in Ireland. The Clarkes were now living in Dublin, where they set up a tobacconist and newspaper shop. The following year they purchased another shop and a third son was born whom they named Emmet, after the Irish revolutionary, Robert Emmet.

Tom Clarke was one of the leaders of the 1916 Rising. He was executed in Kilmainham Gaol, along with Kathleen's brother Ned. Kathleen was pregnant at the time, but subsequently lost the baby.

Kathleen had been a founding member of Cumann na mBan and was one of the main activists in the central branch. She did not take part in the Rising as she had been selected by the IRB to be told of all decisions of the Supreme Council and was entrusted with the names of key men throughout the country. Her role was to coordinate the distribution of support for the families of activists should the fight continue for a number of months. When this was not the outcome of the Rising she became a key organiser in the distribution of aid to prisoners' dependants. Her own family of three sons, the youngest aged seven, was typical of the families affected. The family no longer had an income as their shops had been raided and looted. Suffering poor health, Kathleen went to live with her family in Limerick. Her sister, Madge Daly was president of Cumann na mBan in Limerick. In 1918 Kathleen and her family returned to Dublin. She was arrested for alleged involvement in 'the German Plot' and imprisoned in England from June 1918 until February 1919 with Maud Gonne MacBride and Countess Markievicz.

During the War of Independence she was an active fundraiser, and sheltered men and women on the run. She was a District Justice in the republican courts in Dublin for the North City circuit and was also chairman of the judges on this circuit. In 1919 she was elected an Alderman for Dublin Corporation for the Wood Quay and Mountjoy Wards. In this capacity she served on numerous committees and boards. She was also active in the White Cross from 1920.

She opposed the Treaty and in the fighting of June 1922 she volunteered at the first aid station at the Gresham Hotel. She was chairman of a committee that tried unsuccessfully to negotiate a pact between anti-Treaty and pro-Treaty sides. She was arrested briefly and held in Kilmainham Gaol in February 1923. During the Civil War she ran a shop in D'Olier Street in Dublin which was raided frequently. Her family in Limerick also endured numerous raids; their bakery was taken over by Irish Free State troops.

In 1924 Kathleen went to the United States to lecture and fundraise on behalf of Republicans. Her eldest son was at that time living in Los Angeles for health reasons. A founder member of Fianna Fáil, between 1928 and 1936 she served in the Senate. She opposed the Constitution of 1937, but although she resigned from the Tom Clarke Cumann, she did not resign from the executive of the Party. She was Dublin's first female Lord Mayor, 1939–1943. In 1948, at the age of seventy, she stood unsuccessfully for the Clann na Poblachta party. Throughout the 1940s she served on numerous hospital boards and was a member of the National Graves Association.

In 1965 she left Ireland to live with her youngest son Emmet and his family in Liverpool. She returned in 1966 for the fiftieth anniversary celebrations of the Rising and was presented with an Honorary Doctorate of Law. She died in Liverpool on 29 September 1972 aged ninety-four. She was given a State funeral and is buried in Deansgrange cemetery in Dublin. Her autobiography *Revolutionary Woman* was published in 1991 by The O'Brien Press Ltd, edited by Helen Litton, her grandniece.

DESPARD, CHARLOTTE NÉE FRENCH

(1844–1939)

In *Rebel Irishwomen*, R M Fox said of Charlotte Despard: 'When she was born a girl, a great general was lost to the world, but it gained a worker for social progress'.

Charlotte French, known to the family as Lottie, was born on the family estate in Ripple Vale in Kent in 1844. She was the daughter of naval commander, Captain John Tracey William French and Margaret Eccles, a Glaswegian whose family were wealthy merchants. Charlotte had some Irish lineage as her father was related to the Frenches of Monivea in County Roscommon.

Charlotte's father was dead by the time she was ten and when she was sixteen her mother was committed to a lunatic asylum, where she died five years later. Charlotte was educated but she was not trained to have a career. Now independently wealthy, she and her unmarried sisters travelled extensively in Europe in the 1860s. In 1870, aged twenty-six, she met Maximillian Despard, and after a short courtship they married. Maximillian was a wealthy Irishman, the grand nephew of Colonel Edward Marcus Despard who had been executed for treason in February 1803. The Despards spent their honeymoon in Ireland.

During their married life they visited frequently but made their home in England, purchasing 'Courtlands' in Surrey in 1879.

During the early years of her marriage Charlotte wrote a number of romantic novels, including *Chaste as Ice, Pure as Snow*, which was published in 1874. The childless couple spent their twenty years of marriage travelling extensively. Winters were usually spent abroad as Maximillian Despard suffered from Bright's disease (a degenerative kidney disease). In 1890, when the Despards were returning home from a trip to India, Max Despard's condition deteriorated and he died on Good Friday, 4 April and was buried at sea.

Charlotte was overcome by grief but was encouraged out of her mourning to undertake philanthropic work in the slum district of Nine Elms in London's East End. By 1898 she had established the Despard clubs, community centres set up to advise mothers and provide cheap food. During this period Charlotte converted to Catholicism. This brought her closer to her neighbours in Nine Elms, which was one of Britain's many 'Little Irelands'. She served as a Poor Law Guardian and in this capacity began to visit workhouses.

Charlotte became an active socialist, joining the Social Democratic Federation and later the Independent Labour Party. She began to speak at public meetings on local issues. In 1906 she was recruited to the Women's Social and Political Union. She was arrested following a protest in February 1907 and, because she refused to pay her fine, spent twenty-one days in Holloway Jail along with thirty-one suffragettes. She continued her agitation for female suffrage and in 1909 became president of the Women's Freedom League. That same year she was again imprisoned but was released after five days. Charlotte stood unsuccessfully as a candidate for Battersea in the 1918 General Election but she continued to work tirelessly for equal suffrage, which was achieved in 1928.

During the War of Independence she supported the independence movement and the IRA. She often received letters from people asking her to intercede with her brother, Lord French, who was Viceroy in Ireland at this time. One of the letters came from Maud Gonne MacBride, who wanted her assistance to get her sixteen-year-old son, Seán, out of prison. Charlotte had no influence on her brother but she decided to travel to Ireland and see conditions for herself.

In January 1921 she came to Ireland as a guest of the Irish Women's Franchise League; Maud Gonne MacBride was her hostess. This visit and her contact with Irish activists made her decide to move to Ireland in the summer of 1921.

At the outbreak of the Civil War Charlotte was part of the peace committee that tried to stop the fighting. In August 1922 she and Maud Gonne set up the Women's Prisoners' Defence League (WPDL), with Charlotte as President. That year she moved to Roebuck House, a home she shared with Maud Gonne MacBride. Raids on the house were frequent. When Maud was arrested in 1923 Charlotte, now seventy-eight, mounted a vigil outside the gates of Kilmainham Gaol.

In order to give employment to republicans released after the Civil War, the

Roebuck Jam Factory was set up, but it turned out to be all expenses and no profit. Now in her eighties, Charlotte still embraced new ideas and joined the Irish Worker's Party. She paid Roddy Connolly, James Connolly's son, to be the organiser. The party failed to make an impact. In 1925 she left Sinn Féin, which by then was boycotting all the Free State institutions.

In 1930 she travelled to Russia with fellow members of the 'Friends of Soviet Russia' and made a six-week tour of the Soviet state. Despite being in her late eighties, 'a time when most people would think to give up public life', as she wrote herself, she continued to work for the WPDL until it was disbanded in 1932. She addressed meetings, supported Saor Eire (the republican congress set up by left-wing IRA members), she campaigned for Eamon de Valera in 1932 and for causes such as opposition to General Franco and the Fascist movement.

In 1933 Charlotte sold Roebuck House to Maud Gonne MacBride and moved for a short time to a nursing home in Dublin but soon recovered enough to set up a new home. She continued her socialist activities and founded the Irish Worker's College in Eccles Street, Dublin for the political education of workers. This did not last long; in March 1933 it was ransacked by an anti-communist mob. Her aim even as she entered her nineties was to remain active: 'People think that because of my age I should take things easy now. Why should I? I find life interesting even at ninety-two ... I do not like talking about the past. It has gone. It's the present we should live in'.

She moved to Belfast in an attempt to unite Protestant and Roman Catholic workers. She helped with relief efforts following the violent clashes of 1935. She still attended meetings in London, Bristol, Dublin and even travelled as far as Paris and Antwerp. She was too ill to go to Spain in 1936 but attended a solidarity conference in Belgium and France.

In 1937 Charlotte moved again, to a house at Whitehead, twenty miles outside Belfast. By 1939 she was frequently ill and her finances were not very secure. Bankruptcy proceedings were issued. Six weeks later she had a bad fall; she never regained consciousness and died on 9 November 1939. She is buried in the Republican Plot in Glasnevin cemetery in Dublin.

DUGGAN ROBINSON, HANNAH (PIDGE)

(1901–1987)

Hannah Duggan, always known as Pidge, was born in Cork City on 14 February 1901, one of twelve children of Denis Duggan and his wife, Jane Lyons. Part of her youth was spent in Dublin. At the age of fifteen, with an honours certificate from King's Inn National School in Dublin, Pidge left Ireland. She and her family moved to Scotland when her father was appointed manager of the Glasgow branch of Scottish Legal Life. This was a direct result of the 1916 Rising; the firm's Dublin offices were burnt down during the fighting.

The following year, sixteen-year-old Pidge joined the Anne Devlin Branch of Cumann na mBan in Glasgow. The branch was attached to A Company of the

Volunteers, of which Joe Robinson was captain. Despite an age difference of fourteen years, they began a romance. Over the next few years Joe was frequently imprisoned and during one period of incarceration the couple became engaged. Joe had a ring fashioned out a sovereign as a token for her.

During the years prior to the War of Independence Pidge stored ammunition for the Volunteers. Her home was raided regularly during 1920, and when incriminating material was found, she was imprisoned in Glasgow Central Police Station. As a result she lost what she described as 'a good position'.

Just before the Truce in 1921 she began to courier arms across the Irish Sea, sewing the dangerous cargo into her clothes in order avoid detection. Pidge was opposed to the Treaty of 1921. Like many of her fellow members in Cumann na mBan, she supported the republican side. When Joe Robinson reorganised the republican forces in Glasgow in March 1922 Pidge was one of his ablest comrades.

In March 1923 Pidge Duggan was arrested in Scotland and transported to Ireland, where she was imprisoned in Mountjoy Jail. She was released in June, but re-arrested and sent to Kilmainham Gaol.

Pidge and Joe were married on 10 October 1923 and lived in Glasgow, where they opened a small shop with compensation money paid out by the British government to women who were judged to have been illegally deported. However, neither she nor Joe was business-minded, and the venture failed.

When Pidge became pregnant, Joe sent her back to Dublin so that his first child would be Irish. Their daughter Deirdre was born in 1924. It was Countess Markievicz who took Pidge to the Coombe maternity hospital, hailing a horse and cart to make the journey. A second daughter, Fionnuala, was born in Glasgow in 1927. The family moved to the United States in 1928 and their youngest child, Brenda, was born in New York in 1932. Joe never settled in America. He was offered a job in the Board of Works in Ireland and returned to take up this position in 1934. Pidge and Joe remained in Ireland for the rest of their lives. Joe died in 1955 but Pidge lived for another thirty years, dying on 26 June, 1987 aged eight-six years.

ffRENCH-MULLEN, MADELEINE

(1880–1944)

Madeleine ffrench-Mullen was born in Malta, the daughter of St Laurence ffrench-Mullen, a fleet surgeon of the Royal Navy. When her father retired, the family came to live in Dundrum, County Dublin. Within a short time of the move, Madeleine's parents both died, and, as the eldest of three children, she became the head of the household. She went to Germany where her siblings were educated, but returned to Ireland in 1914. The Great War had begun and Madeleine took a number of Belgian refugees into her new family home of Stradbrook. At this time she became committed to the labour movement and became an early member of the Irish Citizen Army. She was also a member of

Inghinidhe na hÉireann.

Madeleine wrote a children's column using the pen names of Dectora or M O'Callaghan. She met Dr Kathleen Lynn at a lecture on first aid and a lifelong friendship began. For thirty years they shared a house and worked together. In 1916 both took part in the Rising and were imprisoned. After her release, Madeleine became involved with the Connolly Co-operative Society, which provided work for those activists who were unemployed following their participation in the fighting.

During the War of Independence she was briefly arrested on the charge of 'keeping a military patrol under surveillance', and as a result spent a period in the Bridewell prison in Dublin. This is the only record of her involvement in the War of Independence. However, her energies were focused elsewhere during this time. In 1918, along with Dr Kathleen Lynn, she established a temporary hospital, followed in May 1919 by a permanent institution, St Ultan's infant hospital on Charlemont Street, in Ranelagh, Dublin.

Madeleine was also a member of the Rathmines Urban District Council as well as being a founder member of the Joint Committee of Women's Societies and Social Workers established in 1935. She was involved with the Ultan Utility Society and the Charlemont Utility Society – organisations that built new homes for those who had lived in the slums that stood on the site of the ever-expanding hospital. Today a block of apartments on Charlemont Street is called ffrench-Mullen House in her memory. She died on 26 May 1944.

FOLAN, KATHERINE (JAKE)

(1907–1989)

Katherine Frances Folan was born on 13 July 1907, the sixth child of Michael Folan, a carter, and his wife Anne Allen. There were eight girls in the family and one boy, Michael, to whom Katherine was particularly close.

On 12 March 1923, when Katherine was fifteen years old, she was arrested at her home at William Street, Sea Road, Galway. The soldiers had come for her older sister Mary, but she was not at home. Rather than leave empty-handed, they arrested Katherine, who had been known to carry messages for the Irregulars. She was initially imprisoned in Galway Gaol, but it proved embarrassing when the local papers carried reports to the effect that children were being arrested. The governor of the prison was a relative of the Folans, which posed a further difficulty for the authorities.

'Jake', as she became known in prison, was brought to Kilmainham Gaol where she was housed in B Wing, in a cell that had been occupied by Patrick Pearse before his execution in 1916. In later years she recalled her period of imprisonment as one of the happiest times of her life. Her daughter has always maintained that it wasn't political zeal that made prison such a joy, but rather that Katherine no longer had to go to school. Apparently she hated school, as she was not very academic, a particular trial for a child who came from a very studious family. She often recalled that when the rest of the family would be seated around the table doing their homework, she would excuse herself, and creep out the front door to play with her friends. (One of these friends was Tom Savage whom she later married). In fact, the day before her arrest, her mother had gone into the school and had told the nuns to 'beat some knowledge into Kay', so her forcible removal from that environment was quite fortuitous.

However, her prison experience was not without its hardships. On the transfer from Kilmainham Gaol to the North Dublin Union she was beaten by one of the warders. 'Jake' was imprisoned until 28 September 1923.

After her release she remained in Dublin with her eldest sister, Mairéad Murphy, to help with the care of her two young sons. Eventually, Katherine went to America to help another sister, Mary, and her young family in Boston. She worked in the care industry in the United States for a number of years. In 1932, despite being engaged to someone else, she left America and returned to Ireland to marry her childhood friend, Tom Savage. Tom was a dark, handsome six-footer who was an oarsman with the famous Emmets' Rowing Club Eight and a member of the team that took second place at the Tailteann Games in 1928.

The couple began their married life in Galway but moved to London in 1933. It was there that their only surviving child, Eleanor, was born in 1945. They came back to Ireland around 1948 after Tom's health broke down but later returned to England, living firstly in Birmingham and then in Pimlico in London. Tom Savage died in 1956.

Katherine embraced English culture. She always voted Conservative, although she strongly disliked Churchill (she was incensed by his critical speech on the neutrality of Ireland). A keen Royalist, she would go to State processions and attended the Coronation procession in 1953, despite the pouring rain, much to the amusement of her husband and daughter. She did not support the IRA as it evolved after the Civil War and in later years did not approve of a nephew's association with a 'wanted' member of the organisation.

In spite of the fact that her daughter and grandchildren were in England, she was adamant about going back to live in Ireland, which she did in 1982, at the age of seventy-five. Her daughter believes that she wanted to go home to die. She lived firstly in Galway, then in Greystones, County Wicklow and finally moved back to Galway. Although restless and uprooted, she refused to return to England. She died in Ireland, as she had wished, in August 1989.

GAHAN O'CARROLL, MAY

(1898–1988)

May Gahan joined Inghinidhe na hÉireann in her early teens and acted in a number of early productions staged by the organisation. She also participated in performances in the Abbey Theatre. She became a member of Cumann na mBan in 1914 and took part in the Rising, serving with the St Stephen's Green garrison and the GPO garrison. When the women were asked to leave the GPO, she went across to the garrison at Clery's Department Store, where Captain Drennan was stationed with seventy-two men. At the surrender she escaped through Marlborough Street and hid in the vaults of the Pro-Cathedral with Martha Kelly. They were arrested and held in the Customs House and then brought to Kilmainham Gaol. After the Rising, May's activities included campaigning against conscription and collecting for the Prisoners' Dependants' Fund. She was arrested and imprisoned for two months.

May Gahan married fellow volunteer John O'Carroll in May 1917. They opened a milk bar on what is now Cathal Brugha Street. It was called the Republican Bar and painted green, white and orange. The bar was a rendezvous for activists throughout the War of Independence. British soldiers also frequented it and May used the opportunity to buy guns from them. Her greatest success was the purchase of a machine gun. This was lowered over the wall of Ship Street Barracks and taken away by May in a pram.

May was opposed to the Treaty of 1921. During the Civil War she worked for the IRA until the order to dump arms in May 1923. The day after the fighting ceased, she was arrested again and held in Kilmainham. She took part in a number of hunger strikes and was released after the general hunger strike in November 1923.

She and her husband and two children left Ireland in 1924. They spent time in England, South Africa, New Zealand and finally in Australia, where they settled in 1929. In Australia she had eight more children, who were given strongly patriotic names, among them Seamus Connolly O'Carroll (b. 1934), Sean Heuston O'Carroll (b. 1935), Liam Mellowes O'Carroll, (b. 1936), Eamon de Valera O'Carroll (b. 1937), and Peadar Clancy O'Carroll (b. 1942).

GALLAGHER, CECILIA

(1889–1967)

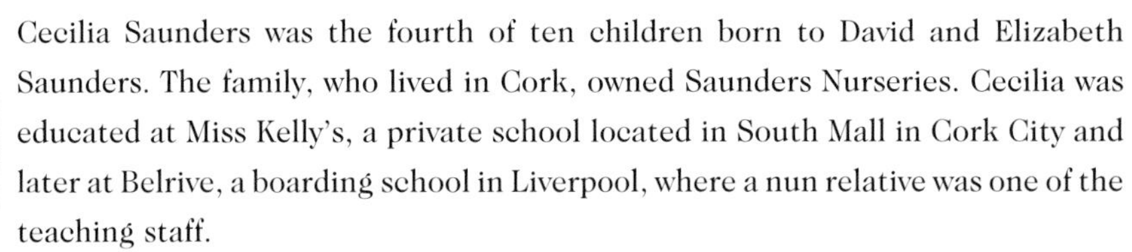

Cecilia Saunders was the fourth of ten children born to David and Elizabeth Saunders. The family, who lived in Cork, owned Saunders Nurseries. Cecilia was educated at Miss Kelly's, a private school located in South Mall in Cork City and later at Belrive, a boarding school in Liverpool, where a nun relative was one of the teaching staff.

In 1911 she went off to teach at a Jewish School in Wiesbaden in Germany. She returned to Ireland the following year and began working in the Provincial Bank in Cork City. Later she took up a position with the National Land Bank in Cork.

Although not politicised herself, from 1914 Cecilia corresponded with Frank Gallagher, a family friend and journalist who was a member of Sinn Féin and worked on the publicity staff of the underground government during the War of Independence. He was imprisoned and went on hunger strike for forty days in March 1920.

Cecilia and Frank (who was six years her junior) were married on 24 May 1922, just as the major hostilities of the Civil War had begun. Cecilia was arrested the following November. She was not a member of Cumann na mBan or any other political organisation, but her husband's stance in opposing the Treaty was well known.

Cecilia was first imprisoned in Dublin's Mountjoy Jail, was transferred to Kilmainham Gaol on 6 February, then to the North Dublin Union Internment Camp and moved back to Kilmainham before she was finally released on 28 September 1923. At that stage she had not seen Frank for a year.

After they were released from prison, the Gallaghers left Ireland and travelled extensively in Europe. Frank found work as a journalist and they lived a nomadic existence in France, Germany and Holland. They returned to Ireland in the late 1920s. They settled first in Raheny House in north County Dublin and later in Sutton. In the 1930s they adopted two little girls, Ann and Mary. Frank worked as Eamon de Valera's secretary and in 1931 when de Valera established the *Irish Press* Gallagher became the first editor. These years were not without their difficulties; in 1931 Frank was again imprisoned for his continued opposition to the Irish Free State.

During World War II Cecilia assisted with the work of the Red Cross in Ireland. Life changed again for the Gallaghers in 1955 when Frank had a stroke. Cecilia nursed him during the period of his illness, assisting him in any way she could – she even learned to drive at the age of sixty-six. They were constant companions until Frank's death in 1962. Cecilia outlived him by five years. Her diary, photographs and memorabilia are housed in Trinity College Dublin.

GAVAN DUFFY, LOUISE

(1884–1969)

Louise Gavan Duffy was born in Nice, France, the daughter of Sir Charles Gavan Duffy and his third wife, Louise Hall. Louise Hall was the daughter of a Protestant banker from Cheshire and was a niece of her husband's second wife. She was in her twenties when she married the fifty-six-year-old Gavan Duffy in 1880. Charles Gavan Duffy had been a prominent member of the Young Ireland movement, founder of *The Nation* newspaper and was the Prime Minister of Victoria, Australia.

In his retirement he had gone to the South of France for health reasons and lived in what he described as 'domestic happiness'. Gavan Duffy had numerous children from his previous marriages and Louise presented him with a daughter and three sons: George (who was one of the signatories of the Anglo-Irish Treaty of 1921), Bryan and Tom. In February 1889, when Louise was just five, her mother died as a result of complications of childbirth. Louise's stepsister Susan, aged forty, came from Australia and took charge of the household. Louise was a gifted student, gaining first place in her examinations.

Charles Gavan Duffy died in 1903 and Louise, now nineteen, travelled to Ireland for the funeral, which was held at the Pro-Cathedral in Dublin. Thousands of people lined the streets as the coffin was carried to Glasnevin cemetery. It was this occasion that inspired her to become part of the Independence movement. She moved to Ireland and attended University College Dublin, where she was one of the first women graduates in 1911. She learned Irish and became an Irish language expert. She taught at St Ita's (Scoil Íde), a bilingual educational institution for girls.

In 1914 she joined Cumann na mBan and was elected to the executive. In 1916 Louise was studying for a Master of Arts degree. She did not approve of the Rising, but nonetheless joined the garrison at the GPO. She spent the time working in the kitchen, although she later admitted that she was not very 'knowledgeable about cooking affairs or on providing food'. Desmond FitzGerald recalled in his memoirs that she worked unceasingly day and night. He also stated that she would not have taken up arms under any circumstances. She evaded arrest following the Rising.

Louise was active during the War of Independence. She supported the Treaty but she turned away from politics on the outbreak of the Civil War and concentrated on her school, Scoil Bhríde, an Irish language secondary school for girls, which she had co-founded in 1917. The school was first located in Dublin city centre but moved to a larger building in the suburb of Ranelagh in 1965. Louise Gavan Duffy was made an Honorary Doctor of Laws of the National University of Ireland for her services to Irish education. She died in 1969 at the age of eighty-five. She never married.

GIFFORD CZIRA, SIDNEY

(1889–1974)

Sidney Sarah Gifford was one of twelve children of solicitor Frederick Gifford and his wife Isabella Burton. The family lived at 8 Temple Villas, Rathmines, Dublin. The youngest of the Gifford sisters, Sidney became politicised at an early age. She was a member of Inghinidhe na hÉireann and was on the Executive Council of Sinn Féin and also a member of the Irish Women's Franchise League. A journalist, her first article was printed while she was still in school; by her early twenties she was contributing to many newspapers, including *Sinn Féin, Bean na hÉireann*, the *Irish Citizen* and *Irish Freedom*. She used the pseudonym 'John Brennan' as she felt that her writing would be seen in a more serious light if she were thought to be a man. Henceforth she was known as 'John' by her friends.

In 1914 she went to the United States to make a career in journalism. Her homes in New York and Philadelphia were described as 'the exiles club'. She worked with Irish-Americans in Clan na Gael and the Irish Progressive League and wrote for the *New York Sun* and the *Irish Press* of Philadelphia.

While in the US she married a Hungarian émigré, Arpad Czira, who had escaped from Russian captivity. The couple had a son, Finian, born in 1917, but they soon separated. The British authorities tried to prevent Sidney from returning to Ireland, but in 1922 she managed to gain entry with her son by using a borrowed passport. She joined the Women Prisoners' Defence League and was active until the 1930s. In later years she worked as a journalist for newspapers such as the *Irish Press*, the *Kerryman* and *An Phoblacht*. She even produced her own newspaper, *News and Views*, (1942–1949) which was made up of reprinted articles from newspapers in various countries. She was a radio journalist on 2RN and Raidio Éireann as the station became known, and in the 1960s she worked on a number of television programmes.

Sidney remained active in social and political causes throughout her life. In the 1940s she was involved in 'Save the German Children', an organisation that found homes for 400 children and raised money to support them. She lived in Ranelagh with her son, who never married. She died in Dublin on 15 September 1974.

GIFFORD DONNELLY, NELLIE

(1880–1971)

Helen Ruth, known as Nellie, was the only one of the Giffords to take part in the Rising, although her sister Grace was engaged to Joseph Plunkett, and another sister, Muriel, was married to Thomas MacDonagh. Nellie was a founder member of the Irish Citizen Army. It was Nellie who accompanied the disguised trade union leader Jim Larkin into the Imperial Hotel on Sackville Street (O'Connell Street). She posed as his niece and assisted him in gaining entry to the balcony where he gave his famous speech that resulted in the lockout of 1913. A domestic economy instructor, she gave lessons to the Irish Citizen Army in 'camp' or 'emergency' cookery. As a member of the St Stephen's Green garrison in 1916, she was in charge of feeding the personnel in the College of Surgeons and the delivery of rations to the various outposts nearby. She was imprisoned in Kilmainham and Mountjoy prisons for a few weeks after the Rising. In Kilmainham Gaol she shared a cell with Julia Grenan and Winnie Carney. She wrote her name on the prison wall; her pencilled inscription can still be seen to this day.

After her release Nellie went to England and eventually made her way to the United States where she undertook a lecture tour on the 1916 Rising. She married Joseph Donnelly from Omagh, County Tyrone in 1918 and had one daughter Maeve, born in 1920. In 1921 Nellie and her daughter returned to Ireland. In 1932, Nellie organised a 1916 exhibition in the National Museum of Ireland during the Eucharistic Congress. It was mainly due to her efforts that a large number of items pertaining to the Rising were donated to the National Museum. In the 1960s she was also a founder member of the Kilmainham Gaol Restoration Society. In later years she attempted to write her biography, which remained unfinished at the time of her death, in June 1971.

GIFFORD PLUNKETT, GRACE

(1888–1955)

Grace Evelyn Mary Vandeleur Gifford is best known as the wife of Joseph Mary Plunkett, one of the leaders of the 1916 Rising. She married Joseph in Kilmainham Gaol just hours before his execution on 4 May 1916.

The second youngest of the twelve Gifford children, Grace, like many young women at the turn of the century, was encouraged in artistic endeavours. She studied at the Metropolitan School of Art, Dublin and later at the Slade in London. When she returned to Dublin, Grace worked as a caricaturist and illustrator. One of the papers to which she contributed was the *Irish Review*, which was edited by Joseph Plunkett. They began a courtship in 1915 and in December Joseph asked Grace to marry him. Despite the fact that he was seriously ill with tuberculosis, Joe was a member of the Military Council that planned the Rising in 1916.

In early April 1916 Grace converted to Catholicism in preparation for her marriage, which was scheduled to take place on Easter Sunday, 23 April. When Joseph was sentenced to death, he sought permission to be married. The ceremony took place in the Catholic chapel of Kilmainham Gaol in the presence of the British military. The tragedy of the event is further underscored by the fact that it is said that Grace had been pregnant but suffered a miscarriage in the weeks following her husband's execution.

In the aftermath of the Rising the story of the Plunkett marriage was seen as a contributing factor in turning the tide of public opinion to one of sympathy. Grace became a public figure and joined in the political arena, becoming a member of the Sinn Féin executive in 1917, a group in which all the disparate elements who supported the Rising gathered.

Grace continued to work as an artist. Her book of caricatures of Irish personalities, *To Hold as 'Twere* was published in 1919. During the War of Independence she used her artistic skills for propaganda purposes. Along with other 1916 widows, she opposed the Treaty that ended that war. During the Civil War she was arrested on 6 February 1923 and imprisoned in Kilmainham Gaol; her elder sister, Katharine Wilson, was a fellow inmate. One of Grace's main occupations while she was incarcerated was drawing and painting on the walls of the cells. She was also imprisoned in the North Dublin Union for a period following her transfer from Kilmainham Gaol in mid August 1923.

In later years Grace pursued her career as an artist and was not active politically. Her best-known works were published in two volumes in 1929 and 1930. She lived in various degrees of poverty throughout these years. She got a State pension in 1932, and in 1935 she finally received money from her husband's estate. This followed a protracted battle with the Plunkett family over Joseph's will, which had been written during the Rising and which left all his possessions to her. The case was settled out of court. Grace never remarried.

When she died in 1955, in her late sixties, she had been widowed for nearly forty years.

GIFFORD WILSON, KATHERINE
(1875–1957)

Katherine Anna, always known as Katie, was the eldest of the Gifford sisters. There is no information on Katie's early education, but she became one of the first generation of Irish women to go to university. She was a gifted linguist, fluent in several languages, and graduated from the Royal University with an honours degree. In 1909, aged thirty, she married Walter Harris Wilson, six years her junior. They went to live in Wales, but Katherine returned to Ireland when her husband died in the 'flu epidemic of 1918, and lived in Philipsburg Avenue, Fairview.

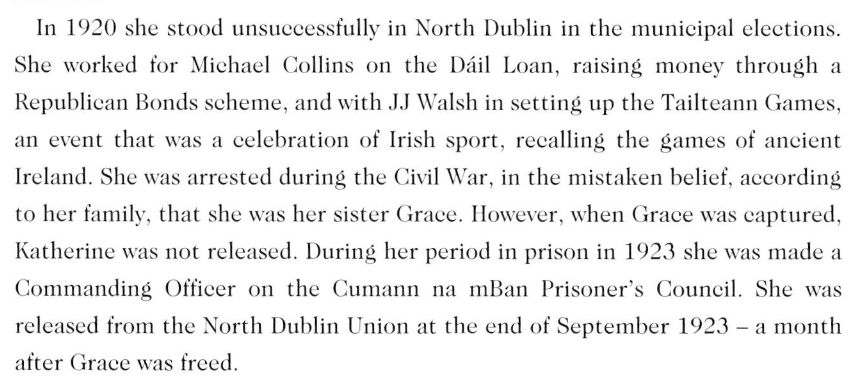

In 1920 she stood unsuccessfully in North Dublin in the municipal elections. She worked for Michael Collins on the Dáil Loan, raising money through a Republican Bonds scheme, and with JJ Walsh in setting up the Tailteann Games, an event that was a celebration of Irish sport, recalling the games of ancient Ireland. She was arrested during the Civil War, in the mistaken belief, according to her family, that she was her sister Grace. However, when Grace was captured, Katherine was not released. During her period in prison in 1923 she was made a Commanding Officer on the Cumann na mBan Prisoner's Council. She was released from the North Dublin Union at the end of September 1923 – a month after Grace was freed.

After the Civil War, Katie was associated with the foundation of 2RN, the precursor of Raidio Éireann. She worked as 'Woman Organiser', but lost this job, possibly because of her political beliefs. In later years she taught French in a technical school near Parnell Square. She was involved in the Irish White Cross, the children's relief organisation, which was active in Ireland from 1920 to 1947. She died in September 1957.

GILL, MAURA (MOLLIE)
(1891– 1977)

Maura Gill, always known as Mollie, was an artist with the Cuala Press, run by the Yeats sisters, Lily and Lolly, and Evelyn Gleeson. The Cuala Press specialised in publishing the work of living Irish writers. It used only Irish materials and employed Irish female workers. The Press was located at Rose Cottage, Churchtown, County Dublin, not far from Mollie's home in Murphystown in the Dublin Mountains.

Mollie was the only one of the seven Gill children involved in the nationalist movement. She was a member of Inghinidhe na hÉireann and later joined Cumann na mBan. She was the organiser of meetings in the area near her home.

There is no documentary evidence of her involvement in the Rising or her activities prior to the Civil War. She was arrested at her home on 9 March 1923 having been found in possession of a notice of a meeting of the Irish Republican Prisoners' Dependants' Fund and Cumann na mBan literature. She was active in the War of Independence and in the Civil War on the anti-Treaty side.

Mollie never married and lived in the Gill family home with her friend Kay Byrne (who had also been in Cumann na mBan) for the rest of her life. Among her treasured mementoes, preserved by her grandnieces, were her Inghinidhe na hÉireann brooch, copies of republican broadsheets printed in the Civil War, an autograph book with signatures collected in Kilmainham Gaol and a photograph album, including a picture of May Gahan O' Carroll and her children, identified by an inscription on the reverse. She died on 15 March 1977 and is buried in St Patrick's cemetery, Glencullen, County Dublin.

GONNE MACBRIDE, MAUD

(1866–1953)

Maud Gonne was born in Tongham, Surrey, England in December 1866, the eldest child of Thomas Gonne, a captain of the Seventeenth Lancers. Maud's earliest memories were of Ireland, where her father was posted in the aftermath of the Fenian Rebellion of 1867. When her father died she became financially independent. Dividing her time between Ireland and France, she became the mistress of Lucian Millevoye, a French journalist and politician.

In 1890 she became active in Irish affairs. Being outside mainstream politics, she lent her support to many causes, including the prevention of evictions. She sought amnesty for 'the Fenian dynamiters', publicising their harsh treatment as convict (rather than political) prisoners through lectures and organising subscriptions for the support of their relatives. She was instrumental in gaining concessions and their early release. In 1891, unknown even to the poet William Butler Yeats, who wished to marry her, she gave birth to Millevoye's son, Georges, who died in infancy. Four years later they had a daughter, Iseult. The birth of her children did not prevent Maud from working for Ireland. Well-placed in political and journalistic circles in Paris, she published a newspaper, *L'Irlande Libre*, and lectured on Irish affairs in Europe and the United States.

When she was excluded from joining existing nationalist groups in Ireland because she was a woman, she founded Inghinidhe na hÉireann in 1900. This group was a catalyst for Irish women involved in the fight for Irish freedom. Active in the Gaelic Revival, she played the lead in Yeats's play *Cathleen Ní Houlihan* in 1902. In 1903 Maud married Major John MacBride, a hero of the Boer War, and they had a son, Seán. Their union was short-lived and she spent much of their married life in France. After MacBride was executed for his part in the 1916 Rising, Maud returned to Ireland, now a hive of political activity. She was imprisoned in Holloway Prison in 1918 for alleged involvement in the 'German

Plot' but her activities were primarily humanitarian, working for the White Cross.

During the War of Independence Maud was instrumental in publicising atrocities committed by the Black and Tans. She was a supporter of the Treaty until the government began executions without trial. She was a member of the committee established by the Lord Mayor of Dublin in an effort to prevent the Civil War. During the Civil War she founded the Women's Prisoners' Defence League, in order to ensure the rights of republican prisoners. She herself was imprisoned in Kilmainham Gaol, where she went on a hunger strike, which secured her release after twenty days. Even when the Civil War was over, Maud supported the republican stance and continued her agitation for political prisoners over subsequent decades. She died in 1953 aged eighty-six.

GORDON, WINIFRED (ÚNA)

(Dates unknown)

Mrs Gordon, as she was known to her fellow inmates in the prisons in the Civil War, was born Winifred Cassidy in The Graan in Enniskillen. Her first marriage was to District Inspector Patrick Gordon. When he died during the Great War, his widow went to Paris and joined the American Ambulance Service and worked for them until 1916. That year she returned to Dublin and took up residence in Lansdowne Terrace.

During the Rising she volunteered to nurse the wounded in the Royal City of Dublin Hospital in Baggot Street. After the executions she attended the requiem Mass for the Pearse brothers and called on their mother to offer her condolences. She also visited Agnes (Úna) Mallin to extend her sympathies. It is said that these contacts brought her in touch with the republican movement. She maintained her friendship with Agnes Mallin in the years following 1916, taking Seamus and Úna Mallin to live with her when Agnes became ill, and when Agnes died in 1930 she again assisted the Mallin children.

Úna Gordon joined the Ranelagh Branch of Cumann na mBan, and she later became an executive member of this organszation. Her home at Strand Road, Ballsbridge became a depot for the making and distribution of first aid material and was also used as a hiding place for wanted men. She sheltered Austin Stack, the well-known prison leader and Deputy Chief of Staff of the IRA (1919–1922) during the War of Independence. She went anti-Treaty and was imprisoned for nine months during the Civil War along with her cousin Fanny O'Dolan. Mrs Gordon and Austin Stack were married in 1925, two years after she was released from prison. Austin Stack was in poor health and died four years later in May 1929.

Although she was childless, Úna Stack was very interested in child welfare and was an active worker in the Infants' Aid Scheme. She was also interested in developing children's playgrounds, in particular that of Clann Mhuire in Foley Street, Dublin. She assisted the work of Dr Kathleen Lynn and Madeleine ffrench-Mullen in St Ultan's Hospital.

GRENAN, JULIA

(D.1972)

Julia Grenan and Elizabeth O'Farrell were lifelong friends, having met during their school days when they were both pupils of the Mercy School, Townsend Street, Dublin. Both were members of Inghinidhe na hÉireann and both joined Cumann na mBan, fighting in the GPO garrison together during the 1916 Rising. After school Julia was a dressmaker in the workroom of a dress salon in Suffolk Street.

Prior to the Rising, James Connolly asked Julia and Elizabeth to attach themselves to the Irish Citizen Army. Julia went to Dundalk, County Louth as one of the many women couriers sent around the country to alert activists to the changed date of the Rising. During Easter week she was a dispatch carrier, bringing information from the GPO to the various garrisons in the city. Together with Elizabeth, she brought the *War News*, a broadsheet produced by the insurgents, to the printers. She was one of the last women in the GPO, remaining until its evacuation, when they made their way to buildings in Moore Street. Julia was arrested and imprisoned in Kilmainham Gaol until 9 May.

In later years Julia was employed in the Irish Hospital Sweepstakes office in Ballsbridge, Dublin with many other women who had been activists, and also worked as a furrier in a large Dublin store. Julia and Elizabeth supported Eamon de Valera until 1927. Maintaining her belief in the republican ideal throughout her life, Julia was a member of Mná na Poblachta and in 1937 wrote to the newspapers attacking the Fianna Fáil Constitution.

She shared a house on Mount Street with Elizabeth O'Farrell until Elizabeth's death in 1957. Julia died in January 1972 and is buried next to her friend in Glasnevin cemetery.

HARTNETT, SHEILA

(1906–1975)

Sheila Hartnett was the second youngest in a family of eight. Born in Dublin, she moved to County Kerry when she was a child. Her father, a chemist, was originally from Limerick, but moved to Kenmare and set up a pharmacy known as 'The Medical Hall'. During the Civil War the family's sympathy to the republican cause was well known and their chemist shop was burnt by Free State troops. Seventeen-year-old Sheila and her younger brother Noel escaped by climbing on to the back roof.

Sheila was arrested on 25 October 1922 and taken by boat to Tralee Jail where she was held for three months. The story of her imprisonment was reported in the *Irish World* and she was delighted to receive 'a lot of fan mail'. When she was released she went to Dublin where her family had moved after the destruction of their home in Kerry. She joined Cumann na mBan. Her duties included travelling by taxi to Broadstone station to deliver pamphlets and leaflets to Sinn Féin and other clubs around the country. She worked from an office run by Countess Markievicz. When the office was raided, she was recognized by one of the soldiers from her previous imprisonment in Tralee Jail and arrested. She was released from the North Dublin Union on 28 September 1923.

Three years later Sheila married Brian Marten, Captain of the First Battalion, Athlone 1916–1921. Like other Republican sympathisers, she found it difficult to obtain work in the Free State. She finally found employment in the Irish Hospital Sweepstakes office where many of those who had been imprisoned with her now worked.

Sheila and Brian had three daughters, Pamela, Sheila and Fionnuala. During the late 1920s and 1930s the family moved frequently, living with Sheila's mother and in a number of different houses in Dublin.

When she was widowed and her children were grown up, Sheila married Robin MacDonald and went to live with him in the highlands of Scotland. She missed Ireland; they parted and she returned to live with her daughter Sheila in Greystones, County Wicklow. It was there that she died suddenly of a heart attack on 12 May 1975. When he heard of her death, Robin MacDonald committed suicide.

HUMPHREYS, MARY ELLEN (NELL) NÉE RAHILLY

(1871–1939)

RAHILLY, ANNA

(1873–1958)

HUMPHREYS, SIGHLE

(1899–1994)

Mary Ellen and Anna Rahilly were the daughters of Richard Rahilly and Ellen Mangan, prosperous shopkeepers in the small town of Ballylongford in County Kerry. Their only brother, Michael (b.1875) changed the family name to the earlier spelling of O'Rahilly, and adopted the style of The O'Rahilly.

Richard Rahilly died in March 1896. He left his family extremely well off, having made shrewd investments in the stock market as well as running an import and distribution business. The widowed Mrs Rahilly moved to Limerick with her daughter Anna (known as Áine or Anno) and purchased Quinsborough House in Ardnacrusha just outside Limerick City. Anna managed the farm and became part of the 'county set', riding and being entertained by the landed families of the area.

In February 1895 Mary Ellen (Nell) had married David Humphreys, an eye surgeon, and settled in Limerick City. The couple had three children, Richard (Dick) (b.1896) Emmet (b.1902) and Sighle who was born on 26 February 1899.

David Humphreys contracted TB shortly after Sighle's birth and her parents spent much time travelling abroad in the hope of a cure. Tragically, David died in May 1903 when Sighle was just four years old. Nell and her children moved in with her mother and aunt in Quinsborough House.

In 1909 the Humphreys family and Anna uprooted from Limerick and moved to 54 Northumberland Road, Dublin. Anna was involved in nationalist activities from her arrival in Dublin. She was a member of the Gaelic League and was involved in Sinn Féin from 1914 onwards. Anna contributed large amounts of money to various nationalist causes, in particular Irish language schools (she was a fluent Irish speaker, as was Nell and her family), and to Patrick Pearse's school, St Endas. Emmet and Dick Humphreys were pupils at St Endas.

During the Rising, Michael O'Rahilly and Dick Humphreys were in the GPO. Dick, aged nineteen, was there only until Tuesday of Easter Week when his mother insisted that he return home. He later recalled that he was safer in the GPO than going home with his mother. (Michael was shot and died during the evacuation of the GPO – *see* Nancy O'Rahilly biog p196) The Humphreys's home was identified as being occupied by sympathisers of the Rebellion, and, following the surrender, the house was raided and Nell was arrested. She was held in a horsebox in the nearby Royal Dublin Society grounds and later imprisoned in Richmond Barracks.

In the aftermath of the Rising, Anna was involved in the support of the prisoners' dependents and with the National Aid Employment Agency. She also campaigned on behalf of Sinn Féin during the General Election of 1918.

Having completed her schooling in Leeson Street and Mount Anville (where she was head girl) Sighle Humphreys spent a year in Paris (1919–1920). She joined Cumann na mBan in 1919 at the age of twenty and during the summer of 1921 became an organiser for Cumann na mBan in County Kerry.

All members of the household opposed the Treaty. Shortly after the commencement of hostilities in the Civil War, Sighle was involved in looking after the wounded, distributing propaganda and finding safe houses for those on the run. In 1922, when Ernie O'Malley was captured in the Humphreys home, Nell and Sighle were imprisoned. Anna, who had been wounded during the raid, was taken to hospital and subsequently sent to prison. Nell was released in July 1923. Sighle and Anna were among the last of the prisoners released on 29 November following a thirty-one day hunger strike.

Nell was a member of the O'Rahilly Sinn Féin Club in Donnybrook until she resigned from the organisation in 1924. She was active in public life as an elected representative of the Pembroke Borough Council and was very committed to assisting the poor in the area. Throughout her life she had a keen interest in design and gardening. It was she who was responsible for the building of their house on Ailesbury Road; today it contains the offices and consulate of the French Embassy.

Anna was treasurer of the O'Rahilly Sinn Féin Club in Donnybrook until she resigned from the organisation in July 1926. She was a committee member of the

Republican Hostess Committee of the Congress of International Women's League for Peace and Freedom in July 1926. From 1917 she was honorary treasurer of the Patriot Graves Associations. In later life she took up golf and belonged to Elm Park Golf Club from 1926 to 1937. She died in 1958.

After the Civil War Sighle remained a committed republican. She organised lectures, first aid demonstrations and generally tried to keep Cumann na mBan going. One of the main activities was trying to influence jurors in republican cases; Sighle was the author of a pamphlet entitled *Ghosts,* which was sent to jurors telling them why the accused should not be found guilty. Sighle was the Cumann na mBan representative on the Republican Council in 1929. As a result of her activities she was imprisoned in Mountjoy Jail in 1926, 1927, 1928 and 1931. In 1928 she went on a six-day hunger strike to be granted the status of a political prisoner. She wrote to her mother from jail: 'I did my best in ways to keep out ... they wanted me to speak at the Easter Commemorations and a million other things and I didn't, but I did write stuff for Cumann na mBan and here I am.'

She continued with Cumann na mBan and was involved in the Easter Lily Campaign from 1926, to 1965. From 1930 she was also involved with the Boycott British Goods campaign. She gave her support to Saor Éire, the socialist republican organisation, serving as co-treasurer in 1931. In 1934 she belonged to the Republican Congress, but resigned when she found that it was critical of the IRA.

In 1935 Sighle married Donal O'Donoghue (1897–1957) a member of the Dublin Brigade of the IRA and later member of the Army Council and editor of *An Phoblacht* from 1934. They had two children, Dara (b.1936) who died at birth, and a daughter, Cróine (b.1939). Donal was imprisoned in 1936 for making seditious speeches. In the 1940s he was involved with Clann na Poblachta, and was chairman of the National Executive and Standing Committee.

When Eithne Coyle resigned as president of Cumann na mBan in 1941, Sighle tried to keep the organisation going but it failed to enrol new members. By this time the organisation was gone in all but name. She continued to be active in other spheres of public life, campaigning on various issues and was in the Ladies Association of the St Vincent de Paul Society from 1937 to 1975 and the Political Prisoners Committee up to 1949. She took part in campaigns promoting the use of the Irish language in the Mass as well as on television, was part of the anti-EEC lobby, and prisoners' dependants campaigns from 1951 until 1989.

She supported republicanism until her death, communicating with prisoners in the H-Block, Long Kesh and Belfast during the 1970s and 1980s. During her latter years she attempted to write a history of Cumann na mBan. Her material for this book as well as her vast collection of papers is housed in University College Dublin Archives. She died in Dublin on 14 March 1994.

JOHNSTON MACMANUS, ANNA (ETHNA CARBERY)

(1864–1902)

Anna Isabella Johnston, who became better known by her pen name Ethna Carbery, was born on 3 December 1864 in the family home at Byran Street, Ballymena in County Antrim. Her father, Robert Johnston, was a successful timber merchant and owner of a number of saw mills. He was known as 'Johnston of the North', because he travelled by foot all over Ulster recruiting members for the Irish Republican Brotherhood. He was later a representative on the Supreme Council of the IRB.

Charles Stewart Parnell and other political figures of the day visited Anna's childhood home in Belfast. It is not surprising, therefore, that Anna developed an interest in the Irish Ireland movement and in Irish nationalism. She and her father were active in the Kickham Literary Society. Anna's poems were published in nationalist newspapers such as the *Irish Nation* and *United Ireland,* under the name of Ethna Carbery. With her friend Alice Milligan she was editor of the *Northern Patriot* (October to December 1895). From 1896 until 1899 they ran their own newspaper, the *Shan Van Vocht* (Poor Old Woman), which was produced in an office in the Johnston timber yard. The newspaper was 'devoted to the fostering and advancing of Irish Patriotism, Irish Literature, Irish Language and Irish Independence.' Alice was editor, while Anna was secretary. Anna and Alice also did much of the writing for the newspaper but other contributors included James Connolly, Dr Douglas Hyde and Seamus MacManus who later became Anna's husband.

In 1898 Anna was active in the centenary celebrations of the 1798 Rebellion. She toured the country, lecturing on the United Irishmen and their Rebellion. During this period she and her family were active members of the Gaelic League, promoting the use of the Irish language. In 1900 she attended the first meeting of Inghinidhe na hÉireann and was appointed a vice-president of the organisation.

Anna married Seamus MacManus in August 1901 and they set up home in a house on the Mount in Seamus's native village, Mountcharles, just outside Donegal town. They moved to Revlon House, closer to Donegal town, shortly afterwards, when Anna became unwell.

Her verses and books on Irish folklore were gaining popularity with Irish Americans but she did not live to enjoy this fame. She died in April 1902 at the age of thirty-seven. She was buried in Frosses graveyard in County Donegal, where, in her husband's words, 'The purple mountains guard her. The valley folds her in'. It would be fifty-eight years before Seamus was laid to rest beside her. She is best remembered for her volume of poetry *The Four Winds of Éirinn*, which was published in 1902 after her death.

KEARNS, LINDA
(1889–1951)

Linda Kearns was born in Cloonagh, Dromard, County Sligo the second youngest of eight children of Thomas Kearns and Catherine Clarke. Named Bridget, she became known as Belinda at school, which became shortened to Linda. She was taught locally until the age of fourteen when she went to Belgium to continue her education. From 1907 she trained as a nurse in the Royal City of Dublin Hospital in Baggot Street. She was a brilliant student, taking first place and first class honours in her final examinations. For a time before the outbreak of the First World War in 1914 she travelled as a private nurse to Lindsay M O'Connor, spending time in France, Switzerland and Egypt. On his death in February 1916 he left her a large legacy.

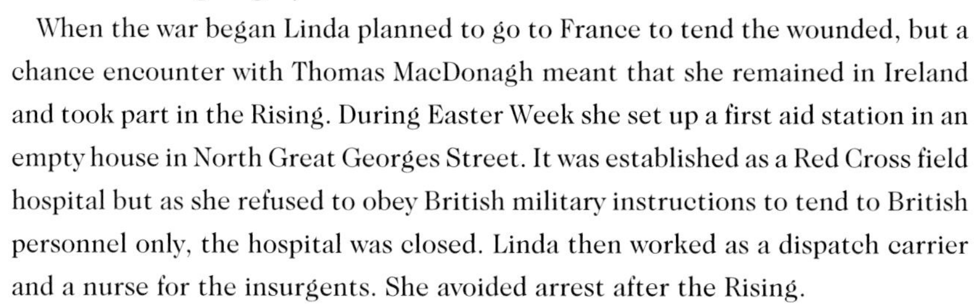

When the war began Linda planned to go to France to tend the wounded, but a chance encounter with Thomas MacDonagh meant that she remained in Ireland and took part in the Rising. During Easter Week she set up a first aid station in an empty house in North Great Georges Street. It was established as a Red Cross field hospital but as she refused to obey British military instructions to tend to British personnel only, the hospital was closed. Linda then worked as a dispatch carrier and a nurse for the insurgents. She avoided arrest after the Rising.

In 1918 Linda was a nurse on Achill Island off the Mayo coast during the influenza epidemic of that year. On her return to Dublin she ran a nursing home in Gardiner Place. Kathleen Clarke was a patient there after her release from prison in 1919. The nursing home also served as a safe house for men on the run. Linda also spied for Michael Collins and carried messages and explosives. Although she lectured for Cumann na mBan, she was never a member of the organisation.

In November 1920, while living with her sister Annie in Sligo, she worked for the IRA. She was arrested in Sligo when she was caught smuggling a large consignment of arms. She was held in a number of prisons in Ireland and also in Walton Prison in Liverpool. She went on hunger strike in Walton and was transferred back to Ireland to finish her sentence in Mountjoy Jail. She escaped from Mountjoy in October 1921 and was sheltered in an IRA training camp in Carlow until the signing of the Anglo-Irish Treaty in December 1921. In 1922 she collaborated with the author Annie M P Smithson on an account of her life, *In Times of Peril: Leaves from the Diary of Nurse Linda Kearns, from Easter Week 1916 to Mountjoy 1921*.

An opponent of the Treaty, Linda attempted to enter the Four Courts when fighting commenced on 28 June 1922. When she failed, she joined the garrison at Barry's Hotel. During the fighting in Dublin from 30 June to 5 July she tended the wounded in various republican garrisons in O'Connell Street. In autumn 1922, at the request of Eamon de Valera, she and a number of other women went to the United States to raise money and support for the republican cause. She returned to Ireland in the spring of 1924, but by the autumn she was on her way to Australia with Kathleen Maloney, (sister of Kevin Barry, killed in the War of Independence). The women spent five months fundraising and lecturing over there.

She became a founder member of Fianna Fáil and was elected to the executive, a position she maintained until her death. In 1929 she married Charles William MacWhinney (known as Wilson) who had been in the IRA in the War of Independence. They had one child, Ann, who was born the following year. Despite her family commitments, during the 1930s Linda continued her role in public life. She was a government appointee to several organisations and committees: the General Nursing Council in 1934; the Visiting Committee of Mountjoy Jail in 1936 and in 1939 the newly-formed Irish Red Cross. Although a supporter of Eamon de Valera, Linda joined the National Council of Women to fight for women's equality when Fianna Fáil introduced the discriminatory Conditions of Employment Bill in 1935 and the Constitution of 1937. In 1938 Linda became a senator, nominated by the Women's Industrial Development Association of which she was a founder member and later president (1938). She was secretary of the Irish Nurses' Association and a member of the National Council of Nurses for many years. In 1941 she cut down on her public activities when Ann became ill with a brain tumour; a condition from which she recovered after almost a year. This period also saw the break up of Linda and Wilson's marriage.

In 1946 Linda fulfilled a long-held ambition when she set up the Kilrock Nurses' Convalescent and Holiday Home in Howth, County Dublin. The International Committee of the Red Cross presented her with the Florence Nightingale Medal in May 1951 for her work on behalf of the nursing profession. At the time Linda was terminally ill with cancer and the medal was presented to her on her sickbed. She died in Howth on 5 June 1951.

LAVERY, HARRIETTE E
(D.1923)

LAVERY, MAYNIE
(1901–1976)

Harriette E Lavery (née Higgins) moved to Dublin from Belfast in 1918. A widow with two children, she was a supporter of the Irish Parliamentary Party and Home Rule. By 1918, Edward Carson was gaining widespread support in the North and the unionist majority dominated. Harriette knew that she and her family could be victimised because of her politics. When a friend alerted her that her house was to 'be torched', she immediately left Belfast, instructing a cousin to close the family's photographic business.

Harriette's daughter, Maynie, who was seventeen when they arrived in Dublin, joined Cumann na mBan. During the War of Independence Maynie took part in Cumann na mBan activities, and although her mother did not belong to the

organisation, she provided a safe house for Volunteers. The Lavery family lived in Howth, a village on the north Dublin coast, nine miles from the city, where they ran a hotel called the 'Dalriada'. A safe room was built in the hotel especially to house men on the run.

On 1 March 1923 Harriette and Maynie were arrested following a raid on their premises in North Earl Street in Dublin, where they ran a photographic business and café at Number 13. They were held in Kilmainham Gaol for a period and later transferred to the North Dublin Union. While Maynie and her mother were imprisoned, Maynie's boyfriend, a Volunteer named Ned Reid (also known as Eamonn), was also in prison in Marlborough Jail (now Portlaoise Prison).

Harriette was released first; she was already suffering from anthrax, a rare infection spread by spores, which the family always believed came from contaminated straw in the North Dublin Union. Maynie went on hunger strike in the North Dublin Union in November 1923 and was released a short time later. Her mother died a few weeks after she returned home, just days after Christmas 1923. Maynie later went on to marry Ned Reid and they had three children, two boys and a girl. They continued to live in Howth where Maynie ran the hotel until it had to be sold in 1944. Ned operated a hardware and general supply shop in the village. The couple were founder members of the Fianna Fáil party. Maynie lived into her seventies and died in October 1976.

LLEWELYN DAVIES, MOYA NÉE O'CONNOR
(1881–1944)

In James Joyces's *Ulysses* Leopold Bloom muses on the sad fate of an O'Connor family who died after being poisoned by mussels from Dublin Bay. This episode is based on the real-life tragedy that befell Moya Llewelyn Davies' family in 1890.

Moya O'Connor was just nine years old when, in the space of one day, she lost her mother and her sisters Annie (13), Aileen, (11), Kathleen (7) and Norah, who was just five years old. On 30 June 1890 the O'Connor children had been sent to the seafront to gather mussels, but instead collected them from a contaminated pool at the rear of their house at Seapoint Avenue, Blackrock. Annie, the eldest girl, prepared the shellfish, and her sisters, mother and a servant all ate the mussels. They died within hours. The family story has always been that Moya was naughty and sent upstairs without her tea.

Moya was one of five daughters of James O'Connor and his wife Mary, known as Molly. By the time of Moya's birth her father had already led an eventful life. He was arrested in 1865, aged twenty-seven, when he was working as a book-keeper in the offices of the *Irish People* newspaper. His crime is noted in the Kilmainham register as 'feloniously conspiring to depose the Queen'. He controlled one of the circles of the Irish Republican Brotherhood in Dublin. He was released from jail in 1869 and began reorganising the Supreme Council of the IRB. He became editor of the IRB newspaper, the *Irishman,* and later of the *Shamrock* and was on the staff of the *United Irishmen* during the Land War. He was arrested again in 1881 and held in Kilmainham Gaol. Moya's great grandfather had been executed in Dunlavin, County Wicklow during the 1798 Rising. It was into this nationalist household that Moya was born in 1881. The writer Charles Kickham, also a member of the IRB, lived with the family, but died when Moya was a baby.

After the tragedy in 1890 Moya and her father immediately left the family home never to reside in it again. It is not recorded what effect the deaths had on Moya, but her father's health went into decline. However, he continued to pursue his nationalist ideals and entered into parliamentary politics to try to achieve change. He served as a Member of Parliament for West Wicklow in Westminster in 1892 and remained an MP until his death in 1910.

Moya became estranged from her father when he married a Miss McBride in 1899. She went to live with her aunt in London and joined the British Civil Service. Moya married Crompton Llewelyn Davies, twenty-eight years her senior, whom she met at a Liberal Party rally. Crompton Llewelyn Davies was Lloyd George's solicitor and Solicitor General of the British Post Office. The couple had two children, Richard (b.1912) and Katherine (b.1915).

Michael Collins became a friend of the Llewelyn Davies's during his time in London. He met Moya at a *céilí* in Islington. During the War of Independence Moya was an activist. She and her husband opened their home to an Irish delegation, which included Michael Collins, that came to London in 1919 hoping to meet with American President Woodrow Wilson who was en route to the Peace Conference in Versailles. The Llewelyn Davies's Dublin home in Furry Park, Killester, which they purchased in 1920, was also frequently used for meetings by Collins and his associates. The house was raided often but no weapons were ever found. Moya carried guns in her car from Cork and Tipperary on behalf of the Irish Republican Army. On one such occasion she got a flat tyre and was helped by the Auxiliaries, but the guns remained undetected. On another occasion she was with Collins and some others in a café in the centre of Dublin when the café was raided by the military. Collins passed his gun to Moya who slipped it into her elasticised underwear and the party was able to leave without it being discovered.

Moya was arrested in 1921 and held in Mountjoy Jail. As a result of her imprisonment her husband was dismissed from his job, but was immediately offered a partnership in a firm of solicitors in London.

It was rumoured that Moya had a relationship with Michael Collins; she wrote her own account of this but it remained unpublished when she received death threats. Her husband assisted Collins by providing information on the British delegates during the Treaty negotiations and later helped him draft the Constitution that was presented during the negotiations. He was appointed Arbitrator and Inspector General in Land Matters in the Irish Free State.

Moya was passionate about the Irish language and, along with George Thomson, she translated Maurice O'Sullivan's autobiography *Fiche Bliain Ag Fás (Twenty Years A-Growing)* which detailed his life on the Great Blasket Island. O'Sullivan's book was published in Irish in Dublin in 1933 and in the same year the English translation was published in London.

Crompton Llewelyn Davies died suddenly of a heart attack in 1936. Moya spent her latter years in Newtownmountkennedy in County Wicklow, living in a house that was owned by her friend, the Danish writer Signe Toksvig and her husband Francis Hackett. She died in 1944.

LYNN, DR KATHLEEN

(1874–1955)

The daughter of an Anglican rector, Kathleen Florence Lynn was born in Mullafarry, near Killala in County Mayo on 28 January 1874. Part of her childhood was spent in County Longford but by the age of twelve she was again living in Mayo. When she was young she noticed that the local doctor was 'the fount of help and hope' and she decided to become a doctor. She received her medical degree from Royal University in 1899. She was the first female resident at the Royal Victoria Eye and Ear Hospital, Dublin. She also worked at a number of other hospitals, including Sir Patrick Dun's Hospital, Dublin city.

In 1904 she set up general practice at 9 Belgrave Road in the suburb of Rathmines. A supporter of the Labour movement during the Lock Out in 1913, she took part in humanitarian aid and joined the Irish Citizen Army, serving as Captain and Chief Medical Officer. In this capacity she served in the garrison at City Hall during the 1916 Rising. She was imprisoned in Mountjoy Jail and later exiled to England for a period. When she returned to Ireland no hospital would employ her. She was elected to the Sinn Féin executive in 1917. During the period of armed resistance that followed, Dr Lynn attended the wounded. She made her house calls in disguise and her house was repeatedly raided. Arrested in 1918, she was released through the intervention of the Lord Mayor of Dublin to help treat patients of the 1918 'flu epidemic.

In 1919 she and her friend Madeleine ffrench-Mullen established Ireland's first infant hospital, St Ultan's. They sought to reduce Ireland's infant mortality, which at the time was one of the highest in the world. Kathleen Lynn pioneered the use of the BCG vaccination and promoted the work of Maria Montessori who visited St Ultan's in 1934. She opposed the Anglo-Irish Treaty of 1921, and although she was elected to the Dáil, she did not take her seat. By 1926 she began to withdraw from active politics but remained a councillor, serving on the Rathmines Urban District Council until 1930.

In her later years Kathleen Lynn was vice-president of *Save the German Children*, an organisation that found homes in Ireland for German children during the Second World War. She was eighty years old when she attended her last clinic in St Ultan's in the spring of 1955. She died the following September and was buried with full military honours.

LYONS THORNTON, BRIGHID

(C.1898–1987)

Brought up in the midlands town of Longford, Brighid's father was a Fenian and had been imprisoned in Sligo for his nationalist activities before she was born. He had married late in life and was already an elderly man when Brighid was a child. Despite his age, he joined the Volunteers as soon as it was formed. Brighid became a member of Cumann na mBan. The first big event in which she was involved was the O'Donovan Rossa funeral, where she sold flags and badges. Brighid was home on holidays from the university in Galway, where she was studying medicine, when news came of the Rising in Dublin. On Tuesday morning, 25 April she accompanied her uncle Frank to Dublin. They joined another uncle, Joe MacGuinness, who was in the Four Courts garrison. Brighid became a dispatch carrier during the fighting. She was arrested and imprisoned in Kilmainham Gaol, but was one of those who obtained early release in May. She returned to Galway and recommenced her studies, qualifying as a doctor in 1922.

In spring 1917 Brighid set up a branch of Cumann na mBan in Galway. During the War of Independence she was attached to the Longford Brigade under General Seán MacEoin. She was given the rank of commandant and was at times personally responsible to Michael Collins in his capacity as Director of Organisation and Intelligence for the Volunteer movement. She supported the Treaty and was invited to join the medical service of the newly formed Free State army. She was given the rank of first lieutenant, thus becoming the first female commissioned officer in the Irish army. She was one of those responsible for establishing the Irish Army Medical Service in 1922. In this capacity she saw the takeover of King George V Hospital (now St Bricins).

Brighid was given responsibility for the anti-Treaty prisoners in Kilmainham Gaol, many of whom were her former comrades. At this time she was suffering with tuberculosis and she went to Nice to recuperate. There she met Edward (Eddie) Thornton, a Free State captain who also had TB. They were married in 1926.

Brighid had studied social and preventative medicine and qualified with a degree in public health from the National University of Ireland in 1927. She spent her medical career in the public health sector. She was State Medical Officer in the department of Maternity and Child Welfare for County Dublin. In the 1930s she was involved in pioneering the use of the BCG vaccination scheme to combat TB in Ireland. She served as medical officer for tuberculosis patients in the Kildare Board of Health, and also in Cork and became Assistant Medical Officer for Dublin Health Authority. She worked as a medical inspector and operated clinics at the Carnegie Centre in Lord Edward's Street, Dublin. In 1946 her husband died. The couple were childless.

After retirement, Brighid worked on medical research in Trinity College. In her late seventies she suffered impaired vision and had difficulty walking but she continued to do voluntary work in the Rotunda Maternity Hospital. She died in 1987.

MACARDLE, DOROTHY

(1889–1958)

Dorothy Macardle was the daughter of Sir Thomas Macardle, owner of the Dundalk Brewery, Macardle, Moore & Co. Ltd. She was educated at Alexandra College, Dublin (1907–1911) and in 1914 was awarded her Teacher's Diploma. Dorothy joined the staff of Alexandra College in 1919 as an English lecturer. Even at this stage she had a very different outlook from other members of staff, who were loyalists and unionists. She encouraged her students to read and perform the writings of WB Yeats and J M Synge. During the War of Independence she lived in a flat in Maud Gonne MacBride's house and was secretly producing publicity for Sinn Féin.

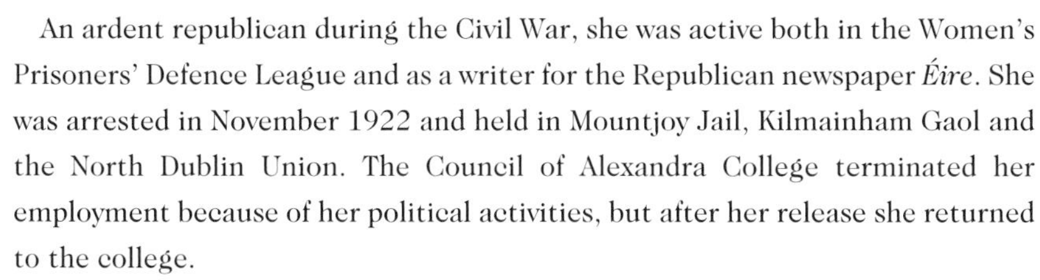

An ardent republican during the Civil War, she was active both in the Women's Prisoners' Defence League and as a writer for the Republican newspaper *Éire*. She was arrested in November 1922 and held in Mountjoy Jail, Kilmainham Gaol and the North Dublin Union. The Council of Alexandra College terminated her employment because of her political activities, but after her release she returned to the college.

A founder member of the Fianna Fáil Party, she served on the National Executive. From the early 1930s she was theatre critic for the *Irish Press*. In 1936 she became vice-chairperson of the National Council for Women. Encouraged by Eamon de Valera, she wrote a history of Ireland 1916–1923, which was published in 1937 as *The Irish Republic*. One of her ghost stories, *Uneasy Freehold,* became a bestseller both in England and the United States and was made into a film entitled *The Uninvited* in the 1940s. In the late 1940s she concerned herself with refugee children and her book *Children of Europe* (London, 1949) recounts the story of children in war-torn Europe. She became vice-president and then president of the Irish Association of Civil Liberties (1949–1951). Dorothy never married. She died aged sixty-nine in December 1958.

MACSWINEY, MARY

(1872–1942)

Mary MacSwiney, the eldest of nine children (seven survived to adulthood), was born in Surrey on 27 March 1872 to John MacSwiney and Mary Anne Wilkinson. When she was six, the family came to Ireland and settled in Cork, where her father started a snuff and tobacco factory. This business failed when Mary was fifteen, and her father left for Australia to seek a better living. His wife set up a corner shop and maintained the family; John never returned, dying in Australia in

October 1895. Mary spent a lot of time in hospital during her early life; once for a period of twelve months. An untreated infection in her foot caused her great pain, eventually it was amputated and she had to wear a surgical boot for the rest of her life.

At the age of twenty Mary gained admission to Cambridge University. After graduation she became a teacher and taught for a time at a boarding school in Farnborough run by the Order of St Benedict. At one point Mary considered joining the Order. Following the death of her mother in 1904, she returned to Cork where she became active in the Munster Women's Franchise League. In time her interest in obtaining the vote for women was replaced by her interest in nationalism, which was inspired by her younger brother Terence. Mary was a founder member of the Gaelic League, and the inaugural meeting of the Cork branch of Cumann na mBan was held in the MacSwiney house in Blackrock.

Her sympathies were well known to the authorities and she was arrested in the aftermath of the 1916 Rising in her classroom at St Angela's, the Ursuline High School. After her release she was dismissed from her teaching post. However, the following year she founded her own private girls school, St Ita's, with her younger sister Annie.

Mary joined Sinn Féin at the Ard Fheis in 1917 and became one of its key workers in Cork. In 1918 she was involved in the anti-conscription movement and campaigned for her brother in the general election of that year. Terence was appointed Lord Mayor of Cork in March 1920, and like many other Sinn Féin supporters who took up office, he was arrested. In August 1920 he was held in Brixton Prison where he went on hunger strike. Mary travelled to London to be with her brother, spending time with him and dealing with the media and talking to interest groups. Terence died after seventy-four days on hunger strike. Following his death, Mary went to the United States to highlight conditions in Ireland, giving evidence before the American Commission in Washington. She remained in the US at the request of Eamon de Valera and promoted the cause of recognition of the Irish Republic.

In May 1921 Mary was elected to the second Dáil. Vehemently opposed to the Treaty, she gave a three hour speech on the subject in the Dáil. When the Treaty was accepted, she joined Eamon de Valera and walked out of the Dáil. During the Civil War Mary was imprisoned on two separate occasions. In November 1922 she was arrested in Nannie O'Rahilly's house and was imprisoned in Mountjoy Jail where she went on hunger strike. She was arrested again in April 1923 en route to Liam Lynch's funeral, and taken to Kilmainham Gaol. She was released on 2 May after spending nineteen days on hunger strike. In August 1923 she was again successful in the elections, but did not take her seat as it would have required taking an oath of allegiance to the British monarch.

After the Civil War she continued to work with Cumann na mBan and Sinn Féin, for whom she became Publicity Director. She defiantly advocated military opposition to the Irish Free State. In 1924 she went on a fundraising tour of the

United States on behalf of republicans. She toured extensively, but by now support and funding had reduced substantially. She supported Eamon de Valera until he broke with Sinn Féin and established Fianna Fáil. In the 1927 elections she ran again in Cork but was defeated; she blamed her poor result on the split in the republican ranks.

For the rest of her life she refused to recognise the legitimacy of the Irish Free State, remaining committed to the Second Dáil, seeing it, as her biographer Charlotte Fallon suggest, 'as the last bastion of true Republicanism'. She still ran her school, but was often in financial difficulties, as it received no government endowments. In 1932 Mary's health began to decline. Her hunger strikes had taken a toll on her digestion and she suffered with heart and kidney problems. That year, Terence's fourteen-year-old daughter, Máire Óg, came to live with her in Cork. For Mary it was a source of great joy as she had been estranged from Máire Óg who had been living in Germany for many years. In 1933 she resigned from Cumann na mBan when the organisation switched allegiance from the Second Dáil. The following year Mary resigned from Sinn Féin because members were accepting government jobs. In 1938 she and the remaining members of the Second Dáil came together, and, with Mary's encouragement, the decision was reached that the authority of the Second Dáil would pass to the Irish Republican Army. She died on 8 March 1942 at the age of seventy. At her own request, her funeral was quiet and devoid of public display. She was buried in St Joseph's cemetery, Cork.

MARKIEVICZ, COUNTESS NÉE CONSTANCE GORE-BOOTH

(1868–1927)

Constance was born into the Anglo-Irish Gore-Booth family of Lissadell, County Sligo and until her late twenties lived a life typical of a woman of her class. She participated in the London and Dublin seasons and in 1887 was presented to Queen Victoria. In 1893 she began studying art at the Slade, London and then in Paris from 1898. From this time onwards Constance began a lifestyle that would ultimately alienate her from her family. In 1900 she married a penniless Polish count, Casimir de Markievicz, a widower with a young son. They lived in his home in the Ukraine for a time before returning to Ireland in 1903. Their daughter, Maeve, was born in 1901; she was given into the care of Lady Gore-Booth and brought up at Lissadell. The Markievicz marriage was not a success; the couple separated and Casimir left Dublin. Thereafter, the Countess, as she was known, became increasingly interested in nationalism and social issues. She joined Inghinidhe na hÉireann in 1907, and contributed to its paper, *Bean na hÉireann*. She later joined Cumann na mBan. Together with Bulmer Hobson, she founded a youth organisation for boys, the Fianna, in 1909. During the Lock Out of 1913, in which workers who supported the union were shut out of their places of employment, the Countess assisted in the soup kitchens and joined the Irish Citizen Army, formed to protect the workers. During the 1916 Rising, she was Second-in-Command at the St Stephen's Green and College of Surgeons garrisons. She was sentenced to death for her part in the Rising, but her sentence was commuted to life imprisonment because she was a woman. She was sent to Aylesbury Jail in England where she was held until June 1917. While in prison she was re-elected president of Cumann na mBan. In the 1918 general election she became the first female elected to the House of Commons. She did not take her seat as she supported the Sinn Féin policy of abstentionism.

She was Minister for Labour in the First Dáil (1919–1921), but spent much of this period in prison. The Countess opposed the Treaty and argued vehemently against its acceptance in Dáil debates. During the Civil War she took part in the fighting, helped to edit the republican newspaper *Éire* from Glasgow, and went on a fundraising trip to the United States. Arrested again in 1923, she was held in the North Dublin Union. Although returned as an abstentionist TD for Dublin City South in the general election of 1923, she refused to take the Oath of Allegiance and so did not enter the Dáil. The Countess joined the Fianna Fáil party at its foundation in 1926, giving up her position in Cumann na mBan to do so. She was elected to the Dáil in 1927 but died on 15 July, 1927 before Fianna Fáil entered government.

MILLIGAN, ALICE
(1866–1953)

Alice Letitia Milligan was born on 14 September 1866 in Gortmore, near Omagh in County Tyrone. She was the daughter of a wealthy Methodist businessman, Seaton Milligan, who had married a widow, Charlotte Burns, four years previously. Alice was the third child in a family of thirteen. Seaton Milligan was an antiquarian and local historian, and a member of the Royal Academy. Alice's sister Charlotte (later Mrs Fox) was a folk music collector and founded the Irish Folk Song Society in London.

The family moved to Belfast when Alice was twelve and she was educated at the Methodist College in Belfast. From 1886 to 1887 she studied English literature at the women's classes at King's College, London. In 1887, at the age of twenty-one, she became a governess at the Ladies' Collegiate in Derry. While her siblings travelled to Europe to further their education, Alice went to Dublin in 1888 to study Irish. During this time she met Michael Davitt, W B Yeats and others who were playing their part in the Irish Renaissance. Returning home, she made her living as a writer and poet, often using the pseudonym 'Irish Olkyrn' or simply I.O. With her father, she co-wrote a guidebook, *Glimpses of Erin,* which was published in 1888. Later she wrote a novel entitled *A Royal Democrat* and contributed a column, 'Notes from the North' to a Dublin newspaper, the *Weekly Independent.*

The Milligan family moved to a new home in the historic area of Cave Hill in

Belfast. In this new community Alice met a number of nationalists, including the woman who for many years was her collaborator and friend, Anna Johnston (Ethna Carbery). Together they were joint editors of the *Northern Patriot*, a nationalist newspaper, in 1895. From 1896 they produced the newspaper the *Shan Van Vocht* (Poor Old Woman) with Alice as editor.

In 1898 she was active in the Belfast commemorations of the 1798 Rebellion. She published a *Life of Theobald Wolfe Tone* and toured the country giving lectures. Alice maintained her interest in the Irish language, which she studied for the rest of her life. She worked as an organiser and then as a lecturer for the Gaelic League. She later recalled that Patrick Pearse objected to her involvement in the Gaelic League because she was not a fluent speaker; he felt she should be raising money and not teaching the Irish language.

Alice was director of a number of *tableaux vivants* staged by Inghinidhe na hÉireann. The Irish Literary Theatre staged her play *The Last Feast of the Fianna* in 1900 and Inghinidhe na hÉireann staged *The Harp that Once* and *The Deliverance of Red Hugh* in 1901. In 1902 her friend Anna Johnston died. In 1903 Alice's unpublished novel *The Cromwellians* was reworked as a play, 'The Daughter of Donagh' and was serialised in the *United Irishman*. This play was staged in Cork in 1905.

She contributed poetry to a number of Irish newspapers and it is as a poet that Alice Milligan is best remembered. 'The Return of Lugh Lamh-Fada' was written in 1893; in 1906 a number of her poems were included in the book *New Songs*. In the foreword Æ (George Russell) describes her writing as 'the best patriotic poetry of Ireland' in his lifetime. Henceforth she wrote in her own name or its Irish form, Eilis Ní Maeleagain. In 1908 her book of poetry, *Hero Lays* was published, it included her most famous poem, 'When I was a Little Girl'.

During this time she was taken up with family responsibilities. As the unmarried daughter, she looked after her aging parents. In 1916 she was to lose both her parents and her sister Charlotte. After the 1916 Rising she visited the prisons, writing a number of poems, including 'Arbour Hill, May 1916'. She travelled to London for the trial of her friend Roger Casement, and was among the crowd that gathered outside Pentonville Prison on the day he was hanged.

Her personal life was difficult; she was in her early fifties, with no steady income or family property. From 1919 she lived with her brother Ernest and his family in Bath. As she wrote to Sinéad de Valera: 'Since the opening of 1919 I have been more or less a prisoner, entirely secluded by circumstances amongst relatives entirely opposed to the Republican cause.' The following year she and her brother William came to live in Dublin. It was during the War of Independence, and William, as a former Captain in the British Army, was given twenty-four hours to leave or be shot. They left Dublin and lived in rented accommodation in the north of Ireland. The Civil War was deeply upsetting to Alice and she wrote 'Till Ferdia Came' which was described by an admirer of her work as the only good thing to come out of the Civil War.

In 1922 Alice and William returned to Bath, where Alice became governess and companion to her nieces. Her nationalist sentiments meant that she was under surveillance by the authorities, but she was estranged from all political activities. She and her brother came back to Ireland in 1932 and lived in the village of Mountfield near Omagh. Her role as carer continued until the late 1930s as she nursed her brother, nephew and sister-in-law through their final illnesses.

By now Alice was virtually destitute, her writings bringing in only a small income. Yet even in old age she sustained the passion of her youth. In 1938 she lobbied against partition, bringing out a pamphlet with the Northern Ireland Council for Unity. In the early 1940s she went to live with friends in Kells, County Antrim. In 1941 the National University of Ireland conferred her with an Honorary Doctorate of Literature. MH Gill & Son Ltd brought out a volume of her verses entitled *We Sang for Ireland* edited by Seamus MacManus. To fulfil her wish that her last days would be spent near her childhood home, she went to live with the McSwiggan family in Tyrcur, outside Omagh. She died there in April 1953.

The following year a volume of her poetry, entitled *Poems*, was published in Dublin. Tragically, Alice Milligan's grave in Drumragh near Omagh has been the focus of sectarian violence; the headstone, which carries the inscription '*Níor car fód eile ach Éirinn*' (she loved no other land but Ireland) has been attacked with chisels and explosives.

MOLONY, HELENA
(1884–1967)

Inspired by a speech given by Maud Gonne in August 1903, nineteen-year-old Helena Molony joined Inghinidhe na hÉireann. From the outset she had a major role in the organisation. As Maud Gonne had two children and was dividing her time between Ireland and France, Helena effectively ran the organisation from 1902 onwards. She adopted the Gaelic name of Emer, and came up with the idea of setting up a newspaper called *Bean na hÉireann,* of which she became editor. It was Helena who recruited Countess Markievicz into Inghinidhe na hÉireann. In 1909 she was one of the founding members of the Fianna, the youth organisation for boys. The original discussions for the formation of this organisation took place in her brother Frank's house.

Helena belonged to Count Markievicz's dramatic company and acted in plays such as *The Devil's Disciple* and *Eleanor's Enterprise.* She also took part in the plays and tableaux staged by Inghinidhe na hÉireann, and, like other members of the organisation, became an actress in the Abbey Theatre. Between 1911–1913 she earned her living as an actress. Helena played the mother in *Cathleen Ní Houlihan* when Lady Gregory made a rare stage appearance as Cathleen.

In 1911 Helena was arrested for protesting against the visit of King George V to Dublin. She was the first female political prisoner since members of the Ladies Land League were arrested in the 1880s. Sentenced to a month in prison for refusing to pay her fine, she served only fourteen days. Ironically, her fine was paid by Anna Parnell of the Ladies' Land League; Helena was editing Anna's history of that organisation, *The Tale of a Great Sham*, and Anna wanted her out of prison to finish the work.

In 1913, the year of the Lockout, Helena joined the labour movement. The following year she did secretarial work for James Connolly at a co-op shop on Eden Quay, and in 1915 he asked her to become secretary of the Irish Women Workers' Union. As a member of the Irish Citizen Army she was part of the City Hall garrison in the 1916 Rising. She was arrested and given one of the longest jail sentences. She was held in Kilmainham Gaol and Mountjoy Jail in Dublin as well as in Lewes and Aylesbury Jails in England. She was released at Christmas, 1916. Throughout 1917 she worked to facilitate the amalgamation of all the nationalist movements under the banner of Sinn Féin. During the War of Independence, while she was working in the Abbey Theatre, she assisted Countess Markievicz in the Ministry of Labour and was a courier for Michael Collins and Liam Mellowes. During this period she also served as a District Justice in the republican courts in Rathmines, dealing with minor crimes and small debts. She was not a member of Cumann na mBan, but later was made an honorary member by Lily O'Brennan.

Helena was organising secretary of the Irish Women Workers' Union from 1929 until 1940. As a member of the Dublin Trade Union Council delegation she visited Russia in 1929 as a guest of the Soviet trade union movement. On her return, she set up the Friends of Soviet Russia and lectured extensively on the Soviet Union. She was involved in politics of the far left and was one of the executive members of Saor Éire, a short-lived breakaway republican socialist organisation. In the 1930s she was active in the Women's Prisoners' Defence League and the People's Rights Association. She was an urban district councillor for Rathmines and Rathgar in Dublin city. She campaigned against the Conditions of Employment Bill (1935), brought in by Fianna Fáil, which saw a curtailment of women's rights. Subsequently she became a member of Mná na hÉireann – seeking equal rights and opportunities for women. In 1936 she became president of the Irish Trade Union Congress, only the second woman to attain this position. Ill health forced Helena Molony into early retirement. She died in January 1967.

O'BRENNAN, ELIZABETH (LILY)

(1878–1948)

Born in Dublin, Elizabeth (Lily) O'Brennan was one of four daughters of Elizabeth Butler and Frank O'Brennan. Frank, a nationalist and a member of the Fenian movement, was originally from County Tipperary. He died when Lily was two years old. Her widowed mother was employed as a nurse in the workhouse. Lily and her sisters were educated by the Dominican nuns and later she set up a small private school herself.

Lily was also a writer and contributed to Irish and American publications. By her mid twenties she had written a play, *May Eve in Stephen's Green*, which was produced by Máire Nic Shiúbhlaigh in Father Mathew Hall, and had authored a number of books. *The Call to Arms* was written under her pen name of Esther Graham.

Like her younger sister Fanny (wife of Eamonn Ceannt), Lily became interested in nationalist politics. She joined Cumann na mBan in 1914. Lily lived with the Ceannts and was aware of the plans for the Rising as her brother-in-law was on the Military Council. She was in the Marrowbone Lane garrison during Easter week. Afterwards she was arrested and held in Kilmainham Gaol. On release she worked for the Volunteer Prisoners' Dependents' Fund and joined Sinn Féin. In 1917 she became an executive member of Cumann na mBan, and in 1918 became the first paid secretary of the organisation.

During the War of Independence Lily was a staff member of the Ministry of Labour. In 1921 she was a secretary for the Treaty delegation at 22 Hans Place London. She became secretary to Arthur Griffith In 1922, but later took an anti-Treaty stance and became private secretary to Erskine Childers. She was arrested at the Sinn Féin offices at 23 Suffolk Street in November 1922 and was held in Kilmainham Gaol, Mountjoy Jail and the North Dublin Union. She was also active in the White Cross.

In later years she wrote a number of plays, short stories, children's stories in Irish and English and contributed articles to Irish periodicals, as well as writing an account of the War of Independence, *Leading A Dog's Life in Ireland*. She was a founder member of the Catholic Writers' Guild, established in November 1947. Lily never married and lived with her sister and nephew until her death in May 1948.

O'CALLAGHAN, KATE NÉE MURPHY
(1885-1961)

Katherine (known as Kate or Kitty) Murphy was born at the Old Forge in Lissarda, Crossmahon, near Macroom in County Cork in October 1885. Her parents, Julia Kelleher and Cornelius Murphy, had fourteen children, six boys and eight girls. Eleven of their children survived to adulthood.

The family valued education and the girls were sent to the Ursuline Convent in Cork before travelling to the Dominican Convent in Eccles Street, Dublin. Kate and her sisters, Máire and Bríd, all obtained degrees from the Royal University, followed by teacher training in Cambridge. Another sister, Elsie, went to University College Cork and qualified as a doctor (Elsie was imprisoned in Kilmainham Gaol in 1923 for opposing the Treaty).

Máire moved to Limerick in 1903 to teach at Mary Immaculate College. She married in 1909 and Kate came to Limerick to replace her in her position as Professor of the Methods of Teaching. Kate held this post until she married Michael O'Callaghan, (whose family owned the city tannery), in July 1914, and passed on the job to another sister, Éilis. The sisters were very close; they joined the Gaelic League together and were active in the suffragette movement.

Kate was a founder member of Cumann na mBan and her husband was active in the Limerick branch of the Irish Volunteers. In the aftermath of the Rising, Kate and her sisters worked with Cumann na mBan, collecting money for the Prisoners' Dependents' Fund and organising commemorative Masses. Kate and her husband supported Dáil Éireann in 1919. He became Lord Mayor of Limerick on 30 January 1920 and throughout his term of office was noted for his uncompromising nationalist stance. He received a number of death threats.

Michael O'Callaghan was killed on 7 March 1921 in front of his wife at their home St Margaret's Villa, Limerick. The masked perpetrators were believed to be Black and Tans. Kate, childless, was left a widow at thirty-five. She immediately began a campaign to countermand the authorities' version that her husband had been killed by an extreme element of the IRA. Her pamphlet, *The Limerick Curfew Murders*, was circulated in Ireland, England and America. Although questions were raised in the House of Commons, there was no official inquiry. Kate's sister Máire was appointed acting Mayor of Limerick from May 1921 until January 1922. In 1921 Kate was elected president of Cumann na mBan in Limerick, but she resigned after a year in office.

As one of the so-called 'Black Widows' Kate O'Callaghan was elected to Dáil Éireann in May 1921. She represented Limerick City and Limerick East in the second Dáil. She opposed the Treaty and in 1922 called for increased women's suffrage. She retained her seat in the General Election of June 1922. She joined Eamon de Valera in October 1922 when he created the Second Dáil. She was made a member of the Council of State in the Second Dáil – an illegal gathering since the establishment of the Irish Free State. She was arrested with Mary MacSwiney en route to Liam Lynch's funeral in April 1923 and was taken to Kilmainham Gaol. She went on hunger strike and was released after nineteen days.

Kate lost her seat in the election of June 1923. She was now out of active politics but remained in the illegal second Dáil. For the rest of her life she lived in Limerick with her sisters. She continued to have an interest in the cultural life of the city and was a member of the Limerick Drama Society, Féile Luimnigh, Limerick Art Gallery and the Gaelic League. When she died in March 1961 members of the old IRA carried her coffin draped with the tri-colour. She was buried in Mount St Lawrence cemetery in Limerick next to her husband.

O'CONNELL, TERESA

(1899–1998)

Teresa O'Connell (known as Tessie by her fellow prisoners) was the second youngest of eleven children born to John O'Connell and Marianne O'Sullivan. Both the O'Sullivan and O'Connell families of Caherdaniel, County Kerry were staunch nationalists; a granduncle, Jeremiah O'Sullivan was involved in the Fenian movement.

In the early 1920s Teresa came to Dublin. Her older sister Kathleen, who was Eamon de Valera's secretary, got her a job in the Sinn Féin offices at 23 Suffolk Street. She became a member of Cumann na mBan and acted as courier, transporting guns from one part of the city to another, concealed under a large overcoat. In the raid on the Sinn Féin offices on 9 November 1922 Teresa was arrested along with Madame Bernard Cogley, Rita Bermingham and Kathleen Devaney. They were sent first to Mountjoy Jail, from there to Kilmainham and later to the North Dublin Union. While imprisoned, she became friendly with Dorothy Macardle. One of the stories in Dorothy's book, *Earthbound*, published in 1924, was dedicated to TOC (Teresa O'Connell).

After her release, one of Teresa's first tasks was to bring a parcel to Eamon de Valera, imprisoned in Kilmainham Gaol. Like many former prisoners, she found it difficult to get work in Ireland, so in the late 1920s she went to Chicago where she was employed as governess to a doctor's family. Whilst there she attended night school and was taught shorthand and typing. She returned to Ireland in the early 1930s and worked at the Irish Hospital Sweepstakes. Later she had a job in the Hospital Commission, known as 'the bed bureau', finding hospital places for doctors.

Teresa never married. She did not own a home, and lived alone in a succession of flats in Dublin. Her last address was in Waterloo Road where she lived until the age of eighty-six, at which time she took up residence in the Holy Family Nursing Home in Roebuck, Dublin. In 1997, aged ninety-eight, she was a guest of honour at the launch by President Mary Robinson of *Guns and Chiffon*, an exhibition on the role of Irish women political activists at Kilmainham Gaol.

O'DALY, NORA NÉE GILLIES
(1883–1943)

Nora Maggie Mary Malcolm Gillies was born on 12 August 1883 at 2 Clapham Villas, Terenure (now Terenure Rd East), a suburb of Dublin city. She was the fifth of eight children of John Malcolm Gillies, a Scots Presbyterian, who came to Ireland in 1878 to take up a position as general manager of the *Freeman's Journal*.

In her youth Nora converted to Roman Catholicism along with six of her siblings. Only one brother remained Presbyterian. Like many of her contemporaries, she became committed to the idea of an Irish Ireland. She and her sisters Kathleen and Daisy were involved in the Gaelic League, which promoted the use of the Irish language. Nora was the Minutes Secretary of An Craoibhín branch from 1906 to 1909, which in the early days was located in McDunphy's Pub in Bolton Street and later moved to Capel Street. It was through the Gaelic League that Nora and Daisy met their future husbands, Seamus and Paddy O'Daly, whom they married in a double wedding on 16 May 1910. Nora and Seamus were active members of the nationalist movement. Seamus was a

Volunteer and Nora was a founder member of the Fairview branch of Cumann na mBan. Their home in Clontarf was used to manufacture bombs and other ammunition. Prior to the 1916 Rising Nora was engaged in intelligence gathering for the attempted destruction of the Magazine Fort in the Phoenix Park.

On Easter Monday 1916 Nora O'Daly reported to St Stephen's Green garrison, which was under the command of Michael Mallin and Countess Markievicz. There she was assigned first aid duties. Later she went with the garrison when it occupied the College of Surgeons. After the surrender Nora was imprisoned in Kilmainham Gaol and was there throughout the time of the executions of the leaders. After the Rising, Nora continued to play a prominent role in the nationalist movement. During the War of Independence she was a judge in the Sinn Féin courts in the Fairview/Ballybough District. Nora supported the Treaty of 1921. With the foundation of the new State she worked as a secretary to the committee that oversaw the completion of the work of the Dáil Courts. She also worked for a time in the newly emerging police department in Oriel House, again in a clerical capacity.

Nora retained her interest in all things Irish, especially Irish literature. She wrote prose and poetry and remained interested in politics right up until her death at her home, 'Clooncoora', Jobstown in County Dublin, on 10 May 1943.

O'FARRELL, ELIZABETH

(1883-1957)

Elizabeth O'Farrell was born at 33 City Quay, Dublin on 5 November 1883. She was the second daughter of Christopher O'Farrell and Margaret Kenneah. While her mother ran a shop on the corner of Balfe Lane, her father was employed by Dublin Port and Docks. He died while she was still in school. Elizabeth wanted to be a nurse, but her father's death put an end to that ambition and she had to go to work. She took a job in Armstrong's, a printing firm in Amiens Street.

In an article in *An Phoblacht* on 26 April 1930 Elizabeth recalled that she had worked for Irish freedom from her sixteenth year. She joined Inghindhe na hÉireann in 1906. Espousing all the ideals of this organisation, Elizabeth was remembered as always wearing Irish tweed and clothes of Irish manufacture. With her friend Julia Grenan she also joined Cumann na mBan. They were taught first aid by Dr Kathleen Lynn, and Countess Markievicz trained them in the use of arms.

They were both involved in preparations for the Rising. Elizabeth was one of the couriers sent around the country by the Military Council advising of the change of date of the Rising. Her destination was Athenry, County Galway.

She was attached to the Irish Citizen Army during the 1916 Rising, serving in the GPO and as a dispatch carrier. She brought the *War News,* a broadsheet published by the insurgents during Easter Week, to the printers.

Elizabeth was selected by Patrick Pearse to bring the surrender documents to each of the garrisons to signal the end of the Rising. In photographs, she can be seen standing beside Pearse as he is presenting the letter of surrender. Her account of delivering the surrender documents to each garrison was published in *The Catholic Bulletin* at Christmas 1916. After the Rising, Elizabeth was held in Ship Street Barracks and Kilmainham Gaol but was released after a short period.

She was engaged to Eamonn Kelly, owner of a silver mine in Chile, but the marriage was called off when she decided that she could not leave Ireland. In later life she regretted her action and questioned her solitary existence, saying to her sister Brighid (who had eight children): 'At least you have all your sons and daughter around you.'

Elizabeth remained an ardent republican all her life. She refused to surrender her ideal of a thirty-two county independent Republic. A member of Sinn Féin, she rejected attempts by Fianna Fáil to recruit her. She trained as a midwife in the National Maternity Hospital, Holles Street and later worked as a district nurse. Today there is a memorial to her in the National Maternity Hospital and each year a medal is presented in her honour to the student who achieves second highest marks in midwifery.

O'MULLANE, BRIGHID (BRIDIE)

(1893–1967)

1918 was a seminal year in Brighid O'Mullane's life; her mother died, she left school and she became politicised. It was also the year in which she served her first prison term. Arrested for selling flags without a permit in aid of the starving of Central Europe, she was imprisoned in Sligo for seven days when she refused to pay the fine imposed.

Brighid was friendly with Alderman Hanley and his wife and when Sligo Corporation decided to confer the freedom of the city on Count and Countess Plunkett, she was asked to help organise the banquet. During their stay in Sligo the Count and Countess had their breakfast at the O'Mullane's home. Countess Plunkett told Brighid about Cumann na mBan and, as Brighid later recalled, 'was most anxious that I should start a branch of Cumann na mBan in Sligo.' This she did. The first meeting was held in the Mayor's parlour and Brighid was made honorary secretary. Subsequently, Brighid was asked by Cumann na mBan headquarters to set up branches throughout the county. She travelled on her push bike to Collooney, Kilmacowen, Ballintogher, Screen, Dromard, Grange, Maugherrow, Rathcormack and Ballintrellick. Her recruitment success was noted by headquarters. and at the annual convention of Cumann na mBan in autumn 1918 she was elected to the executive. At the end of the year she was made an official organiser.

Her activities led to the arrest of her father in 1919. He was held in Sligo Gaol and later given three months for sedition. When she was told of his arrest Brighid went to the gaol to protest that her father was not being treated as a political prisoner. She too was arrested, and, as she described it later, was charged with inciting the people 'to murder the police'. In October 1919 she was sentenced to two months imprisonment with hard labour. Her sentence was served in solitary confinement. Her father was in one cell and she was in another, but they were not allowed to meet each other. The highlight of Brighid's stay in prison was the Christmas dinner sent into her by the Ursuline nuns.

On 29 December 1919 she was released; Kit (Ryan) and Seán T O'Kelly held a reception for her at 19 Ranelagh Road, which was attended by members of the executive of Cumann na mBan. There was also a supper and *céilí* in her honour in Enniskillen. From 1918 until 1921 Brighid was a full time organiser for Cumann na mBan. She was described as 'doing excellent work throughout the country organizing branches', and was responsible for setting up branches in Leitrim, Roscommon, Cavan, Fermanagh, Down, Armagh, South Derry, Antrim, Meath, Westmeath, Kildare, Louth and Wexford. In the early years she stayed in hotels, using a false name and in the guise of a technical inspector. Later, when the Black and Tans were drafted in to assist the police force, she had to seek shelter in safe houses. As she travelled the countryside she was constantly at risk: 'a solitary cyclist like myself, whose work entailed being out late at night, was in continuous danger.' During the War of Independence Brighid narrowly escaped been killed in ambushes and once was almost shot as a spy. She recalled later that it would have been easier if she had allowed herself to be arrested and spent this period in prison, but she was determined to continue her work for Cumann na mBan. The years travelling all over the country, out in all weathers, and eating irregular meals, took their toll. By the time of the Truce, her weight was just six-and-half stone. Her health inevitably broke down and she had to seek medical attention.

At the Cumann na mBan convention held while the Anglo-Irish agreement was being negotiated Brighid was re-elected to the executive. Her memory of this time was that the branches of Cumann na mBan were on alert for the resumption of hostilities. She opposed the Treaty and supported the resolution: 'That the organisation of Cumann na mBan affirms its allegiance to the Republic and refuses to accept the Articles of Agreement as signed in London on 6 December 1921.' Before the Dáil vote on the acceptance of the Treaty, she was sent to County Clare on behalf of Cumann na mBan to 'counteract pro-Treaty influences at work'.

The February 1922 convention of Cumann na mBan appointed Brighid as director of propaganda. She now came to live in Dublin full-time. The position was non-paying, so she took a job as secretary to the National Examining Institute. Brighid became attached to the Ranelagh branch of Cumann na mBan, where many of the key activists, including Úna Gordon, Phyllis Ryan, Sighle Humphreys and Lily O'Brennan, were members. She began a monthly paper called *Cumann na mBan*. Brighid wrote the editorials and contributors included Hanna Sheehy Skeffington and Countess Markievicz.

When Civil War hostilities began, Brighid was on holidays in Sligo. She was about to return to Dublin but was told to take over Sligo barracks in preparation for an invasion of the North, but this did not happen. She then made her way to Dublin and was put to work as a courier. As she cycled around the city, she was constantly at risk of being killed. She was fired at by Free State troops but avoided injury. One of her greatest successes was to remove a machine gun and a number of rifles from an abandoned republican outpost on Whitefriars Street. She continued her dispatch work until the surrender of the hotels in July 1922. Her first task after the surrender was to be part of the guard of honour for Cathal Brugha's body in the Mater Hospital; he had been killed in the fighting at the Gresham Hotel.

In July 1922 Brighid was appointed by Tom Derrig to run a publicity department for the republicans. She commandeered the necessary equipment and set up an office in Clare Street, with a staff of three: Máire McKee (sister of Dick McKee), Nellie Hoyne and a courier. They issued a weekly called *The War Bulletin*, made up of dispatches from IRA headquarters detailing information of military engagements throughout the country. The production of the bulletin and other pamphlets continued until the office was raided by Free State troops on 9 November 1922. Brighid was arrested and imprisoned in Mountjoy Jail, Kilmainham Gaol and North Dublin Union. She became a member of the Prisoner's Council and was Officer Commanding of A Wing of Kilmainham Gaol. She was well known and very popular among the prisoners, having recruited many of them during the War of Independence. She was released in October 1923.

Brighid was arrested again in June 1926 for spreading propaganda – posting handbills highlighting the treatment of prisoners in Maryborough Jail (now Portlaoise Prison). She spent two months in Mountjoy Jail with Sighle Humphreys. She remained on the executive of Cumann na mBan until 1927 when she resigned.

By the mid 1930s Brighid was again involved with the organisation, becoming vice-president of the Association of Old Cumann na mBan. In this capacity she collected records of Cumann na mBan 1917–1923 for historical purposes and assisted members to obtain their Military Service pensions. In 1938 she was nominated to the Senate as a representative of Old Cumann na mBan but her nomination was rejected. She continued to be involved in the Women's Prisoners' Defence League and was a founder member of the Irish Red Cross. Brighid never married. She lived on Leinster Road, Rathmines, Dublin, and earned an income by taking in lodgers. She died at the age of seventy-four and is buried in the Republican Plot in Glasnevin cemetery.

O'RAHILLY, NANCY

(1878–1961)

In 1893, when Nancy Brown (known as Nannie) was fifteen, she spent some time in Ireland before going on to finishing school in Paris. The young American, whose

home was on Fifth Avenue in New York, met Michael Rahilly (later The O'Rahilly), then a medical student. During that summer Michael and Nannie were constant companions. Eventually Nannie had to leave for Paris, but a lucky bet on the horses enabled Michael to visit her there. They did not meet again for another three years, but they corresponded throughout the separation. When Nannie became engaged to another man, Michael decided that it was time for him to move to America to be with her. The successful family business in County Kerry was sold, and with his so-called 'marriage settlement' he travelled to the United States.

The couple married on 15 April 1899 and Michael went to work at the Brown family mills. Nannie's first child was born on 14 March 1900 and christened Bobby. They moved to New York, but by 1902 had decided to return to Ireland. The family had settled in Ireland and Michael had become involved with nationalist activities when Bobby died suddenly in June 1903. Nannie was pregnant again and on 3 July 1903 gave birth to another son. He was christened Richard, but always known as Mac. To recover from their bereavement the couple moved to Paris and a short time later to Brighton, where a third son, Egan, (known in later life as Aodogán) was born in 1904. They then lived in London before coming back to Ireland.

In 1905 Michael was asked to return to the United States to oversee the Brown mills. The family duly moved, but losses at the mills mounted and they closed. A fourth son, Niall, was born in Philadelphia in December 1906.

In spring 1909 the O'Rahillys returned to Ireland with their children and lived near Michael's sisters Nell (Humphreys) and Anna (*see* Humphreys biographies, p173). Michael joined Sinn Féin and assisted Arthur Griffith with his paper, the *Sinn Féin Daily*. He also became a member of the Gaelic League and was involved with its activities for the next number of years. Irish was frequently spoken in the home and Nannie also became proficient in the language.

The O'Rahilly family was continuing to grow and in November 1911, Nannie gave birth to another boy, Maolmuire (Myles). By now, Michael was contributing to the *Irish Freedom* newspaper and arguing that Irishmen must be armed to obtain their freedom. However he refused to join the IRB, as he disagreed with secret societies. In 1913 Michael was managing editor of the Gaelic League newspaper, *An Claidheamh Soluis*. It was in this newspaper, at his instigation, that Eoin MacNeill wrote the article 'The North Began', in November 1913, which was the catalyst for the formation of the Volunteers. Nannie O'Rahilly joined Cumann na mBan when it was formed in 1914 and was elected to the Executive Committee. Their two oldest boys joined the Fianna. Although The O'Rahilly was preparing for the Rising at Easter, the loss of arms in Kerry caused him to agree with MacNeill's decision to cancel. He set out for Limerick, Cork, Kerry and Tipperary with the cancellation order, but when he heard that the Dublin men were going to fight he joined the GPO garrison.

Michael was shot leading the charge up Moore Street when the GPO was being evacuated and died in Sackville Lane. Nannie was not told of his death until the following Tuesday. A relative in Australia knew before she did. Michael wrote a poignant note to his wife as he lay dying, signing off with the words: 'Tons + tons of love dearie to you + to the boys + to Nell + Anna. It was a good fight anyhow. Good bye darling.'

Nannie was pregnant at the time; another son Rory was born the following July.

In 1917 Nannie travelled to America to see her sisters. She returned to Ireland and, in autumn 1917 became a vice-president of Cumann na mBan. During the War of Independence she provided first aid and accommodation for people who lived outside Dublin. She resigned her position in 1922; her appointment to the executive had been merely as a figurehead and she did not take an active role in the organisation. Her family were anti-Treaty. Her teenage son Aodogán was active with the republican forces in the Civil War. Nannie was arrested in November 1922 when her house was raided and she was found to be sheltering Mary MacSwiney. Her sister-in-laws and a number of other relatives were imprisoned for long periods during the Civil War. Nannie was held for a short time and released on 11 November.

She devoted much of her life to the welfare of the poor, in particular to those affected by their involvement with political events. She joined the White Cross organisation in 1920 and was immediately drafted onto the Standing Executive Committee. She was chosen to act on the Winding-Up Commission in 1925. She became joint honorary treasurer of the Children's Relief Association from 1922–1946. She was also in the St Vincent de Paul Society, which distributed food, furniture and clothing to the needy. A noted needlewoman, she made church vestments.

When she died in 1961, forty-four years after her husband, she was buried with him in the Republican Plot in Glasnevin cemetery, Dublin.

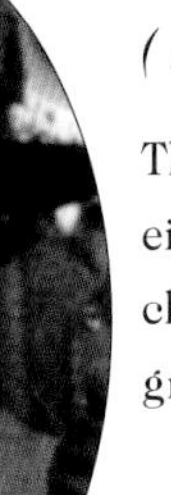

PEROLZ MARY

(1874–c.1950)

The Perolz family were of French Huguenot origin and had come to Dublin in the eighteenth century. Mary Perolz was born in Limerick on 7 May 1874, the third child of Richard Perolz and his wife Bridget Carter. Her father was a printer, as his grandfather had been before him.

Mary was in her late twenties when Maud Gonne founded Inghinidhe na hÉireann in 1900. As a member of the organisation Mary took the part of Meadda in the first play in the Irish language to be produced in Dublin, in December 1902. It was entitled *Eilis agus an Bhean Deirce* (Eilis and the Beggarwoman) and written by PT MacGinley . She taught history and Irish in the classes organised by Inghinidhe na hÉireann for Dublin children. Her classes were conducted by the light of a lantern, something that she felt made them all the more fun.

Mary later became a member of Cumann na mBan and was also a member of the

Irish Citizen Army. She worked closely with both Countess Markievicz and James Connolly. She represented the Irish Women Workers' Union at the Trades Union Congress in Sligo in 1916. She was the registered owner of the *Spark,* a weekly trade union newspaper, published from February 1915 to April 1916, and which was edited by Countess Markievicz. In March 1916 Mary Perolz posed as Countess Markievicz, being similar in stature to her. The Countess had been forbidden to give a lecture at the Fianna Festival in Tralee, County Kerry, by order issued under the Defence of the Realm Act. The Countess urged her friend to 'keep things going and keep the clique together'. Two detectives accompanied Mary to Tralee, thinking that she was the Countess, and, though she was interrogated she managed to keep up the pretence. Mary read the Countess's speech and also the text of the exclusion order. The meeting was a resounding success.

At Easter 1916 Patrick Pearse dispatched Mary to Cork with a message for Tomás MacCurtain that the Rising was going ahead on the Monday. Unable to return to Dublin, she headed for Tralee. She was arrested and brought to Dublin Castle, where she was held with a number of women, including Kathleen Clarke. From there she was taken to Mountjoy Jail and then to Lewes Prison, England. Mary's arrest was a cause of family scandal and some of her relatives changed their name to Prole so as not to be associated with her. When she was released from prison in July 1916 Mary became acting president of the Irish Women Workers' Union in place of Countess Markievicz who was still in prison. She travelled back to England to greet the Countess when she was released from Aylesbury Prison on 17 June 1917.

In 1919 Mary, now forty-five, married James Michael Flanagan, who was known by the nickname 'Citizen Flanagan'. She continued to use her maiden name. The couple lived at 127 Botanic Road in Glasnevin. In her latter years Mary was an advocate of the rights of women in the labour movement. She died *circa* 1950.

PLUNKETT, COUNTESS
(1858–1944)

PLUNKETT, PHILOMENA MARY (MIMI)
(1886–1926)

PLUNKETT DILLON, GERALDINE
(1891–1986)

PLUNKETT, FIONA
(1896–1976)

Countess Plunkett was born Mary Josephine Cranny in 1858, the daughter of Patrick Cranny and Maria Keane. The couple ran a very successful shoe shop at 74 George's Street, Dublin from the 1840s to the 1860s. In 1850 Patrick Cranny also entered the building trade, constructing houses in the expanding Dublin suburbs

of Donnybrook, Rathmines and Ballsbridge. Mary Josephine (known as Jo) had no formal education except for a year spent in a convent in Kensington, but she was considered a beauty and was also an heiress with a considerable fortune.

In 1884 at the age of twenty-six she married George Noble Plunkett (b.1851) the son of a builder. At the time of their marriage George Plunkett had just qualified as a barrister. For her dowry Jo received a number of houses from her father. The couple spent their honeymoon in the United States of America. On their return to Ireland almost two years later they lived in Fitzwilliam Street. The year following their marriage George was created a Papal Count by Pope Leo XIII, an honour bestowed in recognition of his services to the Church, including the gift of a house to the nuns of the Little Company of Mary in Rome.

The couple had seven children, Philomena Mary (Mimi) born in 1886, Joseph Mary (1887), Mary Josephine Patricia (Moya) (1889), Geraldine Mary Germaine (1891), George Oliver (1894), Josephine Mary (Fiona) (1896), and John Patrick (Jack), born in 1897. In 1907 Count Plunkett was made director of the Museum of Science and Art in Dublin. He lectured on art in Europe and was involved in cultural events in Dublin.

Although Countess Plunkett was not political, she assisted, perhaps unwittingly, the nationalist activities with which her children became associated. When Joseph joined the Volunteers, she allowed them to train in the grounds of two of the family properties, at Sandymount Castle and Larkfield in Kimmage. She gave Cumann na mBan the use of Hardwicke Hall, a premises that she owned in Dublin city. The Countess was aware of Eoin MacNeill's order cancelling the Rising; she rang the Imperial Hotel to give the news to her daughter, Geraldine, who was honeymooning with her new husband, Thomas Dillon. The Countess was not active during the Rising but was arrested in the aftermath while searching for news of her sons. After some time in prison she was sent with her husband to live in Oxford.

Joseph Mary Plunkett was executed as one of the leaders of the Rising. The other Plunkett sons, George and Jack, were sent to internment camps. On their return to Ireland, Countess and Count Plunkett moved from Fitzwilliam St to 40 Elgin Rd, Ballsbridge and were subject to constant raids by the Free State Government. The Countess more or less 'managed' her considerable properties, many of which were rented, and in the forties she bought Ballymascanlon House near Dundalk. She lived there until her death in 1944 at the age of eighty-six. Count Plunkett died four years later.

Mimi was the eldest of the Plunkett family. She studied at the Slade Art School in London. She had to return to Ireland in 1914 at the beginning of the First World War. She joined Cumann na mBan, and by 1916 was joint secretary with Min Ryan. Before the Rising she travelled to New York with messages concerning the German consignment of arms and was still there when the Rising took place. On her return to Ireland she resumed her work with Cumann na mBan and also campaigned for her father in the Roscommon by-election in 1917. In 1918 she toured Cork on a recruitment drive for Cumann na mBan. That same year she married a labour activist, Diarmuid O'Laoighre, and had two sons – Rory, who died as an infant, and Colm who became a filmmaker. She contracted TB in her spine and died in 1926 at the early age of forty.

Geraldine was the fourth Plunkett child. She studied medicine at the National University but then switched to chemistry. However, she did not complete her degree as she began to look after her brother Joe, who very ill with TB. Geraldine was his aide-de-camp when he was working with the Volunteers and became a member of the Military Council that planned the Rising. Geraldine herself did not take part in the Rising. On Easter Sunday 1916 she married her former chemistry lecturer, Thomas Dillon. When the Rising began Joe sent word to them to leave the Imperial Hotel. They stayed with Thomas Dillon's mother in Belgrave Road, Rathmines for the duration of the rebellion.

Geraldine was a poet, and in 1917 a volume of her work, entitled *Magnificat,* was published by the Candle Press, Dublin. Prior to this, her poems had appeared in the *Irish Review*. In 1918, when Geraldine was pregnant with their second child, Thomas Dillon was arrested. While he was still in jail in Gloucester he was appointed Professor of Chemistry in the University of Galway. In 1919 Geraldine was sworn into the IRB and was active in the War of Independence. She was jailed in 1920. The Dillons had five children, Moya, Blanaid, Eilís, Michael and Eoin. Geraldine became a founder member of the Galway Arts Club and Taidhbhearc na Gaillimhe. A riverside walk in Galway, for which she had campaigned, is now dedicated to her memory. She died in 1986 at the age of ninety-five.

Josephine Mary (Fiona) was the youngest of the Plunkett girls. She wanted to go to university but was prevented by her mother, who saw her as the beauty of the family, with the potential to make a good match. She was engaged three times but never married. During the 1913 Lockout she was active in Connolly's Free Food organisation. She joined Cumann na mBan and was a key member during the early years, working as an organiser in the Dublin area. Eighteen-year-old Fiona was living with her parents at the time of the Rising and did not take an active part. When her mother was arrested after the Rising, Fiona was brought by the family solicitor to stay with her sister, Geraldine. She accompanied her parents when they were deported to Oxford.

In 1917 Fiona worked as a secretary at Cumann na mBan headquarters, and was a section commander during the War of Independence. She opposed the Treaty and was arrested in Mayo when found to be in possession of anti-government documents and a map. She was imprisoned in Galway and then transferred to Kilmainham Gaol. During her arrest she tried to eat the dispatch she was carrying, and was half-choked as an officer attempted to get her to cough it up. By the time he managed to retrieve it, it was well chewed! When she arrived in Kilmainham her throat was bandaged. After her release from prison, Fiona maintained her involvement with Cumann na mBan and continued to oppose the workings of the Irish Free State. In 1926 she was arrested during a protest; the following year she was imprisoned for two months, having been found loitering near the residence of a judge. During the 1930s she was on the executive of Cumann na mBan. She attended the inaugural meeting of Comhairle na Poblachta in 1936, a short-lived political party formed by the IRA. In 1939, following renewed IRA activity, she was arrested and held in Mountjoy Jail.

Fiona never married and lived with her mother until Countess Plunkett died, when Fiona was nearly fifty. Thereafter she had an income from various houses that she owned and lived a nomadic existence, residing in a number of these houses for the remainder of her life. Sadly, she was regarded by the younger generation as a bit of an oddity and was described as behaving like 'a well-off bag lady.' She was a faithful old comrade to the end and members of Cumann na mBan attended her funeral. She died on 13 July 1977.

POWER, MARGARET (CIS)
[MAIREAD DE PAOR]
(D.1968)

POWER, JOHANNA (JO)
[SIOBHAN DE PAOR]
(D.1969)

The Power sisters of 114 Rock Street, Tralee, County Kerry were the daughters of Patrick and Catherine Power. Their father was one of the leading pig buyers in Munster. They had one brother, John, who became a priest.

The girls were brought up in a house where politics were central. Their uncle, Mick Power, was a well-known Fenian and a Land Leaguer. Their father was also a member of the Land League and counted Charles Stewart Parnell as a personal friend. He was a founder of the Gaelic Athletic Association (GAA) in Tralee and president of the local branch of Sinn Féin. During the War of Independence Patrick Power organised assistance for the IRA.

Cis and Jo joined Cumann na mBan and raised funds for the Prisoners' Dependants' Fund. Along with their father, they opposed the Treaty, and during the Civil War they were involved in producing propaganda, including a weekly republican newssheet called the *Invincible*. (No copies of this newssheet have come to light). On 14 March 1923 the sisters were arrested in Tralee. They were ordered by the military to dig up the garden at Rock Street, in search of the typewriter used to produce the *Invincible*. This proved to be a fruitless exercise, but the girls were taken to Tralee Barracks, where they were held along with their cousin, Han Moynihan. They were then transferred to Kilmainham Gaol and later spent time in the North Dublin Union. The sisters were released in October 1923.

Both Power sisters attended university; Jo obtained an MA degree and worked as a school's inspector in Kerry. The sisters lived all their lives in their family home in Rock Street and took care of their parents when they became elderly.

Their father died in his eighties. Cis Power died in 1968. Some months later, Jo had her sister's memoir of prison life published in three instalments in the *Kerryman* newspaper under the title 'Blaze Away with your Little Gun'. (The original manuscript is now in the Kilmainham collection.)

PRICE DE BARRA, LESLIE
(1893–1984)

Leslie Price became well known as Leslie Bean de Barra, the wife of Tom Barry, guerrilla leader in the War of Independence. Leslie Mary Price was born in Dublin into a nationalist family; her mother was a supporter of Charles Stewart Parnell and later became a member of Sinn Féin. In 1903, when she was eleven, Leslie attended the Patriotic Children's Treat, or as she described it, 'an anti-royalist party' held in Clonturk Park in Dublin. This event coincided with the official entertainments for loyalist children at Phoenix Park during the visit of King Edward to Dublin. Leslie later recalled: 'It was summertime and my mother took us all down there and we got all sorts of cakes and jam and lemonade.'

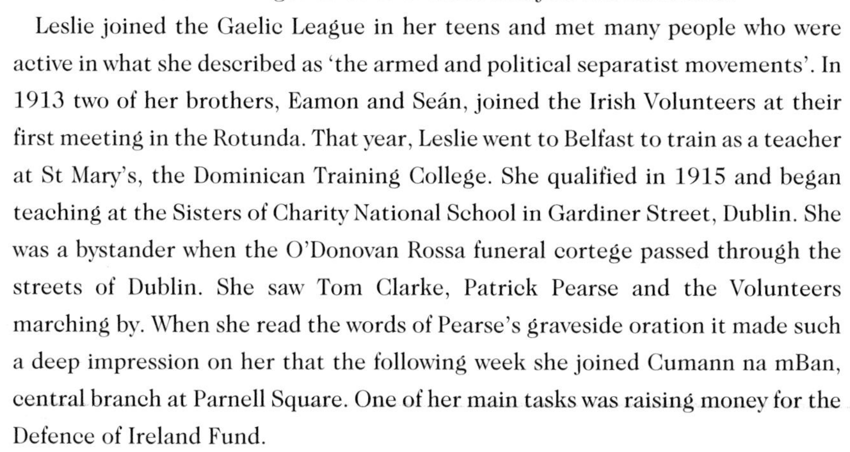

Leslie joined the Gaelic League in her teens and met many people who were active in what she described as 'the armed and political separatist movements'. In 1913 two of her brothers, Eamon and Seán, joined the Irish Volunteers at their first meeting in the Rotunda. That year, Leslie went to Belfast to train as a teacher at St Mary's, the Dominican Training College. She qualified in 1915 and began teaching at the Sisters of Charity National School in Gardiner Street, Dublin. She was a bystander when the O'Donovan Rossa funeral cortege passed through the streets of Dublin. She saw Tom Clarke, Patrick Pearse and the Volunteers marching by. When she read the words of Pearse's graveside oration it made such a deep impression on her that the following week she joined Cumann na mBan, central branch at Parnell Square. One of her main tasks was raising money for the Defence of Ireland Fund.

On Easter Monday 1916, having received no instructions, she went to Mountjoy Street where she met other members of Cumann na mBan. After waiting there for a while, she and her companions made their way to the GPO. Leslie was then sent to the Hibernian Bank where members of the Second Battalion had set up an outpost. When the building was evacuated on Wednesday she became a courier, carrying ammunition and dispatches to Father Mathew Hall in Church Street. Later she went to the church on Marlborough Street to get a priest to attend to men in the GPO. Seán MacDiarmada promoted her to the rank of officer for her work 'in the field.' Leslie was in the GPO on Friday when Patrick Pearse called the women together and told them they had to be evacuated. She was one of those who brought the wounded to Jervis Street Hospital. She was questioned by the military but was not arrested. Her brother Eamon was Captain of C company, 2nd Battalion, and her younger brother Seán was in B company, 1st Battalion. They were arrested and interned in Frongoch, Wales.

In the immediate aftermath of the Rising, Leslie took food parcels and clothes to men being held in Richmond Barracks. She also worked as a collector for the Prisoners' Dependants' Fund. In the autumn of 1916 she was elected to the executive of Cumann na mBan. In 1917 she gave up teaching. The authorities, aware of her political activities, kept her under constant surveillance and she finally quit. She became Director of Organisation and travelled the country recruiting for Cumann na mBan until 1921. Throughout the War of Independence she was a close associate of Michael Collins. While working for Cumann na mBan in County Cork, she met Charlie Hurley of the West Cork Flying Column, to whom she became engaged. He was killed during the War of Independence. After the Truce she married Tom Barry, the leader of the West Cork Flying Column. Barry mentions her just once in his book *Guerilla Days in Ireland*. The couple were married on 22 August 1921 and held their reception in Vaughan's Hotel, Rutland Square, Dublin. Leslie adopted the Irish version of her married name, Leslie Bean de Barra.

The couple settled in Cork. Tom Barry opposed the Treaty and was forced to go on the run, was captured and imprisoned in the Curragh. The couple contemplated leaving Ireland, but in 1927 Tom got a job as General Superintendent of Cork Harbour, a position he held until his retirement in 1965. He remained republican in his beliefs and maintained his links with the IRA until the late 1930s, being arrested several times.

Leslie devoted her energies to humanitarian aid. During the Second World War she oversaw the care of war orphans. She was a member of the Irish Red Cross from its inception in 1939 and became chairman of the society in 1950, a position to which she was reappointed every three years until 1973. In this capacity she travelled all over the world, from Oslo to New Delhi. Her services to humanity were recognised by awards from the German, Italian and Irish governments. She initiated and chaired the 'Freedom from Hunger' campaign. It was so successful that the government decided to make it a long-term project, which became known as 'Gorta', a voluntary third world relief agency. Leslie was national president of Gorta until her resignation in 1968. She was also active in other organisations and committees, including Conradh na Gaeilge. She was a government nominee to the National Health Council and involved in the establishment of the Voluntary Health Insurance Board. She served on the Commission of Enquiry on Mental Illness and was a member of the Cork branch of the Women's Industrial Development Association. She received an honorary LLD (Doctor of Laws) from the National University of Ireland, and in 1978 she received the Henri Dunant Medal, the highest award presented by the International Committee of the Red Cross.

Leslie suffered ill health in her latter years and in 1976 she suffered a stroke that left her with paralysis. She became a long term patient in St Finbarr's Hospital, Cork. She outlived her husband by almost four years and died on 9 April 1984 at the age of ninety-one. She is buried in St. Finbarr's cemetery, Cork.

ROBINSON NORRIS, ÉILIS (ELIZABETH), *(1899–1969)*

ROBINSON KEELEY, SINÉAD (JANE) *(1901–1993)*

Elizabeth and Jane Robinson were born in the seaside town of Skerries in north County Dublin. They left home together as teenagers, and lived in Bray, County Wicklow, where they joined the local branch of Sinn Féin in 1917. On becoming members of the Gaelic League they changed their names to Éilis and Sinéad, and these were the names they used for the rest of their lives. It was at the Gaelic League that Éilis met Séan Norris, who she later married.

The Robinson family had always been active in the nationalist cause. Their father, George, had assisted in the unloading of guns from the *Asgard* in in Howth, County Dublin in 1913. Their uncle, Joe Thornton, took part in the Battle of Ashbourne, County Meath during the 1916 Rising.

By 1918 the sisters had moved to Dublin city and set up a newsagents shop at Harold's Cross bridge. The landlady would not sell them the lease as she thought them too young, so the lease was put in the name of an aunt, Mrs Ó Dalaigh, and the shop was called 'Ó Dalaighs'. Business was difficult during the the years of the War of Independence and the Civil War. The shop was frequently raided and their goods thrown in the street.

Sinéad and Éilis were members of Cumann na mBan. Éilis was a courier and it was said that she carried bullets sewn into her underclothes. In February 1923, whilst transferring guns from one location to another, the sisters were caught up in a raid and arrested. They were stopped outside Oriel House, the headquarters of the Criminal Investigation Division. They were imprisoned in Kilmainham Gaol and later transferred to the NDU. Their sister, Úna, came in from Skerries to run the shop, and continued to work there until her marriage in 1932.

Éílis managed to escape from the NDU with a number of other prisoners and made her way to the nearby Broadstone railway station, where she spent part of the night. While the other escapees decided to wait until morning to leave the station, Éilis headed for home. The following morning all the women were recaptured, with the exception of Éilis and Maureen Power. In order to avoid recapture Éilis went to live with her cousins in County Wicklow and remained there for most of the following year. Sinéad managed to conceal her sister's escape by answering for her at roll call, and remained imprisoned until 28 September 1923.

Éilis married Seán Norris in 1928 and had seven children – Colm, Fintan, Joe, Michael, Brendan and Kevin, and one daughter, Úna. Sinéad married a widower, Jack Keeley, in 1933; they had no children of their own, but she had a stepson. In 1936 Mrs Ryan, former captain of the Ranelagh branch of Cumann na mBan approached the sisters to join an Association of Cumann an mBan. It is not known if they joined or how long they continued their association with Cumann na mBan.

Éilis had left the shop in Harold's Cross on her marriage, while Sinéad continued to run it until 1971. Sinéad also kept lodgers. Éilis was widowed in 1965 and she died in January 1969. In the months before her sister's death, Sinéad began to take care of her nephew Joe Norris, who suffered from depression, and he lived with her for long periods over the next twenty-five years. Jack Keeley died in 1943. Sinéad lived until the age of ninety-two, dying on 14 November 1993.

RYAN, MARY KATE (KIT)
(1878–1934)

RYAN, ELLEN (NELL)
(1881–1959)

RYAN, MARY JOSEPHINE (MIN) [MRS RICHARD MULCAHY]
(1884–1977)

RYAN, PHYLLIS
(1895–1983)

The Ryan sisters of Wexford played an active part in Ireland's revolutionary years. John Ryan and his wife Eliza Sutton, who was originally from Oilgate in Wexford, had a family of twelve, eight girls and four boys. They were a farming family living in the townland of Tomcoole some seven miles west of Wexford town. The household also included the Ryans' maternal grandmother and grandaunt. The family were non political until the turn of the twentieth century when there was a huge revival in Irish nationalism throughout the country. One of the older members of the Ryan household, Martin, a priest based in Wexford, became a member of the Gaelic League.

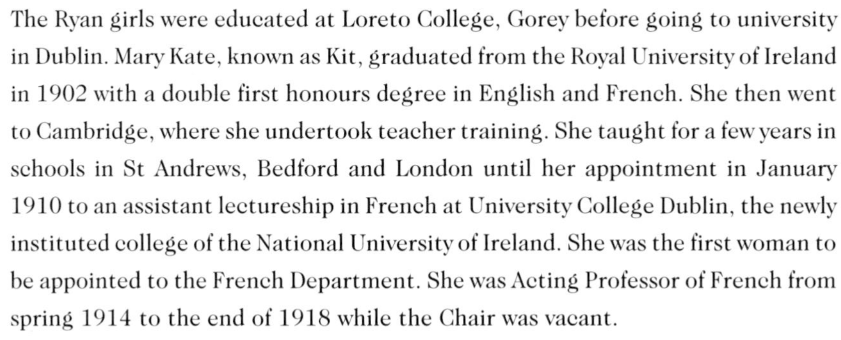

The Ryan girls were educated at Loreto College, Gorey before going to university in Dublin. Mary Kate, known as Kit, graduated from the Royal University of Ireland in 1902 with a double first honours degree in English and French. She then went to Cambridge, where she undertook teacher training. She taught for a few years in schools in St Andrews, Bedford and London until her appointment in January 1910 to an assistant lectureship in French at University College Dublin, the newly instituted college of the National University of Ireland. She was the first woman to be appointed to the French Department. She was Acting Professor of French from spring 1914 to the end of 1918 while the Chair was vacant.

Ellen Ryan (Nell) was the fourth eldest of the family. Five years after she left school, Nell joined the Loreto nuns in Rathfarnham in Dublin, but left after a short time. She taught in Germany in 1900 and was an au pair in San Sebastian in Spain in 1907 before returning to live in Wexford.

Mary Josephine (Min) was the sixth in the family and the fifth girl. She studied French, German and English at the Royal University in Dublin. She spent over a

year in Germany and France as an undergraduate, and, after graduation, taught for four years in London. She returned to Ireland in 1914 at the start of the war and taught in the technical school in Rathmines, Dublin.

Three of the Ryan sisters shared a house at 19 Ranelagh Road: Min, Kit and Phyllis, the youngest of the Ryan girls. Min became involved in nationalist politics and was a founder member of Cumann na mBan. Phyllis went along to the first meeting but decided against joining until she had completed her BSC degree. Kit and another sister, Agnes, were also members of Cumann na mBan and their brother James (Jim), a medical student, joined the Volunteers.

During the 1916 Rising, Phyllis and Min brought food and messages to those stationed in the GPO. Their brother Jim and Min's close friend Seán MacDiarmada were stationed there. MacDiarmada was executed for his part in the Rising; Jim was one of those imprisoned.

Although Kit and Nell Ryan had not taken part in the Rising, they were both sent to prison. Nell was in jail until October 1916; along with Countess Markievicz, Winnie Carney and Helena Molony, she was one the longest serving prisoners. She returned to Wexford and from 1918–1922 was secretary to the local branch of Sinn Féin and was in charge of Cumann na mBan in south Wexford.

Min escaped arrest and was sent by the executive of Cumann na mBan to the US with a message for John Devoy and a report on the Rising. When she returned she became active again in Cumann na mBan. She married Richard Mulcahy, Chief of Staff of the IRA, in June 1919. Their first years of marriage coincided with the War of Independence and Richard Mulcahy spent much of this period on the run. Min and her two small children went for a time to live with Agnes (1888–1967), who was married to Denis McCullough, (president of the IRB before 1916) in Belfast. Min and her husband supported the Treaty. The Mulcahys eventually had a family of six children, three sons and three daughters, and lived in Lissenfield House, Rathmines, a building attached to Portobello Barracks. In 1966 they moved to Temple Villas, Palmerston Road where Min lived until her husband's death in 1971. She then moved to a flat in her son Seán's house in Leeson Park, Dublin where she spent her remaining years. She died at Easter 1977 at the age of ninety-two in Our Lady's Hospice.

Kit had married Sean T O'Kelly, another activist, at Easter 1918. For much of their early married life the couple were separated. Kit remained in Ireland teaching in the University while Sean represented Ireland in Paris during the Peace Negotiations when Ireland was seeking International recognition. He remained there until March 1922. When the Treaty was announced, Kit was in Germany, possibly for her health. Her first reaction was to support the Treaty, but she changed her mind and joined her husband in opposing it. Sean later became vice-president of the executive council of Fianna Fáil. The couple had no children. Kit continued to teach in University College Dublin; she was made Statutory Lecturer in 1925 and was a member of staff until her death. In 1934 she died of rheumatic heart disease in Bad Nauheim in Germany, where she had been sent in search of a cure. She was aged fifty-six.

Nell and Phyllis Ryan also opposed the Treaty, along with their brother Jim. Nell remained at home in Tomcoole and was active with Cumann na mBan. She was a dispatch carrier for the Irregulars. She was arrested in Wexford and held in Kilmainham Gaol. After over thirty days on hunger strike she was released. She returned to the family farm, which was being managed by her brother Jack. She was an active Fianna Fáil party member and served on the National Executive as a representative for South Wexford. She sat on many boards and committees, including the Wexford Harbour Board, County Wexford Vocational Educational Committee and the Wexford Board of Health. She was also a member of Wexford County Council until she retired due to ill health in 1954. Nell never married.She died of stomach cancer on 8 December 1959, aged seventy-eight. She is buried in Glynn cemetery.

Phyllis was awarded an M.Sc. in Chemistry in 1917 and worked for many years as an analyst in her own laboratory in Dawson Street, Dublin. Two years after her sister Kit's death, Phyllis became Sean T O'Kelly's second wife and was known as Phyllis Bean Ui Cheallaigh. The couple did not have any children. She ran a successful business until 1945 when she became First Lady on the election of Seán T O'Kelly as President of Ireland (1945–1959). Her laboratory continued to operate, employing a number of graduates during the 1950s. She survived her husband by seventeen years and died in November 1983.

SHEEHY SKEFFINGTON, HANNA

(1877–1946)

Johanna Sheehy was born on 24 May 1877 in Kanturk, County Cork, the first of seven children of Elizabeth McCoy and David Sheehy. Her early years were spent in County Tipperary. At the time of her birth her father was a mill owner, but during her childhood became a nationalist MP for South Galway. David Sheehy was imprisoned six times for his part in the Land War. Her uncle, Eugene Sheehy, earned himself the title of the 'rebel priest' for his part in the Land League and his support of the Ladies' Land League. He had a great influence and bond with his niece Hanna. He was a member of the IRB and had also been imprisoned for revolutionary activities.

Hanna was educated by the Dominican nuns in Eccles Street, Dublin, where she proved an excellent student. When she was eighteen, incipient tuberculosis sent her to the Rhineland and when she returned to Ireland she enrolled as a student of modern languages. She went to St Mary's University and High School, obtaining her BA degree from the Royal University of Ireland in 1899. In 1902 she achieved a first class honours MA. She became a teacher in Eccles Street and later taught French and German in the Rathmines College of Commerce.

In June 1903 Hanna married Francis Skeffington, a university registrar. Francis was totally committed to equality and, very unusually for the time, took Hanna's surname; thereafter the couple both used Sheehy Skeffington as their name. They were members of the Irish Women's Suffrage and Local Government Association. Five years later the couple became founder members of the Irish Women's Franchise League. They often had to forgo financial security for their principles; Hanna became the main wage earner for a time when Frank resigned from his position as registrar.

In May 1909 Hanna almost died giving birth to her only child, a son named Owen Lancelot. But by early June she was again attending meetings. As well as her teaching, Hanna contributed articles on education and feminist issues for magazines such as the *Nation* and *Bean na hÉireann*. In 1912 she and her husband founded the *Irish Citizen*. Failing to convince Irish Home Rule leaders to support women's suffrage, the IWFL began militant protests and Hanna was arrested in June 1912 for breaking windows. After refusing to pay the fine, she was given a two month sentence and imprisoned in Mountjoy Jail. She was dismissed from her teaching post. This allowed her to become more active in the labour movement, assisting in the soup kitchens set up in Liberty Hall during 1913. She was jailed again for a fracas with a policeman in November 1913. She went on hunger strike and was released after six days.

Hanna and Frank were opposed to the 1914 War, and Francis was jailed for protesting against recruitment. During the Rising, Hanna and her husband did not join the insurgents, but she brought food and messages to the different outposts and Frank tried to set up a citizen's militia to stop looting. He was arrested by the British authorities and shot on the orders of Captain Bowen-Colthurst. Bowen-Colthurst was found 'guilty but insane' at his court martial. Hanna refused the substantial compensation offered and insisted on an enquiry into Frank's death. The enquiry, held in August 1916 and chaired by Sir John Simon, brought out the true facts of the case, but Bowen-Colthurst was never punished. At the end of 1916 Hanna travelled to the United States at the invitation of the Friends of Irish Freedom and spoke at 250 meetings across the continent. Her talk 'British Militarism as I have known it' was later published as a pamphlet. Her tour raised $40,000, which was handed over to Michael Collins who was now a key player in Irish affairs.

Forbidden by the government to return to Ireland, Hanna managed to smuggle herself in via Liverpool in 1918, but was soon detained under the Defence of the Realm Act and imprisoned along with Countess Markievicz, Kathleen Clarke and Maud Gonne MacBride in Holloway Jail in England. She went on hunger strike and was released. In September 1918 she joined Sinn Féin. In November she was appointed to the executive. She was asked to join Cumann na mBan, but while she lent support to their activities, she declined membership, disliking their status as auxiliary to the men.

During the War of Independence she was active in Sinn Féin. In May 1919 she was appointed Organising Secretary. Her main role was as a propagandist, spreading the republican message. She was also a judge in the republican courts.

Throughout this period she lectured for numerous groups, including the Franchise League, the Transport Union and the Socialist Party. She continued to produce the *Irish Citizen*. By 1919 her public speeches against the British administration meant that she had to go on the run for a while. In the local government election in 1920 Hanna was elected to Dublin Corporation, serving on the Technical Education Committee and chairing the Public Libraries Committee. In 1920 she taught French at the Technical Institute in Dun Laoghaire. That year she became involved in the White Cross and was appointed to its executive.

When the Civil War commenced, Hanna, together with other women, made an unsuccessful attempt to stop the fighting. In November 1922 she, Linda Kearns and Kathleen Boland, were sent to the United States by Eamon de Valera, to raise funds on behalf of the American Committee of Irish Republican Soldiers and Prisoners' Dependents Fund. They visited twenty-five states. In September 1923 Hanna attended the League of Nations, where she composed a circular calling on the delegates to reject Irish membership. Her bid was unsuccessful. Hanna was barred from teaching because of her refusal to take the oath of allegiance to the King, but found work as a journalist. In 1925 she was elected to Dublin City Council.

In the 1926 split in Sinn Féin, Hanna supported Eamon de Valera and joined his new political party, Fianna Fáil. She was appointed to its first executive but when de Valera entered the Dáil, declaring the oath to be an empty political formula, she resigned from the party. She now drew closer to republicans like Frank Ryan and Peadar O'Donnell, becoming assistant editor of *An Phoblacht*, the newspaper of the IRA. In 1930 Hanna travelled to Russia in her capacity as secretary of the 'Friends of Soviet Russia'. On her return, following the suppression of *An Phoblacht* and the jailing of Frank Ryan, she became editor of the *Republican File*, a republican socialist journal. She was involved in the first National Aid Association which supported the dependants of republican prisoners and gave continuous support to the Women's Prisoners' Defence League. In January 1933 Hanna travelled to Newry, County Down to speak on behalf of republican prisoners. She was arrested and held for fifteen days in Armagh Jail for defying an order banning her from entering the North.

Her main income came from journalism and occasional lecturing in the United States and Canada. In 1935 she opposed the Conditions of Employment Bill, aware of how its terms would curb the activities of working women. When the Constitution was passed she became a founder member of the Women's Social and Progressive League, which attempted to alert women to the implications of the anti-woman legislation passing through the Dáil. However, they failed to gain support in the 1938 General Elections. She resumed teaching, while continuing to write and to lecture, and in 1943, at the age of sixty-six, Hanna stood as an independent candidate for Dublin. She hoped that she and other candidates would form a Women's Party but all four women failed to get elected. Hanna suffered ill health for much of 1945, and by 1946 she was unable to work. She died on Easter Saturday, 20 April 1946. *The Irish Times* obituary described her as 'the ablest woman in Ireland'.

SPRING RICE, THE HONOURABLE MARY ELLEN *(1880–1924)*

The Honourable Mary Ellen Spring Rice was born on 14 October 1880 to Lord Mounteagle and his wife Elizabeth Butcher, daughter of the Bishop of Meath. The Spring Rice family had lands in Limerick and Kerry. The family seat was Mount Trenchard, Foynes, County Limerick, dating from the late eighteenth century.

During Mary Ellen's childhood the Irish language was still spoken in the Foynes area and she, unlike many of her class, learned the language. Later she joined the Gaelic League in Foynes (a branch established by Dr Douglas Hyde), as well as becoming a member of branches in Dublin and London. She was very committed to the promotion of the Irish language. She employed a gardener who was a native speaker and he assisted her with her spoken Irish. She also travelled to the Gaeltacht to continue her studies. Irish classes were held in Mount Trenchard and she taught some of the classes herself. She hired a native speaker from Kerry to teach at the local school. On behalf of the Gaelic League, she held the Munster Feiseanna on the lawns of Mount Trenchard.

Mary Ellen was also a member of the United Irishwomen, a women's agricultural organisation established in 1910. Her father was a member of the Agricultural Organisation Society and he and his daughter were active in promoting the co-operative movement. Mary Ellen was also interested in Irish politics and believed in Home Rule; later she became a member of Sinn Féin.

In 1914 she proposed to Erskine Childers (whom she had met at a Gaelic League Fair in London) that arms could be run from Germany to Ireland. After the Volunteer Executive agreed to her plan she was on the committee which raised funds for this enterprise. She sailed on the *Asgard*, which landed arms and ammunition at Howth, County Dublin in July 1914.

During the War of Independence she established a branch of Cumann na mBan at Foynes. She offered the hospitality of her stately home to men on the run and had a hideout constructed in the basement. She hosted Cumann na mBan lectures on first aid. She also kept a boat on the Shannon so that the Limerick and Clare brigades could maintain contact across the river. Throughout this period she kept up her acquaintance with English friends and family and entertained many of them in Limerick. She arranged for them to meet with Con Collins, a TD for West Limerick, and the historian Alice Stopford Green who promoted the Irish standpoint in the Anglo-Irish conflict.

In December 1924, having suffered ill health for almost two years, Mary Ellen died in the Vale of Clwydd Sanatorium in north Wales at the age of forty-four. Her body was returned to Ireland. A guard of honour made up of members from the local IRA, Gaelic League and Trade Union officials lined the route to her final resting place in the Protestant graveyard at Loughill near Mount Trenchard.

WYSE POWER, JENNIE NÉE O'TOOLE

(1858–1941)

Jennie Wyse Power was at centre of Irish politics for almost fifty years. She was born Jane O'Toole in May 1858 in Baltinglass, County Wicklow, the youngest of seven children of Edward O'Toole and Mary Norton. As a young child she moved to Dublin. Hers was a nationalist family; her home was a safe house for Fenians and, according to a family story, one of her brothers had taken part in the 1867 Fenian Rising.

In 1881, Jennie joined the Ladies' Land League. As a member of this organisation one of her jobs was to take books to imprisoned members in Kilmainham Gaol and other prisons, and she was a regular visitor to Kilmainham during Charles Stewart Parnell's imprisonment in 1881–1882. She also helped compile the register of evictions and was a Land League organiser in counties Carlow and Wicklow. By the time the Ladies' Land League disbanded, Jennie had become a member of the executive. She remained a staunch supporter of Parnell in the years of his political decline following the O'Shea divorce scandal. After his death in 1892 she published a selection of his speeches and was also responsible for maintaining his grave.

In July 1883 she married journalist John Wyse Power, a member of the Irish Republican Brotherhood and a founder member of the Gaelic Athletic Association. She gave birth to four children in the following decade. The eldest child, a girl, died when she was two; her surviving children were Maura, Nancy and Charles. Despite being the mother of a young family, Jennie remained active in public life. She was a member of the women's franchise movement; she supported Anna Haslam's Dublin Women's Suffrage Association and became a founder member of the Irish Women's Franchise League. She was on the committee that organised the Patriotic Children's Treat in 1900. A founder member of Inghinidhe na hÉireann, she also served as one of its vice-presidents. She was a Poor Law Guardian for North Dublin from 1903 and later, in 1911, a founder and vice-president of Sinn Féin.

In 1899 she opened the Irish Farm Produce Company, a shop and restaurant in Henry Street, Dublin, that was a regular meeting place for political activists and Irish language enthusiasts. It became so successful that she opened three other branches in the city. She was on the provisional committee responsible for setting up Cumann na mBan in 1914. The writing of the 1916 Proclamation was finished in her home. During the Rising she supplied food to the insurgents until her premises in Henry Street was destroyed. In July 1916 tragedy visited Jennie again when her daughter Maura died suddenly.

After the Rising she and her daughter Nancy were active in organising support for the prisoners' dependants. In her capacity as Sinn Féin representative in local government she served as chairman of the Public Health Committee and was on the technical education committee. She also chaired Sinn Féin meetings in the absence of Eamon de Valera. By 1917 she was on the executive of Cumann na mBan. In 1920 she was elected to Dublin Corporation.

Although Cumann na mBan opposed the Treaty, Jennie supported it and became an executive member of the new pro-Treaty organisation. She was made vice-president of Cumann na Saoirse in 1923. In 1924 she was became one of the commissioners appointed to govern the city of Dublin. She joined the pro-Treaty party, Cumann na nGaedheal, but became disillusioned with their policies and attended her last meeting in 1925. Her decision to leave the party was based on factors such as the government policy regarding political prisoners during the Civil War and the apathy towards the Boundary Commission and the northern question. Her husband died in 1926 and she closed her business in 1929. She served as a Free State senator from 1922 until the Senate's dissolution in 1936. In the same year she retired from public life. She was seventy-eight when she died in January 1941.

YOUNG, ELLA
(1865–1951)

Ella Young was born into a Presbyterian family in Fenagh, County Antrim in 1865. During her childhood the family lived on the Bog of Allen and later moved to Dublin. They settled in Rathmines in the 1880s. Ella attended university and took a degree in political science and law. Like other scholars of the day, she developed a consuming interest in Ireland's past. While still in university she joined Æ's Theosophical Society at Ely Place. Later she was in the Hermetic Society; other members included Seumas O'Sullivan, James Connolly, Padraic Colum and Standish O'Grady. It was Æ (the writer George Russell) who encouraged her to pursue an interest in Irish fairy lore. She began to live for part of the year in the west of Ireland, where she collected tales and learnt Irish. In 1900 Ella left the Hermetic Society and set up her own group known as the 'Fine' (the fingers). This group of mystics engaged in meditation and communication with the dead. These events often took place on Ireland's Eye, an island off Malahide in north County Dublin, which Ella believed to be 'the representative of Irish earth'. She wrote a number of children's books on Celtic mythology; *The Coming Of Lugh* was published in 1905 and *Celtic Wonder Tales* in 1910. She also wrote poetry; her book of verse, *The Rose of Heaven*, was published in 1918; the 1920 edition was illustrated by Maud Gonne .

Ella's political sympathies were nationalist. She joined Inghinidhe na hÉireann and wrote frequently for *Sinn Féin*. In 1912 she went to live in Temple Hill, a farmhouse that she renovated in County Wicklow. It was from this house that she stored and distributed guns and ammunition from the Howth gun-running to the

Volunteers. Although Ella spent much of the period 1914–1918 in Achill, County Mayo, she returned to Dublin during the 1916 Rising. In its aftermath she resumed gun running from a pro-British house, which she shared with writer Olive Agnes Fox. As she had become known to the authorities there for her nationalist sympathies, Ella left Dublin for a time. Following Countess Markievicz's release from prison in June 1917, Ella joined Cumann na mBan. In 1919 she came back to Dublin, where she was again involved in hiding arms and ammunition and smuggling weapons. At the Truce she was sent by Erskine Childers to Kerry to meet with representatives of the IRA. During the Civil War she continued to store guns. In her memoirs she recalled how a Thompson sub machine gun was hidden under the floorboards when the house was raided, but remained undiscovered.

In 1925 Ella left for the US to embark on a lecture tour. She gave talks on the east coast and in the mid-west, but finally settled in California where she held a position at the University of California at Berkeley, lecturing in Celtic Mythology and Gaelic Literature. There she studied Mexican and Indian folklore and continued to write, publishing *The Unicorn with Silver Shoes* in 1932 and her memoirs, *Flowering Dusk*, in 1945.

She never married and remained in the United States for the rest of her life. In *Flowering Dusk* she told of how, when she was young, a gypsy had predicted that she would end her days across the water. The prediction came true; Ella died in California in 1951.

ZAMBRA, MAY

(1906–1929)

Mary Ellen Zambra (known as May) lived for only twenty-three years but she packed much into her short life. She was the eldest of seven children of Joe Zambra and Margaret Byrne who lived in Dublin's inner city. May was a noted beauty, probably getting her exotic looks from her North African lineage. The Zambra name is Moorish and the family had come to Ireland from England generations before May was born.

May was fourteen when she entered employment in W & R Jacob & Co Ltd, the biscuit factory close to her family home. The workers there were known as 'The Jacob's Mice' because of their extreme youth. It was in Jacobs that May came into contact with the nationalist movement. She was a member of the girl scouts, Clann na nGaedheal, but was too young to take part in the Rising in 1916. May joined Cumann na mBan in 1922, aged sixteen, against the wishes of her father who was a supporter of the Irish Free State. He, like many of his generation, had joined the British army, and as a Connaught Ranger had seen action in Europe and Palestine. He was wounded during the First World War. His opposition to his daughter's involvement in the illegal organisation meant that there were often arguments in the Zambra household, not least because the family home was constantly raided. May was arrested on 28 February 1923 for the shooting of a CID

(Criminal Investigation Division) man, a fact that came to light from her entry in the autograph book of Bridie Halpin, a fellow inmate at Kilmainham Gaol. She was imprisoned in Kilmainham Gaol until the night of 30 April 1923 when she was one of the female inmates forcibly removed from the gaol to the North Dublin Union. During her period of incarceration in the NDU, May made an unsuccessful escape attempt and was recaptured outside Broadstone railway station. She was one of the youngest inmates to go on hunger strike in November 1923. When that strike was called off and prisoners began to be set free, May was one of the last to be released. She was very weak and had to be nursed back to health by her mother. When she had recovered, she returned to work at Jacob's Biscuit Factory but left the month before she married, in June 1929. May met her husband, James Ryan, an ex-British navy marine, at a dance at a Free State army barracks. The couple moved in next door to the Zambra family home in Cuffe Street. Their marriage was short-lived. May contacted tubercular meningitis later that year and died in the fever hospital, Cork Street, Dublin, on 2 November 1929 at the age of twenty-three. She was five months pregnant; the baby did not survive.

APPENDIX 1

Prisoner List – 1916

Women arrested after the 1916 Rising and imprisoned in Kilmainham Gaol, as recorded in newspapers of the period. Where known, their 1916 garrison, and the organisation to which they belonged, are included.

NAME	1916 GARRISON	ORGANISATION
Barrett, Kitty	City Hall	Irish Citizen Army
Brady, Bridget	City Hall	Irish Citizen Army
Brown, Kate		
Brown, Martha		
Byrne, Eileen		
Byrne, Katie	Marrowbone Lane	Cumann na mBan
Byrne, Mary		
Carney, Winnie	GPO	Cumann na mBan
Carron, Meg (May)	Four Courts	Cumann na mBan
Cooney, Lily	Marrowbone Lane	Cumann na mBan
Cooney, Ann	Marrowbone Lane	Cumann na mBan
Cooney, Eileen	Marrowbone Lane	Cumann na mBan
Cosgrave, Marcella	Marrowbone Lane	Cumann na mBan
Davis, Bridget	City Hall	Irish Citizen Army
Ennis, Ellen	Four Courts	
ffrench Mullen, Madeleine	St Stephen's Green	Irish Citizen Army
Fleming, Kathleen		
Foley, Bridget	St Stephen's Green	Irish Citizen Army
Gahan, Mary	St Stephen's Green	Cumann na mBan
Gifford, Nellie	St Stephen's Green	Irish Citizen Army
Goff, Bridget	St Stephen's Green	Irish Citizen Army
Grenan, Julia	GPO	Irish Citizen Army
Hackett, Rosanna	St Stephen's Green	Irish Citizen Army
Hegarty, Bridget		
Higgins, Annie		
Humphreys, Ellen		
Joyce, Maggie	St Stephen's Green	Irish Citizen Army
Kelly, Kitty	St Stephen's Green	
Kelly, Martha		
Kennedy, Margaret		
Kenny, Bridy		
Liston, Catherine		
Liston, Mary		
Lynch, Bessie		
Lynn, Kathleen	City Hall	
Lyons, Bridget	Four Courts	Irish Citizen Army
MacNamara, Rose	Marrowbone Lane	Cumann na mBan
MacNamee, Agnes	Marrowbone Lane	Cumann na mBan
Maher, Kathleen		
Markham, Pauline		
Markievicz, Countess	St Stephen's Green	Irish Citizen Army
Martin, Brid S	Four Courts	
Martin, Kate		
McCauley, Julia		
McGowan, Josephine	Marrowbone Lane	Cumann na mBan

NAME	1916 GARRISON	ORGANISATION
Barrett, Kitty	City Hall	Irish Citizen Army
McLoughlin, Maggie		
Mead, Florence		
Mitchell, Caroline		
Molony, Helena	City Hall	Irish Citizen Army
Mulhall, Lizzie	Marrowbone Lane	Cumann na mBan
Mullally, Rosa		
Murphy, Kathleen		
Murtagh, Bridget	St Stephen's Green	Cumann na mBan
Norgrove, Annie	City Hall	Irish Citizen Army
Norgrove, Emily	City Hall	Irish Citizen Army
O'Brennan, Lily	Marrowbone Lane	Cumann na mBan
O'Daly, Nora	St Stephen's Green	Cumann na mBan
O'Flaherty, Margaret	Marrowbone Lane	Cumann na mBan
O'Hanlon, Sheila	Marrowbone Lane	Cumann na mBan
O'Keefe, Emily	Marrowbone Lane	Cumann na mBan
O'Keefe, Josephine	Marrowbone Lane	Cumann na mBan
O'Moore, May	St Stephen's Green	Cumann na mBan
Murphy, Mrs S	Marrowbone Lane	Cumann na mBan
O'Sullivan, Louise	Four Courts	
Partridge, Mary		
Perolz, Mary		Irish Citizen Army
Plunkett, Countess		
Quigley, Maria	Marrowbone Lane	Cumann na mBan
Quigley, Priscilla	Marrowbone Lane	Cumann na mBan
Retz, Barbara		
Ryan, Mary Kate		
Ryan, Nellie		
Seary, Kathleen	St Stephen's Green	Irish Citizen Army
Spencer (Spicer), Josephine		
Sullivan, Mary		
Treston, Catherine	GPO	

APPENDIX 2

Prisoner List – Civil War

The list covers prisoners who were held in Kilmainham Gaol, Mountjoy Jail and The North Dublin Union (NDU). Some women spent time in all three prisons; others were held in one or two of these prisons.

The information was compiled mainly from autograph books and other unpublished sources. Many of the details were handwritten or in faded typescript, so some errors of spelling may have occurred in the transcription. Where material is missing or incomplete in the 'details' column, it means that no address, or a partial address only, was found in the sources consulted.

Reference Key: 'LOB letters UCDA' means the letters of Lily O'Brennan in University College Dublin Archives. 'Kilmainham List' is a typescript of prisoner names compiled from memory by former prisoners and held in the Kilmainham Gaol Collection.'D Macardle account' is Dorothy Macardle's account of her imprisonment, in the Kilmainham Gaol Collection. *Jangle of the Keys* by Margaret Buckley was published by James Duffy & Co Ltd., Dublin, 1938.

NAME	DETAILS	REFERENCE
Agnew, Bridie M	Ardnasee, Hackballscross, Dundalk	Military Archives Material Autograph books KGC
Allen, Kathy	Grange, Mooncoin, Co Kilkenny	Autograph books KGC
Alyward, Molly		Autograph books KGC
Anderson, Mrs Annie	9 Ranelagh Road, Dublin	Military Archives Material
Andrews, Anne (Ní Aindriu, Áine)		Autograph books KGC
Barnewell, Brigid	Lyons Cottage, Staffron St, Maynooth, Co Kildare	Autograph books KGC
Barrett, Bridget (Bunty)	67 Rock St, Tralee, Co Kerry	Military Archives Material Autograph books KGC
Barrett, Eileen (Ní Bairead, Eibhlin)	58, Lr Gloucester St, Dublin & London	Autograph books KGC
Barry, Aileen	Mitchelstown, Co Cork	Military Archives Material
Barry, Dotie	Windsor Cottages, St Lukes, Cork	Military Archives Material Autograph books KGC
Barry, Rita (de Barra)	Windsor Cottages, St Lukes, Cork	Military Archives Material Autograph books KGC
Begley, Danni		Autograph books KGC
Behan, Christina (Chrissie)	10 Hackett's Court, Kevin St, Dublin	Military Archives Material Autograph books KGC
Bermingham, Mrs Rita (Lucy)	Dublin	Military Archives Material Autograph books KGC
Bermingham, Margaret	13 Prussia St, Dublin	Military Archives Material
Blackwell, Evelyn (Eileen)	'Wood Farm', Drumbane, Pallasgreen, Co Limerick	Autograph books KGC Military Archives Material
Blake, Crissie		Military Archives Material

NAME	DETAILS	REFERENCE
Blake, Marian	Castlegan	Military Archives Material Autograph books KGC
Bohan, B (Baby)	Market Street, Ballymote, Sligo	Military Archives Material Autograph books KGC
Bourke, Annie	North Circular Road, Dublin	Inscription in cell KG Military Archives Material Autograph books KGC
Bourke, Mary		Autograph book KGC
Bourke-Dowling, Mary	2 Howth Road, Dublin	Military Archives Material Autograph books KGC Jangle of the Keys
Bowe, Mary	Bree, Enniscorthy, Co Wexford	Military Archives Material
Bowen, Mary	13 Melrose, Howth, Co Dublin	Military Archives Material
Bowen, Sighle	6 Killeen Road, Rathmines, Dublin	Military Archives Material Autograph books KGC
Boyle, Eileen U	12 MacMullen Street, Belfast	Military Archives Material Autograph books KGC
Boyle, M		Autograph books KGC
Boyle, Rita	Dungloe, Co Donegal	Military Archives Material Autograph books KGC
Boyle, Sheila	31 Synge Street, Dublin	Military Archives Material
Brady, Claire	Tullycoe, Cootehill, Cavan	Kilmainham List Aug 23 Autograph books KGC Military Archives Material
Brady, Josephine		Autograph book KGC
Brady, Katie (Caitlin)	2 Princess Gardens, Belfast	Autograph book KGC Military Archives Material
Breen, Kate	Grange, Maoineoin, Killarney, Co Kerry	Autograph books KGC Jangle of the Keys Military Archives Material
Brennan, E	1 Shelbourne Road, Dublin	Military Archives Material
Brennan, Gretta	Collooney, Co Sligo	Autograph books KGC Military Archives Material
Brennan, May	Main Street, Swinford, Co Mayo	Autograph books KGC Military Archives Material
Brian, Nora	Birr, Co Offaly	Autograph book KGC
Briar, Margaret	6 Church Road, Dalkey, Co Dublin	Military Archives Material
Brick, Nora	Caherbreagh, Tralee, Co Kerry	Autograph books KGC Military Archives Material
Brock, Eileen	3 Albert Place, Dublin	Military Archives Material
Brock, Elizabeth	5 Albert Place, Dublin	Military Archives Material
Broderick, Moira	Ardcuain, Glenageary, Co Dublin	LOB letters UCDA Military Archives Material D Macardle account, KGC Autograph books KGC
Brogan, Dorothy (Dotie)	Knockmore, Ballina, Co Mayo	Autograph books KGC Military Archives Material

NAME	DETAILS	REFERENCE
Brophy, Brigid (Bea/Bridie)	Tullow Street, Carlow	Military Archives Material Autograph books KGC (in List)
Brosnan, Nora	Castlegregory, Kerry	Autograph books KGC Military Archives Material
Brown(e), Annie	12 Gracepark Gdns, Drumcondra, Dublin	Autograph books KGC Military Archives Material
Brown, Ethel		Inscription in cell KG
Brown, Mary		Inscription in cell KG
Brown, Susie	Bailey Street, New Ross, Co Wexford	Military Archives Material
Browner, Annie	111 Summer Hill, Dublin	Military Archives Material Autograph books KGC
Bryan, Bridget	14 Henrietta Street, Dublin	Military Archives Material
Buckley, Mrs Margaret	24 Marguerite Rd, Dublin	Autograph books KGC Jangle of the Keys Military Archives Material
Bulfin, C (Kid)	Derrinlough House, Birr, Co Offaly	Autograph books KGC Military Archives Material
Burke, Anne	15 North Summer St, Dublin	Military Archives Material Autograph book KGC
Burke, Katie	5 Delahunty Blgs, Lower Mount St, Wexford	Military Archives Material
Burke, Margaret	Parkemore, Castlegar, Co Galway	Military Archives Material Papers UCDA
Byrne, A	Newtown, Wexford	Autograph book KGC
Byrne, Annie	6 Court Street, Enniscorthy, Co Wexford	Military Archives Material Autograph book KGC Kilmainham List
Byrne, Annie	20 Summerhill, Dublin	Military Archives Material
Byrne, Florence R		Autograph book KGC
Byrne, Mrs Mary	1 Lord Edward Street, Dublin	Military Archives Material Kilmainham List
Cadogan, Mary Ellen	Reengarga, Creagh, Skibbereen, Cork	Military Archives Material Kilmainham List
Caffrey, Elizabeth (Lizzie)	17, Church Street, North Wall, Dublin	Autograph book KGC Military Archives Material
Cahalane, Marjorie	'Strathmore', 10 Mount Eden Rd, Donnybrook, Dublin	Autograph book KGC Military Archives Material
Cahill, Mary (Mollie)	Eglinton Asylum, Cork	Military Archives Material Kilmainham List
Campbell, Kathleen	6, Railway Ave, Inchicore, Dublin	Autograph book KGC Military Archives Material
Cantillon, Cathy	'Oakview', Fairgreen, Tralee, Co Kerry	Autograph book KGC Military Archives Material
Carey, Miss (Nora)	Cork	LOB letters UCDA Autograph book KGC Military Archives Material
Carroll, Nora		Military Archives Material
Carroll, T J		Autograph book KGC

NAME	DETAILS	REFERENCE
Casey, Frances	61 Shelbourne Road, Dublin	Military Archives Material Autograph book KGC
Casey, Julia	Ballyvourney Road, Macroom, Co Cork	Military Archives Material
Casey, Letitia (Ní Cathasaigh)	21 Seatown Road, Dundalk, Co Louth	Military Archives Material Autograph book KGC
Cassidy, Kathleen	21 Railway Road, Dalkey, Co Dublin	Military Archives Material
Chamberlain, Maggie	Quarry Hill, Kilmallock, Co Limerick	Autograph books KGC Military Archives Material Inscription in cell KG
Chamberlain, N	Church Lane, Killmallock, Co Limerick	Military Archives Material
Chambers, Mary	Enniscrone, Co Sligo	Military Archives Material
Chambers, Una	Enniscrone, Co Sligo	Military Archives Material
Clancy, Ms	36 Ailesbury Rd, Dublin	Military Archives Material
Clear, Nuala		Autograph book KGC
Cleary, Hannah (Siobhan)	The Eglinton Asylum, Cork	Military Archives Material Kilmainham List Autograph book KGC
Cleary, Lena	White Church, Ballykelly, New Ross, Wexford	Military Archives Material
Cleary, Mollie (Marie)	21 Upper Dorset St, Dublin	Autograph books KGC Military Archives Material
Clifford, Hannah	40 Botherbee, Tralee, Co Kerry	Autograph books KGC Inscription in cell KG Military Archives Material
Clifford, Mary	Holy Cross, Tralee, Co Kerry	Military Archives Material
Coffey, Gretta (Mairéad)	1 Charlemount Ave, Dun Laoghaire, Co Dublin	Kilmainham List Military Archives Material Autograph book KGC
Cogan, Daisy		Military Archives Material
Coghlan, May	2 Frankfort Place	Autograph book KGC Military Archives Material
Cogley, Madame		Autograph book KGC
Colfer, Bridget (Bea)	Killask, Wexford	Autograph books KGC in list
Colgan, Eileen	1 North Strand, Dublin	Autograph books KGC Military Archives Material
Comerford, Máire	9 Merrion Road, Dublin	Autograph books KGC Inscription in KG Military Archives Material
Comyn, Mary	9 Northbrook Rd, Leeson Park, Dublin	Military Archives Material
Condon, Brigid	Ballymacarbry, Co Waterford	Autograph books KGC
Condon, Mary	Gladstone St, Main Guard, Clonmel	Military Archives Material
Connolly, Bridie	Portrane House, Donabate	Autograph books KGC Military Archives Material

NAME	DETAILS	REFERENCE
Connolly, May (Mary)	104 Middle Abbey St, Dublin	Jangle of the Keys Autograph books KGC Kilmainham List Military Archives Material
Connolly, Nellie	10 Morrison Island, Cork	Autograph books KGC Kilmainham List
Connolly O'Brien, N	19 Ely Place, Dublin	Autograph books KGC Military Archives Material
Cooney, Mary	Main Guard, Clonmel, Co Tipperary	Military Archives Material
Corcoran, Crissie (Cressie)	Castle-Hackett, Tuam, Co Galway	Kilmainham List Military Archives Material
Cosgrave, Polly	Taylorstown, Ballycullane, Co Wexford	Autograph books KGC
Costello, Kitty M	16 Joseph's Street, Dublin	Military Archives Material Autograph book KGC
Cotter, Agnes	7 Esmonde Tce, Bray, Co Wicklow	Military Archives Material
Cotter, Criss	Bantry, Co Cork	Military Archives Material
Coventry, Lily	48 Lr Clanbrassil St, Dublin	Autograph books KGC LOB letters UCDA Military Archives Material
Coyle, Eithne (Ní Cumhaill, Irene)		Autograph books KGC
Coyle, Jenny	58 Aughrim Street, Dublin	Military Archives Material Autograph books KGC
Coyle, Kathleen (Kitty)	58 Aughrim Street, Dublin	Kilmainham List Military Archives Material Autograph books KGC
Coyle, Mary	1 Mespil Road, Dublin	Kilmainham List Jangle of the Keys Military Archives Material Autograph book KGC
Coyne, Agnes	1 Lord Edward St, Dublin	Autograph books KGC Kilmainham List Military Archives Material
Cregan, Tilla	4 Tirconnaill St, Inchicore, Dublin	Autograph books KGC
Cremmins, Mrs Beatrice	8 Hardwicke Place, Dublin	Military Archives Material
Cuddihy, Margaret	The Cafe, Harold's Cross, Dublin	Kilmainham List Military Archives Material
Cullinare, J		Autograph book KGC
Cummins, Mary	75 Lr Clanbrassil St, Dublin	Kilmainham List Military Archives Material
Curran, Bridget (Bridie)	Main Street, Killala, Co Mayo	Military Archives Material Autograph book KGC
Daly, A		Autograph book KGC
Daly, Eileen	The Eglinton Asylum, Cork	Military Archives Material Autograph book KGC
Daly, Ellen	69 South Circular Rd, Dublin	Military Archives Material

NAME	DETAILS	REFERENCE
Daly, Katie	Loughbeg, Castlegregory, Co Kerry	Military Archives Material Autograph book KGC
Daly, Mary		Autograph book KGC
Daly, Peg	Kildare	Military Archives Material Autograph book KGC
D'Arcy, Deenie (Teresa)	Woodside, Dalkey, Co Dublin	Autograph book KGC
D'Arcy, Margaret	The Hill, Dalkey, Co Dublin	Military Archives Material
D'Arcy, Mary	Woodside, The Hill, Dalkey, Co Dublin	Military Archives Material Autograph book KGC
D'Arcy, Nellie	Woodside, The Hill, Dalkey, Co Dublin	Autograph book KGC
Dargan, Eilis	Tullow, Co Carlow	Autograph books KGC Military Archives Material
Davis, Esther	40 Cumberland St, Dun Laoghaire, Co Dublin	Military Archives Material
de Barra, Eibhlin (Eileen Barry)		Autograph books KGC LOB letters UCDA.
de Burca, Caithlin	London deportee	Autograph books KGC
de Lappe, Maggie	Annaghvene, Connemara, Co Galway	Military Archives Material
Deegan, Maura	4 Washington Street, Anderson, Glasgow, Scotland and 95 Upper Dorset Street, Dublin	Autograph books KGC Military Archives Material
Delaney, Peg	Station Road, Kildare	Autograph books KGC Military Archives Material
Derham, Mary	Drogheda Street, Balbriggan, Co Dublin	Military Archives Material Autograph book KGC
Devanney, K	36 Upper Dominick Street, Dublin	Military Archives Material
Devlin, Mrs Ann (Annie)	24 Sinnott Place, Dublin	Military Archives Material Autograph book KGC
Doherty, Cissie	Dunloe, Co Donegal	Kilmainham List
Doherty, Lizzie	Dunloe, Co Donegal	Military Archives Material
Dolan, Annie	6 Upper Bridge Street, Dublin	Autograph books KGC Inscription in cell KG Military Archives Material
Dolan, Eilis(h)	81 Manor St, Dublin	Military Archives Material Autograph books KGC
Dolan, Sheila	81 Manor Street, Dublin	Military Archives Material
Donegan, Annie	Church Road, Bantry, Co Cork	Military Archives Material Autograph books KGC
Donnell, M Mary		Autograph books KGC
Donovan, Kitty G (Katie)	24 Nicholas Street, Cork	Military Archives Material Autograph books KGC
Donovan, Madge	Clogheen, Cork	Military Archives Material
Doody, Mrs K	24 Patrick St, Dublin	Military Archives Material Autograph books KGC
Doran, Kitty		Autograph books KGC
Dowling, Sadie	42 Parnell Square, Dublin and 27 Mary Street, Limerick	Military Archives Material Autograph books KGC

NAME	DETAILS	REFERENCE
Doyle, Angela	68 Ring Street, Inchicore, Dublin	Military Archives Material Autograph books KGC Jangle of the Keys
Doyle, Annie	25 Carysfort Road, Dublin	Military Archives Material
Doyle, Maggie (Peg)	Ballinacarrig, Co Carlow	Military Archives Material Kilmainham List Autograph books KGC
Doyle, Mary M (May)	12 Gracepark Gardens, Drumcondra, Dublin	Autograph books KGC
Doyle, Norah 'Montague'	37, North Great George's Street, Dublin	Inscription in cell KG Autograph books KGC Military Archives Material
Doyle, Teresa (Tessie)	42 Ring Street, Inchicore, Dublin	Kilmainham List Autograph books KGC Military Archives Material
Drummy, M	96 Blarney Street, Cork	Military Archives Material Autograph books KGC
Duffy, Molly	Glasgow, Scotland	Autograph books KGC
Duggan, M	Salthill, Co Galway	Military Archives Material
Duggan, Máire (Mary)	Eyre Street, Castlegar, Galway	Military Archives Material Autograph books KGC
Duggan, Pidge	9 Huntley Terrace, Kelvinside North, Glasgow, Scotland	Military Archives Material
Duke, Mairéad	St Margaret's, Co Dublin (Kilbride Camp)	Autograph books KGC Military Archives Material
Dunn(e), Lily	7 Leitrim Place, Grand Canal Street, Dublin	Military Archives Material D Macardle account. Autograph books KGC
Earner, Julia	Knocklehard, Headford, Co Galway	Military Archives Material Kilmainham List 23
Eivers, Josephine (Josie)	28 George's Place, Dublin	Military Archives Material Autograph books KGC Jangle of the Keys
Fagan, Margaret (Maggie)	Mercer Street, Dublin	Autograph books KGC (in list) Military Archives Material
Falconer, Kay (Kitty)		Autograph books KGC Military Archives Material
Falkner, Josie	1 D'Arcy's Cottages, Ballsbridge, Dublin	Military Archives Material
Falkner, Kitty	4 D'Arcy's Cottages, Ballsbridge, Dublin	Military Archives Material
Fallon, Kate	24 Templeshannon, Enniscorthy, Co Wexford	Military Archives Material
Farrell, Dorothea	24 Gardiner Place, Dublin	Military Archives Material
Farrelly, Rita		D Macardle account
Fennell, Nellie	Grattan Villas, Mulgrave Street, Limerick	Military Archives Material LOB letters UCDA Autograph books KGC
Ffrench, Julia	36 Clarendon Street, Dublin	Military Archives Material Autograph books KGC

NAME	DETAILS	REFERENCE
Ffrench, Mary	Smarmore, Ardee, Co Louth	Autograph book KGC Military Archives Material
FitzGerald, E (Lizzie)	28 Fishamble Street, Dublin	Military Archives Material MS, 33,033 NLI
FitzGerald, Máire (Mollie)	4 Ophelia Terrace, The Lough, Cork	Military Archives Material Autograph books KGC
FitzGerald, Peg (Margaret)	Castlegregory, Co Kerry	Military Archives Material Autograph books KGC
FitzPatrick, Maggie	9 Pembroke Street, Irishtown, Dublin	Military Archives Material
Flaherty, Mollie	Clady, Urney, Co Tyrone	Military Archives Material
Flanagan, Peg	Technical Schools, Blackrock, Co Dublin	Autograph books KGC Military Archives Material
Fleming, Mary	Gas Terrace, Tralee, Co Kerry	Autograph books KGC Military Archives Material
Fleury, Dr. Elenora (Norah)	Portrane Mental Hospital	Autograph books KGC Military Archives Material
Flood, Josephine (Josie)	Portester, Blue Bell, Inchicore, Dublin	Autograph books KGC
Flynn, Angela (Angel)	Scart Road, Bantry, Co Cork	Military Archives Material Autograph books KGC Kilmainham List
Flynn, Kate	Youghal, Co Cork	Kilmainham List Military Archives Material
Flynn, Veronica	The Gur, Mayor St	Military Archives Material
Fogarty, Kathleen (Kitty)	Castlebridge, Wexford and 1 Northbrook Road, Dublin	Military Archives Material Autograph books KGC
Folan, Katharine (Jake)	William Street, Sea Road, West Galway	Inscription in cell KG Military Archives Material Autograph books KGC
Foley, Annie	Blennerville, Tralee, Co Kerry	Military Archives Material Autograph books KGC
Foley, Kathleen (Cáit)	49 Norfolk Street, Dublin	Military Archives Material Autograph books KGC
Fox, Annie	124 Upper Abbey St, Dublin	Military Archives Material Autograph books KGC
Freeman, Annie	29 South William St, Dublin	Military Archives Material Autograph books KGC
Freeman, Dolly	29 South William St, Dublin	Military Archives Material
Freeman, Kathleen	29 South William St, Dublin	Autograph books KGC
French, Dora	39 Harcourt Street, Dublin	LOB letters UCDA Military Archives Material
French, Máire	Clady, Co Tyrone	Military Archives Material
Gallagher, Agnes	Westport, Co Mayo and Bridge St, Dublin	Autograph books KGC Military Archives Material
Gallagher, Mrs Cecilia	23 Lr Pembroke St, Dublin	Inscription in cell KG Autograph books KGC Jangle of the Keys Military Archives Material
Gannon, Anna	27 Baggot Street, Dublin	Military Archives Material

NAME	DETAILS	REFERENCE
Garvey, Evelyn	Blackrock, Co Louth	Kilmainham List 23 Military Archives Material Inscription in cell KG
Garvin, Una	1 Prince Arthur Terrace, Rathmines, Dublin	Military Archives Material
Gaughran, Judy	6 St Brigid's Terrace, Dundalk, Co Louth	Jangle of the Keys Inscription in cell KG Kilmainham List 23 Autograph book KGC Military Archives Material
Geoghagan, May (Peg)	4 Seapoint Tce	Autograph book KGC Military Archives Material
Gibney, May	Temple Street, Dublin	Autograph book KGC Military Archives Material
Gill, Mary (Mollie)	Murphystown, Dundrum, Co Dublin	Autograph book KGC Military Archives Material
Gillies, Nora	4 Eagle Hill, Terenure, Dublin	Autograph book KGC Military Archives Material
Gilmore, Mrs F	Billesgarda, Blackrock, Co Dublin	Military Archives Material
Gilroy, Ellie	Killala, Co Mayo	Military Archives Material
Gleeson, Breeid	60 Lr Dominick St, Dublin	Military Archives Material Autograph books KGC
Gleeson, Lily (Lillie)	159 Phibsboro Rd, Dublin	Military Archives Material Autograph books KGC Inscription in cell KG
Gleeson, Margaret	60 Lr Dominick St, Dublin	Military Archives Material
Gleeson, Nora	50 Lr Dominick St, Dublin	Autograph books KGC
Glynn, Katie	Spring Vale, Temple Rd, Dublin	Military Archives Material
Gordon, Mrs Winnie	8 Landsdowne Terrace, Dublin	Autograph books KGC D Macardle account Military Archives Material
Gough (Goff), M A	Enniscorthy, Co Wexford	Military Archives Material Autograph books KGC
Grace, Elizabeth	Graigue, New Inn, Cahir, Co Tipperary	Military Archives Material Kilmainham List
Groarke, Nellie	Swinford, Co Mayo	Military Archives Material Kilmainham List
Grogan, Mary		Military Archives Material
Guilfoyle, Fanny	Clifden, Co Galway	Autograph books KGC Military Archives Material
Guilfoyle, Katie	'Sea View', Clifden, Co Galway	Autograph books KGC Military Archives Material
Halpin, Bridget (Bridie)	4, Nicholas Street, Dublin	Autograph books KGC Military Archives Material
Hanafin, Dorothy	17, Nelson Street, Tralee, Co Kerry	Autograph books KGC Military Archives Material
Hangan, Mary		Autograph books KGC
Hardwicke, Annie (alias of Bridie Clyne)	4, Strand Road, Merrion, Dublin	Military Archives Material
Harley, M.		Military Archives Material

NAME	DETAILS	REFERENCE
Harpur, Kitty	Kildarra Cottages, Dillon Place, Dublin	Autograph books KGC Military Archives Material
Harris, May	3 Holles Place, Dublin	Autograph book KGC LOB letters UCDA Military Archives Material
Harte, P		Autograph book KGC
Hartnett, Sheila	The Medical Hall, Kenmare, Co Kerry	Military Archives Material Autograph books KGC D Macardle account
Hassett, Julia	Kerry	Autograph books KGC Military Archives Material
Hassett, Pauline	Chapel Street, Tralee, Co Kerry	Autograph books KGC Military Archives Material
Hay-Byrne, Mary	10 Lr Mount Street, Dublin	Military Archives Material
Healy Mrs Liam	Ballysaggart, Co Kilkenny	Autograph book KGC
Heffernan, Madge	Gladstone Street, Clonmel, Co Tipperary	Military Archives Material Autograph books KGC
Heffernan, May	Ballinard, Clogheen, Co Tipperary	Military Archives Material Autograph books KGC
Heraghty, Bridget	Dunfore Cottage, Maugheron, Sligo	Military Archives Material Autograph books KGC
Herbert, Bridget	1 Northbrook Road, Dublin	Military Archives Material
Heyburne, Mary	10 Lr Mount Street, Dublin	Military Archives Material
Higgins, Annie	Kilmore, Co Kilkenny	Military Archives Material
Higgins, Eileen	4 Camden Row, Dublin	Military Archives Material
Hills, Caroline	21 Synge Street, South Circular Rd, Dublin	Military Archives Material
Hogan, Annie (Nan)	Cratloe, Co Clare	LOB letters UCDA Military Archives Material Autograph books KGC
Hoyne, Helena Mary (Nellie)	South Circular Rd, Dublin	LOB letters UCDA Autograph books KGC Military Archives Material
Humphreys, Agnes (Nell)	36 Ailesbury Road, Dublin	Jangle of the Keys Autograph books KGC Military Archives Material
Humphreys, Sighle	36 Ailesbury Road, Dublin	Jangle of the Keys Autograph books KGC Military Archives Material
Hurley, Frances	Ballybrack, Co Dublin	Autograph books KGC
Hurley, G Norah	Penny Street, Tralee, Co Kerry	Military Archives Material
Hurley, Jennie	Blackrock (Rd), Bantry, Co Cork	Kilmainham List Military Archives Material
Hurley, Margaret	Galway	Autograph book KGC
Hurley, Maud	Blackrock (Rd), Bantry, Co Cork	Military Archives Material
Hyland, Bridie	101 Pleasant Blgs, Dublin	Military Archives Material
Hyland, Catherine	11 Chester Road, Ranelagh, Dublin	Military Archives Material

NAME	DETAILS	REFERENCE
Hyland, Mollie	11 Chester Road, Ranelagh, Dublin	Autograph books KGC Kilmainham List Military Archives Material
Ivers, Annie J	Loughlinstown Union, Co Dublin	Autograph books KGC
Ivers, Bridie		Autograph books KGC
Ivers, May (Mary Frances)	20 Parnell Tce, Glenageary Rd, Dun Laoghaire, Co Dublin	Autograph books KGC
Jeffares, Dollie	Grove Cottage, 7 Grove Ave, Blackrock, Co Dublin	Autograph books KGC Military Archives Material
Jenkins, Connie	37, Old Kilmainham, Dublin	Military Archives Material
Jenkins, M		Autograph books KGC
Johnson, Kathleen	6 Rosemount Tce, Booterstown, Co Dublin	LOB letters UCDA Military Archives Material
Jones, Mary (May)	10 Spittlesfields, Dublin	Autograph books KGC Military Archives Material
Kavanagh, Josephine	Synge Street, Dublin	Kilmainham List Autograph book KGC
Kavanagh, Kathleen		Autograph book KGC
Keane, Daisy	Anglesea Street, Cork	Kilmainham List Military Archives Material
Keane, Elizabeth (Lily)	117 Stella Gardens, Sandymount, Dublin	Military Archives Material Autograph book KGC
Kearns, May	81 Foley Street, Dublin	Military Archives Material Autograph book KGC
Kelly, Annie	'Bella Vista', Ardbrough Road, Dalkey, Co Dublin	Military Archives Material
Kelly, Bridget (Bridie)	Grangebellew, Dunleer, Co Louth	Military Archives Material Autograph books KGC
Kelly, Chrissie	11 Longford Tce, Monkstown, Co Dublin	Military Archives Material Autograph books KGC
Kelly, Fanny	Abbeyleix, Co Laois	Military Archives Material Autograph books KGC
Kelly, Gretta		Military Archives Material
Kelly, Kathleen	Howth Junction Cottages, Howth, Co Dublin	Military Archives Material
Kelly, May		Autograph books KGC
Kelly, Rosanna (Rosina O'Kelly)	Creeslough, Co Donegal	Kilmainham List Military Archives Material Autograph books KGC
Kenny, Kitty (Cathleen)	New Street, Dublin	MS. 33,033 N.L. Ireland Autograph books KGC
Kenny, Mary	2 York Street, Dublin and 120 Lr Clanbrassil St, Dublin	Kilmainham List Military Archives Material
Keogh, Mary J	17 Parnell Street, Clonmel, Co Tipperary	Autograph book KGC Military Archives Material
Keyes, May (Mai Lily)	4 Market Street, Bantry, Co Cork	Kilmainham List Autograph books KGC
Kiernan Dawson, Lily (L M E)	Elm Grove, Granard, Co Longford	Autograph book KGC Military Archives Material

NAME	DETAILS	REFERENCE
Kiernans, Lily (Jos)	5 Eglington Tce, Dublin	Autograph book KGC
Kinsilla, Rosaline	Gulistan Place, Rathmines, Dublin	Military Archives Material
Kirwan, Mrs Kathleen	64 Harcourt Street, Dublin	Autograph books KGC Jangle of the Keys Military Archives Material
Lally, Kathleen (Kate)	15 New Street, Dublin	Kilmainham List Military Archives Material
Lally, Maggi	15 McCaffery Estate, Mount Brown, Dublin	Military Archives Material Autograph books KGC Inscription in cell KG
Lambert, Nellie	Old Bridge House, Milltown, Co Dublin	Military Archives Material Autograph books KGC
Langan, Mary		Military Archives Material
Langan, Mary (May)	8 Victoria Terrace, Terenure, Dublin	Military Archives Material Autograph books KGC
Lavery, Mrs Harriette	13 Nth Earl Street, Dublin	Military Archives Material
Lavery, Marjorie (Maynie)	13 Nth Earl Street, Dublin and Howth, Co Dublin	Military Archives Material Autograph books KGC
Lawless Moore, Annie	2 Tramway Villas, Terenure, Dublin	Military Archives Material Autograph books KGC
Lawlor, Kathleen		Military Archives Material
Lawlor, Maggie (Peg)	Foulkesmill, Co Wexford	Autograph books KGC Kilmainham List Military Archives Material
Leach, Mary (May)	19 Nth William St, Dublin	Autograph books KGC Military Archives Material
Lehane, Bridget	Scart, Bantry, Co Cork	Military Archives Material
Lehane, Peg	Scart, Bantry, Co Cork	Autograph book KGC Military Archives Material
Lemney, Annie	Garvagh, Co Donegal	Autograph books KGC
Lemney, Cathlin		Autograph books KGC
Lenihan, Minnie	Abbeygate St, Galway	Military Archives Material
Lennon, Margaret	Liverpool, England	Autograph books KGC
Leville, Margaret	Mill St, Galway	Military Archives Material
Livery, Máire	Liverpool, England	Autograph books KGC
Loughney, Nancy	Killala, Co Mayo	Military Archives Material
Lyden, Norah	Clifden, Co Galway	Military Archives Material
Lynch, Jeannie	11 Upper Camden Street, Dublin	Military Archives Material
Macardle, Dorothy	St Margaret's, Dundalk, Co Louth	Autograph book KGC Military Archives Material
MacBride, Maud	Roebuck House, Clonskeagh, Dublin	LOB letters UCDA Autograph book KGC Military Archives Material
MacDermott, Blathnaid		Autograph book KGC D Macardle account
MacDermott, Sorcha	London	Autograph book KGC
MacDonagh, Julia	Lisvernane, Co Tipperary	Military Archives Material
MacDonagh, Marian	Lisvernane, Co Tipperary	Military Archives Material
MacDonnell, Mary (Mrs)	21, Werburgh Street, Dublin	Military Archives Material

NAME	DETAILS	REFERENCE
MacInerney, Sighle (Sinéad)	Kilkee, Co Clare	Autograph book KGC Military Archives Material
MacKeon, Annie		Autograph book KGC
MacMahon, Ciss		Autograph book KGC
MacMahon, Kathleen		Autograph book KGC
MacNamara, Alice	3 Grove Ave, Harold's Cross, Dublin	Autograph book KGC
MacSweeney, Annie	Belgrave Place, Cork	Military Archives Material Autograph book KGC
MacSweeney, Mary	Station House, Tubbercurry, Co Sligo	Military Archives Material Autograph book KGC
MacSwiney, Mary	Moyderwell, Tralee, Co Kerry	Military Archives Material Autograph book KGC
MacSwiney, Mary	Belgrave Place, Cork	Military Archives Material Autograph book KGC
Magee, Kathleen	Dublin	Military Archives Material Autograph book KGC
Maher, Kitty	Botanic Dairy, Glasnevin, Dublin	LOB letters UCDA Military Archives Material
Mahon, Mary	Forster Street, Galway	Military Archives Material Autograph book KGC
Malone, Mary (Máire)	New Street West, Galway	Military Archives Material Autograph book KGC
Malone, Nora(h)	Harborne Hill, Sligo	Military Archives Material Autograph book KGC
Maloney, Ciss	Foley Street, Dublin	Military Archives Material
Maloney, Kathleen (Bessie)	136 Leinster Road, Rathmines, Dublin	Military Archives Material
Maloney, May	Lackelly, Emly, Co Tipperary	Inscription in cell KG Autograph book KGC
Markievicz, Constance	Dublin	Military Archives Material
Martin, Mary	14 McDonagh Street, Wexford	Military Archives Material Autograph book KGC
Martin, Peg	Loughlinstown, Co Dublin	Autograph book KGC
Masterson, E	Newbridge, Co Kildare	Military Archives Material
McBride, Mary (Máire)	Dunloe, Co Donegal	Kilmainham List Autograph books KGC
McBride, Sinéad	13 Holles Street, Dublin	Autograph books KGC
McBride (MacBride), Teresa	13 Holles Street, Dublin	Military Archives Material Autograph books KGC
McCarthy, Mollie	Lattin, Co Tipperary	Military Archives Material Autograph books KGC
McClean, Elizabeth (Lillian)	5 Ross Road, Dublin	Military Archives Material Autograph books KGC
McCormack, Eilis	20 Monck Place, Dublin	Military Archives Material Autograph books KGC
McDermott, F	37 Kenilworth Park, Dublin	Military Archives Material
McDonnell, Mary	12 Holles Street, Dublin	Military Archives Material Autograph books KGC LOB letters UCDA
McDonnell, Nellie	Stillorgan Road, Co Dublin	Military Archives Material Autograph books KGC

NAME	DETAILS	REFERENCE
McGarry, Florrie	17 Carlisle Street, S C R, Dublin	Military Archives Material
McGee, Kathleen (Kate/Kitty/Kathy)	Tymore, Creeslough, Co Donegal and 55 Fontenoy St, Dublin	Autograph books KGC Military Archives Material Kilmainham List
McGee, Mary	Tymore, Creeslough, Co Donegal	Kilmainham List Military Archives Material
McGee, Sadie	Tymore, Creeslough, Co Donegal And 38 Blackhall Place, Dublin	Military Archives Material Autograph books KGC
McGeehan (Nic Aodain), Teresa	Kingarron, Fenton, Co Donegal	Autograph books KGC Kilmainham List Military Archives Material
McGrane, Eileen	21 Dawson Street, Dublin	Autograph books KGC Jangle of the Keys Military Archives Material
McGrath, Alice (Nan)	Farron, Emly, Co Tipperary	Autograph books KGC Kilmainham List Military Archives Material
McGrath, Josie (Joe)	Farron, Emly, Co Tipperary	Autograph book KGC
Nan	Same address	
McGrath, Polly	8 St Patrick's Road, Dalkey, Co Dublin	Autograph book KGC
McGrath, Siobhan	Emly, Co Tipperary	Autograph book KGC
McGreakin, Celia (Sile)	Killyclogher, Co Leitrim	Military Archives Material Autograph book KGC
McHale, Mary	Ballina, Co Mayo	Military Archives Material
McInerney, Rose	13 Augustine Street, Dublin	Autograph books KGC Kilmainham List
McInerney, S	Kilkee, County Clare	Military Archives Material
McKeown, Annie	117 Strand Road, Sandymount, Dublin	D Macardle account Military Archives Material Autograph book KGC
McMahon, Ciss		Autograph book KGC
McManamon, Emma	George's Street, Newport, Co Mayo	Military Archives Material Autograph book KGC
McNeary (MacNeary), Maud(e)	10 Melbourne Ave, Drumcondra, Dublin	Military Archives Material Autograph book KGC
McSweeney, May	Hanratty's Hotel, Limerick	Military Archives Material
Meaney, Lillie	Church Cross, Macroom, Co Cork	Military Archives Material
Medlar, Peg	29 Adelaide Road, Dublin	LOB letters UCDA Military Archives Material
Melfee, Kitty		Autograph books KGC
Merrigan, Elizabeth		Autograph books KGC
Merrigan, Kathleen		Autograph books KGC
Merrigan, Marie		Autograph books KGC
Merrigan, Nellie		Autograph books KGC
Merrigan, Susan		Autograph books KGC

NAME	DETAILS	REFERENCE
Millar, Sarah	62 Upper Clanbrassil St, Dublin	Military Archives Material
Moloney, Bessie	136 Leinster Road, Rathmines, Dublin	Military Archives Material
Moloney, Chrissie	Dublin	Autograph book KGC
Moloney, Kathleen	136 Leinster Road, Rathmines, Dublin	Military Archives Material
Moloney, Lizzie	83 Foley Road, Dublin	Military Archives Material
Monahan, Bridget	Marino Street, Bantry, Co Cork	Military Archives Material
Mooney, Rosie	17 Rutland Cottages, Lr Rutland Street, Dublin	Autograph books KGC Military Archives Material
Moore, Annie	Rathbride Bridge, Co Kildare	Jangle of the Keys Autograph books KGC Military Archives Material
Moore, Mrs Kathleen	6 Lr Columba's Road, Dublin	Military Archives Material
Moore, Mary (May)	422 North Circular Rd, Dublin	Autograph books KGC Military Archives Material
Moore, Maureen C	Dungannon, Co Tyrone	Autograph books KGC/A3 Military Archives Material
Moran, Eileen	3 South Richmond Street, Dublin	Military Archives Material
Moran, Mrs Eilis (Lizzie)	10 Robson Street, Glasgow, Scotland	Military Archives Material Autograph book KGC
Moran, Kathleen	89 Pembroke Cottages, Dublin	Military Archives Material
Morgan, Annie	12 Bridge Street, Dundalk, Co Louth and 10 Grays Street, Dublin	LOB letters UCDA Military Archives Material Autograph books KGC
Morrisey, Margaret	West Limerick	Autograph books KGC
Morrisey, Mona	6 High Street, Dublin	Military Archives Material
Moynihan, Hanna	Ballymullen, Tralee, Co Kerry	Autograph books KGC Military Archives Material
Mulhern, Annie	Bridge Street, Dundalk, Co Louth	Autograph books KGC Military Archives Material
Mullen, Annie (Nano)	Church Street, Sligo	Kilmainham List Autograph books KGC Military Archives Material
Mulligan, Rosalind (Rose)	32 Monck Place, Phibsboro, Dublin	Military Archives Material Autograph books KGC Inscription in cell KG
Mullins, Bridie	Coolnashaughtna, Myshall, Co Carlow	Military Archives Material
Murphy, Constance (Connie)	Garville Ave, Rathgar, Dublin	Military Archives Material Autograph books KGC
Murphy, Dr Elsie	Carraroe, Connemara, Co Galway	Military Archives Material Autograph books KGC
Murphy, Kathleen	Blackpool Buildings, 17 Commons Road, Cork	Military Archives Material Autograph books KGC
Murphy, Nora	Pouladuff Road, Cork	Military Archives Material
Murphy, Peggy	20 Hope Street, Dublin.	Military Archives Material Autograph books KGC

NAME	DETAILS	REFERENCE
Murray, May	9 Montague Place, Dublin	Military Archives Material Autograph books KGC
Murray, Nellie	282 Blarney Street, Cork	Military Archives Material
Nagle, Sheila (Sinéad/Jennie)	Castlemaine, Kerry &. 71, Cabra Road, Dublin	Military Archives Material Autograph books KGC
Nally, Theresa	Eyre Square, Mary St. Galway and Caltra House, Claremorris, Co Mayo	Military Archives Material Autograph books KGC
Nelson, Mary Agnes	Glasgow, Scotland	Autograph book KGC
Neville, Margaret	Mill Street, Galway	Autograph books KGC LOB letters UCDA Military Archives Material
Nolan, Mrs M	49 Synge Street, S C Rd, Dublin	Military Archives Material
Nolan, Nell	Rathmore, Tullow, Co Carlow.	Military Archives Material Autograph book KGC
Noonan, Sarah	Liscarroll, Cork	Military Archives Material
Nunne, L		Military Archives Material
O'Beirne, F	Roebuck House, Clonskeagh, Dublin	Military Archives Material
O'Brennan, Eileen	30 Oakley Road, Ranelagh, Dublin	Autograph books KGC
O'Brennan, Lily	44 Oakley Road, Ranelagh, Dublin	Autograph books KGC Military Archives Material
O'Brien, Julia (Juggie)	Silvermines, Nenagh, Co Tipperary	Autograph books KGC Military Archives Material
O'Brien, Kathleen	68 Patrick's Street, Cork.	Autograph books KGC Military Archives Material
O'Brien, Lena	Dublin	Autograph books KGC
O'Brien, Lily	68 Albert Road, Dalkey, Co Dublin	Military Archives Material LOB account UCDA Kilmainham List Autograph books KGC
O'Brien (Ní Bhriain), Margaret	6, Church Rd, Dalkey, Co Dublin	Military Archives Material Autograph books KGC
O'Brien (Ní Bhriain), N	55 Pimlico, Dublin	Military Archives Material
O'Brien, Rosie	31 Upper William Street, Limerick	Autograph books KGC Military Archives Material
O'Byrne, Bridget	17, Berentine Ave, Heresford, England	Military Archives Material
O'Byrne, Florence	Dublin	Autograph books KGC
O'Callaghan, Anna	27 Lr Baggot Street, Dublin	Military Archives Material
O'Callaghan, Annie	Chapel Street, Dublin	Military Archives Material
O'Callaghan, Mrs Kate	Limerick	Autograph books KGC Military Archives Material
O'Carroll, Eileen	Washington Lodge, Grange Rd, Rathfarnham, Co Dublin	Military Archives Material Autograph books KGC
O'Carroll, Ethna	21 Belvedere Road, Bray, Co Wicklow	Autograph books KGC Military Archives Material
O'Carroll, Kathleen	The Lawn, Peter Place, Adelaide Road, Dublin	Military Archives Material LOB letters UCDA Autograph books KGC

NAME	DETAILS	REFERENCE
O'Carroll, Mary	55, North Clarence St, Dublin	Autograph books KGC Kilmainham List
O'Carroll, Moya	St Aidans Tce, Bray, Co Wicklow	Autograph books KGC Military Archives Material
O'Carroll, Nora	St Aidans Tce, Bray, Co Wicklow	Autograph books KGC Military Archives Material
O'Connell, Maureen	Blarney, Co Cork	Military Archives Material
O'Connell, Sadie	12 Bushy Park Rd, Rathgar, Co Dublin	Military Archives Material
O'Connell, Teresa	Caherdaniel, Co Kerry	Autograph books KGC
O'Connor, Bridie	5 Moyderwell, Tralee, Co Kerry	Autograph books KGC Military Archives Material
O'Connor, Mrs Eileen	1a Lyon Street, Fauclough Lane, Liverpool	Military Archives Material
O'Connor, Fanny	Elm Hall, Celbridge, Co Kildare	Autograph book in KGC
O'Connor, Hanna	Castle Desmond, Ballymullen, Tralee, Co Kerry	Autograph books KGC Military Archives Material
O'Connor, Kathleen		Autograph books KGC
O'Connor, Madge	Upper Bansha, Co Tipperary	Autograph books KGC
O'Doherty (Doherty), Cissie	Dungloe, Co Donegal	Autograph books KGC Military Archives Material
O'Doherty, Lena	Newtown Cottages, Church Street, Bundoran, Co Donegal	Autograph books KGC Military Archives Material
O'Doherty, Nora(h)	McCurtain Street, Cork	Autograph books KGC Military Archives Material
O'Dolan, Frances	8 Landsdowne Tce, Dublin	Military Archives Material
O'Donnell, Eliza	Castlegregory, Co Kerry	Autograph books KGC Military Archives Material
O'Donnell, Rose (Róísin)	Meemore, Dunloe, Co Donegal	Military Archives Material Kilmainham List Autograph books KGC
O'Donovan, Annie (Kitty)	24 Nicolas Street, Cork	Autograph books KGC Military Archives Material
O'Farrell, Dorothea		Military Archives Material
O'Farrelly, Annie	Oakley, Vernon Ave, Clontarf, Dublin	Military Archives Material
O'Farrelly, Rita	Oakley, Vernon Ave, Clontarf, Dublin	Autograph books KGC D Macardle account Military Archives Material
O'Flaherty, Mollie		Military Archives Material
O'Grady, Bridget	George St, Newport, Co Mayo	Military Archives Material
O'Halloran, Mary	Granny, Co Galway	Military Archives Material
O'Halloran, Maura	Limerick	Autograph books KGC
O'Hanlon, Sheila	7 Camac Place, Dolphins Barn, Dublin	Military Archives Material
O'Harte, Bridie	24 Gardiner's Place, Dublin	Military Archives Material
O'Higgins, Aileen	Joy Cottage, Ticknock, Sandyford, Co Dublin	Autograph books KGC

NAME	DETAILS	REFERENCE
O' Hora, Ida	Ballina, Co Mayo	Autograph books KGC Military Archives Material
O'Keefe, Nora	Fairview, Dublin	Kilmainham List
O'Keefe, Noreen	Goolds Cross, Tipperary	Autograph books KGC
O'Kelly, Cis		Autograph books KGC
O'Kelly, May	93 Harold's Cross Rd, Dublin	Military Archives Material Autograph books KGC
O'Kelly, Peggy		Autograph books KGC
O'Moore, Cathleen		Autograph books KGC
O'Mullane, Bridie (Brigid)	73 Heytesbury Street, Dublin	Inscription in cell KG Autograph books KGC Military Archives Material
O'Neill, Annie	The Asylum, Enniscorthy, Co Wexford	Military Archives Material Autograph books KGC
O'Neill, Frances (Fanny)	8 Maples Place, Dublin	Military Archives Material Kilmainham List Autograph books KGC
O'Neill, Mrs Hanna(h)	7 Park Terrace, Francis St, Dublin 8	Military Archives Material Autograph books KGC
O'Rahilly Anna (Annie)	36 Ailesbury Road, Dublin	Military Archives Material Autograph books KGC
O'Rahilly, Kitty	Spitland House, Ballyneaty Rd, Limerick	Autograph book KGC
O'Rahilly, May	Spitland House, Ballyneaty Rd, Limerick	Military Archives Material Autograph books KGC
O'Reilly, Bridget	8 Temple Bar, Dublin	Military Archives Material
O'Reilly, Molly	Dalkey, Co Dublin	Autograph books KGC
O'Rourke, Eileen		Autograph books KGC
O'Shaughnessy, May	Jances Harbour, Grand Canal	Military Archives Material
O'Shea, Eileen	Tomervane, Blennerville, Tralee, Co Kerry	Military Archives Material Autograph books KGC
O'Shea, Nora	134 Parnell Street, Dublin	Military Archives Material Autograph books KGC
O'Sullivan, Florence (Flo/Blathnaid)	246, North Circular Road, Dublin	Military Archives Material Autograph books KGC
O'Sullivan, Kitty	The Eglington Asylum, Cork	Kilmainham List Autograph book KGC
O'Sullivan, Mary	Glengarriff Road, (Bantry), Cork	Military Archives Material Autograph books KGC
O'Sullivan (Sullivan), Nora	5 Devonshire St (Nth), Cork	Military Archives Material Autograph books KGC
O'Toole, Mrs A		Autograph books KGC
O'Toole, Bea (Bridie)	6 Priory St, New Ross, Co Wexford	Military Archives Material Autograph books KGC
O'Toole, Jennie	9 Leinster Ave, North Strand, Dublin	Military Archives Material Autograph books KGC
O'Toole, Maggie	Tomduff, Borris, Co Carlow	Military Archives Material
O'Toole, Maureen (May)	9 Leinster Ave, North Strand, Dublin	Military Archives Material Autograph books KGC
Owens, Katie	Douglas Road, Cork	Military Archives Material
Penrose, Kitty	Cecil Street, Limerick	Military Archives Material

NAME	DETAILS	REFERENCE
Perry, Eva	18 Batchelor's Quay, Dublin	Military Archives Material
Perry, J	18 Batchelor's Quay, Dublin	Military Archives Material
Phelan, Maeve (Melina)	14, Wexford Street, Dublin	Military Archives Material D Macardle account Autograph books KGC
Plunkett, Fiona	Upper Fitzwilliam St, Dublin	Inscription in cell in KG Autograph books KGC
Plunkett, Mrs Grace	40 Philipsburg Ave, Fairview, Co Dublin	Military Archives Material Autograph books KGC
Powell, Bridie	11 Mark Street, Dublin	Military Archives Material
Powell, Molly	11 Monck Street, Dublin	MS. 33,033 NLI Military Archives Material
Powell, Nellie	Grattan Villa, Mulgrave St, Limerick	Military Archives Material
Power, Johanna (Jo) (de Paor, Siobhán)	Rock Street, Tralee, Co Kerry	Military Archives Material Autograph book KGC
Power, Margaret (Cis) (de Paor, Mairéad)	Rock Street, Tralee, Co Kerry	Autograph books KGC
Power, Mary Jo (M J)	Bremor House, Piltown, Carrick-on-Suir, Co Tipperary	LOB letters UCDA Military Archives Material Autograph books KGC
Power, Maureen (Máirín)	21 Ely Place, Dublin	Military Archives Material
Quinn, Florrie	Claregalway, Co Galway	Military Archives Material Autograph books KGC
Quinn, Mary	Swinford, Co Mayo	Military Archives Material Autograph books KGC
Quinn, Peg	19 Monck Place, Drumcondra, Dublin	Military Archives Material Inscription in cell KGC Autograph books KGC
Ramsbottom, May	164 Deansgrange, Blackrock, Co Dublin	Military Archives Material Autograph books KGC
Redmond, M A (Máire)	19 Carlisle St, South Circular Rd, Dublin	Military Archives Material Autograph books KGC
Reid, Bridget	Dublin	Autograph books KGC
Reid, Mrs Margaret	3 Nicholas Street, Dublin	Autograph books KGC Military Archives Material
Reid, Mrs Mary	17 Carlisle St, South Circular Rd, Dublin	Military Archives Material Autograph books KGC
Reilly, Brigid	6 Temple Bar, Dublin	Military Archives Material Autograph books KGC
Reilly, May		Autograph book KGC
Richmond, Mary Anne	19 Carlisle St, South Circular Rd, Dublin	Military Archives Material
Robinson, Elizabeth	Harold's Cross Bridge, Dublin	Military Archives Material
Robinson, Sinéad	Harold's Cross, Bridge, Dublin	Military Archives Material Autograph books KGC
Rogers, Mrs Nora	24 Gardiners Place, Dublin and Kilmore House, Silvermines, Nenagh, Co Tipperary	Military Archives Material Autograph books KGC

NAME	DETAILS	REFERENCE
Rossiter, Helen	Wexford and 168 Rathgar Rd, Dublin	Military Archives Material Autograph books KGC
Ryan, C	Filemore, Caherciveen, Co Kerry	Autograph books KGC
Ryan, Eileen	32 Leinster Road, Dublin	LOB letters UCDA Military Archives Material Autograph books KGC
Ryan, Esther	Sweetmount, Dundrum, Co Dublin	Military Archives Material
Ryan (O'Ryan), Nellie	Tomcoole, Wexford	Autograph book KGC LOB letters UCDA Military Archives Material
Ryan, Róisín (Rose)	2, Adelaide Rd, Dublin	Autograph book KGC LOB letters UCDA Military Archives Material
Ryan, Susan	58 Church Street, Dublin	Autograph book KGC Military Archives Material
Scanlon, Mary (Molly)	21 Raglan Road, Dublin and Cork	Autograph book KGC Military Archives Material
Sheehan, Winnie	Belgrave Place, Cork	Military Archives Material
Sheehy, Agnes (Big Aggie)	3 Urban Cottages, Boherbee, Tralee, Co Kerry	Autograph book KGC Military Archives Material
Shelly, Eileen	Loreto Hall, Dublin	Autograph book KGC Military Archives Material
Simpson, Matilda (Tilley)	Upton Cottage, Goose Green, Drumcondra, Dublin	Autograph book KGC LOB letters UCDA Military Archives Material
Sinnott, Annie	Clover Hill, Tralee, Co Kerry	Autograph book KGC Military Archives Material
Skinnider, Margaret	Dublin	Autograph book KGC Military Archives Material
Smith, Sheila	59 Pembroke Cottages, Donnybrook, Dublin	Autograph book KGC Military Archives Material
Snoddy. Essie (Lizzie)	Black Bog, Carlow	Military Archives Material
Somers (Summer), Mrs Margaret	The Forge, Anna Liffey, Lucan, Co Dublin	Autograph book KGC Military Archives Material
Spain, Margaret	37 Sandwich St, Dublin	Autograph book KGC LOB letters UCDA Military Archives Material
Spillane, Nora	Lough Tiltane, Killarney, Co Kerry	Autograph books KGC
Spillane, Nora	Liverpool, England	Autograph books KGC
Stafford, Christina (Chrissie)	23 Drumcondra Road, Dublin	Military Archives Material Autograph books KGC
Stuart, Mrs Iseult	Roebuck House, Clonskeagh, Dublin	Military Archives Material
Sweeney, Margaret (Mary/Mairéad)	Pearse Street, Ardagh, Ballina, Co Mayo	Military Archives Material Autograph books KGC
Taaffe, Aoife (Effie)	Dublin	Kilmainham List Autograph books KGC Military Archives Material

NAME	DETAILS	REFERENCE
Tallon, Mary-Kate (Mary)	24 Templeshannon, The Colloyne, Enniscorthy, Co Wexford	Kilmainham List Autograph books KGC Military Archives Material
Tallon, May	123 Deansgrange, Blackrock, Co Dublin	Autograph books KGC Military Archives Material
Thewliss, Lillian (Lily)	Chapelizod, Co Dublin	Autograph books KGC Military Archives Material
Thornley, Mary	3 Dean Swift Square, Dublin	Autograph books KGC Military Archives Material
Timmons, Mrs Mary (Maggie)	16 Pembroke Street, Irishtown, Dublin	Autograph books KGC Military Archives Material
Timoney, Annie	Garvagh, Barnes Mor, Co Donegal	Autograph books KGC LOB letters UCDA Military Archives Material
Timoney, Claire	Killala, Co Mayo	Military Archives Material
Tubbert, Alice	1 Estate Cottage, Shelbourne Rd, Ballsbridge, Dublin	Autograph books KGC Military Archives Material
Tubbert, Annie	1 Estate Cottage, Shelbourne Rd, Ballsbridge, Dublin	Autograph books KGC Military Archives Material
Tubbert, Eileen (Eilis)	1 Estate Cottage, Shelbourne Rd, Ballsbridge, Dublin	Autograph books KGC Military Archives Material
Tucker, Eileen	37 Capel Street, Dublin	Inscription in cell KG Autograph books KGC Military Archives Material
Twamley, Mary	Dublin	Autograph books KGC Military Archives Material
Twohig, Betty	Canty's Hotel, Bantry, Co Cork	Military Archives Material
Tyndall, Annette	Blennerville, Tralee, Co Kerry	Military Archives Material Autograph books KGC
Ua Mordha, Caithlin	6 Lr St Columbus Rd, Drumcondra, Dublin	Autograph book KGC
Valentine, Emily	3 Temple Street, Dublin	Military Archives Material
Wallace, Eileen (Nellie/Elizabeth)	Eyre Street, Newbridge, Co Kildare	Military Archives Material Autograph book KGC
Wallace, Lily	Newbridge, Co Kildare	Military Archives Material
Walsh(e), Kathleen	'Mervone House', Mervone Park, Ballybane, Galway	Autograph books KGC Military Archives Material
Walsh, Peg (alias Vera Flynn)		Autograph books KGC
Webb, Mrs Kate	17 Wellington Quay, Dublin	Military Archives Material
Whelan, Elizabeth (Eilis/Lizzie)	Staplestown Rd, Carlow	Military Archives Material
Whelan, Maura (Mary/Maria)	17 Foster Cottages, Phibsboro Rd, Dublin	Autograph book KGC Military Archives Material
Whelan, Peg	17 Foster Cottages, Phibsboro Rd, Dublin and Staplestown Rd, Carlow	Autograph books KGC
Whitty, Margaret		Autograph books KGC

NAME	DETAILS	REFERENCE
Wilson, Mrs Catherine	40 Phillipsburg Ave, Fairview, Dublin	Autograph books KGC Military Archives Material D Macardle account
Woods, Mrs Mary Anne	19 Wynne's Tce, Dundalk, Co Louth	Military Archives Material Autograph books KGC
Woods, Nellie	Russelstown Park, Benneykerry, Co Carlow	Military Archives Material Autograph books KGC
Zambra, May	41 Cuffe St, Dublin	Military Archives Material Autograph books KGC

Notes

Notes to Chapter 1: Women Activists (1900–1916)

1. Nancy Cardozo, *Maud Gonne*, London, Victor Gollancz, 1979, p188.
2. Máire, 'Inghinidhe na hÉireann, The First Meeting', in *In Their Own Voice, Women and Irish Nationalism, (*ed.) Margaret Ward, Dublin, Attic Press, 1995, p18.
3. Ella Young, *Flowering Dusk*, London, Dennis Dobson Ltd, 1945, p70.
4. The Bureau of Military History CD 119/3/1, Military Archives.
5. Maud Gonne MacBride, *Servant of the Queen*, Dublin, Golden Eagle Books Ltd, 1950, p279.
6. Máire Nic Shiúbhlaigh, *The Splendid Years*, Dublin, James Duffy & Co., Ltd, 1955, p3.
7. Ibid, p6.
8. Ibid, p16.
9. Ibid, p14.
10. Eithne Ní Chumhaill, 'The History of Cumann na mBan', *An Phoblacht*, 8 April 1933.
11. Ella Young, *op. cit.*, p70.
12. Helena Molony, Unpublished Autobiographical Account, Kilmainham Gaol Collection.
13. Diana Norman, *Terrible Beauty, A Life* of Constance Markievicz, London, Hodder & Stoughton, 1987, p53.
14. Countess Markievicz, 'Buy a Revolver', in *In Their Own Voice* (ed.) Margaret Ward, pp46-47.
15. Helena Molony, Unpublished Autobiographical Account.
16. Diana Norman, *Terrible Beauty*, p59.
17. Helena Molony, Unpublished Autobiographical Account.
18. Author's interview with Honor O'Brolchain, granddaughter of Geraldine Plunkett Dillon, 2003.
19. Countess Markievicz, 'James Connolly's Connection with Belfast', (undated), Francis McKay collection.
20. Brian Feeney, *Sinn Féin, A Hundred Turbulent Years*, Dublin, The O'Brien Press, 2002, p42.
21. Margaret Ward, *Hanna Sheehy Skeffington, A Life,* Cork, Attic Press, 1997, p37.
22. Margaret Ward, *Unmanageable Revolutionaries*, Kerry, Brandon Book Publishers Ltd., 1983, p72.
23. Ibid, p70.
24. Countess Markievicz, *Women, Ideals and the Nation.*
25. Diane Urquhart, *Women in Ulster Politics 1890-1940*, Dublin, Irish Academic Press, 2000, pp22-23.
26. Ibid, p64.
27. Jennie Wyse Power 'Cumann na mBan', *Leabhar na mBan*, p4.
28. Margaret Ward, *Unmanageable Revolutionaries*, p91.
29. Barry O'Delany, 'Cumann na mBan', William Fitzgerald (ed.), *The Voice of Ireland*, London, Virtue & Co Ltd., undated, p162.
30. Ibid.

31. Cumann na mBan Leaflet, 1919.
32. Eithne Ní Chumhaill, 'The History of Cumann na mBan', *An Phoblacht*, 8 April 1933.
33. Kenneth Griffith and Timothy O'Grady, *Curious Journey, An Oral History of Ireland's Unfinished Revolution,* Cork, Mercier Press, 1998, p23.
34. Mary Colum, 'The Allies of the Volunteers', in *In Their Own Voice* (ed.) Margaret Ward, p45.
35. Aodogán O'Rahilly, *Winding the Clock, O'Rahilly and the 1916 Rising,* Dublin, The Lilliput Press, 1991, p118.
36. Helen Landreth, *The Mind and Heart of Molly Childers*, Boston, privately published, 1965, p14.
37. Jennie Wyse Power 'Cumann na mBan', *Leabhar na mBan*, p5.
38. Margaret Ward, *Unmanageable Revolutionaries*, p101.
39. Jennie Wyse Power 'Cumann na mBan', *Leabhar na mBan*, p5.
40. Margaret Ward, *Unmanageable Revolutionaries*, p103.
41. Madge Daly, 'Gallant Cumann na mBan of Limerick', *Limerick's Fighting Story 1916-1921,* Tralee, the *Kerryman*, p202.
42. Jennie Wyse Power 'Cumann na mBan', *Leabhar na mBan*, p6.
43. Hazel P Smyth, 'Kathleen Lynn MD FRCSI (1874-1955)', *The Dublin Historical Record,* Vol XXX, 1976-78, p52.
44. Ruth Taillon, *When History was Made: The Women of 1916,* Belfast, Beyond the Pale Publications, 1996, p16.
45. Kenneth Griffiths and Timothy O'Grady, *op. cit.,* p41.
46. Una Bolger was sworn into the IRB in Wexford at the insistence of her fiancé Robert Brennan. He was later told that there was one other female in the organisation. He thought it was Maud Gonne MacBride. Robert Brennan, *Allegiance*, Dublin, Browne and Nolan Ltd, p11. In *When History was Made: The Women of 1916,* p7 Ruth Taillon suggests that it was Kathleen Clarke.
47. Helen Litton (ed.), *Revolutionary Woman, Kathleen Clarke*, Dublin, The O'Brien Press, 1991, p71.

Notes to Chapter 2: The Women of the Rising

1. Aodogán O'Rahilly, *Winding the Clock, O'Rahilly and the 1916 Rising*, Dublin, The Lilliput Press, 1991, p234.
2. Brian Barton, *From Behind a Closed Door, Secret Court Martial Records of the 1916 Easter Rising*, Belfast, The Blackstaff Press, 2002, p6.
3. Ibid., p 7.
4. Ruth Taillon, *op. cit.,* pp 81-82.
5. Uinseann MacEoin, *Survivors*, Dublin, Argenta, 1987, p200.
6. RM Fox, *Rebel Irishwomen*, Dublin, Progress House, 1935, p70.
7. Ruth Taillon, *op. cit.,* p54.
8. RM Fox, *Rebel Irishwomen,* p71.
9. Author's interview with Tony Roche, grandson of Nora Gilles O'Daly, 2000.
10. Nora O'Daly, 'Cumann na mBan in Stephens' Green and in the College of Surgeons', *An t-Óglach,* April 1926.
11. Máire Nic Shiúbhlaigh, *op. cit.*, p166.

12. Francis McKay, 'Clann na nGaedheal Girl Scouts', the *Irish Press,* 3 May 1966.
13. Margaret Ward, *Unmanageable Revolutionaries*, pix.
14. Lily M O'Brennan, 'The Dawning of the Day', *The Capuchin Annual*, 1936.
15. Unpublished list of the Marrowbone Lane Garrison, Dublin, private collection.
16. Sean O'Mahony, *Frongoch University of Revolution*, Dublin, FDR Teoranta, 1987, p17.
17. Unpublished 1916 diary of Rose McNamara, Dublin, private collection.
18. Ruth Taillon, *op. cit.,* p 61.
19. Unpublished 1916 diary of Rose McNamara.
20. Unpublished written account by Anne Cooney of her political activities 1916-1921, Dublin, private collection.
21. Éilis Bean Uí Chonail, 'A Cumann na mBan recalls Easter Week', *Capuchin Annual*, 1966.
22. Julia Grenan, 'Julia Grenan', *Voices of Ireland*, Donncha Ó Dúlaing (ed), Dublin, The O'Brien Press, 1984, p70.
23. May Gibney O'Neill, 'Statement of her involvement in 1916.' Kilmainham Gaol Collection.
24. Kenneth Griffith & Timothy O'Grady, *op. cit.,* pp59-60
25. Ibid., p86.
26. Anon., Sinn Féin Rebellion 1917 Handbook, p15.
27. Louise Gavan Duffy, 'Ins An GPO: Cumann na mBan', *In their own Voice,* [ed.] Margaret Ward p60.
28. 'The Petticoat Heroine', the *Evening Herald*, 13 April 1966.
29. Anon., 'Cumann na mBan in Easter Week; Tribute from a Hostile Source', *Wolfe Tone Annual:* Special 1916 Number, undated, p43.
30. Margaret Skinnider, *Doing my Bit for Ireland*, New York, The Century Co., 1917, p165.
31. 'The Petticoat Heroine', the *Evening Herald*, 13 April 1966.
32. Anon., 'Cumann na mBan in Easter Week; Tribute from a Hostile Source', *Wolfe Tone Annual: Special 1916 Number*, undated, p43.
33. Ibid, p44.
34. Ibid.
35. Helen Woggon, 'Silent Radical, Winnie Carney 1887-1943 : A Reconstruction of her Biography, Dublin, SIPTU, 2000, p15.
36. Anon., 'Cumann na mBan in Easter Week; Tribute from a Hostile Source', *Wolfe Tone Annual*, undated, p43.
37. Helena Molony, Unpublished Autobiographical Account.
38. Helena Molony, 'Women of the Rising', Radio Telefís Éireann radio interview, 16 April 1963, RTÉ Sound Archive.
39. Margaret Skinnider, *op. cit.*, p137.
40. Ibid, p148.
41. Seumas Ó Dubhghaill, 'Activities in Enniscorthy', *The Capuchin Annual*, 1966.
42. Lil Conlon, *Cumann na mBan and the Women of Ireland 1913-1925,* Kilkenny, the Kilkenny People Ltd, 1969, p26.
43. Roger McHugh, *Dublin 1916*, London, Arlington Books, 1966, p68.
44. 'Joe' to John Caffey, 5 May 1916, Asquith Papers, MS 43, Bodleian Library, Oxford University cited in Brian Barton, *op. cit.,* p58.
45. Ibid, p154.

46. Ibid, p8.
47. RM Fox, 'How the Women Helped', *Dublin's Fighting Story 1916-1921, Told by the Men who Made it*, Tralee: The Kerryman Ltd, undated, p209.
48. Máire Comerford 'Women in the Van', the *Irish Press*, 9 April 1966.
49. Gertie Colley Murphy, Unpublished Account of 1916, Kilmainham Gaol Collection.
50. Louise Gavan Duffy, 'In San GPO: Cumann na mBan', *In their own Voice*, (ed.) Margaret Ward p61.
51. Julia Grenan, 'Julia Grenan', *Voices of Ireland*, (ed.) Donncha Ó'Dúlaing, p73.
52. Anon., Unidentified Commemorative Article, Kilmainham Gaol Collection.
53. Elizabeth O'Farrell, 'Events of Easter Week', *The Catholic Bulletin*, May 1917 pp329-300.
54. M Reynolds, 'Cumann na mBan in the GPO', *An t-Óglach*, 27 March 1926.
55. Hazel P Smyth, *op. cit.*, p53.
56. Ibid, p53.
57. Dr Kathleen Lynn diary 24 April 1916, cited in Medb Ruane, 'Kathleen Lynn (1874-1955)', *Female Activists, Irish Women and Change 1900-1960*, Mary Cullen & Maria Luddy (eds.), Dublin, The Woodfield Press, 2001, p72.
58. Máire Nic Shiúbhlaigh, *op. cit.*, p185.
59. Nora O'Daly, 'Cumann na mBan in Stephens' Green and in the College of Surgeons', *An t-Óglach,* April 1926.
60. Maureen Field, Unpublished History of Kilmainham Gaol, Kilmainham Gaol Collection.
61. Unpublished written account by Anne Cooney of her political activities 1916-1921.
62. RM Fox, 'How the Women Helped', *op. cit.*, p210.
63. Unpublished 1916 diary of Rose McNamara.
64. Ibid.
65. Brian Barton, *op. cit.,* p187.
66. Roger McHugh, *op. cit.*, p78.
67. Brian Barton, *op. cit.,* p23.
68. Robert Livingston Chapman, Unpublished 1916 Journal, Dublin, private collection.
69. Brian Barton, *op. cit.,* p18.
70. Ibid, p20.
71. Eitne McKeown, 'A Family in the Rising' *Electricity Supply Board Journal,* 1966.
72. Interview by Niamh O'Sullivan with Maureen O'Carroll, daughter of May Gahan O'Carroll, 1999.
73. Ruth Taillon ppxxi-xxvii – A list of 188 women who took part in the Rising.
74. Nora O'Daly, 'Cumann na mBan in Stephens' Green and in the College of Surgeons', *An t-Óglach,* April 1926.
75. Eitne McKeown, 'A Family in the Rising' *Electricity Supply Board Journal,* 1966.
76. Unpublished 1916 diary of Rose McNamara.
77. Nora O'Daly, 'Cumann na mBan in Stephens' Green and in the College of Surgeons', *An t-Óglach,* April 1926.
78. Kenneth Griffiths & Timothy O'Grady, *op. cit.,* p78.
79. Nora O'Daly, 'Cumann na mBan in Stephens' Green and in the College of Surgeons', *An t-Óglach,* April 1926.
80. Elizabeth O'Farrell, 'Events of Easter Week', the *Catholic Bulletin*, May 1917.

81. Unpublished 1916 diary of Rose McNamara.
82. Nora O'Daly, 'Cumann na mBan in Stephens' Green and in the College of Surgeons', *An t-Óglach,* April 1926.
83. Ruth Taillon, *op. cit.,* p102.
84. Unpublished 1916 diary of Rose McNamara.
85. Nora O'Daly, 'Cumann na mBan in Stephens' Green and in the College of Surgeons', *An t-Óglach,* April 1926.
86. Julia Grenan, 'Events of Easter Week', the *Catholic Bulletin*, June 1917.
87. Brian Barton, *op cit.*, p72.
88. Diana Norman, *op cit.*, p155.
89. Julia Grenan, 'After the Surrender' *Wolfe Tone Annual:* Special 1916 Number, p 22.
90. Nora O'Daly, 'Cumann na mBan in Stephens' Green and in the College of Surgeons', *An t-Óglach,* April 1926.
91. Letter from General John Maxwell to The Secretary of the War Office, 30 May 1916, Class WO141/19, PRO.
92. Ibid.
93. Lil Conlon, *op. cit.*, p35.
94. Unpublished 1916 diary of Rose McNamara.
95. Eitne McKeown, 'A Family in the Rising' *Electricity Supply Board Journal,* 1966.
96. Letter from General John Maxwell to the Secretary of the War Office, 30 May 1916, Class WO141/19, PRO.
97. Ibid.
98. Brian Barton, *op. cit.,* p57.
99. Letter from General John Maxwell to the Secretary of the War Office, 30 May 1916. Class WO141/19, PRO.
100. Ibid.
101. RM Fox, *Rebel Irishwomen*, p67.
102. Lil Conlon, *op. cit.*, p22.
103. Sile Bean Ui Dhonnachadha, 'Memories of Easter Week' *An Phobhlacht/Republican News,* 27 March 1986.
104. National Archives Ireland, Chief Secretary's Office Registered Papers, 1916, 25889.
105. Anon., 'Annie Higgins', the *Capuchin Annual*, 1936.
106. Lil Conlon, *op. cit.*, p23.
107. Unpublished 1916 diary of Rose McNamara.
108. Author's interview with Honor O'Brolchain, 2003.
109. Anna Kinsella, *Women of Wexford 1798-1998*, Wexford, Courtown Publications, 1998, p25.
110. Bernard Browne, 'The Browne Families of County Wexford', (ed.) Kevin Whelan, *Wexford: History and Society*, Dublin, Geography Publications, 1987, p486.
111. Letter from County Inspector PJ O'Hara, 25 July 1916, NAI, CSORP, 1916, 13205.
112. Ibid.
113. Piaras F Mac Lochlainn, *Last Words*, Dublin, The Stationery Office, 1990, p170.
114. Risteárd Mulcahy, *Richard Mulcahy (1886-1971) A Family Memoir*, Dublin, Aurelian Press, 1999, p275.
115. Piaras F Mac Lochlainn, *Last Words*, p171.
116. Jennie Wyse Power, 'Cumann na mBan', *Leabhar na mBan*, p6.

117. Phyllis Ryan to James Ryan, 19 May 1916, p88/5 (1), University College Dublin Archives Department.
118. Author's interview with, grandniece of Mary Kate (Kit) Ryan, 2002.
119. Letter from Kathleen Browne to her mother, 23 May 1916, Wexford, private collection.
120. Ibid.
121. Anna Kinsella, *op. cit.,* p95.
122. Ibid.
123. Ibid., pp95-96.
124. Author's interview with Honor O'Brolchain, 2003.
125. Marie Mulholland, *The Politics and Relationships of Kathleen Lynn*, Dublin, The Woodfield Press, 2002, p48.
126. Ibid.
127. Letter from General John Maxwell to the Secretary of the War Office, 5 June 1916, Class W0141/20. PRO.
128. Notice Regulation Order 14B.1916. Class H0144/1457/314179. PRO.
129. Helena Molony, Unpublished Autobiographical Account.
130. Class 10 114/1455/313106/0 PRO.
131. NAI, CSORP, 1916, 13205.
132. NAI, CSORP, 1916, 14387.
133. NAI, CSORP, 1916, 13503.
134. Letter from Agnes Ryan to Nell Ryan, 27 July 1916, Dublin, private collection.
135. Winifred Carney's petition to the Secretary of State for the Home Department, 6 December 1916, Class HO 144/1457/314179. PRO.
136. Telegram to the Ryan family, 13 October 1916, Dublin, private collection.
137. A blank statement, Winifred Carney's File, Class Ho 144\1457\314179, PRO.
138. Helena Molony, Unpublished Autobiographical Account.
139. Letter from Helena Molony to Nell Ryan, January (1917), Dublin, private collection.
140. Ibid.
141. Diana Norman, *op. cit.,* p163.
142. Prison Letters of Countess Markievicz (ed.), Esther Roper, London, Virago, 1986, pp150-151.

Notes to Chapter 3: Women and the Road to Independence (1917–1921)

1. Brian Feeney, *Sinn Féin, A Hundred Turbulent Years*, p57.
2. Sean O'Mahony, *op. cit.*, p58.
3. Anonymous, 'Cumann na mBan in Easter Week; Tribute from a Hostile Source', *Wolfe Tone Annual*, Special 1916 Number, undated, p44.
4. Letter from Eileen Dempsey Hawley to Emily Norgrove Hanratty, undated, Kilmainham Gaol Collection.
5. Letter from Kathleen Clarke to Eamon, 19 August 1965, copy, author's collection.
6. Helen Litton (ed.), *op. cit.*, p132.
7. Ibid.

8. Anonymous, 'Report of the Irish National Aid and Volunteer Dependants' Fund' the *Catholic Bulletin,* August 1919.
9. Ibid.
10. Letter from Eileen Dempsey Hawley to Emily Norgrove Hanratty, undated.
11. Éilis Ní Chorra, 'A Rebel Remembers', *The Capuchin Annual*, 1966.
12. Anonymous, 'Report of the Irish National Aid and Volunteer Dependants' Fund', the *Catholic Bulletin,* August 1919.
13. Brian Feeney, *op. cit.*, p61.
14. Letter from Emmet Clarke to the author, 25 March 1995, Author's collection.
15. Meda Ryan, *Michael Collins and the Women in His Life*, Cork, Mercier Press, 1996, p33.
16. Helen Litton (ed.), *op. cit.*, p133.
17. Grace Plunkett scrapbook of Press Cuttings and Memorabilia, NLI MS. 21,593.
18. Plunkett/Gifford Marriage Certificate, 1916.
19. Grace Plunkett Scrapbook, NLI MS. 21,593.
20. Madge Daly, 'Gallant Cumann na mBan of Limerick', *Limerick's Fighting Story*, p202.
21. Helena Molony, Unpublished Autobiographical Account.
22. Nell Regan, 'Helena Molony (1883-1967)', *Female Activists*, p154.
23. Margaret Ward, 'The League of Women Delegates and Sinn Féin', *History Ireland,* autumn 1996.
24. Medb Ruane, 'Kathleen Lynn (1874-1955)', *Female Activists, Irish Women and Change 1900-1960*, Mary Cullen & Maria Luddy (eds.), p74.
25. Margaret Ward, *History Ireland,* autumn 1996.
26. Lil Conlon, *op. cit.,* pp 52-53.
27. Margaret Ward, *Unmanageable Revolutionaries*, p131.
28. Meda Ryan, *op. cit.,* p41.
29. Lil Conlon, *op. cit.,* p62.
30. Ibid., p62.
31. The *Freeman's Journal*, June 10, 1918.
32. Jacqueline Van Voris, op.cit., p250.
33. Ernie O'Malley, *On Another Man's Wound*, London, Rich & Cowan Ltd, p81.
34. Lil Conlon, *op. cit.,* p70.
35. Helen Litton (ed), *op. cit.,* p150.
36. Margaret Ward, *Hanna Sheehy Skeffington, A Life*, p156.
37. Leah Levenson & Jerry H. Natterstad, *Hanna Sheehy Skeffington: Irish Feminist,* Syracuse, Syracuse University Press, 1986, p115.
38. Lil Conlon, *op. cit.,* pp73-74.
39. Diane Urquhart, *Women in Ulster Politics 1890-1940,* p113.
40. Helen Woggon, *op. cit.*, p19.
41. Diana Urquart, *op. cit.*, p114.
42. Brian Feeney, *op.cit.,* p116.
43. Ibid., p117.
44. Margaret Ward, *Unmanageable Revolutionaries,* p138.
45. Margaret Ward, *Hanna Sheehy Skeffington A Life*, p202.
46. Humphreys Papers, UCDAD, P106/1166.
47. The Bureau of Military History, MA, WS 450.

48. Kate O'Callaghan, 'Limerick City Curfew Murders', *Limerick's Fighting Story*, pp136-137.
49. Margaret Ward, *Unmanageable Revolutionaries,* p139.
50. The Bureau of Military History, MA, WS 450.
51. Ibid.
52. Author's interview with Peggy Jordan, daughter of Áine Heron, 1994.
53. Cumann na mBan Activities South County Dublin, Undated, Eithne Coyle O'Donnell Papers P61/4(9).
54. Louise O'Hanrahan and Patricia O'Reilly (eds.), *Talking Liberties, Dublin,* SICCDA Heritage Centre, 1995, pp 44-45.
55. Uinseann MacEoin, *Survivors,* p152.
56. Unpublished written account by Anne Cooney of her political activities 1916-1921.
57. Cumann na mBan Activities South County Dublin, Undated, Eithne Coyle O'Donnell Papers P61/4(9).
58. Report given at Annual Convention of Cumann na mBan, 1921.
59. Ibid.
60. The Bureau of Military History, MA, WS 450.
61. Lily Gleeson autograph book, 1923, Kilmainham Gaol Collection.
62. Author's interview with Peggy Jordan, daughter of Áine Heron, 1994.
63. Louise Ryan, '"Drunken Tans" representations of Sex and Violence in the Anglo-Irish War (1919-1921)', *Feminist Review*, No 66, p81.
64. Interview by Niamh O'Sullivan with Patrick Pearse O'Daly, son of Catherine Wisely, 1996.
65. Author's interview with Peggy Jordan, daughter of Áine Heron, 1994
66. *Margaret Ward, Unmanageable Revolutionaries,* p141.
67. Mary Kotsonouris, *Retreat from Revolution: The Dáil Courts, 1920–1924,* Irish Academic Press, p38.
68. Louise Ryan, *Feminist Review*, p83.
69. Author's interview with Ita O'Gorman Draper, 1994.
70. Maryanne Valiulis, *Richard Mulcahy*, p69
71. Louise Ryan, *Feminist Review*, p84.
72. The Bureau of Military History, MA, WS 450.
73. Risteárd Mulcahy, *op. cit.,* p296.
74. Ibid., p 296.
75. Author's interview with Ita O'Gorman Draper, 1994.
76. Batt O'Connor, *With Michael Collins*, London, Peter Davies Ltd, 1929, p139.
77. Louise Ryan, *Feminist Review*, p91.
78. Uinseann MacEoin, *Survivors,* p43.
79. Batt O'Connor, *op. cit.,* p153.
80. Lil Conlon, *op. cit.*, p224.
81. Ibid., p222.
82. Eilís Dillon, *Inside Ireland*, Hodder and Stoughton, 1982, p73.
83. Ibid.
84. Ibid., p75.
85. Madge Daly, unpublished account, *War on Women in Ireland,* author's collection.
86. Lil Conlon, *op. cit.*, p143.

87. Joanne Mooney Eichacker, *Irish Republican Women in America,* Dublin, Irish Academic Press, 2002, pp236-261.
88. Áine Ceannt, *The Story of the Irish White Cross 1920-1947*, Dublin, At the Sign of the Three Candles, undated, p10.
89. Lil Conlon, *op. cit.,* p205.
90. Áine Ceannt, *op. cit.*, p38
91. Lil Conlon, *op. cit.,* p224.
92. Meda Ryan, *Michael Collins and the Women of Ireland,* p61.
93. Lil Conlon, *op. cit.,* p249.
94. Meda Ryan, *The Tom Barry Story,* Cork, The Mercier Press, 1982, pp64-65.
95. Helen Litton, (ed.), *op. cit.,* p177.
96. Lil Conlon, *op. cit.,* p225.
97. Margaret Mulvihill, *Charlotte Despard*, London, Pandora, 1989, p5.
98. Ibid., p8.
99. Report given at the Annual Convention of Cumann na mBan, 1921.
100. Proinnsíos Ó Duigneáin, *Linda Kearns*, Manorhamilton, Drumlin Publications, 2002, p46.
101. Lil Conlon, *op. cit.,* p223.
102. Ibid., p194.
103. Ibid., p207.
104. Unpublished written account by Anne Cooney of her political activities 1916-1921.
105. Proinnsíos Ó Duigneáin, *Linda Kearns*, p59.
106. Unpublished written account by Anne Cooney of her political activities 1916-1921.
107. Uinseann MacEoin, *Survivors,* p55.
108. Margaret Buckley, *Jangle of the Keys*, p 7. Note: Margaret Buckley incorrectly identifies Aileen Keogh as Eileen Keogh and calls Frances Brady 'Frank'.
109. Unpublished written account by Anne Cooney of her political activities 1916-1921.
110. Ibid.
111. Ibid.
112. Margaret Buckley, *op. cit.,* p7.
113. Uinseann MacEoin, *Survivors,* p152.
114. Unpublished written account by Anne Cooney of her political activities 1916-1921.
115. Tim Pat Coogan, *Michael Collins*, p284.
116. Unpublished written account by Anne Cooney of her political activities 1916-1921.
117. Tim Pat Coogan, *op. cit.*, p284.
118. Ibid., p285.
119. Unpublished written account by Anne Cooney of her political activities 1916-1921.
120. Margaret Buckley, *op. cit.,* p8.
121. Ibid., p7.
122. Proinnsíos Ó Duigneáin, *Linda Kearns*, p59.
123. Proinnsíos Ó Duigneáin, 'Linda Kearns – The Sligo Nurse in the 1916 Rising', the *Sligo Champion,* 5 April 1991.
124. Linda Kearns, 'Arrest – Two Experiences', in *In Their Own Voice*, Margaret Ward (ed.), p99.
125. Proinnsíos Ó Duigneáin, *Linda Kearns*, p44.
126. Ibid., p58.

127. This is the number of women prisoners held in September 1921 according to Michael Collins, cited in Uinseann MacEoin, *Survivors,* p159.
128. Ibid., p153.
129. Ibid.
130. Margaret Buckley, *op. cit.,* p11. Note: Buckley uses the spelling of Mae. The author has opted for the common spelling of May used elsewhere.
131. Linda Kearns gives the date of the escape as 30 October 1921. The author has used Eithne Coyle's date of 31 October, as it appears in other accounts, including *The Jangle of the Keys*.
132. Margaret Buckley, *op. cit.,* p11.
133. Proinnsíos Ó Duigneáin, *Linda Kearns*, p62.
134. Uinseann MacEoin, *Survivors,* p154.
135. Proinnsíos Ó Duigneáin, *Linda Kearns*, p65.
136. Frank Pakenham, *Peace by Ordeal*, London, Sidgwick & Jackson, 1972, p77.
137. Uinseann MacEoin, *The IRA in the Twilight Years 1923-1948,* p203.
138. Margery Forester, *Michael Collins, The Lost Leader,* London, Sphere Books Ltd, 1972, p212.
139. Uinseann MacEoin, *Survivors,* p151.
140. Ibid., p154.
141. Margaret Ward, *Unmanageable Revolutionaries*, p166.
142. *The Treaty Debates*, Public Session, 20 December 1921.
143. *The Treaty Debates*, Public Session, 21 December 1921.
144. *The Treaty Debates*, Public Session, 3 January 1922.
145. Author's interview with Aodogán O Rahilly, son of The O'Rahilly, 1997.
146. The Bureau of Military History, MA, WS 450.
147. Humphreys Papers, UCDAD, P106/1735(1).
148. Anonymous Newspaper Cutting, "Women in Council", (1921), Kilmainham Gaol Collection.
149. William Fitzgerald (ed.), *op. cit.,* p161.
150. Lil Conlon, *op. cit.,* p268.

Notes to Chapter 4: The Civil War (1922–1923)

1. Statement from Cumann na mBan, 14 February 1922, Kilmainham Gaol Collection.
2. Unpublished written account by Bridie Clyne of her political activities 1919-1926, undated, Author's collection.
3. Author's interview with Ita O'Gorman Draper, 1994.
4. Uinseann MacEoin, *Survivors*, p211.
5. Ernie O'Malley, *The Singing Flame*, Dublin, Anvil, 1978, p130.
6. Diana Norman, *op. cit.,* p244.
7. Jacqueline Van Voris, op. cit., p325
8. Nancy Cardozo, *op. cit.,* pp350-351.
9. C S Andrews, *Dublin Made Me*, Cork, The Mercier Press, 1979, p233.
10. Ernie O'Malley, *The Singing Flame*, p131.
11. Uinseann MacEoin, *Survivors*, p47.

12. Unpublished written account by Bridie Clyne of her political activities 1919-1926, undated.
13. Edward Purdon, *The Civil War 1922-23*, Cork, Mercier Press, 2000, p40.
14. Kenneth Griffith & Timothy O Grady, *op.cit.*, p263.
15. Edward Purdon, *op. cit.*, p49.
16. Uinseann MacEoin, *Survivors*, p48.
17. Edward Purdon, *op. cit.*, pp47-48.
18. Ernie O'Malley, *The Singing Flame*, p160.
19. Ibid., p174.
20. Nell Humphreys to Aunt Annie, 17 November (1922), the Humphreys Papers UCDAD, P106/390(1).
21. Report from Mountjoy Jail, Miss MacSwiney's Condition, Kilmainham Gaol Collection.
22. Humphreys Papers, UCDAD, P106/979.
23. Charlotte Fallon, 'Civil War Hungerstrikes: Women and Men', *Eire*, Vol 22, 1987.
24. Anonymous, The Women's Prisoner's Defence League Leaflet, Undated, private collection.
25. Margaret Mulvihill, *Charlotte Despard.*, pp143-144.
26. Margaret Mulvihill, *op. cit.*, p145.
27. *Report from Mountjoy Jail, Miss MacSwiney's Condition*, Kilmainham Gaol Collection.
28. *A Message from Mountjoy: An Appeal on behalf of Mary MacSwiney*, Kilmainham Gaol Collection.
29. Charlotte Fallon, *Republican Hunger Strikes during the Irish Civil War and its Immediate Aftermath*, MA Thesis, University College Dublin 1980.
30. Uinseann MacEoin, *Survivors*, p49.
31. *Irish Independent*, 9 January 1923 cited in Charlotte Fallon, MA Thesis *op cit.*, University College Dublin 1980.
32. Charlotte Fallon, 'Civil War Hungerstrikes: Women and Men', *Éire*, Vol 22, 1987.
33. Ibid.
34. Madge Daly, 'Gallant Cumann na mBan of Limerick', *Limerick's Fighting Story 1916-1921*, p205.
35. Edward Purdon, *op. cit.*, p54.
36. Margaret Buckley, *op. cit.*, pp14-15
37. Ibid., p15.
38. Ibid.
39. Ibid., p16.
40. Ernie O'Malley, *The Singing Flame*, p171.
41. Letter from Áine Ceannt to Lily O'Brennan, 25 February 1923. O'Brennan Papers, p13\34.
42. Letter from Áine Ceannt to Lily O'Brennan, 3 April 1923. O'Brennan Papers, p13\47.
43. Nancy Cardozo, *op. cit.*, pp 354-355.
44. Margaret Buckley, *op. cit.*, pp1-2.
45. *Poblacht na hÉireann* War News, No 90, 11 November 1922, Kilmainham Gaol Collection.
46. Humphreys Papers UCDAD P106/979

47. Ibid.
48. Unpublished written account by Hanna O'Connor of her imprisonment during the Civil War (copy), undated, Kilmainham.
49. Margaret Buckley, *op. cit.,* p33.
50. Ibid., p19.
51. The Bureau of Military History, MA, WS 485.
52. Margaret Buckley, *op. cit.,* p18.
53. Uinseann MacEoin, *Survivors*, p49.
54. Margaret Buckley, *op. cit.,* p31.
55. 'Kildare Men Executed', *Leinster Leader*, 23 December 1922.
56. Margaret Buckley, *op. cit.,* p17.
57. Humphreys Papers UCDAD, P106/1052.
58. Author's interview with Ann Gallagher, daughter of Cecilia Gallagher, 2002.
59. Nellie O'Cleirigh, 'A Political Prisoner in Kilmainham Jail - The Diary of Cecilia Saunders Gallagher', *Dublin Historical Record* Vol. LVI, No1, Spring 2003, p5.
60. Margaret Buckley, *op. cit.,* p27.
61. Nellie O'Cleirigh, *op. cit.*, p6.
62. Cecilia Gallagher, Prison Diary, 20 June 1923. TCD MS10056.
63. Margaret Buckley, *op. cit.,* p36.
64. Ibid., p36.
65. Ibid.,p34.
66. Ibid., p37.
67. Ibid., p38.
68. Eithne Coyle O'Donnell, Undated Account on the Scottish Branch of Cumann na mBan,. Eithne Coyle O'Donnell Papers, UCDAD, P61/4/(68)
69. Ibid.
70. Ibid.
71. See appendix for list of 562 women imprisoned at this time.
72. Letter from Eithne MacSweeney to the Archbishop, 26 February 1923, Mary MacSwiney Papers, UCDA P48a/195 (2)\3.
73. Letter from Lily O'Brennan to Rónán Ceannt, 14 March 1923, O'Brennan Papers, UCDA P13\44.
74. Cis Power & Jo Power, Undated Account of imprisonment 'If Winter Comes' (copy), Kilmainham Gaol Collection.
75. Cis Power & Jo Power, 'Blaze Away with your Little Gun', the *Kerryman*, 21 December 1968.
76. Unpublished Civil War Diary by Hannah Moynihan. Kilmainham Gaol Collection.
77. Cis Power & Jo Power, 'Blaze Away with your Little Gun', the *Kerryman*, 21 December 1968.
78. Ibid.
79. Dorothy Macardle, *Tragedies of Kerry 1922-1923*, p16.
80. Cis Power & Jo Power, 'Blaze Away with your Little Gun', the *Kerryman*, 21 December 1968.
81. Unpublished Civil War Diary by Hannah Moynihan. Kilmainham Gaol Collection.
82. Bridie Halpin, Autograph Book, 1923.

83. Unidentified press cutting, 'The Women Prisoners, Some Particular of Women in Colonial Gaols', (1923), Francis McKay collection.
84. Author's interview with Laura McGuirk, granddaughter of Hannah O'Neill, 1995.
85. Unpublished written account by Hanna O'Connor of her imprisonment during the Civil War (copy), undated.
86. Ibid.
87. Cecilia Gallagher prison diary, 20 June 1923, TCD MS10056.
88. Hannah Moynihan diary.
89. Cis Power & Jo Power, 'Blaze Away with your Little Gun', the *Kerryman*, 28 December 1968.
90. Hannah Moynihan diary.
91. Hanna O'Connor, Account.
92. Margaret Buckley, *op. cit.*, pp 45-46.
93. Account by Sheila Hartnett, Coyle O'Donnell Papers, UCDAD, p61\4 (85).
94. Sheila Hartnett, 'Comradeship Kilmainham', The *Irish Press*, 30 Dec 1971.
95. Maureen Field, *op. cit.*
96. The Bureau of Military History, WS 485.
97. Margaret Buckley, *op. cit.*, p41.
98. Unpublished Civil War diary by Hannah Moynihan. Kilmainham Gaol Collection.
99. Cecilia Gallagher prison diary, 20 June 1923. MS10056. Trinity College Dublin.
100. Cis Power & Jo Power, 'If Winter Comes'.
101. Letter from Fanny Kelly to Crissie, 17 April 1923, Kilmainham Gaol Collection.
102. Letter from Áine Ceannt to Lily O'Brennan, 7 February 1923, O'Brennan Papers, UCDAD, P13/30.
103. Unpublished written account by Hanna O'Connor of her imprisonment during the Civil War (copy), undated.
104. Author's interview with Nora Brosnan, 1994.
105. Margaret Buckley, *op. cit.*, p101.
106. Hanna O'Connor, Account.
107. Letter from Fanny Kelly to Crissie, 29 April 1923. Kilmainham Gaol Collection.
108. Letter from Peter Berresford Ellis to the author, 5 April 1996, Author's collection.
109. Hanna O'Connor, Account.
110. NDU Record Book, MA, Dublin.
111. Eithne Coyle O'Donnell Account, undated, Coyle O'Donnell Papers, UCDAD, P61\21.
112. Margaret Buckley, *op. cit.*, p29.
113. Lily O'Brennan diary, 13 February 1923, O'Brennan Papers, UCDAD, P13\1.
114. Author's interview with Eleanor Hunt, daughter of Katherine (Jake) Folan, 1994.
115. Interview by Niamh O'Sullivan with Eileen O Neill and Mary Leavey, daughters of Eileen Tucker, 1997.
116. Lily O'Brennan diary, 23 February 1923, O'Brennan Papers, UCDAD, P13\1.
117. Cecilia Gallagher prison diary, 19 September 1923, MS10056. TCD.
118. Hannah Moynihan diary.
119. Humphreys Papers UCDAD, P106/979.
120. Anonymous Report to Director of Intelligence Cumann na mBan, 8 August (1923), Kilmainham Gaol Collection.
121. Ibid.

122. Margaret Buckley, *op. cit.*, p83.
123. Lily O'Brennan diary, 10 March 1923, O'Brennan Papers, UCDAD, P13\1.
124. Letter from Lily O'Brennan to Rónán Ceannt, 14 March 1923, O'Brennan Papers, UCDAD, p13\44.
125. Lily O'Brennan diary, 26 February 1923, O'Brennan Papers, UCDAD, P13\1.
126. Letter from Lily O'Brennan to Rónán Ceannt, 14 March 1923, O'Brennan Papers, UCDAD, p13\44.
127. Hannah Moynihan diary.
128. Hanna O'Connor, Account.
129. Author's interview with Eleanor Hunt, daughter of Katherine (Jake) Folan, 1994.
130. Hanna O'Connor, Account.
131. Hannah Moynihan diary.
132. Maggie Timmins, Susan Ryan Autograph Book, (copy), Kilmainham Gaol Collection.
133. Fanny O'Connor Autograph Book, private collection.
134. Author's interview with Michael Purcell, son of Essie Snoddy Purcell, 1996.
135. Cis Power & Jo Power, 'If Winter Comes'.
136. Hannah Moynihan diary.
137. Charlie Keegan, 'Pat Purcell laid to rest in 98th Year', *Nationalist and Leinster Times*, 11 November 1994.
138. Charlie Keegan, 'War Veteran Laid to Rest', *Nationalist and Leinster Times*, 16 October 1987.
139. Photographs 1960s, Kilmainham Gaol Collection.
140. Letter from Lily O'Brennan to Rónán Ceannt, 14 March 1923, O'Brennan Papers, UCDAD, p13\44.
141. Hannah Moynihan diary.
142. Margaret Buckley, *op. cit.*, p27.
143. Hannah Moynihan diary.
144. Letter from Ellen Masterson to Bridie (O'Mullane), 1923, Kilmainham Gaol Collection.
145. Hannah Moynihan diary.
146. Hanna O'Connor, Account.
147. Ibid.
148. Letter from Fanny Kelly to Crissie, 17 April 1923, Kilmainham Gaol Collection.
149. Margaret Ward, *Unmanageable Revolutionaries*, p284.
150. Ibid., p192.
151. Letter from Fanny Kelly to Sheila, 10 April 1923, Kilmainham Gaol Collection.
152. Hannah Moynihan diary.
153. Letter from Ellen Masterson to Bridie (O'Mullane), 1923, Kilmainham Gaol Collection.
154. Margaret Buckley, *op. cit.*, p30.
155. Cis Power & Jo Power, 'Blaze Away with your Little Gun', the *Kerryman*, 28 December 1968.
156. Margaret Buckley, *op. cit.*, p79.
157. Ibid., p82.
158. Mary Twamley's Autograph Book, Kilmainham Gaol Collection.
159. Margaret Buckley, *op. cit.*, p105.

160. Lily Gleeson, Autograph Book, 1923, Kilmainham Gaol Collection.
161. Angela Doyle Memorial Card, 1925, Kilmainham Gaol Collection
162. Margaret Buckley, *op. cit.*, p83-84
163. Ibid.
164. Nellie O'Cleirigh, *op. cit.*, p12.
165. Letter from Catherine O'Donovan to the Governor of the North Dublin Union, 1923, Margaret Burke Papers, UCDAD, P30/12.
166. 'Dr Elenora Fleury' (1960), Unidentified Press Cutting, Author's collection.
167. Kate O'Callaghan biographical note, Kilmainham Gaol Collection.
168. Cis Power & Jo Power, 'If Winter Comes'.
169. Lily O'Brennan diary, 28 February 1923, O'Brennan Papers, UCDAD, P13\1.
170. Letter from Lily O'Brennan to Áine Ceannt, 8 April 1923, O'Brennan Papers, UCDAD, P13\50.
171. Hannah Moynihan diary.
172. Ibid.
173. Ristéard Mulcahy, *op. cit.*, pp 285-286.
174. Letter from Kit Ryan O'Kelly to Liz Ryan, (1923), private collection.
175. Letter from Lily O'Brennan to Áine Ceannt, 4 April 1923, O'Brennan Papers, UCDAD, P13\49.
176. Charlotte Fallon, 'Civil War Hungerstrikes: Women and Men', *Eire*, Vol 22, 1987.
177. Dr Brian Murphy OSB 'Kate O'Callaghan (1885-1961)', a lecture given at Limerick City Library, 14 January 2003.
178. Letter from Mary MacSwiney to Austin Stack, 21 November 1923. Kilmainham Gaol Collection.
179. Charlotte Fallon, MA Thesis, *op. cit.*
180. Hannah Moynihan diary.
181. Charlotte Fallon, 'Civil War Hungerstrikes: Women and Men', *Eire*, Vol 22, 1987.
182. Ibid.
183. Hannah Moynihan diary.
184. Letter from Lily O'Brennan to Áine Ceannt, 8 April 1923, O'Brennan Papers, UCDAD, P13\50.
185. Hannah Moynihan diary.
186. Unidentified newspaper cutting, 'The Murder of Margaret Duggan', Francis McKay collection.
187. Nora Connolly O'Brien, *We Shall Rise Again*, London, Mosquito Press, 1981, p.56.
188. Letter from Lily O'Brennan to Áine Ceannt, 4 April 1923, O'Brennan Papers, UCDAD, P13\49.
189. Hanna O'Connor, Account.
190. Ibid.
191. Letter from Lily O'Brennan to Áine Ceannt, 25 April 1923, O'Brennan Papers, UCDAD, P13\60.
192. 'Speech by Nora Connolly O'Brien', 12 May 1923, *Éire*, Kilmainham Gaol Collection.
193. 'Easter Week in Kilmainham', Ibid.
194. Concert Programme 24 April 1923, Kilmainham Gaol Collection.
195. Hanna O'Connor, Account.
196. Nellie O'Cleirigh, *op. cit.*, p12.

197. 'Civil Strife and the Hunger Striker from Cratloe', *Clare Champion*, 11 May 2001.
198. Dorothy Macardle, *The Kilmainham Tortures.*
199. Ibid.
200. Letter from Fanny Kelly to Crissie, undated, Kilmainham Gaol Collection.
201. Cis Power & Jo Power, 'Blaze Away with your Little Gun', the *Kerryman*, 28 December 1968.
202. Letter from Fanny Kelly to Crissie, undated, Kilmainham Gaol Collection.
203. Dorothy Macardle, *The Kilmainham Tortures.*
204. Hanna O'Connor, Account.
205. Dorothy Macardle, *The Kilmainham Tortures.*
206. Ibid.
207. Annie Hogan, 19 May 1923, *Éire.*
208. Dorothy Macardle, *The Kilmainham Tortures.*
209. Author's interview with Joe Tierney, nephew of May Zambra, 1997.
210. Author's interview with Eleanor Hunt, daughter of Katherine (Jake) Folan, 1994.
211. Annie Hogan, 19 May 1923, *Éire.*
212. Dorothy Macardle, *The Kilmainham Tortures.*
213. The Bureau of Military History, MA, WS 485.
214. Dorothy Macardle, *The Kilmainham Tortures.*
215. Hannah Moynihan diary.
216. Letter from Fanny Kelly to Crissie, undated, Kilmainham Gaol Collection.
217. Lily O'Brennan Diary, 1 May 1923, O'Brennan Papers, UCDAD, P13\1.
218. Charlotte Fallon, 'Civil War Hungerstrikes: Women and Men', *Eire*, Vol 22, 1987.
219. Hannah Moynihan diary.
220. Margaret Buckley, *op. cit.,* p47.
221. Ibid., pp47-48.
222. Nora Spillane, 'Savaging Women Prisoners', *Éire,* 19 May 1923.
223. Margaret Buckley, *op. cit.,* p50.
224. Mary Duggan, untitled article, the *Donegal Democrat,* 1923, Frances McKay collection.
225. Margaret Buckley, *op. cit.,* p53.
226. Mary Duggan, untitled article, the *Donegal Democrat,* 1923, Frances McKay collection.
227. Margaret Buckley, *op. cit.,* p60.
228. Author's interview with Mary Heffernan, granddaughter of Harriette Lavery, 1997.
229. Letter from Mary A Woods to Bridie (O'Mullane), 30 July 1923, Kilmainham Gaol Collection.
230. 'Civil Strife and the Hunger Striker from Cratloe', *Clare Champion*, 11 May 2001.
231. Margaret Buckley, *op. cit.,* p55.
232. Hannah Moynihan diary.
233. Cis Power & Jo Power, 'If Winter Comes'.
234. Ibid.
235. Cis Power & Jo Power, 'Blaze Away with your Little Gun', the *Kerryman*, 28 December 1968.
236. Margaret Buckley, *op. cit.,* p60.
237. Hannah Moynihan diary.

238. Margaret Buckley, *op. cit.,* p56-58.
239. Hannah Moynihan diary.
240. Cis Power & Jo Power, 'Blaze Away with your Little Gun', the *Kerryman*, 3 January 1969.
241. Kenneth Griffith & Timothy O' Grady, *op. cit.,* p304.
242. Hannah Moynihan diary.
243. Margaret Buckley, *op. cit.,* pp65-72.
244. Hannah Moynihan diary.
245. Brother Fintan Norris, Account (1997) of Escape of Éilis Robinson from the North Dublin Union, Author's collection.
246. Margaret Buckley, *op. cit.,* p63.
247. Brother Fintan Norris, Account (1997) of Escape of Éilis Robinson from the North Dublin Union, Author's collection.
248. Hannah Moynihan diary.
249. Ibid.
250. 'Women Prisoners in Hospital and Miss Broderick (sic), 19 May 1923, *Éire.*
251. Humphreys Papers UCDA, p106/1046.
252. Letter from Sally Foere to author, 18 September 1995, Author's collection.
253. Ibid.
254. Pádraig Ó Loinsigh, unpublished biography, The Hon. Rebel, Ó Loinsigh Family collection.
255. Albinia Brodrick, The NDU Invincible, 1923, Kilmainham Gaol Collection.
256. Margaret Buckley, *op. cit.,* p64.
257. Hannah Moynihan diary.
258. CS Andrews, *Dublin Made Me,* p251.
259. Dorothy Macardle, *The Irish Republic*, Dublin, the Irish Press Ltd., 1951, p861.
260. Anonymous Captured Papers, 1923, MA, A/1129 Lot 39.
261. Margaret Buckley, *op. cit.,* p79.
262. Cecilia Gallagher, Prison Diary, 18 June 1923, TCD, MS10056.
263. Ibid., 20 June 1923.
264. Hannah Moynihan diary.
265. Letter from Mary A Woods to Bridie (O'Mullane), 30 July 1923, Kilmainham Gaol Collection.
266. Uinseann MacEoin, *Survivors*, p49.
267. Ibid.
268. Hannah Moynihan diary.
269. Ibid.
270. Sinéad McCoole, *Hazel, A Life of Lady Lavery*, Dublin, The Lilliput Press, 1996, p105.
271. Cecilia Gallagher, Prison Diary, 28 June 1923. TCD, MS10056.
272. Letter from Fanny Kelly to Crissie, 17 April 1923, Kilmainham Gaol Collection
273. Ibid.
274. Letter from Áine Ní Fairceallaigh to Bridie (O'Mullane), 29 July 1923. Kilmainham Gaol Collection.
275. Letter from Kay Freeman to Bridie (O'Mullane) , 8 August 1923, Kilmainham Gaol Collection.
276. Hannah Moynihan diary.

277. Ibid.
278. Mary Duggan, untitled article, the *Donegal Democrat,* 1923, Frances McKay collection.
279. Cecilia Gallagher, Prison Diary, 3 July 1923. TCD, MS10056.
280. Nellie O'Cleirigh, *op. cit.*, p12.
281. Cecilia Gallagher, Prison Diary, 15 July 1923. TCD, MS10056.
282. Margaret Buckley, *op. cit.,* p85.
283. Unpublished Civil War Diary by Hannah Moynihan, Kilmainham Gaol Collection.
284. Margaret Buckley, *op. cit.,* p18.
285. Cecilia Gallagher, Prison Diary, 25 July, 1923, TCDMS10056.
286. Margaret Buckley, *op. cit.,* p87.
287. Ibid., p88.
288. Ibid., p93.
289. Nellie O'Cleirigh, *op. cit.*, p13.
290. Letter from Annie McKeon to Bridie (O'Mullane), 30 July 1923, Kilmainham Gaol Collection.
291. Letter from Áine Ní Fairceallaigh to Bridie (O'Mullane), 29 July 1923, Kilmainham Gaol Collection.
292. Letter from Maggie Timmins to Bridie (O'Mullane), 30 July 1923, Kilmainham Gaol Collection.
293. Letter from Áine Ní Fairceallaigh to Bridie (O'Mullane), 29 July 1923, Kilmainham Gaol Collection.
294. Letter from Catalina Bulfin MacBride to Bridie Halpin, 27 October 1976, Kilmainham Gaol Collection.
295. Concert Programme 19 August 1923, Kilmainham Gaol Collection.
296. Nellie O'Cleirigh, *op. cit.*, p14.
297. Nora Connolly O'Brien, *We Shall Rise Again,* London, Mosquito Press, 1981, p56.
298. Cis Power & Jo Power, 'Blaze Away with your Little Gun', the *Kerryman*, 3 January 1969.
299. Uinseann MacEoin, *The I.R.A. in the Twilight Years 1923-1948*, p86.
300. Humphreys Papers, UCDA, P106/1172
301. Ibid.
302. Ibid., P106/198
303. *Prison Letters of Countess Markievicz*, Esther Roper (ed.), London, Longmans, Green & Co, 1934, pp 304-305.
304. Charlotte Fallon, MA Thesis, *op. cit.*
305. Humphreys Papers, UCDAD, P106/1053
306. Ibid., P106/201
307. Uinseann MacEoin, *Survivors,* p347.
308. Letter from Polly Cosgrave to Bridie Halpin, 19 July 1923, Kilmainham Gaol Collection.

Bibliography

Guide to further reading

Primary and secondary sources used in this publication are clearly listed in the Notes. Each woman who features in the biography section has a separate individual bibliography to assist in further research. These are by no means exhaustive lists.

Kilmainham Gaol Museum now houses one of the largest collections of material relating to political women. The vast majority of the source material for this book may be found in this collection. Although many papers relating to women of this period are held in national repositories, a considerable amount of material is still in private hands. Where possible, I have cited it, although in some cases there are only partial references. My interviews also proved a valuable original source of material. In compiling the biographies the work undertaken by the Women's History Project web on National Archives www.nationalarchives.ie/wh/whp.html has been invaluable.

In 2003, a major new source of material for women political activists became available: *An Introduction to The Bureau of Military History 1913-1921,* Dublin, Military Archives, Defence Forces Printing Press, 2003 will greatly enhance research in this area.

Anonymous, *Sinn Féin Rebellion Handbook,* Dublin, Fred Hanna, 1917.

Anonymous, 'Cumann na mBan in Easter Week; Tribute from a Hostile Source', *Wolfe Tone Annual,* undated.

Anonymous, 'Report of the Irish National Aid and Volunteer Dependants' Fund,' *The Catholic Bulletin,* August, 1919.

Andrews, C S, *Dublin Made Me*, Cork, Mercier Press 1982.

Andrews, C S, *Man of No Property,* Dublin, Lilliput Press, 2001.

Barton, Brian, *From Behind a Closed Door, Secret Court Martial Records of the 1916 Easter Rising,* Belfast, The Blackstaff Press, 2002.

Boylan, Henry, (ed.), *A Dictionary of Irish Biography*, Dublin, Gill and Macmillan, 1999.

Boyle, Andrew, *The Riddle of Erskine Childers,* London, Hutchinson, 1977.

Brennan, Robert, *Allegiance*, Dublin, Browne and Nolan Ltd, 1950.

Broderick, Marian, *Wild Irish Women*, Dublin, The O'Brien Press, 2001.

Browne, Bernard, *Living by the Pen, The Author, Poets and Writers of Wexford,* Wexford, Privately published, 1997.

Browne, Bernard, 'The Browne Families of County Wexford,' in *Wexford: History and Society,* Whelan, Kevin, (ed.), Dublin, Geography Publications, 1987, pp485-489.

Buckley, Margaret, *Jangle of the Keys,* Dublin, James Duffy & Co Ltd., 1938.

Cardozo, Nancy, *Maud Gonne,* London, Victor Gollancz, 1979.

Carey, Tim, *Hanged for Ireland,* Dublin, Blackwater, 2001.

Caulfield, Max, *The Easter Rebellion,* Dublin, Gill and Macmillan, 1995.

Ceannt, Áine, *The Story of the Irish White Cross 1920–1947,* Dublin, At the Sign of the Three Candles, undated.

Clancy, Mary, 'Aspects of Women's Contribution to the Oireachtas Debate in the Free State 1922-37', in *Women Surviving, Studies in Irish Women's History in the 19th and 20th centuries,* edited by Maria Luddy and Cliona Murphy, Dublin, Poolbeg Press, 1990.

Clarke, Kathleen, *Revolutionary Woman, Kathleen Clarke,* edited by Helen Litton, Dublin, The O'Brien Press, 1991.

Conlon, Lil, *Cumann na mBan and the Women of Ireland,* Kilkenny, Kilkenny People Ltd., 1969.

Connolly O'Brien, Nora, *We Shall Rise Again*, London, Mosquito Press, 1981.

Connolly-Heron, Ina, 'James Connolly, The Search for Roots', *Liberty*, May 1966.

Coogan, Tim Pat, *Michael Collins*, London, Hutchinson, 1990.

Coxhead, Elizabeth, *Daughters of Erin,* Gerrard's Cross, Colin Smythe Ltd., 1985.

Cullen, Mary and Luddy, Maria, *Female Activists, Irish Women and Change 1900-1960,* Dublin, The Woodfield Press, 2001.

Czira, Sidney, *The Years Fly By*, Dublin, Gifford & Craven, 1974.

Daly, Madge, 'Gallant Cumann Na mBan of Limerick,' in *Limerick's Fighting Story 1916-1921*, Kerry, The Kerryman Ltd., 1948, p201-205.

De Paor, Mairéad and Siobhán, (Cis and Jo Power) 'Blaze Away with your Little Gun', the *Kerryman*, 21 December 1968; 28 December 1968; 3 January 1969.

Doyle, Jennifer, Clarke, Frances, Connaughton, Eibhlis, Somerville, Orna, (eds.), *An Introduction to The Bureau of Military History 1913-1921,* Dublin, Military Archives, Defence Forces Printing Press, 2003.

Fallon, Charlotte, *Soul of Fire, A Biography of Mary MacSwiney,* Cork, Mercier Press, 1986.

Fallon, Charlotte, 'Civil War Hungerstrikes: Women and Men,' *Eire*, Vol. 22, 1987.

Feeney, Brian, *Sinn Féin, A Hundred Turbulent Years,* Dublin, The O'Brien Press, 2002.

Fitzgerald, Desmond, *The Memoirs of Desmond FitzGerald 1913-1916,* London, Routledge & Kegan Paul, 1968.

Fitzgerald, William G, (ed.), *The Voice of Ireland*, London, Virtue and Company Ltd, undated.

Forester, Margery, *Michael Collins, The Lost Leader*, London, Sphere Books, 1972.

Foster, R F, *Modern Ireland 1600-1972,* London, Penguin Books, 1989.

Fox, R M, *Rebel Irishwomen,* Dublin, Progress House, 1935.

Fox, R M, 'How the Women Helped', in *Dublin's Fighting Story 1916-1921, Told by the Men who Made it*, Tralee, the *Kerryman*, undated.

Gonne MacBride, Maud, *The Servant of the Queen*, Dublin, Golden Eagle Books Ltd., 1950.

Grenan, Julia, 'Events of Easter Week', *The Catholic Bulletin*, June 1917.

Grenan, Julia, 'After the Surrender', *Wolfe Tone Annual*: Special 1916 Number.

Griffith, Kenneth and O'Grady, Timothy, *Curious Journey, An Oral History of Ireland's Unfinished Revolution,* Cork, Mercier Press, 1998.

Hartnett, Sheila, 'Comradeship Kilmainham', The *Irish Press*, 30 December 1971.

Haverty, Anne, *Constance Markievicz, An Independent Life*, London, Pandora Press, 1988.

Hayes, Alan, (ed.), *The Years Flew By, Recollections of Madame Sidney Gifford Czira,* Galway, Arlen House, 2000.

Hickey, DJ & Doherty, JE, *A Dictionary of Irish History 1800-1980,* Dublin, Gill and Macmillan, 1987.

Johnston, Sheila Turner, *Alice A Life of Alice Milligan,* Omagh, Colourpoint Books, 1994.

Jones, Mary, *These Obstreperous Lassies, A History of the Irish Women Workers' Union,* Dublin, Gill and Macmillan, 1988.

Kotsonouris, Mary, *Retreat from Revolution, The Dáil Courts 1920-1924,* Dublin, Irish Academic Press, 1994.

Kinsella, Anna, *Women of Wexford 1798-1998*, Wexford, Courtown Publications, 1998.

Landreth, Helen, *The Mind and Heart of Mary Childers*, Boston, Privately published, 1965.

Levenson, Leah and Natterstad, Jerry H, *Hanna Sheehy Skeffington: Irish Feminist*, Syracuse, Syracuse University Press, 1986.

Levenson, Samuel, *Maud Gonne,* London, Cassell & Co. Ltd., 1977.

Linklater, Andro, *An Unhusbanded Life: Charlotte Despard, Suffragette, Socialist and Sinn Féiner*, London, Hutchinson, 1980.

Lowth, Cormac F, 'James O'Connor, Fenian, and the Tragedy of 1890.' *The Dublin Historical Record*, Vol IV, No. 2, Autumn 2002.

Lowth, Cormac F, 'The O Connor Tragedy', *The Dun Laoghaire Borough Historical Society Journal*, No. 10, 2001.

Luddy, Maria, *Women in Ireland 1800-1918, A Documentary History,* Cork, Cork University Press, 1999.

Luddy, Maria, *Hanna Sheehy Skeffington*, Historical Association of Ireland, Life and Times Series No 5, Dundalk, Dundalgan Press Ltd, 1995.

Macardle, Dorothy, *The Irish Republic,* Dublin, The Irish Press Ltd., 1951.

Macardle, Dorothy, *Tragedies of Kerry 1922-1923*, Dublin, Irish Freedom Press, 1998.

MacEoin, Uinseann, (ed.), *Survivors,* Dublin, Argenta, 1980.

MacEoin, Uinseann, *The I.R.A. in the Twilight Years 1923-1948,* Dublin, Argenta, 1997.

MacLochlainn, Piaras F, *Last Words,* Dublin, The Stationery Office, 1990.

McCoole, Sinéad, *Guns and Chiffon, Women Revolutionaries and Kilmainham Gaol 1916-1923,* Dublin, Stationery Office, 1997.

McCoole, Sinéad, *Hazel, A Life of Lady Lavery*. Dublin, Lilliput Press, 1996.

Meehan, Helen, *'Ethna Carbery: Anna Johnston McManus'*, *Donegal Annual*, No. 45, 1993.

McHugh, Roger, *Dublin 1916,* London, Arlington Books, 1966.

McKeown, Eitne, 'A Family in the Rising,' Dublin, Electricity Supply Board Journal, 1966.

Markievicz, Countess Constance, *Cumann na mBan* 11, no 10, 1926.

Markievicz, Countess Constance, *Prison Letters of Countess Markievicz,* London, Virago Press, 1987.

Markievicz, Countess Constance, *Women, Ideals and the Nation.* Dublin: Inghinidhe na hÉireann, 1909.

Marreco, Anne, *The Rebel Countess: The Life and Times of Constance Markievicz*, London, Weidenfeld and Nicolson, 1967.

Mooney Eichacker, Joanne, *Irish Republican Women in America, Lecture Tours, 1916-1925*, Dublin and Portland, Irish Academic Press, 2003.

Mulcahy, Risteárd, *Richard Mulcahy (1886-1971), A Family Memoir,* Dublin, Aurelian Press, 1999.

Mulholland, Maria, *The Politics and Relationships of Kathleen Lynn,* Dublin, Woodfield Press, 2002.

Mulvihill, Margaret, *Charlotte Despard*, London, Pandora, 1989.

Ní Chorra, Éilis, 'A Rebel Remembers', *The Capuchin Annual,* 1966.

Nic Shiúbhlaigh, Máire, *The Splendid Years,* Dublin, James Duffy & Co. Ltd., 1955.

Norman, Diana, *Terrible Beauty, A Life Constance Markievicz,* London, Hodder & Stoughton, 1987.

O'Brennan, Lily M, 'The Dawning of the Day', *The Capuchin Annual*, 1936.

O'Callaghan, Kate, The Treaty Debates, Public Session, 20 December, 1921.

O'Callaghan, Kate, 'A Curfew Night in Limerick,' in William G. Fitzgerald, (ed.), *The Voice of Ireland, Dublin and London, Virtue and Company Ltd.*, 1925.

O'Callaghan, Kate, 'The Limerick City Curfew Murders of March 7th, 1921,' in *Limerick's Fighting Story 1916-1921*, Kerry, The Kerryman Ltd., 1948.

Ó Céirín, Kit and Cyril, *Women of Ireland*, Galway, TírEolas, 1996.

O'Cleirigh, Nellie, 'A Political Prisoner in Kilmainham Jail, The Diary of Cecilia Saunders Gallagher', *Dublin Historical Record* Vol. LVI, No1, Spring 2003.

O'Connor, Anne V, and Parkes, Susan M, *Gladly Learn and Gladly Teach, A History of Alexandra College and School 1866-1966,* Dublin, Blackwater Press, 1986.

O'Connor, Batt, *With Michael Collins*, London, Peter Davies Ltd., 1929.

O'Daly, Nora, 'Cumann na mBan in Stephens' Green and in the College of Surgeons', *An t-Óglach*, April 1926.

Ó Dubhghaill, Seumas, 'Activities in Enniscorthy', *The Capuchin Annual*, 1966.

Ó Duigneáin, Proinnsíos, *Linda Kearns*, Manorhamilton, Drumlin Publications, 2002.

Ó Duigneáin, Proinnsíos, 'Linda Kearns, The Sligo Nurse in the 1916 Rising', *The Sligo Champion,* 5 April 1991.

Ó Dúlaing, Donncha, (ed.), *Voices of Ireland,* Dublin, The O'Brien Press, 1984.

O'Farrell, Elizabeth, 'Events of Easter Week', *The Catholic Bulletin,* 1917.

O'Hanrahan, Louise and O'Reilly, Patricia (eds.), *Talking Liberties*, Dublin, SICCDA Heritage Centre, 1995.

O'Mahony, Seán, *Frongoch University of Revolution,* Dublin, FDR Teoranta, 1987.

O'Malley, Ernie, *On Another Man's Wound,* London, Four Square, 1936.

O'Malley, Ernie, *The Singing Flame*, Dublin, Anvil, 1978.

O'Neill, Marie, *Grace Gifford Plunkett and Irish Freedom,* Dublin, Irish Academic Press, 2000.

O'Neill, Marie, *From Parnell to de Valera, A Biography of Jennie Wyse Power,* Dublin, Blackwater Press, 1991.

O'Rahilly, Aodagán, *Winding the Clock, O'Rahilly and the 1916 Rising*, Dublin, The Lilliput Press, 1991.

Pakenham, Frank, *Peace by Ordeal*, London, Sidgwick & Jackson, 1972.

Power, Cis & Jo, 'Blaze Away with Your Little Gun - Memoirs of Three Jails, Tralee, Kilmainham, and the North Dublin Union, by "Two of Them"', Kilmainham Gaol Collection.

Purdon, Edward, *The Irish Civil War 1922-23,* Cork, Mercier Press, 2000.

Regan, Nell, 'Kathleen Lynn (1874-1955)', in Cullen, Mary and Luddy, Maria, *Female Activists, Irish Women and Change 1900-1960,* Dublin, The Woodfield Press, 2001.

Reynolds, M, 'Cumann na mBan in the GPO', *An t-Óglach*, March, 1926.

Roche, Anthony J, (ed.), *A Family in Revolution,* Dublin, McGiollaíosa Publications, 2000.

Roper, Esther, 'Biographical Sketch', in *Prison Letters of Countess Markievicz*, London, Virago Ltd., 1987.

Ruane, Medb, 'Kathleen Lynn', in *Ten Dublin Women*, Dublin, Women's Commemoration and Celebration Committee, 1991.

Ruane, Medb 'Kathleen Lynn (1874-1955)', in Cullen, Mary and Luddy, Maria, *Female Activists Irish Women and Change 1900-1960,* Dublin, The Woodfield Press, 2001.

Ryan, Louise, "Drunken Tans" representations of Sex and Violence in the Anglo-Irish War (1919-1921)', *Feminist Review* No 66, 2000.

Ryan, Meda, *Michael Collins and the Women in his Life,* Cork, The Mercier Press, 1996.

Ryan, Meda, *The Tom Barry Story*, Cork, Mercier Press, 1982.

Ryan-Smolin, Wanda, Mayes, Elizabeth, and Rogers, Jenni, (eds.), *Irish Women Artists,* Dublin, National Gallery of Ireland and The Douglas Hyde Gallery, 1997.

Skinnider, Margaret, *Doing my Bit for Ireland*, New York, Century, 1917.

Smyth, Hazel P, 'Kathleen Lynn, M.D., FRCSI, (1874-1955)', *Dublin Historical Record*, Vol XXX, 1976-1978.

Smyth, Sally, *Kilmainham Suite*, Wicklow, Privately printed, 1999.

Taillon, Ruth, *When History was Made, The Women of 1916*, Belfast, Beyond the Pale Publications, 1996.

Thornton, Comdt. Brighid Lyons, 'Women and the Army', *An Cosantóir*, November 1975.

Tierney, Mark, *Ireland since 1870,* Dublin, CJ Fallon, 1993.

Tremayne, Peter, 'A Reflection of Ghosts', in *Gaslight and Ghosts*, edited by Stephen Jones and Jo Fletcher, London, Robinson Publishing, 1988.

Uí Cheallaigh, Phyllis Bean, 'The Story of Eight women of 1916, Women of the Revolution,' 8 April 1971, *RTE Sound Archive.*

Uí Chonaill, Éilis Bean, 'A Cumann na mBan recalls Easter Week', The *Capuchin Annual*, 1966.

Ulry Colman, Anne, *A Dictionary of Nineteenth Century Poets*, Galway, Kenny's Bookshop and Art Gallery, 1996.

Urquhart, Diane, *Women in Ulster Politics 1890-1940,* Dublin, Irish Academic Press, 2000.

Van Voris, Jacqueline, *Countess Markievicz: in the Cause of Ireland,* Amherst, University of Massachusetts, 1967.

Ward, Margaret, *Unmanageable Revolutionaries,* Kerry, Brandon Book Publishers, 1983.

Ward, Margaret, *Maud Gonne,* California, Pandora, 1990.

Ward, Margaret, *In Their Own Voice,* Dublin, Attic Press 1995.

Ward, Margaret, *Hanna Sheehy Skeffington, A Life*, Cork, Attic Press, 1997.

Wilkinson, Burke, 'Erskine Childers: Boston Connections', Dublin, *Capuchin Annual*, 1977.

Wilkinson, Burke, *The Zeal of the Convert, The Life of Erskine Childers,* Washington and New York, Robert B Luce Co., Inc., 1976.

Woggan, Helga, *Silent Radical, Winifred Carney, 1887-1943: A Reconstruction of her Biography,* Dublin, SIPTU, 2000.

Young, Ella, *Flowering Dusk*, London, Dennis Dobson Ltd., 1945.

Young, John N., *Erskine H. Childers, President of Ireland,* Gerrard's Cross, Colin Smythe Ltd., 1985.

Theses (unpublished)

Dempsey, Jacqueline, *Jennie Wyse Power (1858-1941),* MA thesis presented to the Department of Modern History, St Patrick's College, Maynooth, 1993.

Doherty, Shuna, *'Elizabeth O'Farrell and the Women of 1916.'* Unpublished MA thesis presented to The National University of Ireland, 1995.

Fallon, Charlotte, *Republican Hunger Strikes during the Irish Civil War and its Immediate Aftermath,* MA thesis, University College Dublin, 1980.

Manley, Therese, *Sighle Humphreys, Her Republican Beliefs*, MA thesis presented to the History Department, National University of Ireland, Maynooth, 2002.

Morris, Catherine, *From the Margins: Alice Milligan and the Irish Cultural Revival, 1888-1905,* PhD, University of Aberdeen, September 1999.

Individual Bibliographies

The Honourable Albinia Lucy Brodrick

Ó Céirín, Kit and Cyril, *Women of Ireland*, Galway, TírEolas, 1996.

Ó Loingsigh, Pádraig, unpublished biography, 'The Hon. Rebel', Ó Loingsigh Private Collection.

Buckley, Margaret, *Jangle of the Keys*, Dublin, James Duffy & Co Ltd, 1938.

Kathleen Browne

Browne, Bernard, *Living by the Pen, The Authors, Poets and Writers of County Wexford*, privately published, Wexford, 1997, pp13-14.

Browne, Bernard, 'The Browne Families of County Wexford,' in *Wexford: History and Society,* Whelan, Kevin, (ed.), Dublin, Geography Publications, 1987, pp485-489.

Browne, Kathleen, letter to her mother, 23 May 1916, Bernard Browne Collection, Wexford.

Entry for Seanad Electors, Bernard Browne Collection, Wexford, undated.

Obituary, 'Prominent Wexford Lady's Death', 16 October 1943, Bernard Browne collection, Wexford, unidentified publication.

Clancy, Mary, 'Aspects of Women's Contribution to the Oireachtas Debates in the Free State 1922-37', in *Women Surviving, Studies in Irish Women's History in the19th and 20th Centuries,* Dublin, Poolbeg Press, 1990, pp206-232.

Kilmore Parish Journal 1981–1982, No.10, pp13. Bernard Browne collection, Wexford.

Kinsella, Anna, *Women of Wexford 1798-1998,* Wexford, Courtown Publications, 1998, pp25-27.

Margaret Buckley

Anon., 'Republican Women's Jail Journal', unidentified newspaper cutting, (1938), Judy Gaughran collection, Dublin.

Anon., 'Buckley, Margaret, President of Sinn Féin', *Saoirse – Irish Freedom*, July 1998.

Anon., '50 Years Ago', *Saoirse – Irish Freedom*, April 2003.

Buckley, Margaret, *Jangle of the Keys*, Dublin, James Duffy & Co Ltd, 1938.

Buckley, Margaret, *Sinn Féin 1905-1956,* Sinn Féin, 1956.

Gonne, Maud, *Servant of the Queen,* Dublin, Golden Eagle Books Ltd, 1950.

MacEoin, Uinseann, *The I.R.A. in the Twilight Years 1923-1948,* Dublin, Argenta, 1997.

Catalina Bulfin MacBride

Andrews, C S, *Man of No Property,* Dublin, Lilliput Press, 2001, p29.

Interviews with Anna MacBride White, daughter of Catalina Bulfin MacBride, 1997 and March 2001.

McCoole, Sinéad, *Guns and Chiffon, Women Revolutionaries and Kilmainham Gaol 1916-1923*, Dublin, The Stationery Office, 1997, p2.

Ward, Margaret, *Maud Gonne,* California, Pandora, 1990.

Winifred Carney

Ó Céirín, Kit and Cyril, *op. cit.*, pp38-39.
McCoole, Sinéad, *op. cit.*, p20.
Taillon, Ruth, *When History was Made: The Women of 1916,* Belfast, Beyond the Pale Publications, 1996.
Urquhart, Diane, *Women in Ulster Politics 1890-1940,* Dublin, Irish Academic Press, 2000.
Woggan, Helga, *Silent Radical, Winifred Carney, 1887-1943: A Reconstruction of her biography,* Dublin, SIPTU, 2000.

Áine Ceannt

Ceannt, Áine, *The Story of the Irish White Cross 1920-1947,* Dublin, At the Sign of the Three Candles, undated.
Henry, William, unpublished biography, *Supreme Sacrifice The Story of Eamonn Ceannt 1881-1916*, William Henry Collection, Galway.
Interview with Máirín O'Connor (née Kent), niece of Eamonn Ceannt, 1997.
Kelly, Seamus G, *The Glorious Seven,* Commemorative Pamphlet, 2nd edition, 1966, Copy in Kilmainham Gaol collection.
Kent, Richard, Account of his brother Eamonn Ceannt's last hours, Copy in Kilmainham Gaol collection.
Kent, Richard, Biographical notes on Eamonn Ceannt (16 April 1917), Copy in Kilmainham Gaol collection.
O'Brennan Papers, P13, University College Dublin Archives Department.
O'Connor, Batt, *With Michael Collins,* London, Peter Davies, Ltd., 1929.
Ward, Margaret, *Unmanageable Revolutionaries, Women and Irish Nationalism,* Kerry, Brandon Book Publishers Limited, 1983.

Molly Childers

Boyle, Andrew, *The Riddle of Erskine Childers,* London, Hutchinson, 1977.
Ceannt, Áine, *The Story of the Irish White Cross 1920-1947,* Dublin, At the Sign of the Three Candles, undated.
Landreth, Helen, *The Mind and Heart of Mary Childers*, Boston, Privately published, 1965.
Wilkinson, Burke, 'Erskine Childers: Boston Connections', Dublin, *Capuchin Annual*, 1977.
Wilkinson, Burke, *The Zeal of the Convert, The Life of Erskine Childers,* Washington and New York, Robert B Luce Co., Inc., 1976.
Young, John N, *Erskine H. Childers, President of Ireland,* Gerrard's Cross, Colin Smythe Ltd., 1985.

May Coghlan MacMahon

Interviews with Anne MacMahon, daughter-in-law of May Coghlan MacMahon, 1996/1997.

Interviews with Aoife MacMahon, granddaughter of May Coghlan MacMahon, 1996/1997.

Interviews with Louie O'Brien, sister of May Coghlan MacMahon, 1996/1997.

McCoole, Sinéad, *op. cit.*, p49.

Van Voris, Jacqueline, *Countess de Markievicz in the Cause of Ireland*, Amherst, University of Massachusetts, 1967.

Máire Comerford

Comerford Papers, LA18, University College Dublin, Archives Department.

Comerford, Máire, Account of her Service for the Irish Nation 1917-1923, Kilmainham Gaol collection.

Comerford, Máire, 'Republican Courts' and 'In the Four Courts', in Ward, Margaret, *In Their Own Voice,* Dublin, Attic Press, 1995.

Griffith, Kenneth and O'Grady, Timothy, *Curious Journey, An Oral History of Ireland's Unfinished Revolution,* Cork, Mercier Press, 1998.

Interviews with Joe Comerford, nephew of Máire Comerford, 1996, 1997, 2003.

MacEoin, Uinseann, *Survivors,* Dublin, Argenta, 1987.

Ó Céirín, Kit and Cyril, *op. cit.*, pp44-45.

Nora Connolly O'Brien

Connolly O'Brien, Nora, *We Shall Rise Again,* London, Mosquito Press, 1981.

Connolly-Heron, Ina, 'James Connolly, The Search for Roots', *Liberty*, May 1966.

Ó Dúlaing, Donncha, *Voices of Ireland* , Dublin, The O'Brien Press, 1984.

Fox R M, *Rebel Irishwomen,* Dublin, Progress House, 1967, pp51-64.

Interview with Seamus Connolly, nephew of Nora Connolly O'Brien, 2003.

MacEoin, Uinseann, *Survivors,* Dublin, Argenta, 1987.

Anne, Lily, Eileen Cooney

Interviews with Eitne McKeown, daughter of Anne Cooney, 1995, 1996.

McCoole, Sinéad, *op. cit.,* p26.

McKeown, Eitne, 'A Family in the Rising,' Dublin, Electricity Supply Board Journal, 1966.

Unpublished written account by Anne Cooney of her political activities 1916-1921, Dublin, Private collection.

Marcella Cosgrave

Cosgrave, Marcella, Biographical notes, 1996, Kilmainham Gaol collection.

Gonne, Maud, *Servant of the Queen,* Dublin, Golden Eagle Books Ltd., 1950.

Interview with Frances Fleming, grandniece of Marcella Cosgrave, 2002.

Levenson, Samuel, *Maud Gonne,* London, Cassell & Co. Ltd., 1977.

McCoole, Sinéad, *op. cit.*, p25.

Eithne Coyle O'Donnell

Anon., 'Republican Women on Hunger Strike', *Éire,* 10 November 1923. Copy in Francis McKay collection, Donegal.

Buckley, Margaret, *Jangle of the Keys*, Dublin, James Duffy & Co Ltd, 1938.

Eithne Coyle O'Donnell Papers, P61, University College Dublin Archives Department.

Conlon, Lil, *Cumann na mBan and the Women of Ireland*, Kilkenny, Kilkenny People Ltd., 1969, p205.

Coyle O'Donnell, Eithne, www.searcs-web.com/odonn4.html, 11 December 2002.

MacEoin, Uinseann, *Survivors,* Dublin, Argenta, 1987.

Kathleen Daly Clarke

Clarke, Kathleen, *Revolutionary Woman, Kathleen Clarke*, edited by Helen Litton, Dublin, The O'Brien Press, 1991.

Clarke, Emmet, letter to Sinéad McCoole, 25 March 1995, Author's collection.

Ó Céirín, Kit and Cyril, *op. cit.*, pp41-42.

Ruane, Medb, 'Kathleen Clarke', *Ten Dublin Women, Dublin, Women's Commemorative and Celebration Committee,*1991, pp33-40.

Charlotte Despard (née French)

Fox R M, *Rebel Irishwomen*, Dublin, Progress House, 1935, pp99-103.

Linklater, Andro, *An Unhusbanded Life: Charlotte Despard, Suffragette, Socialist and Sinn Féiner*, London, Hutchinson, 1980.

Mulvihill, Margaret, *Charlotte Despard,* London, Pandora, 1989.

Ó Céirín, Kit and Cyril, *op. cit.*, pp60-62.

Pidge Duggan Robinson

Duggan Robinson, Pidge, Undated Account on the Scottish Branch of Cumann na mBan.

Eithne Coyle O'Donnell Papers, University College Dublin Archives Department, P61/4/(67)

Jordan, Deirdre, letter to Sinéad McCoole, 25 March 2002.

Robinson, Pidge. Undated Account of her Service for the Irish Nation 1917-1923, (copy), Author's collection.

Madeleine ffrench-Mullen

Clancy, Mary, 'Aspects of Women's Contribution to the Oireachtas Debates in the Free State 1922-37', in Maria Luddy and Cliona Murphy (eds.), *Women Surviving, Studies in Irish Women's History in the19th and 20th Centuries,* Dublin, Poolbeg Press, 1990, p229.

Conlon, Lil, *Cumann na mBan and the Women of Ireland*, Kilkenny, *Kilkenny People* Ltd., 1969, p109.

'Death of Miss M. ffrench-Mullen' unidentified newspaper cutting, [May 1944], MacMahon Family collection, Dublin.

'It happened when two women met', *Sunday Express* [1953], St Ultans Hospital Archive, Royal College of Physicians of Ireland.

Memorial card for Madeleine ffrench-Mullen, 1944, MacMahon Family collection, Dublin.

Mulholland, Marie, *The Politics and Relationships of Kathleen Lynn,* Dublin, Woodfield Press, 2002.

Katherine 'Jake' Folan

Gleeson, Lily, Autograph Book, 1923, Kilmainham Gaol Collection.

Interviews with Eleanor Hunt, daughter of Katherine Folan, November 1994 and 2003.

McCoole, Sinéad, *op. cit.*, p44.

May Gahan O'Carroll

Gahan O'Carroll, May, letter to the Minister of Defence, 28 June 1943, copy, Author's collection.

Gahan, Robert K, Recollections of May Gahan O'Carroll by her nephew, December 1999, Kilmainham Gaol collection.

O'Carroll, Maureen, Recollections of May Gahan O'Carroll by her daughter, November 1999, Kilmainham Gaol Collection.

Whitaker, Dr Anne-Maree, letter to Sinéad McCoole, 20 December 1994, Kilmainham Gaol collection.

Cecilia Saunders Gallagher

Gallagher, Ann, Biography of Cecilia Gallagher née Saunders, Kilmainham Gaol collection.

Interview with Ann Gallagher, daughter of Cecilia Gallagher, 2002.

O'Cleirigh, Nellie, 'A Political Prisoner in Kilmainham Jail - The Diary of Cecilia Saunders Gallagher', *Dublin Historical Record* Vol. LVI, No1, Spring 2003, p5.

Cecilia Saunders Gallagher Papers, Trinity College Dublin, MS10050-10055.

Louise Gavan Duffy

Fitzgerald, Desmond, *The Memoirs of Desmond FitzGerald 1913-1916,* London, Routledge & Kegan Paul, 1968.

Gavan Duffy, Louise, 'In San GPO: Cumann na mBan', in Margaret Ward (ed.), *In Their Own Voice,* Dublin, Attic Press, 1995, pp60-61.

Ó Broin, Leon, *Charles Gavan Duffy, Patriot and Statesman,* Dublin, James Duffy & Co. Ltd, 1967.

Ó Céirín, Kit and Cyril, *op. cit.*, pp68-69.

Pearl, Cyril, *The Three Lives of Gavan Duffy*, Kensington, NSW, New South Wales University Press Ltd, 1979.

Ward, Margaret, *Unmanageable Revolutionaries, Women and Irish Nationalism*, Kerry, Brandon Book Publishers Limited, 1983.

Sydney Gifford Czira

Boylan, Henry, *A Dictionary of Irish Biography*, Dublin, Gill and Macmillan, 1999, p92.

Czira, Sidney, *The Years Fly By,* Dublin, Gifford & Craven, 1974.

Hayes, Alan, (ed.), *The Years Flew By: Recollections of Madame Sidney Gifford* Czira, Galway, Arlen House, 2000.

Ó Céirín, Kit and Cyril, *op. cit.*, pp56-57.

Nellie Gifford Donnelly

Czira, Sidney, *The Years Fly By,* Dublin, Gifford & Craven, 1974.

Hayes, Alan, (ed.), *The Years Flew By: Recollections of Madame Sidney Gifford* Czira, Galway, Arlen House, 2000.

Interview with Maeve Donnelly, daughter of Nellie Gifford Donnelly, December 1996.

Molony, Helena, unpublished Autobiographical Account, Kilmainham Gaol collection.

McCoole, Sinéad, *op. cit.*, p24.

Grace Gifford Plunkett

Czira, Sidney, *The Years Fly By,* Dublin, Gifford & Craven, 1974.

Hayes, Alan, (ed.), *The Years Flew By: Recollections of Madame Sidney Gifford Czira*, Galway, Arlen House, 2000.

Interview with Maeve Donnelly, daughter of Nellie Gifford Donnelly, December 1996.

McCoole, Sinéad, *op. cit.*, pp32-33.

Ó Céirín, Kit and Cyril, *op. cit.*, pp82-84.

O'Neill, Marie, *Grace Gifford Plunkett and Irish Freedom*. Dublin, Irish Academic Press, 2000.

Plunkett, Grace, Undated, Scrapbook of Press Cuttings and Memorabilia, MS. 21,593, National Library of Ireland.

Ryan-Smolin, Wanda, Mayes, Elizabeth, and Rogers, Jenni, (eds.), *Irish Women Artists*. Dublin, National Gallery of Ireland and The Douglas Hyde Gallery, 1997.

Katherine Gifford Wilson

Gifford Wilson, Katherine, Unidentified Obituary, 20 September 1957, copy, Author's Collection.

Hayes, Alan, (ed.),*The Years Flew By: Recollections of Madame Sidney Gifford Czira,* Galway, Arlen House, 2000.

McCoole, Sinéad, *op. cit.*, p48.

Mollie Gill

Gill, Marie, Captured Papers, 1923, A/1020 Lot No.23, Military Archives, Dublin.

Interview with Ann Clarke, grandniece of Mollie Gill, 1995.

Interview with Celine Doyle, grandniece of Mollie Gill, 1995.

McCoole, Sinéad, *op. cit.*, p50.

Maud Gonne MacBride

Cardozo, Nancy, *Maud Gonne*. London, Victor Gollancz, 1979.

Coxhead, Elizabeth, *Daughters of Erin,* Gerrard's Cross, Colin Smythe Ltd., 1985, pp19-77.

Gonne, Maud, *Servant of the Queen,* Dublin, Golden Eagle Books Ltd., 1950.

Levenson, Samuel, *Maud Gonne*, London, Cassell & Co. Ltd., 1977.

McCoole, Sinéad, *op. cit.*, p53.

Ó Céirín, Kit and Cyril, *op. cit.*, pp86-88.

Ward, Margaret, *Maud Gonne,* California, Pandora, 1990.

Úna (Winifred) Gordon

Gordon, Úna, 'Mrs. Winifred Stack', Unidentified Obituary, Kilmainham Gaol collection, undated.

Interview with Moira Mallin Phillips, daughter of Michael and Agnes Mallin, 2002.

Moynihan, Hannah, Unpublished Civil War Diary, [1923], Kilmainham Gaol collection.

Letters from Austin Stack to Winifred Gordon, Austin Stack Papers, 1920-1928, National Library of Ireland, MS22, 398.

Julia Grenan

Elizabeth Farrell & Julia Grenan, Memorial Card, 1972, Kilmainham Gaol collection.

Grenan, Julia, 'Events of Easter Week', *The Catholic Bulletin*, June 1917.

McKay, Francis, Information on Mná na Poblachta, 1999, Francis McKay collection, Donegal.

Ó Dúlaing, Donncha, *Voices of Ireland,* Dublin, The O'Brien Press, 1984.

Sheila Hartnett Marten

The Eithne Coyle O'Donnell Papers, P61/4 (85), Sheila Hartnett statement, undated, University College Dublin Archives Department.

Hartnett, Sheila, 'Comradeship Kilmainham', The *Irish Press*, 30 December 1971.

Interview with Sheila Fortune, daughter of Sheila Hartnett Marten, 2002.

Mary Ellen (Nell) Humphreys née Rahilly
O'Rahilly, Anna
Sighle Humphreys O'Donoghue

Humphrys, Dr Mark, Unpublished Genealogy of the Humphreys/Humphrys and Family History.

Interview with Cróine Magan, daughter of Sighle Humphreys, 2000.

Interview with Aodogán O'Rahilly, son of The O'Rahilly, 1997.

Manley, Therese, *Sighle Humphreys, Her Republican Beliefs*, MA Thesis presented to the History Department, National University of Ireland, Maynooth, 2002.

MacEoin, Uinseann, *Survivors,* Dublin, Argenta, 1987.

O'Malley, Ernie, *The Singing Flame*, Dublin, Anvil, 1978.

The Humphreys Papers, P106, University College Dublin Archives Department.

Ui Dhonnachadha, Sile Bean, to Francis McKay, Francis McKay collection.

Anna Johnson (Ethna Carbery).

Meehan, Helen, 'Ethna Carbery: Anna Johnston McManus', *Donegal Annual*, No. 45, 1993.

Ó Céirín, Kit and Cyril, *op. cit.*, p38.

Johnston, Sheila Turner, *Alice: A Life of Alice Milligan,* Omagh, Colourpoint Books, 1994.

Ulry Colman, Anne, *A Dictionary of Nineteenth Century Poets,* Galway, Kenny's Bookshop and Art Gallery, 1996, pp122-123.

Linda Kearns

Kearns, Linda, 'Arrest – Two Experiences', in *In Their Own Voice,* Margaret Ward (ed.), Dublin, Attic Press, 1995.pp99-101.

Mooney Eichacker, Joanne, *Irish Republican Women in America, Lecture Tours, 1916-1925, Dublin and Portland, Irish Academic Press, 2003,* pp156-181.

Ó Céirín, Kit and Cyril, *op. cit.*, pp156-181.

Ó Duigneáin, Proinnsíos, 'Linda Kearns – The Sligo Nurse in the 1916 Rising', the *Sligo Champion,* 5 April 1991.

Ó Duigneáin, Proinnsíos, *Linda Kearns*, Manorhamilton, Drumlin Publications, 2002.

Hariette and Maynie Lavery

Anon., 'CID Officers Active, Captures in Dublin Raid', *Irish Independent*, 2 March 1923.

Heffernan, Dr Mary, letter to the author, 28 May 1997, Author's collection.

Interview with Dr Mary Heffernan, daughter of Maynie Lavery, 1998, 2003.

Susan Ryan's Autograph Book, (copy), Kilmainham Gaol collection.

Moya Llewelyn Davies

Unpublished written account by Anne Cooney of her political activities 1916-1921, Dublin, Private collection.

Interview with Melissa Llewelyn Davies, granddaughter of Moya Llewelyn Davies, 2003.

Lowth, Cormac F, 'James O'Connor, Fenian, and the Tragedy of 1890.' *Dublin Historical Record*, Vol IV, No. 2, Autumn 2002.

Lowth, Cormac F, 'The O Connor Tragedy', *The Dun Laoghaire Borough Historical Society Journal*, No 10, 2001.

Pihl, Lis, (ed.), *Signe Toksvig's Irish Diaries 1926-1937,* Dublin, The Lilliput Press, 1994.

Ryan, Meda, *Michael Collins and the Women in His Life*, Cork, Mercier Press, 1996.

Dr Kathleen Lynn

Ó Céirín, Kit and Cyril, *op. cit.*, pp131-132.

Ruane, Medb, 'Lecture on the life and times of remarkable Mayo Woman', Undated, Unidentified newspaper cutting, Author's collection.

Ruane, Medb,. 'Kathleen Lynn', *Ten Dublin Women,* Dublin, Women's Commemoration and Celebration Committee, 1991, pp33-40.

Ruane, Medb 'Kathleen Lynn (1874-1955)', in Cullen, Mary and Luddy,Maria, *Female Activists Irish Women and Change 1900-1960*. Dublin, The Woodfield Press, 2001.

Smyth, Hazel P, 'Kathleen Lynn, M.D., F.R.C.S.I. (1874-1955)', *Dublin Historical Record*, Vol XXX, 1976-1978.

Mulholland, Marie, *The Politics and Relationships of Kathleen Lynn,* Dublin, Woodfield Press, 2002.

Brighid Lyons Thornton

Griffith, Kenneth and O'Grady, Timothy, *Curious Journey, An Oral History of Ireland's Unfinished Revolution*, Cork, Mercier Press, 1998.

Irish Medical and Hospital Directory, 1958, Dublin, The Parkside Press Limited, 1958, p123.

Irish Medical and Hospital Directory, 1970, Dublin, General Publications Limited, 1958, p128.

Ó Céirín, Kit and Cyril, *op. cit.*, pp213-214.

Thornton, Comdt. Brighid Lyons, 'Women and the Army', *An Cosantoir*, November 1975, Military Archives.

Dorothy Macardle

MS Minutes of the Council of Alexandra College, 1919-1923, Alexandra College, Dublin.

Macardle, Dorothy, *The Kilmainham Tortures,* Undated, Kilmainham Gaol collection.

McCoole, Sinéad, *op. cit.*, p47.

Ó Céirín, Kit and Cyril, *op. cit.*, 1996, pp132-133.

O'Connor, Anne V, and Parkes, Susan M, *Gladly Learn and Gladly Teach, A History of Alexandra College and School 1866-1966,* Dublin, Blackwater Press 1986.

Tremayne, Peter, 'A Reflection of Ghosts,' in *Gaslight and Ghosts'*, (eds.), Stephen Jones and Jo Fletcher. London, Robinson Publishing, 1988.

Mary MacSwiney

Fallon, Charlotte, *Soul of Fire A Biography of Mary MacSwiney*. Cork, The Mercier Press, 1986.

Fox R M, *Rebel Irishwomen,* Dublin, Progress House, 1935, pp31-40.

Hickey, DJ & JE Doherty, *A Dictionary of Irish History 1800-1980,* Dublin, Gill and Macmillan, 1987, pp346-347.

Mary MacSwiney Papers, P48a, University College Dublin Archives Department.

Mooney Eichacker, Joanne, *Irish Republican Women in America, Lecture Tours, 1916-1925,* Dublin and Portland, Irish Academic Press, 2003.

Ó Céirín, Kit and Cyril, *op. cit.*, 1996, pp141-142.

Countess Markievicz (née Gore Booth),

Coxhead, Elizabeth, *Daughters of Erin,* Gerrard's Cross, Colin Smythe Ltd., 1985, pp79-123.

Haverty, Anne, *Constance Markievicz, An Independent Life*, London, Pandora Press, 1988.

Lewis, Gifford, *Eve Gore Booth and Esther Roper, A Biography*, London, Pandora, 1988.

Roper, Esther, 'Biographical Sketch', in *Prison Letters of Countess Markievicz*, London, Virago Ltd., 1987, pp1-123.

Markievicz, Countess Constance, 1926. *Cumann na mBan* 11, no 10.

Markievicz, Countess Constance, 1909. *Women, Ideals and the Nation*. Dublin: Inghinidhe na hÉireann.

Marreco, Anne, *The Rebel Countess, The Life and Time of Constance Markievicz*, London, Weidenfeld and Nicolson, 1967.

Mooney Eichacker, Joanne, *Irish Republican Women in America, Lecture Tours, 1916-1925*, Dublin and Portland, Irish Academic Press, 2003.

Norman, Diana, *Terrible Beauty, A Life Constance Markievicz*, London, Hodder & Stoughton, 1987.

Ó Céirín, Kit and Cyril, *op. cit.*, 1996, pp142-145.

Van Voris, Jacqueline, *Countess de Markievicz in the Cause of Ireland*, Amherst, University of Massachusetts, 1967.

Alice Milligan

Alice Milligan Collection, the Allen Library, Dublin.

Anon., 'Interview with Alice Milligan', the *Sunday Press*, 21 October 1951, The Allen Library, Dublin.

Johnston, Sheila Turner, *Alice: A Life of Alice Milligan*, Omagh, Colourpoint Books, 1994.

Morris, Catherine, 'In the enemy's camp, Alice Milligan and Fin de Siécle Belfast', in *Cities of Belfast*, Nicholas Allen and Aaron Kelly (eds), Dublin, Four Courts Press, 2003.

Morris, Catherine, *From the Margins: Alice Milligan and the Irish Cultural Revival, 1888-1905*, PhD, University of Aberdeen, September 1999.

Nic Shiúbhlaigh, Máire, *The Splendid Years*, Dublin, James Duffy & Co. Ltd., 1995.

Ó Céirín, Kit and Cyril, *op. cit.*, pp150-151.

Ulry Colman, Anne, *A Dictionary of Nineteenth Century Poets*, Galway, Kenny's Bookshop and Art Gallery, 1996, pp156-158.

Helena Molony

Fox R M, *Rebel Irishwomen*, Dublin, Progress House, 1935.

Molony, Helena, Unpublished Autobiographical Account, Undated, Helena Molony collection, Kilmainham Gaol collection.

Molony, Helena, 'Women of the Rising'. 16 April 1963, Radio Telefís Eireann Sound Archive.

Ó Céirín, Kit and Cyril, *op. cit.*, pp152-153.

Regan, Nell, 'Kathleen Lynn (1874-1955)', in Cullen, Mary and Luddy Maria, *Female Activists, Irish Women and Change 1900-1960*, Dublin, The Woodfield Press, 2001, pp141-168.

Lily O'Brennan

Henry, William, unpublished biography: *Supreme Sacrifice, The Story of Eamonn Ceannt 1881-1916*, William Henry private collection, Galway.

Hickey, DJ, & Doherty, JE, *A Dictionary of Irish History 1800-1980,* Dublin, Gill and Macmillan, 1987, p411.

Leabhar na mBan, 1919, Kilmainham Gaol collection.

Nic Shiúbhlaigh, Máire, *The Splendid Years,* Dublin, James Duffy & Co. Ltd., 1995.

O'Brennan, Lily, 'Letter to the Editor, an Appreciation of Erskine Childers', *Irish Independent*, 21 November 1922.

O'Brennan, Lily M, www.seares-web.com/obrenn.html 11 December 2002.

O'Brennan Papers, P13 University College Dublin Archives Department.

Kate O'Callaghan

Daly, Madge, 'Gallant Cumann Na mBan of Limerick,' in *Limerick's Fighting Story 1916-1921*, Kerry, The Kerryman Ltd., 1948, p201-205.

Murphy, Dr. Brian P, OSB, 'Kate O' Callaghan (1885-1961)', Lecture given in the Limerick City Library, 14 January 2003.

Murphy, Séan, Biographical Note on Kitty O'Callaghan by her nephew, Kilmainham Gaol collection.

O'Callaghan, Kate, 'A Curfew Night in Limerick,' in William G. Fitzgerald, (ed.), *The Voice of Ireland, Dublin and London, Virtue and Company Ltd,* 1925.

O'Callaghan, Kate, 'The Limerick City Curfew Murders of March 7th, 1921,' in *Limerick's Fighting Story 1916-1921,* Kerry, The Kerryman Ltd, 1948, pp115-139.

Teresa O'Connell

Interview with Kathleen O'Farrell, niece of Teresa O'Connell, 2003.

Interview with Marie O' Neill, niece of Teresa O Connell, 2002.

Interviews with Teresa O' Connell, 1994-1997.

McCoole, Sinéad, *op. cit.*, p1.

O'Connell, Teresa, letter to Sinéad McCoole, 15 July 1994, Kilmainham Gaol collection.

Nora Gillies O'Daly

Interviews with Anthony J Roche, grandson of Nora O'Daly, 1997, 2002.

McGarry, Patsy, 'An Irishman's Diary', *The Irish Times*, 16 July 1998.

Roche, Anthony, J, (ed.), *A Family in Revolution,* Dublin, McGiollaíosa Publications, 2000.

Elizabeth O'Farrell

Henderson, Fr Enna, Cistercian Abbey Roscrea, Testimony, 1997, Kilmainham Gaol Collection.

Interview with Tove O'Flanagan and Jill Andrews of the National Maternity Hospital, 2003.

O'Farrell, Elizabeth, 'Events of Easter Week', *The Catholic Bulletin,* 1917, Kilmainham Gaol collection.

O' Farrell, Elizabeth & Grenan, Julia, 1972, Memorial Card, Kilmainham Gaol collection.

Shuna Doherty, *'Elizabeth O'Farrell and the Women of 1916.'* Unpublished MA Thesis presented to the National University of Ireland, 1995.

Brighid (Bridie) O'Mullane

Interview with Bill McDonald, nephew-in-law, 2003.

Interview with Myra McGowan, niece of Bridie O'Mullane, 2003.

Leabhar na mBan, 1919, Kilmainham Gaol collection.

Macardle, Dorothy, *The Irish Republic,* Dublin, The Irish Press Ltd., 1951.

Old Association of Cumann na mBan, letter to An Taoiseach, Eamon de Valera, 27 April 1938, Department of the Taoiseach, National Archives of Ireland, S10081.

Brighid O'Mullane papers, Kilmainham Gaol Collection.

Brighid O'Mullane papers, Ms 22,631, National Library of Ireland.

O'Mullane, Brighid, letter to An Taoiseach, Eamon de Valera, 28 July 1938, Department of the Taoiseach, National Archives of Ireland, S10737.

O'Mullane, Brighid, Witness Statement, 450, Bureau of Military History, Military Archives.

O'Mullane, Brighid, Witness Statement, 485, Bureau of Military History, Military Archives.

Report on Cumann na mBan Convention 1920-21, Kilmainham Gaol collection.

Nancy (Nannie) O'Rahilly

Interview with Aodogán O'Rahilly, son of Nannie O'Rahilly, 1997.

Interview with Blanaid O'Rahilly, daughter-in-law of Nannie O'Rahilly, 2003.

Ceannt, Áine, *The Story of the Irish White Cross 1920-1947,* Dublin, At the Sign of the Three Candles, undated.

O'Rahilly, Aodogán, *Winding the clock: O'Rahilly and the 1916 Rising,* Dublin, The Lilliput Press, 1991.

The Humphreys Papers, P106, University College Dublin Archives Department.

Ward, Margaret, *Unmanageable Revolutionaries, Women and Irish Nationalism,* Kerry, Brandon Book Publishers Limited, 1983.

Mary Perolz

Clarke, Kathleen, *Revolutionary Woman, Kathleen Clarke,* edited by Helen Litton, Dublin, The O'Brien Press, 1991.

Conlon, Lil, *Cumann na mBan and the Women of Ireland.* Kilkenny, Kilkenny People Ltd., 1968.

Genealogy of the Perolz Family compiled by Eileen Bostle, Robert Prole, Colin Sagar, copy, author's collection.

Jones, Mary, Biographical Note on Mary Perolz, Irish Labour History Society.

Jones, Mary, *These Obstreperous Lassies, A History of the Irish Women Workers' Union,* Dublin, Gill and Macmillan, 1988, p23.

Norman, Diana, *Terrible Beauty, A Life of Constance Markievicz*. London, Hodder & Stoughton, 1987.

Taillon, Ruth, *When History was Made: The Women of 1916*. Belfast, Beyond the Pale Publications, 1996.

Ward, Margaret, *Unmanageable Revolutionaries, Women and Irish Nationalism*, Kerry, Brandon Book Publishers Limited, 1983.

Ward, Margaret, *Maud Gonne,* California, Pandora, 1990.

Countess Plunkett, Mimi Plunkett, Geraldine Plunkett Dillon, Fiona Plunkett

Buckley, Margaret, *Jangleof the Keys*, Dublin, James Duffy & Co Ltd, 1938.

Interview with Honor O'Brolchain, granddaughter of Geraldine Plunkett Dillon, 2003.

MacEoin, Uinseann, *The I.R.A. in the Twilight Years 1923-1948*, Dublin, Argenta, 1997.

O'Neill, Marie, *Grace Gifford Plunkett and Irish Freedom*. Dublin, Irish Academic Press, 2000.

The Humphreys Papers, P106, University College Dublin Archives Department.

Ulry Colman, Anne, *A Dictionary of Nineteenth Century Poets,* Galway, Kenny's Bookshop and Art Gallery, 1996, p190.

Ward, Margaret, *Unmanageable Revolutionaries, Women and Irish Nationalism*, Kerry, Brandon Book Publishers Limited, 1983.

Cis Power and Jo Power

Anon., 'Death of Veteran Kerry Patriot, The late Mr. Patrick Power', the *Kerryman*, Undated, Kilmainham Gaol collection.

Anon., 'Late Miss Jo Power, Lower Rock Street', the *Kerryman*, 8 February 1969.

Anon., 'Obituary Patrick Power', the *Kerryman* 29 January 1938.

Anon., 'Our Views', (the death of Michael Power) the *Kerry Press,* 4 March 1915, Kilmainham Gaol collection.

De Paor, Mairead and Siobhan, 'Blaze Away with your Little Gun', the *Kerryman*, 21 December 1968; 28 December 1968; 3 January 1969.

Moynihan, Hannah, Unpublished Civil War Diary, [1923], Kilmainham Gaol collection.

Power, Cis & Jo, Undated, Account of imprisonment, 'If Winter Comes', (copy), Kilmainham Gaol collection.

Power, Cis & Jo, *Blaze Away with Your Little Gun - Memoirs of Three Jails, Tralee, Kilmainham, and the North Dublin Union*, by "Two of Them"', Kilmainham Gaol collection.

Power, Margaret, 'Late Miss M. Power 114, Rock Street', Unidentified newspaper cutting, 2 March 1968, Kilmainham Gaol collection.

Leslie Price de Barra

Boylan, Henry, *A Dictionary of Irish Biography*, Dublin, Gill and Macmillan, 1999, p97.

Coogan, Tim Pat, *Michael Collins,* London, Hutchinson, 1990.
de Barra, Leslie Price Bean, Bureau of Military History, Witness Statement 1754, Military Archives.
de Barra, Leslie Bean, Death Notice, [1984], The Irish Times, File on Leslie Bean de Barra, Local Studies Section, Cork Library.
de Barra, Leslie Price, homepage.tinet.ie/~corkredcross/natl/history.html, 28 March 2003.
Griffith, Kenneth and O'Grady, Timothy, *Curious Journey, An Oral History of Ireland's Unfinished Revolution,* Cork, Mercier Press, 1998.
The Humphreys Papers, P106, University College Dublin Archives Department.
Neeson, Geraldine, 'The GPO in 1916 – Leslie Price was there', Unidentified newspaper, File on Leslie Bean de Barra, Local Studies Section, Cork Library.
Ó Céirín, Kit and Cyril, *op. cit.*, p57.
Ó Dúlaing, Donncha, *Voices of Ireland* , Dublin, The O'Brien Press, 1984.
Ryan, Meda, *The Tom Barry Stor,y* Cork, Mercier Press, 1982.

Éilis Robinson Norris and Sinéad Robinson Keeley

Interviews with Brother Fintan Norris, son of Éilis Robinson Norris and nephew of Sinéad Robinson Keeley, 2003.
Interviews conducted by Geraldine Stout with Brother Fintan Norris, 2002, copy, Author's collection.
Ní Riain, P, letter to Mrs Norris, 4 December 1936, Kilmainham Gaol collection.
Norris, Brother Fintan, Account of Escape of Éilis Robinson from the North Dublin Union, Kilmainham Gaol collection, 1997.
Norris, Michael, Account of Escape of Éilis Robinson from the North Dublin Union. Author's collection, 2002.

Kit Ryan, Nell Ryan, Min Ryan, Phyllis Ryan

Interviews with Dr Phyllis Gaffney, grandniece of the Ryan sisters, 2002.
Kenny, Eibhlin, letter to Sinéad McCoole, 21 May 2003.
Kinsella, Anna, *Women of Wexford 1798-1998*. Wexford, Courtown Publications, 1998.
Leabhar na mBan, 1919, Kilmainham Gaol collection.
Mulcahy, Risteárd, *Richard Mulcahy (1886-1971) A Family Memoir*, Dublin, Aurelian Press, 1999.
Ryan Family Papers, private collection.
Ui Cheallaigh, Phyllis Bean, 'The Story of Eight women of 1916, Women of the Revolution', 8 April 1971, Radio Telefís Êireann Sound Library & Archives.

Hanna Sheehy Skeffington

Fox R M, *Rebel Irishwomen,* Dublin, Progress House, 1967, pp73-81.
Luddy, Maria, *Hanna Sheehy Skeffington*, Historical Association of Ireland, Life and Times Series No 5, Dundalk, Dundalgan Press Ltd, 1995.
Mooney Eichacker, Joanne, *Irish Republican Women in America, Lecture Tours, 1916-1925,* Dublin and Portland, Irish Academic Press, 2003.

Ó Céirín, Kit and Cyril, *op. cit.*, pp201-203.

Ward, Margaret, Hanna Sheehy Skeffington, A Life, Cork, Attic Press, 1997.

Mary Spring Rice

Anon., The Spring Rice Family of Mount Trenchard', in the *Annual Observer*, Newcastle West Historical Society, 1983, pp12-14.

Anon., 'The Death of the Hon. Mary Ellen Spring Rice', the *Limerick Chronicle*, 4 December 1924.

Delia, Sr., 'Mount Trenchard – Stella Maris', in *St Senans Fourth Community Annual*, Limerick, Fitzsimons Printers, Shanagolden, 1982, pp7-21.

Duane, Mary, 'Mount Trenchard,' in Etienne Rynne (ed.), *North Munster Studies*, Limerick, The Thomond Archaeological Society, 1967, pp335-341.

Hickey, DJ & Doherty, JE, *A Dictionary of Irish History 1800-1980,* Dublin, Gill and Macmillan, 1987, p547.

Ó Céirín, Kit and Cyril, *op. cit.*, pp209-210.

S.B., 'The Honourable Mary Spring Rice', in *Limerick's Fighting Story 1916-1921*, Kerry, The Kerryman Ltd., 1948, pp169-170.

Ella Young

Gonne, Maud, *Servant of the Queen,* Dublin, Golden Eagle Books Ltd, 1950.

Colman, Anne, *A Dictionary of Nineteenth Century Poets,* Galway, Kenny's Bookshop and Art Gallery, 1996, 244.

Young, Ella, *Flowering Dusk,* London, Dennis Dobson, 1945.

May Zambra

Halpin, Bridie, Autograph Book, Kilmainham Gaol ollection

Interview with Joe Tierney, nephew of May Zambra, 1996, 2000, 2002.

Tierney, Kathleen née Zambra, Reminiscences of her sister, May Zambra Ryan, Author's collection.

Picture Credits

Illustrations from the Kilmainham Gaol Collection: pages 2, 3,4,6, 8,10,11,14, 21 (bottom), 23, 24 (bottom), 25 (both), 27, 28, 31 (bottom), 32, 33, 34 (top and bottom), 36, 40 (top), 42, 44, 45, 47, 48, 49, 50, 59, 60 (top and bottom), 63 (top), 64, (photographic copy,) 66, 69, 70, 72, 73, 76 (top), 80, 81, 85, 88 (both), 89, 91 (bottom), 92, 93, 97, 101, 105, 106, 108, 109, 112, 113 (all), 114 (top and bottom), 119 (top), 121, 122, 128, 131, 133, 135 (both), 137, 142 (bottom), 145, 147, 163, 168, 171, 172 (bottom), 183 (bottom), 185, 189, 191, 211; Kilmainham Gaol Collection with the following – Anna MacBride White p24 (top), p144, Seamus Connolly pp26, 90, 151, Eitne McKeown pp39, 153, The Catholic Bulletin pp40 (bottom), 41, 62, 172 (top), 193, Joe Craven p47, Rhoda Draper pp74 (top), 75 (bottom), Máirín O'Connor pp61, 146, Nora and Mairead de hÓir p77, Teresa O'Connell p78, Sally Smyth p79, Sally Foere p117, Kate Lowe p124, Esther O'Moore p139, Brother Fintan Norris pp127 (top), 205 (both), MacMahon family pp91, 149 (top), 161, Frances Fleming p154, Emmet Clarke p156, John Power pp102 (both), 202, Ann Gallagher p103 (top), Deirdre Jordan pp103 (bottom), 104, 160, Eleanor Hunt pp162, 164, Maeve Donnelly pp167, 168 (top), Ann Clarke P169 (bottom), Leabhar na mBan p194.

Illustrations courtesy of the following persons and institutions: The Pearse Museum Collection pp1 and 75 (spectacles and lace), pp5, 7, 99, the National Library of Ireland p20, the Loretta Clarke Murray Collection pp1 (locket), 9, 21 (top), 31 (top), 74 (bottom), 75 (locket), 119 (bottom), from *The Fair Winds of Éirinn*, courtesy of Gill and Macmillan Ltd p22 (bottom), Kilmainham Gaol Museum p29, The Old Dublin Society, from the *Dublin Historical Record*, pp 46, 181, Imogen Stuart pp52, 188, Honor O Brolchain/The Geraldine Plunkett Dillon Collection pp53, 76 (bottom), 199, 200 (top two), Dr Phyllis Gaffney pp55, 206 (all), 207, Melissa Llewelyn Davies pp82, 179 (bottom), Delia McDevitt/Drumlin Publications pp83, 84, 155, 177, University College Dublin Archives Department pp87, 200, 203 (bottom), Blon Uí Rathaille pp95, 96, 173 (both), Noel Guilfoyle p110, Dr Mary Heffernan pp125, 178, 179 (top), John 'Buddy' FitzGerald pp127 (bottom), 141, Bernard Browne p142 (top), Joe Comerford p149 (bottom), the Sheehy Skeffington family pp158, 208, Ruth Taillon p165, Ann Clare pp166, 197, Cróine Magan p174, Helen Meehan, pp176, 186, The Military Archives p182, Alexandra College p183 (top), from *Limerick's Fighting Story* courtesy of Limerick City Library p190, Anthony J Roche p192, Irish Labour History Society p198, Eoin P O'Neill and Marie O'Neill p212, from *Flowering Dusk*, Dennis Dobson, 1945 p213, Joe Tierney, p214.

Photographs pp11,19, 21 (top), 24, 28, 31, 34 (bottom), 36, 42, 44, 45, 47, 49, 54, 57, 60 (bottom), 63, 72, 73, 74, 75, 81, 99, 105, 106, 107, 109, 112, 113, 114, 115, 116, 118, 119, 120, 121, 133 134, 135, 137 by Emma Byrne.

Index

D

K

L

M